DIMENSIONS OF POLITICS
AND ENGLISH JURISPRUDENCE

Understandings of law and politics are intrinsically bound up with broader visions of the human condition. Sean Coyle argues for a renewed engagement with the juridical and political philosophies of the Western intellectual tradition, and takes up questions pondered by Aristotle, Plato, Augustine, Aquinas and Hobbes in seeking a deeper understanding of law, politics, freedom, justice and order. Criticizing modern theories for their failure to engage with fundamental questions, he explores the profound connections between justice and order and raises the neglected question of whether human beings in all their imperfection can ever achieve truly just order in this life. Above all, he confronts the question of whether the open society is the natural home of liberals who have given up faith in human progress (there are no ideal societies), or whether liberal political order is itself the ideal society?

SEAN COYLE is Professor of English Laws at the University of Birmingham.

DIMENSIONS OF POLITICS AND ENGLISH JURISPRUDENCE

SEAN COYLE

CAMBRIDGE
UNIVERSITY PRESS

CAMBRIDGE UNIVERSITY PRESS
Cambridge, New York, Melbourne, Madrid, Cape Town,
Singapore, São Paulo, Delhi, Mexico City

Cambridge University Press
The Edinburgh Building, Cambridge CB2 8RU, UK

Published in the United States of America by Cambridge University Press, New York

www.cambridge.org
Information on this title: www.cambridge.org/9780521196598

First published 2013

Printed and bound in the United Kingdom by Clays, St Ives plc

A catalogue record for this publication is available from the British Library

Library of Congress Cataloguing in Publication data
Coyle, Sean.
Dimensions of politics and English jurisprudence / Sean Coyle.
pages   cm
Includes bibliographical references and index.
ISBN 978-0-521-19659-8 (Hardback)
1. Jurisprudence–Great Britain.   2. Jurisprudence–United States.
3. Law–Philosophy.   4. Liberalism.   I. Title.
KD640.C69 2013
349.41–dc23
2012047170

ISBN 978-0-521-19659-8 Hardback

To my parents

'I think we have real progress in philosophy when a disputant thinks little of victory as compared with the discovery of what is just and true'
– attributed to Licentius
(Saint Augustine, *Contra Academicos*, Bk 1.3)

CONTENTS

PREFACE

The origins of this book lie in an ambition to explore a sceptical attitude toward modern jurisprudence and political thought. Modelled upon a kind of Academic scepticism (avoidance of positive doctrines), the intention was to subject key aspects of legal and political thought to question. This gave the book as initially conceived a somewhat looser structure, as a series of more or less independent arguments addressed to each subject in turn. As the book progressed, I decided to change this strategy. Increasingly, there were arguments or ideas that demanded to be affirmed. They could be subjected to question, but not denied. Positive doctrines began to assert themselves in the book's main line of analysis.

As a result of this, I decided (at quite a late stage) to rewrite the book almost from the ground up. I am grateful to Cambridge University Press for allowing me the extra time it took to complete this process. The result is a book that is more cohesive, but which perhaps retains vestiges of its earlier incarnation. The relationship between the chapters, particularly in the second part of the book, now resembles more a series of reflections upon a body of interrelated ideas: law, liberty, order, community, justice (and others). Each dimension of law and politics is pushed temporarily into the foreground, to be examined and then replaced, whereupon another is called forth. The reflections are underpinned by a vision of law and politics that is developed in the Introduction and the early chapters of the book. The book's overarching concern, though I did not know it at first, is with justice.

It was necessary to restrict the scope of the book. I consider first and foremost the legal and political experiences of the liberal social order. I have very little to say about established criticisms of liberalism, such as communitarianism, preferring to develop my own line of criticism. My question is above all whether liberalism represents a deepening of man's moral predicament or, as some liberals seem to suggest, a resolution.

I would like to take this opportunity to thank a number of people whose input has been invaluable to me over the course of writing the

ix

book. For discussions of some of the book's ideas, I am grateful to audiences at the University of Antwerp's Centre for Law and Cosmopolitan Values, Birmingham Law School, the University of Minnesota School of Law, LSE, and Emory University. I owe special thanks to John Witte Jr and colleagues at the Center for the Study of Law and Religion, Emory University, for hosting me as a visiting scholar during April 2010, and for a very illuminating debate on some of the book's concerns. Brian Bix, Anna Grear, Joel Hanisek, George Pavlakos, the late Amanda Perreau-Saussine, Esther Reed, Veronica Rodriguez-Blanco, Nigel Simmonds and Melanie Williams read and commented upon a number of chapters. Tobias Schaffner offered some very helpful suggestions on two key chapters, and I am grateful for a very interesting correspondence on justice and virtue. Fiona Smith and Margaret Martin read virtually the whole of the manuscript, sometimes in successive versions, and were an unfailing source of encouragement and ideas. I am grateful to my editors at Cambridge University Press, Finola O'Sullivan and Richard Woodham, for their advice and support, and their patience. Finally, but most of all, Allison. I thank you all.

Earlier incarnations of some of the book's arguments have appeared in print elsewhere. An early version of Part I, Chapter 1 was published in *The Canadian Journal of Law and Jurisprudence*, 2010. Elements of Part II, Chapters 7 and 8 appeared in a long article in *The Australian Journal of Legal Philosophy*, 2010. Two articles in the 2009 *Northern Ireland Legal Quarterly* contain earlier versions of the arguments in Part II, Chapter 10 and Part III, Chapter 13. Part III, Chapter 15 appears in *New Blackfriars* in 2012. I am grateful to the editors of those journals for permission to reprint or adapt material.

INTRODUCTION

This book aims to illuminate various dimensions of politics and English jurisprudence. The terms 'politics' and 'jurisprudence' do not have a constant meaning in the Western intellectual tradition. In the Hellenic philosophies of the classical period, the associations of law and politics were considerable: they pointed simultaneously to the context of the city, the Latin *civitas* which Hobbes later identifies with 'that great Leviathan called a Common-wealth, or State',[1] and inwardly to the constitution and dispositions of the soul. If justice depended upon the development of proper order in the soul, nevertheless it could only be positively beneficial to the individual if it sprang from a decorous and principled political regime.[2] The city itself demanded attention not as a physical, but as a metaphysical, entity, which if natural and belonging to the natural order, nevertheless has to be built by the efforts of men. Politics gestured toward heaven as well as to the material fate of the earthly life. These ideas achieved their highest expression in the Catholic scholastic philosophy of the Middle Ages, culminating in the works of Aquinas. The English jurisprudential tradition of the common law in particular, witnessed a remarkable flowering of Thomist ideas in Henry de Bracton's influential *De Legibus* (1235), Fortescue's *In Praise of the Laws of England* (c.1470), and Saint Germain's *Doctor and Student* (1518).[3] Centuries later, these associations remain visibly present in the work of the greatest English political philosopher, Hobbes, where they are the subject of intense anxieties. Of the possible states of existence in the sublunar world, it is only the condition of civic peace that offers an experience of justice.[4]

---

[1] Hobbes, *Leviathan* [1651], introduction.

[2] Plato, *Republic*, 427c–445e. See also the Penguin Classics edition (London, Penguin, 2007), xxiii.

[3] See inter alia: HA Rommen, *The Natural Law* (Indianapolis IN, Liberty Fund, 1998), 100ff; N Doe, *Fundamental Authority in Late Medieval English Law* (Cambridge University Press, 1990), 112–13.

[4] Hobbes, *Leviathan*, ch 13.

But whilst the famous frontispiece of *Leviathan* restricts the experience of justice to a commonwealth composed of both sword *and* sceptre, civil *and* ecclesiastical authority, that of *De Cive* suggests a more complex and ambivalent relationship between *imperium*, the state of civic peace, and the final justice of the Last Judgment.[5]

At the hands of Locke and Hume, the province of jurisprudence progressively narrowed in order to accommodate a more austere depiction of the possible boundaries of human understanding. Increasingly it is artifice, in place of nature, that is to provide the form and limits of these ideas.[6] Building upon their efforts in the eighteenth century, Bentham thunders his disapproval of the entire natural rights tradition.[7] By the middle of the twentieth century, HLA Hart quietly dismisses these questions from reflection upon law as being 'too metaphysical for modern minds'.[8] More recently, legal philosophers barely whisper criticisms of a dead tradition, limiting their attention to a call for 'constructive' interpretations of law as an expression of liberal values, or insisting upon the separability of the very concept of law even from these thin associations.[9]

Are these arguments and interpretations actually significant to the main questions and fears of our times? Do we clearly perceive our own modernity? The liberal order is endlessly debated, but are the nature of its blessings fully understood? Thinkers who dwell upon the interpretation of law as the seed-bed of liberal values have shown remarkably little interest in the ultimate direction of liberalism. One might put this down to the character of liberalism itself, in being non-directive; but this would not explain why the plurality of directions is not the subject of lively debate. Thus we are drawn to a fundamental ambivalence in liberalism's deeper characteristics: liberalism has both a pessimistic version (there are no ideal societies or better forms of life, merely endless alternatives) and an optimistic version (the liberal order is *itself* the ideal society). In the face of this ambivalence, it is necessary to consider what the purpose of

---

[5] Hobbes, *De Cive* [1642], frontispiece.

[6] See e.g. Locke, *An Essay Concerning Human Understanding* [1690], III.5; Hume, *An Enquiry Concerning the Principles of Morals* [1777], III.2.

[7] Jeremy Bentham, 'Nonsense Upon Stilts', in P Schofield et al (eds.), *Rights, Representation, and Reform: Nonsense Upon Stilts and Other Writings on the French Revolution* (Oxford University Press, 2002), 317–35.

[8] HLA Hart, *The Concept of Law*, 2nd edn (Oxford, Clarendon Press, 1994), 192.

[9] See e.g. R Dworkin, *Justice in Robes* (Cambridge MA, Harvard University Press, 2007); J Raz, *Between Authority and Interpretation* (Oxford University Press, 2009).

liberal politics is. In an address to Western politicians, business leaders and intellectuals in 1997, the President of the Czech Republic, Vaclav Havel, said: 'It cannot suffice to invent new machines, new regulations, new institutions. It is necessary to understand differently and more perfectly the true purpose of our existence on this Earth, and of our deeds.'[10]

It is with these questions, and others which arise from them, that this book is concerned. One might say that it attempts to put modern juridical and political culture 'in context'. This is a difficult task if only because liberalist philosophies reject the idea of context. The eyes of the Christian jurists had fastened upon heaven as the final end of politics and of all human endeavour. The liberal jurists lowered their gaze, looking around themselves, and to man himself as the source and architect of future possibilities. Liberalism implies a more open view of the future, but what does this imply about the human condition? One of the principal ideas of liberalism is that of the human being as an 'individual', who has escaped the tyranny of class, of nature and of church. The condition that is 'proper' to this being is one, not simply of 'free will', but of freedom. But how should one respond to this sense of propriety? Is it an achievement of liberal society, or its goal? Concrete experience or nebulous piety? A feast for the soul, or apocalyptic emptiness?

English jurisprudence

What will help us understand the situation with which we are presented? One may be tempted to turn to Kant, following a familiar route. The profundity of what Kant has to say about the condition of individuality is such that his vision of the autonomous self might almost be equated with the liberal subject itself. But Kant himself casts doubt upon the reliability of this equation, for he in fact has very serious doubts about the possibility of human beings ever achieving anything close to 'autonomy'.[11] A politics premised upon the attributes of this character is therefore inappropriate to enduring realities of the human condition, and must in some ways distort our understanding. Kant's remarks nevertheless coincide with the liberal political tradition in associating the 'properness',

---

[10] Vaclav Havel, Address to FORUM 2000 Conference, Prague Castle, 4 September 1997.

[11] Kant, 'Religion Within the Boundaries of Mere Reason', in AW Wood (ed.), *Religion and Rational Theology: The Cambridge Edition of the Works of Immanuel Kant* (Cambridge University Press, 1996), 39–216.

and thus the phenomenon, of freedom with the characteristics of the individual as such. But if freedom is 'proper', it nevertheless requires a nexus of rules and entitlements to define and sustain it. If attributed to individuals, this cannot be in sheer recognition of their individuality, for it concerns their interrelations and thus presupposes an already-instituted community. To speak of freedoms, or of rights, is always to implicate the institutional realities which support them. England and its philosophies did indeed succeed in displacing the historical condition of its subjects. The liberal state is no longer responsible for the articulation and defence of revealed truth, but the defence of the individual himself (through his property). The freedom of the individual was therefore created institutionally. It is as inhabitants of Western democracies that we have become more autonomous.

Kant's philosophy is not as insensitive to this point as may be supposed, for he is above all a *juridical* philosopher. But if we want to understand the extent and meaning of liberal freedom fully, asking what it means to exhibit this condition, it is necessary to turn elsewhere. If we look to recent writing in the Anglo-American tradition of jurisprudence, we appear to encounter the suggestion that one must at all costs avoid contextualizing the problem historically or institutionally. Raz, for example, equates the truth of philosophical ideas with their universality: '[philosophical] theses, if true, apply universally, that is, they speak of all law, of all legal systems; of those that exist or will exist, and even of those that can exist or never will. Moreover, [such] theses are advanced as necessarily universal.'[12] An incautious reading of this statement can encourage the belief that philosophies of law and politics, in being concerned with questions and standards that are universal or categorical, are *not* directed toward specific arrangements: that philosophy 'must transcend the local concepts of a particular place and time.'[13]

What is meant by the statement that philosophy must 'transcend' particular arrangements? Obviously, philosophy seeks to uncover the nature of the human being and of the human condition in its fullest sense, and not merely that of particular historical conditions. Philosophical reflection involves the 'expansion and clarification of consciousness' in a way that 'helps to distance us from the concealed assumptions and prejudices characteristic of our own place and time, and so to get a

---

[12] Raz, 'On the Nature of Law', *Archiv fur Rechts und Sozialphilosophie* (1996), 1.
[13] R Tur, 'The Notion of a Legal Right: A Test-Case for Legal Science', *Juridical Review*, 21 (1976), 183.

critical purchase on them'.[14] If the liberal subject is free, it is because *man* is free. Liberalism may set him free, but he possesses freedom because his soul is in every way unspecified. Passages such as Raz's can lead us to assume that the questions raised by the philosopher are in some sense prior to the questions asked by the political historian, the cultural anthropologist, or the lawyer. But if we think of law and politics as being unconditioned by contextual possibilities, we risk the propulsion of analysis into an unhelpful abstraction to which it is constantly vulnerable. Plato reminds us that in the case of the philosopher, 'only his body has its place and home in the city and can be found there, while his mind disdains all these matters, seeing them as petty and worthless, and is borne in all directions, as Pindar says, "from beneath the earth to above the heavens"'.[15] This is a correct image, of an embodied state comprehending its true and fullest meaning in reaching beyond itself. If we are not careful, it is possible to distort this insight into its opposite: the city becomes irrelevant, the enquiry begins and is conducted in the abstract, and all values are deciphered and settled so that they do not become circumstantially or historically negotiable.[16] How much blood will be spilt in the defence of freedom and justice, when interpreted in this way!

The transcendence of philosophical questions is not the same as their priority. Certainly the issues which preoccupy the writer of a scholarly text on the English law of property (for example) are not directly philosophical, even if they are acknowledged as sometimes raising philosophical questions. On these occasions, the legal writer feels justified in placing such questions to one side. But the implication of this ought to be obvious: the philosophical enquiry *arises from* the lawyer's concepts and classifications, it consists in an extension and a deepening of his activities and suppositions. It is not an enquiry that is logically *prior to* such activities, the lawyer innocently continuing about his business until instructed by the philosopher that his suppositions are ill-founded. In an early essay on the philosophy of law, HLA Hart recognized that:

> [n]o very firm boundaries divide the problems confronting [the doctrinal lawyer] from the problems of the philosophy of law. This is especially

---

[14] H Meynell, 'In Defence of the Humanities', *New Blackfriars*, 81 (2007), 327.

[15] Plato, *Theaetetus*, 173e.

[16] It is interesting to observe how short is the journey from the supposed consensus of the 'original position' in *A Theory of Justice* to the aggressive defence of American foreign policy against 'outlaw states' in J Rawls's later work, *The Law of Peoples* (Cambridge MA, Harvard University Press, 2001).

true of the conceptual schemes of classification, definition, and division introduced by the academic study of law ... [I]t is more important to distinguish as belonging to the philosophy of law certain groups of questions which remain to be answered even when a high degree of competence or mastery of particular legal systems of the empirical and dogmatic studies ... has been gained.[17]

Hart is undoubtedly correct. Familiarity with both legal practice and academic legal scholarship shows lawyers demonstrating an interest not only in the interpretation of 'black-letter' rules and the substance of legal doctrine, but also in questions of justice, of the difference between 'good' law and 'bad' law, and of the many and varied political consequences of particular rules and decisions. It is very doubtful whether any set of fixed and (supposedly) universal standards could meaningfully illuminate such questions. Either we will discover them to be of too abstract a character to be genuinely informative for our specific needs, or they will turn out to be, upon reflection, but idealized generalizations of our 'local and particular' concepts. Pierre Manent argues that 'the "methodological" intemperance that characterizes it, and that spreads to the other "human sciences," stems first of all from [a] two-fold contradictory movement: a deliberate and forceful distancing from any familiarity with what is real in order to achieve the distance and height of Science, and a no less deliberate and forceful effort to recover that familiarity'.[18]

Although it is prone to the same abstractionism,[19] Hart's own legal philosophy can be interpreted as a contribution to a long-running argument in English jurisprudence. One might reflect upon the problems of jurisprudence as a series of constantly shifting perspectives on the city and the soul. In *The Concept of Law*, we find Hart seeking to draw out universal or generalized truths from deep reflection upon the conceptual structures and institutions of English law (and not vice versa). In two celebrated essays, we find him at pains to clarify the differences which separate American jurisprudence ('that is, American speculative thought about the general nature of law'[20]) from the English tradition to which he

---

[17] Hart, 'Problems of the Philosophy of Law', in *Essays in Jurisprudence and Philosophy* (Oxford University Press, 1983), 88.

[18] P Manent, *The City of Man*, M LePain (trans.) (Princeton University Press, 1998), 55.

[19] See e.g. Hart (above n 8), 240.

[20] Hart, 'American Jurisprudence Through English Eyes: The Nightmare and the Noble Dream', in *Essays* (above n 17), 123. See also '1776–1976: Law in the Perspective of Philosophy', ibid., 145–58.

is conscious of belonging.[21] These passages are suggestive of one who understands that, in deepening our understanding of the historical contexts of philosophical arguments concerning law and politics, we are not thereby led to abandon the idea that such arguments address permanent questions of the world and of the human condition. Our very ideas of politics must begin with an experience of life as inhabitants of a city.

At other times, Hart's reflections seem to point to an entirely different conclusion. His 'analytical' jurisprudence is written in the shadow of Hume and Locke. '[T]here is no view of human life or of the condition of mankind', declares Hume, 'from which, without the greatest violence, we can infer the moral attributes, or learn the divine benevolence'.[22] The very idea of survival itself, Hart tells us, is not 'something antecedently fixed which men necessarily desire because it is their proper goal or end'. Its central place in human thinking is 'a mere contingent fact which could be otherwise'.[23] How does one explain its grip on the mind, on the very being of man? Because it is 'reflected in whole structures of our thought and language, in terms of which we describe the world and each other'. We cannot subtract the wish for survival and leave these structures intact. The fundamental truth about man is that he is a thinker: *homo linguisticus*. Man as an artificer! His emergence can be traced to Locke, who places him in this condition in Book I of *An Essay on Human Understanding* when he pours scorn on the idea of a 'bounteous nature' supplying man with 'general truths' about his condition.[24] Man perceives the world through 'simple ideas' which come to him via the senses: these alone conform to nature.[25] Through the labour of the mind, he transforms these ideas into complex ones, out of which all his understanding flows. Nothing in nature corresponds to 'murder' or 'incest': these are the names of complex associations of ideas, and the relations between them (e.g. pulling the trigger of the gun and the other ideas that make up the act of 'murder') are entirely manufactured by the mind in 'its free choice [giving] a connexion to a certain number of ideas'.[26] On this basis, Locke is able to assert that all of man's ideas are 'arbitrary'. Man's character as a thinker and artificer consumes the whole of his nature.

---

[21] Though see, interestingly, biographical fragments in Nicola Lacey's book on Hart, which reveal his defensiveness over his Jewishness, and consequent sense of un-belonging: N Lacey, *A Life of HLA Hart: The Nightmare and the Noble Dream* (Oxford University Press, 2004).

[22] Hume, *Dialogues Concerning Natural Religion* (Oxford University Press, 1993), XI.

[23] Hart (above n 8), 192. [24] Locke, *An Essay Concerning Human Understanding*, I.2.

[25] Ibid., II.2. [26] Ibid., III.5. The example is Locke's, drawn from III.9.

This leaves us with a very serious problem. Man is the author of his cities. But because his constructions are arbitrary, nothing can be inferred about the nature of the city's values, of its laws, or of its justice. One cannot look to the city, because this is a mere reflection of the soul; but one cannot look to the soul, for it is entirely free and undetermined. Everything Hart has to say on the subject of law and justice is compromised by this. For every insight he plucks from an understanding of 'elementary truths' about human beings, he must finally withhold commitment from it, assenting to its validity only for 'as long as these [truths] hold good'.[27] The very forging of ideas, in becoming so 'free', seems to be trivialized. Indeed, a world that is centrally composed of 'free ideas' is one in perpetual danger of unravelling.

There is something innately unsatisfactory about this explanation. If the Lockean argument is to be believed, society is not natural to man. In his soul, in his very essence, man is the builder of his own world: but if he is 'free' to do so (if his constructions are arbitrary), as Humboldt reminds us, in the very act of building, man builds cages for his own intellect. The emergence of 'common' notions upon which the city is established and organized introduces an order into the soul, qualifying its freedom, affecting man's ability to 'think'. But what else is language except a system of communication that is irreducibly 'common'? Man can only be essentially a 'thinker' if he is also essentially social. His 'freedom' is established upon the existence of a form of 'order' that is derived in *some* sense from outside, from the civil condition in which it has its being. The order that is implied by this relationship is not necessarily equivalent with any of the values or political phenomena that form the object of investigation, but it must have some connection with them, however remote or corrupted this connection. In an early argument in the *Republic*, Socrates establishes an indispensable relationship between justice and the existence of order, even in a very depraved culture: 'For had [men] been completely unjust, they would never have kept their hands off one another, and there must have been some element of justice amongst them which prevented them from wronging each other at the same time as those whom they attacked; they were in fact only half corrupted when they set about their misdeeds, for had their corruption been complete, their complete injustice would have made them incapable of achieving anything.'[28] The very existence of the city requires a soul that is appropriate to its order, one that is not in its essence 'free'.

---

[27] Hart (above n 8), 193.   [28] Plato, *Republic*, 352c.

Jurists and political philosophers ought not to be so impressed with the understandings implied by analytical jurisprudence. Pursuit of understanding of the modern political condition, and of its relationship to questions of justice, of order and of civility, should cause them to reconnect with an older tradition of juridical thought in which the enquiry is shaped by engagement with the ideas of the 'great' philosophies of the West. It is recognized clearly in Plato, in Saint Augustine, Aquinas and even Hobbes, that the question of the city and of the soul is central to the problems of political philosophy. The tensions implicit in this question make themselves felt not only in Locke (who fails to resolve or understand them), but at various points in the English tradition. Writing in c.1810, the poet and thinker Samuel Coleridge invokes the 'heroic Luther' over the 'crazy dreamer' Rousseau, when he declares that 'universal principles ... necessarily suppose uniform and perfect subjects, which are to be found in the *Ideas* of pure geometry and (I trust) in the *Realities* of Heaven, but never, never in creatures of flesh and blood'.[29] If we wish to understand permanent values such as order and justice, we cannot turn to the city, or to human beings, for enlightenment, for there we will meet only with corruptions of these ideas: we can only raise our imagination to the contemplation of ideal societies, achieving enlightenment in the perfection of the soul in its journey toward God. A little under two hundred years earlier, we see the Christian Platonist Thomas Jackson, later president of Corpus Christi College, Oxford, asserting a position that is clearly at variance with Coleridge's, though perhaps not fully incompatible with it: 'we cannot contemplate incorporeal substances without the imagination of some corporeal form'.[30] Christians must seek the divine, not by turning away from the visible world, but by looking toward it.[31]

The positions of Jackson and Coleridge are immensely difficult to reconcile, but in bringing them alongside one another, one gains a glimpse of how the city can be at once endlessly variable and contingent, yet at the same time a possible point of departure for reflection upon more permanent ideas. When seeking to establish a truth that is

---

[29] Samuel Taylor Coleridge, *The Friend: A Series of Essays to Aid in the Formation of Fixed Principles in Politics, Morals and Religion*, vol. I, B Rooke (ed.) (Princeton University Press, 1969), 202. The references to Luther and Rousseau occur at 132.

[30] Thomas Jackson, *Treatise of the Divine Essence and Attributes* [1628], in *The Collected Works of Thomas Jackson*, vol. V (Oxford University Press, 1844), VI.i.4.40.

[31] See D Hedley, *Living Forms of the Imagination* (London, T & T Clark, 2008), 264, and more generally ch 8.

'unconditional', the attempt is not to affirm an argument without conditions, but rather one that holds in all conditions. But this is hugely problematic. Human beings cannot know or discover *all* conditions. Experience is in that sense irrevocably 'contextual'. Knowledge of philosophical truth is thus properly understood as proceeding from reflection upon the institutions and practices which supply the context of one's immediate experience. Unless they are very barbaric, we can expect such reflection to produce general insights into the human condition: insights which in this sense can be expected to hold just as much of (say) German law and politics as of English law. In the words of Isaac Pennington: 'All truth is a shadow, except the final truth . . . But every truth is substance in its own place.'[32] But the philosopher who seeks such lessons by first abstracting his understanding from all that divides German and English structures of law and politics (and from all other contexts of governance), and taking as premises whatever general impressions are left over, is likely to become ensnared by their very sterility. For the differences between alternative systems of governance can be made to vanish only by losing what is specific and essential. This can be conceived as a basis for an understanding of the human condition only by ignoring the fact that it is itself a 'condition' manifested and experienced specifically.

Dimensions of the problem

Do we truly understand what justice is? The question of our 'modernity' often seems to resolve itself in Western man's self-conscious achievement of a just society. The tension described above is overcome in the thought that the perfection of justice is to be found nowhere but in the liberal form itself. Humanity's last great effort lies in the exportation of this achievement across the world, to set the world free.[33] We see justice perfectly *because* we are liberals, even if our own liberal condition is itself yet to be fully perfected. Liberalism inherits from utilitarianism the belief that 'the natural instincts of solidarity and friendship would return after faulty political institutions and religious superstition had been abolished, and humanity would be blessed with lasting harmony and conflict-free order'.[34] The abolition of faulty institutions means the abolition of evil.

---

[32] Quoted in WR Inge, 'Theism', 23 *Philosophy* (1948), 38–59.

[33] See e.g. Dworkin (above n 9), 138–9; Rawls (above n 16).

[34] L Kolakowski, *Modernity on Endless Trial* (University of Chicago Press, 1990), 46.

In exhibiting this belief, liberals recall the Platonic philosopher, described in the *Republic* as one who:

> contemplates a world of unchanging and harmonious order, where reason governs and nothing can do or suffer injustice; and like one who imitates an admired companion, he cannot fail to fashion himself in its likeness. So the philosopher, in constant companionship with the divine order of the world, will reproduce that order in his soul and, so far as a man may, become godlike; though here, as elsewhere, there will be scope for detraction.[35]

Liberals are both too proud and too dismissive of the city. Impatient of the injustices and inequalities of present society, they theorize models in which such imperfections are removed; but pride in the liberal ideal leads them to associate too readily the concrete liberal arrangements of the present day with the impressive qualities of the model. Present arrangements are not to be understood as constituting a form of order on their own terms (with its various advantages and disadvantages), but as a partial and as yet imperfect realization of the ideal model of order. It is significant that, in contemplating the idea of justice, Rawls is drawn to an image of deliberators who reproduce its order in their souls because their souls are first emptied of all order. They are seeking a virtuous set of arrangements, in Kant's phrase, 'of which the world has never had an example',[36] and must first be deprived of all worldly associations. We can contrast this image of society and its members being reborn into justice, with the words of Saint Bernard of Clairvaux on the subject of ecstatic love: 'I would count him blessed and holy to whom it has been given to experience such a thing in this mortal life at rare intervals or even once, and this suddenly or scarcely for the space of a single moment. In a certain manner to lose yourself as though you were not, and to be utterly unconscious of yourself and to be emptied of yourself and, as it were, brought to nothing, this pertains to heavenly intercourse, not to human affection.'[37] These words are suggestive of a different interpretation of Plato's remarks on the philosopher in the *Republic*. They depict human access to pure insights as rare and fleeting glimpses, scarcely experienced before they are taken away. If only one could really manufacture such experiences by contemplating an 'original position'!

---

[35] Plato, *Republic*, 500c–d.
[36] Kant, *Groundwork of the Metaphysics of Morals*, Section II.
[37] Saint Bernard of Clairvaux, *On Loving God* [c.1121], ch X.

Modern liberal philosophies owe to Kant the thought that the cardinal values of freedom, equality and justice are not to be found in the city (which is corrupted and unjust), but in the soul alone (in the form of reason), shorn of earthly attachments. The 'original position' has such a powerful attraction over the mind because it establishes justice on the basis of something philosophers understand and respect above all else: *arguments*. Since values exist in detachment from the unjust arrangements of the earthly polity, what else but argument can win people over to justice? Amongst philosophers it is Aristotle who best understands the limitations of argument in the movement of minds. In chapter IX of the tenth book of the *Nicomachean Ethics*, he recalls that 'if arguments were in themselves enough to make men good, they would justly ... have won very great rewards'.[38] Though arguments may 'have power to encourage and stimulate' those *already* possessed of nobility and good character, 'they are not able to encourage man to nobility and goodness ... It is hard, if not impossible, to remove by argument the traits that have long since been incorporated in the character.' For arguments to become powerful, 'the soul of the student must first have been cultivated by means of habits'.[39] If the values of the earthly city are imperfect, or even positively corrupted, they nevertheless establish the nexus within which the individual is directed to think and behave justly.

If we wish to understand the position of the 'modern man' who resides at the centre of politics, it is necessary to realize that he is neither to be trusted as being in the possession of the truth of his situation, nor abandoned to a world in which there is no truth. If Rawls and other liberal philosophers are too quick to identify the truth, Hart is nevertheless too willing to abandon the world to ultimate meaninglessness. How, as historical beings, can we hope to uncover the nature of the human being and of the human condition in its fullest sense, and not merely that of particular historical conditions? Philosophy aims to reveal something other than a history of ideas: 'it aims at Truth as such, and not at somebody's truth'.[40] But when we try to conceive the truth, it is always somebody's thought. This entails an interesting situation. We begin to perceive the nature of philosophical problems when we come to realize that they are of infinite depth. Being infinite, such problems lack definitive starting points. The conception of such problems is thus always

---

[38] Aristotle, *Nicomachean Ethics*, Book X, ch 9.   [39] Ibid.
[40] A Kolnai, *Ethics, Value and Reality* (New Brunswick NJ, Transaction Publishers, 2008), 23.

shaped by 'someone's conception' of where one must begin, and of the way in which the problem may be temporarily reduced to finite dimensions for the sake of thought.

Faced with these difficulties, it is not hard to understand why some liberal philosophers might feel anxiety that the world may not contain final truths. There appear to be no ultimate perspectives from which political efforts make sense. If we do not think of values such as justice, or equality, as having merely a local, contingent meaning, neither should we think of politics as being aligned to such values directly: 'politics is not about doing what is good or rational or beneficial *simpliciter* ... but about the pursuit of what is good in a particular concrete case by agents with limited powers and resources, where the choice of one thing to pursue means failure to choose and pursue another'.[41] The cynicism of certain liberals in this regard can be compared to the ancient scepticism of the Phyronnians, for whom philosophy is incapable of furnishing knowledge of a 'reality' that exists behind appearances. Accepting that arguments about reality are irredeemably opposing, the Phyronnians suspended judgment and elected to live according to appearances. Their scepticism was not dogmatic, but premised upon the avoidance of all dogma.[42] This form of scepticism is in essence anti-philosophical. Recognizing the infinite nature of philosophical problems, it despairs of ever discovering deeper truths and instead finds solace of mind in the suspension of judgment. In a diary entry, Hart recollects an exchange with the future Labour cabinet minister, Richard Crossman. Upon Hart's return to New College, Oxford, Crossman is reported as having laughed at his philosophical ambitions: 'Still worrying about the truth, I suppose?'[43] If Crossman's cynical indictment of 'truth' (or perhaps of the relevance of its pursuit) seems to betoken a Phyronnian form of scepticism, Hart's response might seem to embody its antithesis: 'I was all that Crossman hated: that's to say, balanced, fair, worrying about the truth.'[44] But taken another way, Hart's statement itself implies a sceptical

---

[41] R Geuss, *Philosophy and Real Politics* (Princeton University Press, 2008), 30–1.

[42] The principal source on the Phyronnian philosophers is Diogenes Laertius, *Lives of Eminent Philosophers* (Cambridge MA, Loeb Classical Library, 1925), esp. Bk IX. See also JC Laursen, *The Politics of Skepticism in the Ancients, Montaigne, Hume and Kant* (New York, Brill, 1992).

[43] Quoted in Lacey (above n 21), 24.

[44] Ibid., 284. The reminiscences are brought alongside each other in A Perreau-Saussine, 'An Outsider on the Inside: Hart's Limits on Jurisprudence', *University of Toronto LJ*, 56 (2006), 386 n 37.

attitude, that of Socratic (or so-called 'Academic') scepticism. The Socrates of Plato's early *Dialogues* questions the opinions of all men, and refrains from offering positive doctrines. The Academic sceptics were therefore critical of both Plato and Aristotle for departing from this method, in seeking and claiming to know the truth.[45]

Hart's anxieties are preferable to the triumphalist visions sometimes proclaimed by advocates of the liberal ideal. At the same time, it is doubtful whether either form of scepticism can provide a basis for politics unless it is contained within certain limits. Socrates' method is not incompatible with the existence of truth, but it too is subject to a fundamental despair if left unbounded. Augustine, who greatly admired Plato, recognizes the difficulties that face the philosopher: 'the fact is that, whether because we have deserved it, or because this is necessary by nature, the divine spirit that is united to our mortal bodies can never reach the harbour of wisdom ....'[46] Augustine constantly worries about our 'pretensions to insulate ourselves from temporality and mortality', recognizing (as does Montaigne) that experience forever outstrips all efforts to order and classify it.[47] But, writing to Romanianus, he nevertheless expresses hope that human reason can uncover truth: 'You were born ... into this earthly life, abounding as it does in all error, with such talent – obvious even from your earliest youth when reason's progress is but weak and faltering – as always makes me marvel.'[48] Augustine's concern is not therefore ultimately to deny that human beings can participate in truth, but that 'men, wrongly thinking that they have already found truth, do not seek with diligence'.[49]

The ultimate assurance of knowledge, for Augustine, is the supernatural grace by which human beings are enabled to participate in a truth that is finally divine.[50] Human reason, being finite, is incapable of discovering truth in its entirety, but may nevertheless perceive something of truth, and derive hope from the search for truth. In a broader sense, it is Augustine's acceptance of and submission to *authority* (in his case, the authority of the Church and of the Gospels) that sets limits to an entirely negative and sceptical picture of human knowledge. The sceptical and questioning disposition is essential to the avoidance of an

---

[45] Laursen, 'Oakeshott's Skepticism and the Skeptical Traditions', *European J of Political Theory*, 4 (2005), 37–55, 38.

[46] Augustine, *Contra Academicos*, JJ O'Meara (ed.) (Westminster MD, Newman Press, 1951), Bk I.1.

[47] T Fuller, 'Introduction', in M Oakeshott, *Religion, Politics and the Moral Life* (New Haven CT, Yale University Press, 1993), ix.

[48] Augustine, *Contra Academicos*, Bk I.1.   [49] Ibid., Bk II.1.   [50] Ibid., Bk III.18–19.

ever-threatening *superbia* (or pride) to which humans too easily succumb; but limits must be set to scepticism if we are not to indulge an equally damaging pride which conceives the limits of human knowledge and experience to coincide with the totality of what may be known.

In being either too pessimistic about a *summum bonum* or correct way of living, or too optimistic in identifying this form of life with their current imaginings of the liberal ideal, liberals can easily miss the deeper significance of the liberal political order in the human condition. As its historians have pointed out, a free society requires a measure of confidence in the ability of men to reach some measure of accommodation between their competing interests, and to arrive at certain shared ideas of justice which transcend their particular interests.[51] The subjects of liberal political orders are neither wholly depraved nor especially saintly: 'men are not devils, neither are they angels'.[52] Too great a pessimism regarding the moral character of men will result in governments of an authoritarian character, for it will be sensed that only highly centralized and concentrated forms of order will serve to coerce variant interests into harmonious relationships in which vulnerabilities are held in check. Its central principle is *organization*. But too great an optimism in the capacity for justice without centralized interventions aggravates the problems associated with *disorder*: the lack of a unified direction, the situation of not being controlled, can produce feelings of powerlessness and helpless subjection to the tyranny of unpoliced interests.[53] Thus if a free society is allowed to wander too far out of control, it may invite the alternative evil of authoritarian rule: the overwhelming desire for an architect that one finds in Hobbes, for example.

A philosophical explanation of politics (in common with any subject) is the discovery and exploration of its orderliness. It is probably unintelligible to think that there could be an explanation of *disorder*, for explanation is precisely the perception and narration of order. The presence of order is undoubtedly felt more strongly in some areas of political life, and certain arrangements or institutions come to be regarded as the source or the precondition of the further patterns of orderliness in which we move.

---

[51] See R Niebuhr, 'The Children of Light and the Children of Darkness', in R McAfee Brown (ed.) *The Essential Reinhold Niebuhr: Selected Essays and Addresses* (New Haven CT, Yale University Press, 1986), 160.

[52] Hart (above n 8), 196.

[53] See Kolakowski, 'The Self-Poisoning of the Open Society', in *Modernity on Endless Trial* (above n 34), 162–74.

Nevertheless, political order is without 'foundations' as such: our perception of or belief in the orderliness of politics proceeds from no fixed or well-defined starting point. Lacking such starting points, it is strictly incorrect to speak of legal and political understandings as being 'grounded' in certain ideas which it is the duty of philosophy to call forth in a more conscious form. Instead, philosophy must be thought of as seeking a more explicit awareness of the 'orientation' of thought and experience, and as willingly and honestly questioning the beliefs which sustain this orientation. Thinking and experience seldom proceed in one direction at a time, however. A central task of the philosopher must be to identify and probe those 'neuralgic' points at which our sense of the orderliness of thought and experience is most visibly threatened: where we feel the attraction of conflicting tendencies or outlooks, which represent, simultaneously, the limits of our adherence to the primary orientation of our thinking, and the loss of our immediate ability to give a good account of the reason for our beliefs.

For example, optimistic liberals need to cultivate with care a sense of the character and ultimate purpose of order as against the disordered state of 'freedom' that is said to be the birthright of the individual. If he is not careful, the liberal can end up deriving the demand for a just order *and* the demand for the recognition of freedom from the same source: equality. Socialists and conservatives share with liberals the belief that all human beings are equal and equally precious; but if they agree on the ethical meaning of this insight, its political meaning remains shrouded in conflicts and arguments. One cannot posit a truly just and free political ideology upon the basis of equality without resolving all that lies between conservatives and socialists. Upon the one hand, liberals recognize that human beings must choose how to live here and now. On the other hand, they express agnosticism over the issue of what man is trying to become. The price that liberals pay for this benevolence is the creation of societies that tend to be rather venal in character, for the political focus rests upon what a man *has*, not what he *is*. Liberal societies, in tolerating all identities (within reason), will constantly invite the abandonment of individual efforts to adhere to a scale of values that is spiritual in nature rather than material. Because there is nothing that a man *must* have in order to grow, unnecessary material acquisitions fill the void and become his 'vital needs'.[54] But the same tolerant attitude depends upon the belief

---

[54] H Marcuse, *One-Dimensional Man: Studies in the Ideology of Advanced Societies* (London, Routledge, 1964), 5.

that, whichever way humans choose to live, they are at a basic level 'good' rather than twisted and evil. Perhaps the true predicament of the modern individual is that of failing to do what one ought to do, because one is constantly diverted into doing what one is free to do. Do optimistic liberals join with pessimists in making it impossible for politics to transcend its own present conditions?

In this book, I offer a series of reflections on the themes and problems I have just described. I have divided these into three parts. The first consists of chapters which consider the central problems of jurisprudence in a liberal society, and try to indicate the path that must be taken in order to address them. The second part attempts to isolate certain dimensions of the problem of modern law and politics, and to explore their significance from a broader perspective that is too often absent from recent philosophical debate. Finally, a third part considers the idea of justice from a number of distinct but related perspectives.

PART I

Jurisprudence

1

Jurisprudence and the liberal order

The Western tradition of jurisprudential reflection on the nature of law stands amongst the most significant intellectual and cultural achievements in history. The subjects of law and politics appear in the earliest philosophical texts as a source of perplexities and questions, and in none amongst the 'great' philosophies of the West are they ever wholly absent as a concern. Both Plato and Aristotle took the nature of law and justice as a central question, and in consequence developed what may be referred to as 'philosophies of law'. Aquinas and Kant both produced a treatise on law. Amongst the pantheon of great thinkers, other philosophers produced no systematic reflections on law, but mused upon its nature and its distinctive qualities in the course of meditations upon the subjects of morality, of society and politics, and of grace. Such connections help to illustrate the intimate relationship of juridical ideas to our broader cultural inheritance. The fundamental forms of human judgment may in fact be viewed as juridical in origin.[1] Hence the notion of 'law' seems to be inseparable from the phenomenon of human rationality generally, and of the mind's conformity to standards of sensibility or of reason.

We might nevertheless ask exactly *how* law and reason are linked. In Book I of the *Politics*, Aristotle draws a striking contrast between those who live in a state, and are thus 'perfected' by living according to justice and virtue, and those who, separated from law and justice, become 'the worst of all . . . the most unholy and the most savage of animals, and the most full of lust and gluttony'.[2] Because man is 'by nature' a political animal, law is not in Aristotle's view separated from nature. But 'nature' was not an impartial interpreter or judge of the regime, for (as the first two books of the *Nicomachean Ethics* make clear) man only fulfils his 'nature' when in the presence of law, and as modified by it so that he

---

[1] G Rose, *The Dialectic of Nihilism: Post-Structuralism and Law* (Oxford, Blackwell, 1984).
[2] Aristotle, *Politics*, I.2.

'lives under a certain confusion of nature and law'.[3] The worse Aristotle
thinks human beings are capable of becoming, the more law is needed for
their modification and improvement. The more savage man's nature
when 'uncivilized', the harder it will be for him to coerce society into
civilized order. Picking up on this theme, Aquinas observes that the
achievement of social order is a relative one pertaining to man's com-
parative goodness as a citizen, rather than his absolute goodness as a
man.[4] The unity of society is not an organic but a relative order. Thus, in
his commentary on Aristotle's *Ethics*, Aquinas suggests that politics,
ethics and economics cannot be considered as constituent sub-elements
of a single science, but retain a distinctiveness which prevents their
reconciliation into a unified 'social' science.[5]

   These reflections might lead to a certain anxiety about the character of
jurisprudential thinking. Philosophical analysis, by its very nature, sup-
poses the realms of law and politics to be amenable to coherent expos-
ition and rationalization. This inevitably involves a degree of 'rational
reconstruction', of amending the inconsistencies of social practices.
Efforts which seek to give a concrete form to the justice spoken of by
Aristotle must in a sense complete the order of society.[6] If they do not
treat a society's tensions as illusory, then they must envisage them as
temporary, or else transmute them through the enumeration of 'compossible' domains of autonomy. Societies in general, but liberal societies
in particular, must establish unity within conditions of freedom, but
also contain the disorder of freedom within the scope of a superior
order. Especially where the market is concerned, there are limits to
rationalization. Markets are specifically *unstructured*. They embody a
form of competition, a struggle between conflicting interests in which
the stronger prevails. The behaviour of the market is notoriously resistant
to models. It is spontaneous rather than determined. A considerable
amount of the market's 'order' is due not to control, but to countless

---

[3] P Manent, *The City of Man*, M LePain (trans.) (Princeton University Press, 1998), 180.
[4] Aquinas, *Summa Theologiae*, I–II, 92.1: 'the law does not make men good simply, but in
respect to that particular government'.
[5] Aquinas, *Commentary on Aristotle's Nicomachean Ethics*, CI Litzinger (ed.) (Chicago,
Dumb Ox Books, 1993), I.1. See also E Fortin, 'The Political Thought of St Thomas
Aquinas', in JB Benestad (ed.) *Classical Christianity and the Political Order: Collected
Essays*, vol. II (Lanham MD, Rowman & Littlefield, 1996), 161.
[6] Finnis notes this tendency: see J Finnis, *Natural Law and Natural Rights*, 2nd edn (Oxford,
Clarendon Press, 2011), 192–3.

negotiable instruments. One can at most offer predictions, and ex post facto explanations.

Liberals who like to think of their society as informed by an overarching theory of justice will not readily accept this description. Where some see tensions and disorganization, they will perceive the existence of 'valid' domains of freedom structured by sound principles and institutions. Where socialists (and others) feel deep anger at the cruelty of the market, liberals will focus upon the emancipatory character of looser political controls. They will suggest that, having become sufficiently civilized, modern man can be let loose to negotiate his own arrangements without acting in a beastly way.[7] Socialists are less sure. In order to maintain their position, liberals must stress the systematic quality of society, a perspective from which everything finally makes sense. If it is to be an expression of a system of justice, the terrain of law and politics must appear fully consistent. If, by contrast, the terrain of modern politics is of an internally complex and only superficially coherent nature, why should one expect a theoretical understanding of it to be any less complex, or less subject to numerous lines of development existing only in tension? Have liberals confused the realities of the open society with its ideology?

It would be easy to suggest that modern-day liberals have forgotten Machiavelli's observation that it is

> more fitting to go to the effectual truth of the thing than to the imagination of it. And many have dreamt of republics and principalities that have never been seen or known to exist in truth; for it is so far from how one lives to how one ought to live that he who renounces what is done for what should be done learns his ruin rather than his preservation.[8]

But Machiavelli does not entirely get to the heart of the problem. All moral positions are 'imaginative' in requiring some re-imagination of social conditions. Liberals do not agree with Machiavelli that the present form of the liberal order is 'so far' from the condition of life that is required. But liberals have also too frequently identified the required condition with the abolishment of the ills of society.[9] In this, the philosophers of liberal order have misunderstood the nature of philosophical problems. Philosophical problems are essentially infinite. Thinkers are

---

[7] See in particular Montesquieu, *L'Espirit des Lois*, XX.1: 'Commerce cures destructive prejudices, and it is almost a general rule that everywhere we find agreeable manners, commerce flourishes, and that wherever there is commerce, there are agreeable manners.'

[8] Machiavelli, *The Prince* [1532], ch 15.

[9] See esp. F Fukuyama, *The End of History and the Last Man* (London, Penguin, 1993).

always (so to speak) in the middle of such problems, never finding their way back to a definitive beginning, or to a final end wherein further questions are exhausted. One can hardly avoid the imagination of philosophical truths! The imagination of truth is itself dependent upon a kind of faith. Faith is intrinsic to philosophical enquiry, for if the truth or rationality of philosophical problems were finally demonstrable, philosophical problems would disappear. It is for this reason that philosophical arguments are so intractable. Standpoints on questions that are truly 'philosophical' cannot be eliminated through mere argument, but only made more or less attractive to those who contemplate them. As with religious faith, it is sometimes possible to alter belief by bringing to light the tacit assumptions on which the beliefs rest; but very often this is not the case. Faith is not, at the same time, *opposed* to reason, but must itself be rational if it is to be recognized as philosophical. Philosophical thinking enjoys no well-defined end point beyond which reason terminates in an exercise of 'sheer' faith: that which is believed may be ultimately mysterious, but belief is not itself inarticulate and sets no final boundaries to the activity of speculation.

Where liberals have identified the final moral and political form of social life, it is because they have misunderstood the nature of faith. When we read Rawls's A Theory of Justice, are we more impressed by its architectonic coherence, or its author's steadfast confidence in its doctrines? Twenty years after the book's first publication, Rawls remains convinced that (with only minor modifications), his work offers a general standpoint from which central political questions 'can be reasonably decided'.[10] In the modern world, it is certainty rather than doubt which is the enemy of faith. This is seen most clearly in religion: the man of certainty, wrote Pope Pius X in his inaugural encyclical, 'has with infinite temerity put himself in the place of God, raising himself above all that is called God ...'.[11] The same is true of all instances of faith. Faith must encounter doubt. If it does not, its true nature becomes hidden, seeming to take on the characteristics of 'knowledge' but within narrower intellectual horizons.

By way of illustration, in the final chapter of his *Natural Law and Natural Rights*, Finnis asks whether the argument defended in the body of the book, concerning basic dimensions of human flourishing, is yet

---

[10] J Rawls, *A Theory of Justice*, revised edn (Cambridge MA, Harvard University Press, 1999), xvi. (Rawls's remarks are contained in the revised preface, dated 1990.)
[11] The encyclical *E Supremi*, 4 October 1903, 5.

questionable from a broader perspective. Having enumerated seven basic objective goods, each representing a distinctive form of human flourishing (life, knowledge, play, aestheticism, sociability, practical reasonableness and religion), Finnis says that each is

> obvious to anyone acquainted, whether through his own inclinations or vicariously through the character and works of others, with the range of human opportunities. And the general requirements of reasonableness (itself one of those basic forms of good) are, likewise, as obvious as the norms of rationality, principles of logic, and canons of explanation that are presupposed in *any* explanation, whether in our practical context or in natural science or analytical philosophy.[12]

Having shown such goods to be insusceptible of rational denial, Finnis asks: 'what further explanations are required?'

Assuming that Finnis's characterization of human flourishing is correct, for such goods to make sense as dimensions of this flourishing they must appear not only as *abstracta* or general ideas, but as actually present dimensions of the flourishing of individuals. Similarly, the idea of 'the common good' must manifest itself in a range of potentialities open to individuals with shared opportunities and vulnerabilities, and must indicate the concrete conditions under which the wellbeing of individuals may be favoured, advanced, and preserved.[13] But the participation of each individual, and therefore of every community, in those forms of flourishing is actually extremely limited (death, in particular, intervening before anything great can be accomplished). We might then ask whether pursuit of the good by individuals or communities has any *further* point, beyond such limited self-enrichment? Finnis invites us to suppose that the good of my relations, or of my community, necessitates my own ruin or destruction. What is the meaning of such self-sacrifice? The question does not seek to challenge the reality of the other's good. It asks if any further sense can be made of the whole situation, some more remote or ultimate condition to which that good, and the self-sacrifice, contribute? Does not all the resultant wellbeing, even that of the community, come to an end sooner or later? Even great civilizations wane and collapse. What then is *its* purpose, and meaning?

It is not necessary to embrace the particulars of Finnis's argument in order to appreciate the force of the question. Whatever understanding we

---

[12] Finnis (above n 6), 371.   [13] Ibid., 372.

have of the nature of law, it behoves us to ask what purpose is served, in the end, by its having that nature? The 'noble dream' of liberalism,[14] even if it has not addressed the question, is in some way responsive to it. The question, 'what *further* point is there?' (to our definitions, concepts, categories, experiences) has in recent times generated 'a ready market for interpretations of history which allow the questioner to believe that he and his community, race, class or party are contributing to the attainment of some future plateau to which History will, with his assistance, progress'.[15] As Finnis also observes, Kant noted early the corrupting and defective character of all noble dreams:

> What remains disconcerting about all this is first, that the earlier generations seem to perform their laborious tasks only for the sake of the later ones, so as to prepare for them a further stage from which they can raise still higher the structure intended by nature; and secondly, that only the later generations will in fact have the good fortune to inhabit the building on which a whole series of their forefathers (admittedly without any conscious intention) had worked without themselves being able to share in the happiness they were preparing.[16]

It is in some ways ironic that liberals have taken such a view of history. Liberalism celebrates the individual as one who genuinely selects, and lives according to, an end chosen by himself, rather than having an end dictated to him. Does the individual exercise this freedom only to find that he has, all along, been the unwitting tool of a constructive imperative that is larger than himself, and than any of his dreams? Does the lack of organization in liberal regimes finally redound to a superior *order*?

I would like to suggest that liberalism is sometimes animated by a tacit theodicy, and thus also a corresponding soteriology. Appropriately, liberals imply ideas of superior order within apparently disorganized processes of individual choice, when they seek to articulate a *juridical* vision. The idea of a 'liberal' is of course a very broad one. I shall therefore concentrate on the example of Rawls.

---

[14] See HLA Hart, 'American Jurisprudence Through English Eyes: The Nightmare and the Noble Dream', in *Essays in Jurisprudence and Philosophy* (Oxford, Clarendon Press, 1983), 123.

[15] Finnis (above n 6), 373.

[16] Kant, 'Idea for a Universal History with a Cosmopolitan Purpose', HB Nisbet (trans.) in H Reiss (ed.) *Kant's Political Writings* (Cambridge University Press, 1970), 44. Quoted by Finnis (above n 6), 373–4.

History and direction

This tacit theodicy can be brought to light by considering some of the deep intellectual commitments of modern juridical thought. We might reveal something of those commitments by considering the relationship of present thinking about morality and law to its immediate past. The juridical thought of any age embodies certain understandings of those aspects of the human condition it seeks to clarify: in this case, the gradual self-transformation of society under the rule of law.[17] Each generation of jurisprudential thinking can be expected to reflect its own philosophical biases, by regarding certain questions as central to philosophical progress whilst marginalizing or suppressing others. The processes by which philosophical doctrines wax and decline are not straightforward, but they are worth studying because they reveal much about the deepest commitments of the present age, and the challenges that face it.

To modern writers, the distinctive achievement of twentieth-century jurisprudence can be viewed as its emancipation from the narrow confines of English utilitarianism, and the subsequent development of perspectives rooted in the fundamental values of justice and rights. The central jurisprudential task of the new century is thus the exploration of a deeper, more elusive moral standpoint whose most profound intellectual commitments are yet to be fully digested and understood.

The publication in 1971 of Rawls's *A Theory of Justice* in some ways marks a watershed in political theory. In that book, Rawls conceives of himself as responding to a political scene dominated by utilitarianism.[18] Utilitarian arguments form the focus of his attack, to such an extent that 'his criticisms of utilitarianism go to inform the structure and

---

[17] See e.g. R Dworkin, *Law's Empire* (London, Fontana, 1986), ch 11: 'Law Beyond Law'; L Fuller, *The Law in Quest of Itself* (Chicago, Foundation Press, 1940), 140, who writes of 'the eternal process by which the common law works itself pure and adapts itself to the needs of a new day'.

[18] See Rawls (above n 10), ch 1. Rawls also targets 'intuitionistic' theories of justice, but he devotes far less attention to these than to utilitarianism. Hart, too, noted: 'I do not think that anyone familiar with what has been published in the last ten years, in England and the United States, on the philosophy of government can doubt that this subject ... is undergoing a major change. We are currently witnessing, I think, the progress of a transition from a once widely accepted old faith that some form of utilitarianism ... *must* capture the essence of morality. The new faith is that the truth must lie ... with a doctrine of basic human rights, protecting specific basic liberties and interests of individuals.' Hart, 'Between Utility and Rights', in *Essays* (above n 14), 198.

assumptions of his own theory'.[19] The effect of Rawls's work was indeed to bring about a sea change in Anglo-American political thought. To a great extent, the political project of the current age is not that of maximizing overall satisfaction of an array of conflicting preferences, but of discovering a theory of justice capable of grounding a common framework for the pursuit of competing preferences whilst maintaining the equal value of each person. Progress in such an endeavour is thus a matter of refining understandings of justice as they apply to a context of actually functioning institutions.

Progress in philosophy is seldom linear. The nature of philosophical argument nevertheless lends itself especially easily to forms of narrative history. Philosophy is centrally concerned with truth, but since the philosophical efforts of previous generations have manifested that truth at best only imperfectly and incompletely, it is constantly tempting for the modern age to regard itself as being in the most favourable position to detect it: standing on the shoulders of giants, we command a clearer view of the terrain than any before us. It would not be difficult to construct a history of Western jurisprudence which would seem to bear out this sense of progression.

The ancient writers had focused upon the question of how we can lead an excellent and valuable life. Consequently their ethical thought gave a central place to the idea of 'the good life', and explored the ways in which politics and law might foster and sustain that life. Requiring political institutions for its realization, the nature of the good life was thought to be intrinsically social, capable of full expression only within the bounds of a common existence and not when pursued 'individually'.

In the wake of the Reformation, a new and essentially Protestant view of the world began to take shape which rejected key elements of the classical philosophy of the past.[20] Amongst the ideas which came to be rejected was the idea that the social world is animated by a single conception of 'the good life', understood to be embedded within and actively promoted by institutions such as the law. Law was to be regarded instead as an unfortunately necessary framework of rules for the maintenance of order and social stability in a world where each person has their *own* idea of the good or worthwhile life, which they pursue in

---

[19] NE Simmonds, *Central Issues in Jurisprudence*, 3rd edn (London, Sweet & Maxwell, 2008), 62.

[20] See HJ Berman, *Law and Revolution, Volume I: The Formation of the Western Legal Tradition* (Cambridge MA, Harvard University Press, 1983).

competition with others. Those who sought to identify a solid foundation for the law's neutrality between these competing projects discovered an answer in the idea of natural equality. The premise that all men are by nature juridical equals proved to be a splendidly rich and adaptable idea. Important philosophical questions nevertheless persisted in relation to the character of such equalities. On one side stood Grotius and his intellectual descendants, arguing that basic equalities were rooted in the *suum*, or domains of self-ownership in which a person is able to make autonomous decisions independently of the will of others. The Grotian philosophy insisted upon the reality of a framework of non-overlapping entitlements which logically preceded the authority of the state, and which were grounded in notions of self-preservation and the potential for human flourishing. No one (and hence no law) may violate the *suum* of another in pursuit of his interests.[21] On the other side was Hobbes, who regarded such basic rights as all-encompassing. All men were equal in that all were equally free to exert their will in whatever way they chose, 'even [over] one another's body'.[22] The function of law was not to realize basic rights but to restrict them, by *creating* protected spheres in which each person enjoys certain freedoms from the will of others.

Despite diverging in many ways, the philosophies of Hobbes and Grotius both paved the way for utilitarian accounts of law that Rawls takes as the object of his attack. Both, for example, transformed the understanding of law as an object of moral reflection, in which one might come to certain conclusions about the nature of a common good, towards a picture wherein law is presented as an otherwise self-standing intellectual framework to which various notions of the good life might subsequently be applied. More importantly, both Grotius and Hobbes made decisive steps towards a secular view of morality. In founding his philosophy on human equalities, Hobbes depicted a lawless world of chaotic competition in which 'notions of Right and Wrong, Justice and Injustice have ... no place', unless as artificial products of 'men in Society'.[23] Grotius famously remarked that theoretical knowledge of God was unnecessary for an understanding of moral truth, for such understanding derives from reflection upon the qualities of the *suum*: an observation for which he was criticized by Pufendorf. Yet in seeking to retain the centrality of a theocentric framework of divine law, Pufendorf

---

[21] Grotius, *De Iure Belli ac Pacis*, I.2.1.6.
[22] Hobbes, *Leviathan*, R Tuck (ed.) (Cambridge University Press, 1991), ch 14.
[23] Ibid., ch 13.

himself articulated a standpoint which facilitated the development of secular moralities. For Pufendorf, actions are not good or evil in themselves, but only as they affect rights: 'That reason should be able to discover any morality in the actions of a man without reference to a law, is as impossible as for a man born blind to choose between colours.'[24] Once it came to be recognized that such a law need not be divine, but merely human in origin, then any remaining ties to the classical conception of ethics could be finally cut.

Those in the Grotian tradition of juridical thinking regarded the function of law as being ultimately protective of fundamental rights, and thus as seeking an ideal ordering or balancing amongst the competing conceptions of the good life to be found in post-Reformation societies. Such an ordering would give central place to conceptions of justice, right and equality. But in the light of Pufendorf's modulation of the moral foundations of the position, the only possible source of the moral values which would inform notions of justice and right was the will of the 'autonomous agent': a view which reached its highpoint in Kant's *Groundwork of the Metaphysics of Morals*, and which was inherited in a slightly modified form by Rawls and his intellectual allies. The Hobbesian tradition, meanwhile, regarded the function of law as that of achieving some reasonable accommodation or balancing between the competing conceptions of the good life. This was eventually to develop into the thought of the English utilitarians, who noticed that the premise of divine law in the earlier moral theories served only to link ideas of the human good to that of human felicity, so that the moral injunction to seek the good represented a curiously roundabout way of saying that one should aim to maximize welfare.

Other aspects of the Grotian position indicated possible grounds for a utilitarian standpoint. Despite Pufendorf's castigation of Grotius for his 'impious hypothesis', other interpreters (such as Barbeyrac) had recognized in Grotius's remarks a commonplace of seventeenth-century moral philosophy, that the obligatory force of natural law derives from the divine will, whereas its content is founded upon the nature of the human condition. This independence of the force of moral laws from determination of their content (as it appeared to the utilitarians) meant that the whole of the weight of morality's rational intelligibility was to be borne by considerations of utility. If God's will does not establish any

---

[24] Pufendorf, *De Iure Naturae et Gentium*, I.2.6.

intellectual basis for morality, then considerations of human wellbeing or felicity must themselves ground standards of right and wrong. Law, as well as other social institutions, must be interpreted as human conventions whose function is to maximize welfare in society.[25]

Having removed the theological foundation from ethics, utilitarians developed the idea of natural equality in a different way. Rather than interpreting such equalities as establishing equal rights to pursue and realize certain dimensions of value, utilitarianism viewed individuals as potential maximizers of units of 'utility', the value of which derives from their being the object of preferences. Not only persons, but also values, were to be considered equals. One man's conception of 'the good' is no more or less valuable than anyone else's, and thus no more or less worthy of legal protection. The reasonable ordering or balancing of competing interests is to be considered as one in which the allocation of rights and obligations tends to realize the greatest levels of utility across society. Modern liberals who have flocked to the Rawlsian banner dismiss utilitarianism as misconceived and unsuccessful. But they remain deeply fascinated by its central moral idea: equality.

Utilitarianism sought to give expression to equalities between *persons* by recognizing the equality of the objects of their pursuit, *goods*. Utilitarians raised the idea of 'good' to an absolute position, higher than 'right', whilst maintaining a neutral position over the identity of 'the good' by referring to it only in very abstract ways ('utility', 'welfare', etc.) Modern liberals, by contrast, regard the 'value' of personal equality as finding a clearer and more profound expression in a theory of rights. How significant is this shift? Rawls is entirely correct to emphasize that the essential focus of an account of rights falls upon questions of the institutional structure of society. A politics which delivers 'rights' must take as its object the regime. Liberals are famously opposed to the Aristotelian idea that the regime delivers goods that complete and perfect the nature of man. States represent individuals, not the salvation of spiritual masses. But liberals treat the regime as perfective in another way. Only through it do men become truly 'individuals'; only the regime offers stability, freedom, equality. Precisely because it does not ground itself upon any despotic opinion about 'the good', the liberal political order delivers the 'ideal' condition, the freedom of each person to pursue their own chosen ends. The idea that liberal orders secure only an escape from the evils of

---

[25] See e.g. JS Mill, *An Examination of William Hamilton's Philosophy* [1865], in J Robson (ed.) *The Collected Works of John Stuart Mill*, vol. IX, ch VII (London, R&K Paul, 1963–91).

'mere' nature, and not the pursuit of what must be recognized jointly as truly 'good', may therefore be mistaken.

Though it does not specifically cultivate any particular qualities, one might say that the idea of 'the good' in a liberal political order is preserved in the idea of a coherent system of political values ('freedom', 'equality', etc.) in which the interpretation of each value serves to reinforce the others.[26] Liberals regard so-called 'right-based' liberalism as an advance over utilitarianism because a political order realized along these lines approximates more closely to a perception of an ideal condition in which injustice will disappear. Politics cannot seek the perfection of men without flying into the arms of despotism; it must instead seek the perfection of liberal social order. Injustice and despotism are evils that a correct politics can destroy.

The end of legal order

Liberal philosophers have been slow to connect their immediate concerns about justice with a deeper sense of the evils they wish to eradicate. Partly this is because liberals specifically wish to separate questions of temporal power from questions of spiritual direction. Partly, it is because the character of the 'open society' is not thought to imply any particular notions of 'evil' except those associated with 'closed' societies, or anti-social behaviours which threaten society's 'openness'. Liberals by and large assume that they understand these evils very well. Correct order will eliminate them. Progress toward this order equals human beings' historical progress.

Pursuing an agenda indicated by these ideas, liberal philosophers have not asked themselves what it is about the order they are proposing which will deliver us from evil. Does evil have its origin in *disorder*, or too much order? To what extent can evil be overcome by reason's imposing a correct order? These questions are ultimately linked to the ancient problem of evil as raised by the early Christian theologians. If God is creator of the universe, then is God also the source of evil? The presence of evil in the world (hunger, suffering, war, death) would seem to testify to the imperfection, even malevolence, of God. If He is not the source of evil, then God's omnipotence is undermined, for then sin is not permitted to exist but rather suffered. Similarly, if evil is an expression of free

[26] See e.g. Dworkin, *Justice in Robes* (Cambridge MA, Belknap Press, 2006), 161.

will, then in what sense can free will count as a 'gift' of God? These dilemmas surrounding the existence of evil had been the subject of philosophical and theological debate since ancient times.

It was Pierre Bayle who, in his *Dictionnaire Philosophique*,[27] suggested that the only possible way out of the problem was to admit that the presence of evil cannot be rationally explained: it is to faith, not reason that we must turn for enlightenment and salvation. Bayle's arguments were subjected to criticism by Leibniz, who saw in Bayle's attack upon human reason a more profound source of scepticism than any of the difficulties associated with the rational explanation of evil. According to Leibniz, evil was to be understood as an unavoidable but essentially negative phenomenon,[28] and its presence in the world was to be taken as evidence that, of all possible worlds, our world contains and preserves the utmost order that is consonant with the utmost beauty and truth.[29] The world was not created solely for human happiness, but in accord with a divine plan that transcends human needs and interests; therefore, the world must be interpreted as the best of all possible worlds.[30]

This optimistic view of the world was regarded by later writers, such as Voltaire, as generating an ultimately fatalistic, and hence paradoxically pessimistic, philosophy.[31] For if the world of the present is understood to embody the *best* possible conditions, then it would seem that all human endeavour (and therefore law) must be directed, if at anything, towards the preservation of current arrangements. Such an apology for the status quo makes impossible any general belief in the transformational capabilities of law and society to achieve progress.

Those aspects of the jurisprudence of the present day which take the achievement of the just society as a central aim, are characterized by just such an ethic of progress. Consequently, such efforts cannot be altogether shielded from these broader questions. We must ultimately face the

---

[27] P Bayle, *Dictionnaire Philosophque et Critique* [1697]. Bayle's text has a multi-layered arrangement making it notoriously difficult to read. Some relevant sections are gathered in Bayle, *Political Writings*, SL Jenkinson (ed.) (Cambridge University Press, 2008).

[28] GW Leibniz, *Theodicy* (New York, Open Court, 1988), II.20.

[29] See H Mason, 'Optimism, Progress and Philosophical History', in M Goldie and R Wokler (eds.), *The Cambridge History of Eighteenth Century Political Thought* (Cambridge University Press, 2006), 195–217.

[30] Leibniz (above n 28), II.21–3 and especially III.117–18.

[31] See Mason (above n 29), 196 and 199–200. The term 'optimism' apparently comes from Leibniz's view that our world represents an 'optimum'. I am very grateful to Mason's essay for shaping my thinking on the connections between Leibniz, Voltaire and Locke.

question of why progress towards a just society is thought possible, or even desirable. Can the history of human society not equally be viewed as a gradual loss of innocence, in the manner of a Rousseau, or of freedom, in the manner of a Nietzsche or (in some ways) a Kant? Or as a fall from classical Athenian civility into barbarism (or away from God), the recovery of the former state demanding unfortunately necessary laws in place of true virtue or Christian love? These questions can be suppressed but not eliminated. Philosophical perspectives which regard them as mistaken or irrelevant must themselves defer to a cosmology that is, in its own terms, equally fundamental.

The possibility of human progress demanded a philosophical vision of the worldly predicament radically different from that of Leibniz. At the heart of this altered vision lay a shift in philosophical thinking of profound importance for the development of utilitarianism and subsequent developments in ethics and jurisprudence. The ground of morality was no longer a theology or a metaphysics, but epistemology. In his *Essay Concerning Human Understanding*, Locke had argued that human knowledge of the world derived entirely from sensory experience. The human mind at birth was, therefore, a *tabula rasa* that is morally neutral in its essence. On this basis, Voltaire suggested that improvement of the human lot comes from an increased knowledge of the environment with which human beings interact, so that the mind may profit from the sensory data it receives. Education was of fundamental importance in securing human progress.[32] Further developing the idea of sensory experience as the basis of human knowledge, Helvetius asserted that mankind is motivated by the love of pleasure and the fear of pain. A system of laws was therefore required if otherwise morally neutral human beings were to be inclined towards virtuous conduct, by creating an environment that is in harmony with basic human impulses, creating agreeable incentives and disagreeable disincentives. By a series of short intellectual steps, this theory was to develop into the source of English utilitarianism in the writings of Mill.

The notion of utility amounted to an alternative resolution of the problem of evil. The ultimate assurance of progress was the accumulation of knowledge, which made possible the ascription of a meaning to history that was independent of divine rewards and punishments. As Turgot put it in his 1750 address to the Sorbonne,

---

[32] Ibid., 200.

Empires rise and fall ... Self-interest, ambition, and vainglory continually change the world scene and inundate the world with blood; yet in the midst of their ravages manners are softened, the human mind becomes more enlightened ... and the whole human race, through alternative periods of rest and unrest, of weal and woe, goes on advancing, although at a slow pace, towards greater perfection.[33]

On the basis of these reflections, I would like to suggest that the central questions of jurisprudence in the modern age are not concerned with the extent to which utilitarian thought has been displaced by theories of justice or rights, but with understandings of the relationship between law and human progress. The most profound intellectual commitments of modern jurisprudence revolve around a deep-seated fixation with epistemologically orientated notions of ethics, and a theodicy that is both tacit and startling.

Proper order?

Retracing our steps, let us consider again Aristotle's perception of the relationship between law, reason and progress. Social institutions (such as law) were regarded by Aristotle as nourishers of human potential. By providing a set of constraints upon permissible behaviour, the law would serve to incline persons of average temperament towards virtue and goodness through the development of good habits: 'when all the influences by which we are thought to become good are present, we get some tincture of excellence'.[34] Human history contained the potential for the diminution of evil in human affairs. By cultivating virtuous dispositions in people forced into habitual obedience to its norms, the law would play a central part in this process. Law was then *both* a civilizing influence *and* an embodiment of the values that would underpin the just and excellent polity.

Later eras of political thought modulated, but did not abandon, these ethical assumptions. Hobbes (for example) wrote that 'whatsoever is the object of any man's appetite or desire ... he for his part calleth *Good*: And the object of his hate and aversion, *Evil*'.[35] Nothing in nature was to be regarded as 'good' or 'evil' in an absolute sense, but merely in relation to its status as an object of someone's desire or aversion. Because each person would perceive good and evil in the world in different ways,

---

[33] Quoted by Mason (above n 29), 203.   [34] Aristotle, *Nicomachean Ethics*, Book X ch 9.
[35] Hobbes, *Leviathan*, ch 6, 39.

therefore, a reduction of evil (or 'infelicity') would require 'an Arbitrator or Judge, whom men disagreeing shall by consent set up, and make his sentence the rule thereof'.[36] Despite the darker picture that is offered by Hobbes, jurisprudential thought has never altogether abandoned its sense of law's aspirational quality: in confronting legal and political institutions, we encounter not only a set of factual arrangements but also a body of transformative ideals.[37]

This aspirational quality is part of the *idea* of law. Our reasons for having law appear to testify to the implication that it achieves certain desirable ends (the establishment and preservation of good order, the placement of limits on violence, reduction of arbitrariness and so forth). Without such achievements, humanity would find itself in a state of barbarism which, from our perspective as cultured beings, can be imagined only in terms of loss. Law represents the attainment of human progress. But the many and various imperfections that present legal arrangements embody force thoughtful people to interpret this as a partial attainment, awaiting further fulfilment as factual circumstances are brought more closely into alignment with certain aspirational ideals. Juridical categories of thought are perhaps inevitably infused with a spirit of optimism concerning the further perfectibility of the human condition. What else could underlie the motivation for judicial refinement or legislative change?[38] Law appears as the instrument of human progress *par excellence.*

Jurisprudential writers have at various times sought to distance themselves from these wider assumptions about the human condition. Calling attention to the hard lives and the atrocities that political regimes can produce, they have questioned whether one can correctly point to an intrinsic relationship between law and the progress of the species. Imagining that they had produced a genuinely new political form, outside the regime-taxonomies discussed by writers like Aristotle and Aquinas, liberals celebrated the emancipatory and progressive genius of the human mind to resolve its central problems. Others stressed caution,

---

[36] Ibid. Hobbes's characterization of the infelicitous conditions of the state of nature is found in ch 13.

[37] For an insightful discussion see R Geuss, *History and Illusion in Politics* (Cambridge University Press, 2001).

[38] One might conceive such adjustments to concern only a response to changing conditions, motivated not by the desire for improvement but by avoidance of decline. But whilst this might mark the ambition of a caretaker government, it is not easy to see how political stasis (or vacuum) could exist in 'normal' contexts of governance.

reminding liberals of how dark and depraved the human imagination can be. Their arguments strove to emphasize that law is merely an instrument which can be employed in the service of many different ends, evil as well as good.[39] More recently, advocates of the law's moral 'neutrality' have conducted inquiries in the spirit of offering a 'scientific' or 'analytical' account of law that is shielded from 'normative' concerns. The extent to which such efforts at analysis can maintain a scientific neutrality is debatable. For any analysis must base itself upon certain assumptions about the object, law, that is to be analyzed. Such assumptions are not axioms of a 'science', but rather depend upon an understanding of the role of law as a distinctive kind of social institution. Understandings of this kind are, in effect, abstractions from an experience of the world and hence involve an interpretation of that world which cannot, in the end, remain insulated from judgments about the purposes and ends served by law and government in human history.[40] A view of the law that was morally 'neutral' could not therefore achieve its neutrality through scientific detachment, but through an understanding of the human condition *itself* as intrinsically neither good nor evil.

The connection of ideas of moral progress with a historical 'journey' from barbarism to civility has long been an implicit soteriological assumption of Western thought. Equally however, it may be that the development within jurisprudence of 'neutral' or 'scientific' perspectives on law can occur only in situations where there is widespread perception and fear of cultural decline. Then the achievement of the law-state (or rechtsstaat) will seem to possess no historical significance in its own right, but to be a mere harbinger of possibilities: both of civility and of cruelty and destruction. In such instances, one might be inclined to separate beliefs about law and government from any aspirational ideals, viewing the latter as connected to the former only contingently. 'Evil' empires flourish. Great civilizations crumble and fall into ruin. Nothing lasts forever! What sense is to be made of the impermanence of even the greatest human achievements? Did Augustine (for example), in writing *The City of God*, realize that the Roman Empire was truly at an end? In Book III he discusses the impotence of Rome's sacred symbols and objects in preventing the ruin of that city from fire, natural disaster

---

[39] See e.g. MH Kramer, *In Defence of Legal Positivism: Law Without Trimmings* (Oxford University Press, 2003), and *Where Law and Morality Meet* (Oxford University Press, 2004).

[40] See M Oakeshott, *Experience and its Modes* (Cambridge University Press, 1933).

and attack. His remarks concerning the status and interpretation of such symbols might well apply also to juridical theories in which present manifestations of law and government are transmuted into permanent symbols of human progress:

> We Christians would not bring the same objections against such sacred objects, if it was said that they were appointed not for the preservation of temporal goods but to point to goods that are eternal, and therefore though those physical and visible things are fated to perish, their disappearing entails no impairment of the things which were the purpose of their appointment. They can be replaced, to fulfill the same purpose. But as it is, they think, in their astonishing blindness, that by those perishable sacred objects their earthly life and the temporal felicity of their city can be preserved imperishably. Then, when it is proved that the preservation of those objects has not in fact protected men's lives from the onset of extinction or of unhappiness, they are ashamed to change a belief which they are unable to defend.[41]

Augustine's words abound with significance. For we may read him as offering a warning against the pessimism that results from the tendency to sublime the concrete achievements of the world into necessary historical stages of human development. Too enthusiastic an idealism, when circumstances cause it to collapse in ruins around us, leads to the opposite 'blindness': a positivism which detaches law from all ideals. Faced with the realities of cultural fragmentation, we may seek to detach the ideas of law and government from the cultural forms of which they were previously thought to be a part. Denuded of such associations, law appears as a general idea that can be comprehended and analyzed *prior* to immersion within specific cultural or political contexts.[42] Thus equipped, we are able to retain a sense of the form and function of law as a means of realizing and preserving a mode of earthly life or temporal felicity, whilst at the same time adopting a detached attitude toward the desirability of certain social forms.

The divided intellectual inheritance found in the legacies of Hobbesian and Grotian juridical thought must be understood in the light of these considerations. Hobbes's conception of law, in seeking a reasonable ordering or balancing as between conflicting interests in society, seems

---

[41] Augustine, *De Civitate Dei*, III.18. For an interesting discussion of the development of Kelsen's positivism, see C Jabloner, 'Hans Kelsen', in AJ Jacobson and B Schlink (eds.), *Weimar: A Jurisprudence of Crisis* (Berkeley, University of California Press, 2000), 67–76.

[42] See e.g. Hart, *The Concept of Law*, 2nd edn (Oxford, Clarendon Press, 1994), 239.

to force upon us the conclusion that the particular ordering that is achieved is the product of the will of an earthly ruler whose values may be those of a Gandhi, or those of a Hitler. There being no intrinsic moral content to the idea of legality, we will regard the meaning of 'law' as being determined on the basis of a 'family resemblance' amongst various existing systems of law whereby typical conditions for the existence of a functioning legal order can be identified. The concept of law 'is not tied to any particular legal system or legal culture, but seeks to give an explanatory and clarifying account of law as a complex social and political institution'.[43] Law is a feature of the human world that is present in social conditions both of good and of great evil, and may be employed in the creation or perpetuation of either kind of circumstance. The outlook associated with this view is essentially pessimistic.

On the other hand, the Grotian understanding of law (in seeking some ideally just ordering or balancing) can be regarded as giving priority to the law's aspirational qualities. If left unmodulated, it can lead to a view in which law is not to be conceived as an abstraction from experience but rather depends upon the elaboration of abstract models, none of which is perfectly embodied in experiential conditions: law as a domain of ideas in which a theory of justice is gradually realized and perfected. We are therefore said simultaneously to confront 'two forms or stages of the same system of law, the nobler form latent within the less noble, the impure, present law gradually transforming itself into its own purer ambition'.[44] The presence of evil in human affairs is something of which law holds out the promise of eradication: it is a taint affecting 'the purer form of law within and beyond the law we have'.[45] This standpoint can be described as optimistic.

The position adopted by Rawls's positivist opponents has some complex connections to the pessimistic outlook. As Amanda Perreau-Saussine has observed, something of this pessimism surfaces occasionally in the writings of Hart. Hart's suggestion that there is a 'necessary minimum' of natural law within any legal order indicates that for him, 'law exists to uphold society and society can be upheld only by sustaining communal *mores*: insofar as there is no morality other than communal *mores*, law and morality are inseparable'. In the face of such pessimism, 'Hart seems to have striven to keep jurisprudential thought open to a moral truth that he feared might not exist, aware that our capacity to

---

[43] Ibid.   [44] Dworkin (above n 17), 400.   [45] Ibid., 407.

understand what does exist is rooted in our own self-definitions and, hence, in what we are.'[46]

Noble dreamers, such as Rawls, instead advance a position that is underwritten by a form of optimism. Increasingly, they call not for lack of order, but correct order. If the liberal regime is the fulfilment of freedom, this can only be because it is also the fulfilment of justice. Under Rawls's encouragement, liberals are becoming less wary of organizing social and economic conditions. As their efforts fail time and again to establish the society of which they dream, will liberals relapse into a more pessimistic way of thinking?

Wiser than the regimes they analyzed, the Christian writers understood that the laws of the state themselves, in being products of human imagination, can be relied upon to produce injustice. Because man lives under a certain confusion of nature and law, his character will always have a degree of injustice woven into it. Without law, man is 'the most dangerous of animals'. In the presence of law he is less dangerous. But he is never completely tamed. Anarchy and despotism equally involve the rule of men. No regime, lying in between these possibilities, is ever perfectly just. Evil can never be entirely confronted, and will never be completely eradicated. A liberal regime has the virtue of allowing man to explore every aspect of his predicament. It does not hold forth the virtue of allowing him to escape it. The 'meaning' of politics and jurisprudence lies in something more than passively understanding this predicament, but in less than its resolution.

It is necessary to consider what follows from the nature of liberal society understood in these terms. The following chapter offers some reflections upon the 'open' character of liberal society, what this says about its philosophies, and what can be deduced about its 'meaning'.

---

[46] See A Perreau-Saussine, 'An Outsider on the Inside: Hart's Limits on Jurisprudence', *University of Toronto LJ*, 56 (2006), 371–88, at 388. Hart himself treated this as a question 'which cannot be investigated here': (above n 42), 201.

2

Concept and reality in jurisprudence

How should the purpose of jurisprudential arguments be understood today? Certain remarkable features of modern liberal societies exercise a definite influence on jurisprudential thought. It is not simply that liberal politics has been detached from truth. Liberalism ensured that the truth was no longer the goal of politics. Individuals might pursue and even discover truth, but they would not find it in any conscious aspect of their collective arrangements. The market, responsive to interests, inevitably creates a market in ideas, and not a collective pursuit of truth. Politics is grounded only on consensus. The very 'openness' of the liberal society excludes any question of its significance.

From a certain point of view, one can say no more about law than that it is the instrument of a politics. Under the politics of a totalitarian society, law will put on a terrible character. The law of a liberal society is less terrible, but does this touch the human situation in any really deep way? Politics cannot eliminate suffering. The fate of humanity is to suffer. Evil is everywhere. No essential improvement of the human condition can be expected. Faced with an understanding of the human condition as an inescapable predicament, we might be tempted to ask whether there is any point in a *normative* jurisprudence?

At first, liberals desired one thing above all: peace. A way to live together in the face of disunity. There is no right way to live. Ideologies are not truth. The extinction of the market in ideas must absolutely be avoided. Great vigilance is necessary to prevent the irrevocable victory of values or manifestos. Social institutions must constantly watch over one another, balancing and limiting their achievements. 'Normative' theories are essential to the success of liberalism in this sense. In the absence of numerous sincere recommendations for the amendment of present social arrangements, the market in ideas would cease to function. One viewpoint would dominate. But the normative theories themselves are in a certain sense incompatible with liberalism. Each one of them expresses a single viewpoint. If they are genuinely sincere about seeking an ideal institutional basis for pluralism, they must base politics on something more insidious than either truth or consensus: *reason*. Modern liberals think of peace as flowing from a more basic need: justice. The basis of the just society is not consensus, but a *rational* consensus. Its origin is not found in history or politics, but an 'original position' or 'discourse ethics'. The open society is permitted to exist because it can be rationalized. Its pluralism is not absolute but bounded. Its openness is completed in its ultimate synthesis of all values and energies. Each vision of its agnosticism terminates in an eventual reconciliation of all things!

Legal positivists have called upon others to recognize that an understanding of the legal order of liberalism cannot be identified with any of these 'normative' explanations. The concrete circumstances of liberal order correctly appear only when described in isolation from normative rationalizations. Are the descriptions of legal positivists any less 'rationalizations'? In a letter to his father in which Marx wrote of his early attempts to arrive at a general philosophical outlook on law, he noted that:

> From the outset an obstacle to grasping the truth here was the unscientific form of mathematical dogmatism, in which the author argues hither and thither, going round and round the subject dealt with, without the latter taking shape as something living and developing in a many-sided way. A triangle gives the mathematician scope for construction and proof, it remains a mere abstract conception in space and does not develop into anything further. It has to be put alongside something else, then it assumes other positions, and this diversity added to it gives it different relationships and truths. On the other hand, in the concrete expression of a living world of ideas, as exemplified by law, the state, nature, and philosophy as a whole, the object itself must be studied in its development; arbitrary divisions must not be introduced, the rational character of the object itself must develop as something imbued with contradictions in itself and find its unity in itself.[1]

Marx demonstrates an awareness that the subject-matter of enquiry, 'law', is not an independent datum that is observable as a 'type' or 'instance'. At the same time, its unique particularity is not resistant to all efforts at demarcation, all attempts to discover unity or rationality within it. As Marx later came to believe, the methods and assumptions of the social sciences functioned in a way opposed to that of ordinary perception. Acquaintance with what is 'real and concrete' in the case of

---

[1] Marx, Letter from Karl to his father in Trier (1837) quoted in D McLellan (ed.), *Karl Marx: Early Texts* (Oxford University Press, 1971), 1–10.

social science derives from the progressive refinement of abstractions where it is the latter that are the primary givens. Thus, in economics for example, we begin with the population, which is the foundation and subject of the act of production. But on closer analysis, 'the population' is an abstraction which demands reduction into its various classes. Classes in turn are but empty abstractions if not determined by reference to wage labour, capital and other matters.[2] Perception of the 'concrete', in this way, is the outcome rather than the raw given of analysis.

Jurisprudential arguments inevitably function as abstractions. In seeking to give form and intelligibility to legal practices, a degree of regimentation is unavoidable. The jurist's arguments necessarily summarize and abridge certain dimensions of the practices only. Analysis demands order. Explanations must be coherent. Every analysis of liberal order is a containment of its openness: a resolution of its intrinsic *disorder*. Marx's remarks in one sense point in the wrong direction. Dissatisfied with generalization, he seeks a concrete truth. For analysis to lose its abstraction, it must introduce finer distinctions. The relationship of the abstract to the concrete is one involving separation and multiplicity. An abstraction is a representation of one element of a concrete reality that consists of numerous and possibly infinitely distinguishable parts. Proceeding in this fashion, Marx hoped to engage in minute study of reality in all its aspects. Modern positivists have tended to share this impression. Nevertheless, an alternative strand of Western philosophy, encompassing Hegel and the British idealists, has steadily contemplated a position that is in most respects the antithesis of Marx's. According to it, what is 'real' or 'concrete' is always a single, complete whole, incapable of differentiation. It is abstractions that are numerous, distinguishable and always incomplete. Abstractions never serve to isolate *parts* of reality. They offer instead a partial view of the *whole* of reality: that is, a view of reality from a particular standpoint.[3] At best, theoretical insights offer incomplete views of the whole of legal practice and of the wider social reality into which that practice fits. If such insights can participate in truth, nevertheless they are unable to state the truth in a complete or final form.

The 'open' nature of liberal society, its capacity for development along numerous lines that can only be predicted up to a point, exaggerates this

---

[2] Marx, *The Grundrisse: Foundations of the Critique of Political Economy*, new edn, M Nicolaus (trans.) (London, Penguin Classics, 1973), Introduction.
[3] See M Oakeshott, *Experience and its Modes* (Cambridge University Press, 1933).

limitation of analytical arguments. A 'closed' society, seeking the realization of a particular truth, cannot be finitely described. Liberal societies refuse to accept that anything essential can be captured even by these descriptions. Positivists' much-vaunted distinction between description and evaluation has if anything obscured this underlying situation. Christian jurists and philosophers were more aware of the problem. Mindful of the Fall, they stressed the disordered state of the soul and its effect on human knowledge. Once deprived of justice, human beings do not even understand true order. They will fail to see the world correctly, perceiving it through the lens of depravity.[4] Human beings better understand what is eternally important (with the aid of divine providence) than the material arrangements of present life. All understanding involves distortion. Liberalism implied a different intellectual basis for the problem of human knowledge, but its conclusions were much the same. Human beings were not depraved but 'autonomous'. As beings who select their own ends, their image of the world is affected by something just as deep: their interests. Depictions of liberal society must avoid intrinsic commitment to any person's 'truth', at the risk of becoming despotic.

Both the Christian and the liberal visions are underpinned by a basic idea: the world is experienced as a world of ideas. 'Experience' is always significant. Consciousness is not passive and receptive, as a flower is acted upon by the elements. It is active, and its processes of thought are inseparable from what is experienced as 'reality'. Every aspect of human experience is a processing of reality. As fleshly beings, humans' experience of the world can become distorted in a thousand ways. One might say that since reality consists in a world of ideas, there can be no distortion inherent in a theory simply by virtue of its being an idea. Its shortcoming is not that of distortion, but of incompleteness. But as finite beings, humans are constantly tempted to mistake their limited and partial vision for the larger and indisputable whole from which it is drawn. This is the vice that concerned Augustine above all others: *superbia*, the pride which corrupts the very understanding itself.

The idea of a 'theory' of the social world need not imply any further distortion. In being finite and bounded, theories are abstractions from the larger whole represented by one's 'experience'. The theory is the finite and systematically reordered expression of certain dimensions of this

---

[4] See e.g. Saint Anselm of Canterbury, *Opera Omnia* (Edinburgh, Thomas Nelson & Sons, 1940–61), 149 (though Anselm is ultimately optimistic about human beings uncovering the truth.)

experience. Human knowledge proceeds by means of abstractions. By developing multiple abstractions of the same thing (i.e. reality), and by constantly moving between and overlaying various abstractions, human knowledge is advanced. The central problem of jurisprudence is that of progressing towards an ever more complete and coherent understanding of the significance of law as it belongs to reality. I will attempt to explain this last sentence.

Law, reality, truth

The impulse toward philosophical contemplation of law is often aroused by perceptions, sometimes half-perceptions, of its imperfection. The philosophic impulse generally arises where an awareness is manifested, sometimes indirectly, of certain gaps or forms of incoherence in our outlook on life. It is an attempt to make sense of things that currently fall short of total comprehension. Or it can offer reassurance that existence *has* some sense, or some final point. Life under the rule of law is an aspect of existence, and thus to reach a philosophical understanding of law is not to expose its 'foundations' but to clarify its meaning in relation to life in all its aspects. The classical philosophies of law and society proceeded in this way. Aristotle (for example) sought to comprehend the role of law in fostering virtuous dispositions such as would lead persons towards 'the good life'. Philosophy is never 'descriptive' even when it is attempting to describe conditions in a deep and penetrating way.[5] In attempting to uncover the good life, the form and purpose of the enquiry moved beyond a mere pursuit of 'understanding' but sets out upon the quest to attain the grand prize. As Oakeshott observed, we 'seek in philosophy what wiser men would look for in a gospel, ... some convincing proof that there is nothing degrading in one's being alive, something to make the mystery of human existence less incomprehensible'.[6]

Philosophers feel a deep need to ascribe to reality a rational character, thereby presenting reality as being amenable to philosophical explanation and justification. Philosophers do not *impose* reason upon the world, but uncover its rational order. But apparently chaotic features of the world and of history have repeatedly sent philosophers into the arms of an equally powerful doubt. How do earthquakes redound to greater order?

---

[5] See HLA Hart, *The Concept of Law*, 2nd edn (Oxford, Clarendon Press, 1994), v, where he observes that his book 'may also be regarded as an essay in descriptive sociology'.
[6] Oakeshott (above n 3), ch 1.

Does war create more than it destroys? Do we not witness meaningless cruelty? The rationalization of such events disguises their arbitrary and senseless character. Reality is simply a *factum brutum* which may be described but not explained or justified.[7] The emergence of analytical philosophy, armed with new and powerful techniques of formal logic and analysis, brought about a general shift away from the idea of reality as an integrated whole and instead emphasized the 'atomic' nature and endless particularity of the world.[8] The political events of the first half of the twentieth century gave impetus to these developments, for the brute atrocities of global conflict were commonly supposed to defy, rather than to exhibit, reason. Thought is not confined to the intellectual search for meaning, but becomes the desire to *realize* meaning, to impose one's will upon the practical world. Often it has appeared to philosophers that the quest for understanding can be separated from other aims.

Can one 'understand' without making judgments about the object considered? May we understand the world as we find it and leave it unchanged (whilst increasing our knowledge of it), leaving to others the search for principles by which human effort may be directed so as to *improve* the world? To jurists it has seemed that law, too, demanded contemplation from these twin perspectives. We wish both to understand law, *and* to discover ways by which it may be moved further towards some imagined ideal. Everything about the liberal order of society appears to uphold the viability of this distinction. If politics has an 'open' character then so must its instrument, law. But I wonder whether this is a fair description of what philosophers understand. The suggestion that law must be moved into closer approximation to an ideal is also a recognition that the 'realities' of legal order sometimes fail to promote that ideal. Law is not a concrete manifestation of an imagined ideal. Some reordering is required. Those aspects of law which promote the ideal are not an exhaustive description of the law's reality. Taken alone they represent an abstraction from the law's total character. At the same time, a description of this 'total character' cannot avoid reference to the pursuit of the ideal, without also distorting or abridging that character.

---

[7] See E Skidelski, 'The Strange Death of British Idealism', *Philosophy & Literature*, 31 (2007) 41–51, esp. at 46.

[8] See e.g. JA Coffa, *The Semantic Tradition from Kant to Carnap: To the Vienna Station* (Cambridge University Press, 1993), and P Hylton, *Russell, Idealism and the Emergence of Analytic Philosophy* (Oxford, Clarendon Press, 1990).

Let us think about how the same philosophers might attempt to describe an avaricious man. Scrimping and saving, and lack of generosity are characteristic of one whose life is given to avarice. But if the man does not also steal instead of paying for food, or murder to obtain money, then one may admit that avarice has not consumed his whole character. Not only vice, but virtues are exhibited. He is not completely corrupted. Avarice has not determined him. No one is beyond redemption! His motives can pull him in different directions. Without this understanding, one cannot correctly perceive the human being. He becomes 'one-dimensional'. A caricature. Yet what would it say about a man to observe that he exhibits certain vices or virtues only contingently? Because no single vice or virtue is constantly and necessarily true of a man, do we describe him more aptly by excluding all reference to his predilections? Do we not leave out everything that is interesting and important about a man? We do not make less of a judgment when we declare that we know what a man is when we have described his biology, or the shape of his nose, without paying attention to matters of character or soul. He is no less of an 'abstraction' as a result. Attention to his avariciousness does not distort our understanding unless it overwhelms and blinds us to other qualities. We understand better when we see that he is avaricious *despite* the fact that he is not *essentially* avaricious.

Something similar holds true of the law of a liberal social order. Law is not understood more clearly when described in detachment from its policies and ideas. Little is learned by pointing simply to the contingency of ideas. The idea of liberal neutrality itself is not without limits, because it must coexist alongside other ideas and priorities. One can only begin by considering the contingency of its presently defined limits. In one sense, positivists have failed to consider contingency seriously enough. Conceptual categories such as 'positive law', 'natural law' and 'rechtsstaat' are not simply rival ways of characterizing an agreed object, but expressions of the dimensions of meaning that we take to constitute the object. There is no neutral and independent substance to be given to 'the realities' apart from the conceptual categories through which they are perceived. It might be thought easy to pinpoint 'real' things and events which belong to the law: such as legislation in force, courts, judicial rulings and decided cases. But in being real, such things do not fail also to be ideas. To be an 'event' or a 'ruling' or a 'case' (to be one thing rather than another) is to possess a meaning or significance. This meaning or significance of an object is in no way and at no point detachable from its 'reality'.

The statements we make about law (or about the avaricious man) are all 'rationalizations'. They draw attention to a certain order in the object described. This order cannot be thought of as entirely discovered, because in drawing attention to certain features of the object we impose a particular way of looking at it. Certain features are selected for attention as more significant than others. Explanations are much more limited than the objects they describe. We cannot fathom the deepest reaches of the soul. But even here, order is not entirely 'imposed'. We speak truths about the object only when we actually describe its characteristic patterns of order. If the truths do not become distorted in our speaking of them, nevertheless they are only ever fragments of a more complete truth.

A line of thought connecting Plato and Aristotle to Hegel (and beyond) considered human experience of the world to be verbal in nature.[9] Some remarks of Gadamer's capture the idea:

> [T]he verbal world in which we live is not a barrier that prevents knowledge of being-in-itself but fundamentally embraces everything in which our insight can be enlarged and deepened ... but in whatever traditions we consider it, it is always a human – i.e. verbally constituted – world that presents itself to us.[10]

This supposition has been in one way or another a central feature of most philosophies since the earliest times: Plato's allegory of The Cave, for instance, can be understood as a metaphor of the relationship between the expressible, human world and the absolute, inexpressible reality that lies beyond. One must treat this contrast with great care.

Expressions of a belief in an 'external world' lying outside present experience give to one's experience a particular meaning: one structured by a belief that what is 'known' or 'experienced' is not exhaustive of existence. When we attempt to formulate such thoughts, to regard them as deep truths, it is to assert that they are necessary for the coherence of experience. There is no 'end' to human knowledge. It does not become perfect and complete. At no point do we perceive the world except as a series of 'views' of the world. At times, relativism threatens to crash down upon us. Such infinitely extendible vistas may be considered as 'relative' in being opposable to one another. But they are never so in virtue of being comparable to 'the world'. The 'relativism' of experience does not

---

[9] I do not want to overplay the depth or purity of this connection as, to my mind, does H-G Gadamer: see *The Idea of the Good in Platonic–Aristotelian Philosophy* (New Haven CT, Yale University Press, 1986).

[10] Gadamer, *Truth and Method*, new edn (London, Continuum Books, 2004), 444.

permit the assumption that alternative views of reality are equally valid. It is of the nature of a 'view' of reality that each person inhabits *the same* reality, albeit one capable of being understood in different, incompatible ways. The coherence of the world depends upon the necessity of supposing that experience of it is shared. Because all understandings are abstracted from the *same* whole they are not independent of one another. They are not private fantasies. One must believe in the relativity of one's own experience in order to give coherence to the world. It is necessary to accept the relativity of one's knowledge of an absolute.

The idealist philosophers sought to recognize the inexpressible character of reality by calling it 'the absolute'. There is no means of ridding human thought of absolutes. Even in denial, absolute status is implied. To admit nothing to reality except immanent cognition is to give absolute status to cognitive propositions, for all others must ultimately reduce to these. Those who assert that material objects, or sensory data, or empirical propositions are the absolute givens will believe these things to be the only possible reality, by reference to which all else must finally be understood. Our starting point determines what we end up with: 'once we stand upon an absolute, that is where we stay; we cannot progress beyond it'.[11] The ineliminability of absolutes displays the falsity of empiricist 'refutations' of metaphysical speculation as the ground of morality.[12] The atomistic viewpoint of analytical philosophers represents a decision to adopt a metaphysical view of the world in which each fact or event is treated as having a separate and absolute existence.

Understanding this relationship of thoughts to 'the world', the aim and direction of jurisprudential reflection is made clear. Law does not itself have an absolute status in the human world. It exists alongside other significant dimensions of life. Some areas of life (such as social life, politics, and the administration of public services and government) have a greater prominence than others. Understandings of law must be coherent with these other dimensions of experience. They do not seek a comprehensive view of an isolated part of reality, but a partial view of the whole of reality. They illuminate all aspects of life under the rule of law. Similarly, political thought does not exist to clarify a discrete and autonomous body of experience, 'politics', but instead presents a view

---

[11] L Kolakowski, 'The Priest and the Jester', in *The Two Eyes of Spinoza* (South Bend, IN, St Augustine's Press, 2004), 250.

[12] See Iris Murdoch, *Metaphysics as a Guide to Morals* (London, Chatto & Windus, 1992), esp. ch 2.

of all experience from the political standpoint. It is not easy to render these standpoints coherent with one another. Marx's observation that the nature of law must be recognized through its possession of 'contradictions in itself' as well as 'unity in itself', expresses a central problem of jurisprudence. Liberal legal thought cannot hope to simplify a contested subject-matter without producing great distortion. Liberal societies are not agreed upon the interpretation of central values. On a certain level, one must appreciate the number and the difficulty of the disagreements which structure understanding of law. At the same time, the very idea of law is an idea of its organized unity. Law is characterized above all by its systematic character, internal order and integrated structure.

Especially in liberal societies, coherence is bought at a high price. The presence of grand unified visions of politics equals the presence of partisan visions. The more contradictions are ironed out, the greater the appearance of 'normative' concerns having ousted 'descriptive' sensitivities. Liberal order is full of noble dreamers. Small wonder that some liberals have given up on the idea of truth. They perceive clearly that political and social realities do not have a fixed or grounded meaning. Experience is too open for its meaning to be declared. It is not wholly subjective: experience of material objects, of pain, or of law, is in one sense 'private', but it is necessary to suppose that in another way they are 'shared' and up to a point commonly understood. Aspects of jurisprudential views can be expected to bestir and influence others, to whom they are intelligible in belonging to a single world. But the result of this interaction does not distil a truth from amid abundant falsities. Discourse on law and politics – on the meaning of social life – is a mutual and constant adjustment of abstractions which are being ceaselessly overlaid and opposed to one another. The life of liberal legal order approaches Hobbes's observation that life consists in the continual motion of thoughts and minds that terminates only in death.[13]

The mutability of political forms is a long-recognized touchstone of Western thought. Christians as much as liberals insisted upon the detachment of politics from truth. Political systems distribute earthly rewards, but they are not divine. Unlimited pursuit of political objectives is a path to hell. Previously, Christians insisted that a life centred upon the pursuit of truth must be orientated toward the Church. Then they qualified their call, demanding reforms and counter-reforms to address

[13] See Hobbes, *Leviathan*, ch 6.

an imperfect and corrupted Church. Eventually, individuals were told that the road to their redemption lay in their own hands. Amid so many individual opinions, one may easily despair of truth. Many liberals were willing to regard the Church's social teachings as indeed no wiser than those of political movements, even to the extent of judging them to be an unwonted 'interference' in the material realm. Does the significance of social life require a higher unity? Was Marx not correct in pointing to the limited unities of social order as serendipitous convergences in ever-shifting judgments?

In looking at the world, we might wonder whether time and history are nothing but a collection of successive events, each of which possesses meaning only during its finite appearance; or whether the significance of events extends beyond their mere occurrence, lying in their relationship to a greater whole. Interpreted jurisprudentially, the question is whether human efforts can make any significant mark upon the world, to change it for good or ill, or whether we are but helpless pawns at the mercy of historical forces beyond our conception or control. Must we, as Hamlet asked, 'suffer the slings and arrows of outrageous fortune, or ... take arms against a sea of troubles, and by opposing end them?'[14] These alternatives are not mutually exclusive opposites, but contrary poles between which human thought oscillates. When examining values such as legality, justice or order, do we suppose that we are the architects of the earthly paradise, or simply the playthings of despots upon a ship of fools?

The interpretation of law

The 'open' character of liberal society created uncertainty over the ultimate direction of jurisprudential reflection. Some aspects of this openness appeared to vindicate the views of Turgot, Voltaire and others, that the limitless possibilities of the human imagination would slowly bring the human race into a better condition. Freedom is a more ingenious solver of human problems than the schemes of dictatorial dreamers. Reflections on law and government would eventually produce notable improvements to the human condition. Other aspects of the open society suggested a more depressing possibility. Perhaps the Christian jurists were correct: there is no ideal regime. Progress is an illusion. Even the greatest advancements of political thought merely permute existing

---

[14] Shakespeare, *Hamlet*, Act 3, Scene 1.

injustice into new and more insidious forms. The recommendations of the jurists and political philosophers can only ever be provisional. Politics is corrupt. The man of good character cannot endorse any of its schemes for the improvement of society, but only perceive its real nature more closely. He must know his enemy. Passive understanding of his predicament is all that may be sought. Liberals are not constructing heaven on earth. Confronted with the manifest injustices of tyrannical regimes, they may only sigh for the folly of the world and decide, I would rather be my sort of fool than his.

How are we to understand this problem? Disconnecting politics from truth, the Christian writers made room for a truth that is more enduring than any human opinions, but in some ways unsatisfactory. Christians are called upon not merely to know but also to live the truth, by taking its law into their own hearts. It is not a truth that is remote and far off, but immediately experienced and closer than our own breath. Its laws are those of fellowship and good relations with one's neighbours. Its meaning is not personal, but founded in a community: ultimately the heavenly community of the celestial Jerusalem, but capable of expression in the life of good men here and now.[15] But politics is unjust. Living in a corrupted environment, the Christian experiences the truth personally rather than communally. None of its endless interpretations can become the principle of politics.

Left unbounded, these thoughts can culminate in an all-consuming despair. Confronted with injustice, good men who realize that their wisest solutions are unlikely to be less harmful than present arrangements may choose to devote their energies entirely to prayer rather than works. Their dilemma resembles that of Plato's ideal rulers in the *Republic*: having escaped from the cave, why will the philosophers return there in order to rule? Plato's answer seems to be that men of good character will not be able to prevent themselves from intervening. They will not be driven by 'unhealthy illusions'[16] but by the much deeper stirrings of mercy. Despite its depravities, the city is not beyond saving. Its very existence demonstrates that it is not irredeemable.

> For had men been completely unjust they would never have kept their hands off each other, and there must have been some element of justice among them which prevented them from wronging each other as well as

---

[15] See Augustine, 'Letter to Nectarius', in M Atkins and R Dodaro (eds.), *Augustine: Political Writings* (Cambridge University Press, 2001), 18.

[16] Plato, *Republic*, 520c.

their victims, and brought them what success they had. They were in fact only half corrupted when they set about their misdeeds, for had their corruption been complete, their complete injustice would have made them incapable of achieving anything.[17]

The city could be worse. Good men will wish to exercise their influence over politics in order to avoid being ruled by anyone worse.[18] Their education is owed to the city, which in consequence cannot be entirely corrupted.[19] Finally, it is through saving the city that the philosopher saves himself.[20]

Plato's remarks act as a reminder that a central tendency in liberalism must be constantly resisted: the tendency to absolutize the individual. Liberals do not conceive of legal order by reference to the realization and improvement of a common condition. Common aspects of existence are to be kept to a minimum so as to give maximum scope to the developmental efforts of the individual. The 'individual' of modern political thinking is conceived as an entity apart from the world, and confronting it. Social life is a world of separately operating units interfering with each other in random ways and occasionally fostering more or less stable alliances, at other times diverging in effort and coming into conflict. In such a world, law appears as a set of external impositions upon the person's activities, serving at once to limit patterns of destructive interference and to offer further stability to forms of cooperation. It can have no more significance than as a marker of domains of convergence or compromise between otherwise divergent wills. A world made up of separate units remains a world of independent wills. All notions of 'law', 'power', 'morality' and so on must appear as the varying expression of such wills. No deeper and finally satisfactory idea of law is possible within such a framework. The gap between wills is unbridgeable. In a world in which the will is absolute, there is no more fundamental transmitter of energy. One can save oneself but *not* the city. It will never conform to one's personal vision of the truth.

Seizing upon the notion of worldly imperfection, Protestants emphasized the necessity of a personal relationship with God as a path to salvation. Liberals, in placing the individual at the heart of politics, inherited a similar sense of separation between 'truth' and 'society'. Beginning from such a frame of reference, these problems are more or

---

[17] Ibid., 352c.   [18] Ibid., 347a–d.
[19] Ibid., 520a–c (though Plato is here talking in the context of the ideal society).
[20] Ibid., 497a.

less intractable, for their existence (rather than their solution) is presupposed by the framework of thought in which they figure. They forgot or suppressed the idea that a personal relationship with God, or truth, is not fully independent of community. Entrenching the dichotomy of 'individual' and 'society', 'man' and 'world', they did not see that men, however wilful, belong to and are completed by a common world of ideas. Their truths are not limited by the common resources of education and of language, but they are unimaginable without them. Men do not have an uninterrupted view of the truth. Their opportunities for pursuing it are created as well as limited by society. However corrupting social influences might be, the individual cannot in losing them discover himself: he is not an *ens completum* but a social being. His very identity is formed only in continuity with society, history and tradition.

Keeping in mind these continuities we can begin to glimpse the need for jurisprudential arguments to demand certain changes to the world, above and beyond seeking to understand it. Human beings will endlessly debate the meaning of the social world without reaching settled conclusions. Their schemes for its improvement will turn out not to be 'progress'. But they are not independent of the world. They should care about its arrangements because they are not significantly 'above' its influences. Men cannot put on the character of 'liberal individuals' in a totalitarian society. In a capitalist society, they cannot avoid becoming 'consumers'. Retreat from society is not possible for the vast majority of people. One must be on terms with one's fellow citizens. The principles of one's engagement with others cannot avoid becoming the terms on which one believes that all relationships must be conducted. A person's course through life is not without effect on others. One's efforts and ideals constantly meet with resistance and compromise. Often they are deflected by 'invisible hands'. Precisely because the present life of humanity must be lived out in conditions that are impoverishing to the spirit and to one's efforts, the current situation cannot be passively accepted. Constantly we strive to place a rational order upon our social life. We are not indifferent to the nature of this order. It is intrinsically aspirational in one form or another.

At times, even liberals have sought to identify their sense of order with the deeper order of history. History has no grand plan or cumulative strategy, but this has not prevented philosophers from offering historical interpretations in which the human efforts of the past represent a confused and semi-blind groping towards the social conditions of the present. Aware also that individuals disagree very profoundly about the meaning of present conditions, liberals frequently reduce their understanding of the social sphere to a series of average conditions.[21] Realizing that law must represent a domain of continuity in a divided world, they have sometimes exaggerated the level of agreement which sustains it. Law is a domain structured by a convergence in otherwise opposing judgments. It is defined by shared practices of 'recognition',[22] or by 'constructive interpretation'.[23] An overlapping consensus. Dismissive of Marx's idea of law being imbued by 'contradictions in itself', they have stressed the importance of the law's 'unity in itself'. Individuals do not agree on many things; but the possibility of their individual lives is maintained by the law having a settled and agreed meaning. Law cannot reflect more agreement than there is without becoming despotic. It cannot reflect less agreement than there is without prescinding from the order of society. Have liberals misunderstood the nature of this 'consensus'?

Liberals are correct to talk about coincidence in judgments or the overlapping of outlooks. But they are wrong to speak of consensus or settled meaning. Each person's outlook is constituted by a world of ideas. The values and judgments that are necessary for the coherence of one person's world are not necessarily identical with what is necessary for another's. In belonging to a common world, a good measure of coincidence in judgments is to be anticipated. But the resultant 'common world' is not an average. Legal order, which reflects this level of agreement, is not a domain of compromise but of continuity. Each person's understanding of these continuities will be different. There is no single or 'correct' interpretation. Whatever the law has to say will be contentious. Except in unusual cases, there will be few people who feel completely alienated by the law. Few will find within the law no shadow of their outlook and values. But there will be none who find there a perfect reflection of their beliefs.

Once this is fully understood, it must be concluded that the functional possibilities of legal values fall short of the realization of the 'ideal society'. They can relate only to the real society in which disagreement and contention are ineliminable. Values and beliefs can be reflected in the law only unevenly and incompletely, and may on occasion be

---

[21] See Oakeshott, *Religion, Politics and the Moral Life* (New Haven CT, Yale University Press, 1993), 51.
[22] Hart (above n 5), 100–10.
[23] See R Dworkin, *Law's Empire* (London, Fontana, 1986), ch 6.

distorted horribly. Those who administer the law must interpret it, and in doing so they must regard the law as an element of a common reality which does not fully conform to their desires and ambitions. But they must fashion and articulate its provisions. They cannot avoid decisions. The present state of the law is inevitably advantageous on some occasions to those who live under its rule, and damaging on others. Every conscientious effort to bring about improvement to the human lot will result in further unforeseen harm, wrong turnings and backward steps elsewhere. Life can resemble a comedy of errors. The realities of comedy can be harsh, and the suffering caused very real. In the same way, theatrical comedy can be appreciated by the audience only at the expense of the frustrations and reversals of those on stage. Comedy is what results from the observation of complexities being constantly thrown in the way of actors who must nevertheless continue to move forward. Plato was correct to assume compassion on the part of philosopher-rulers. Human beings are not mere observers but also participants in this mode of existence. Responses to these complexities may appropriately vary from vexation, amusement, righteous anger and other emotions. But it is by maintaining, at the same time, a sense of the irony of existence and the absurdity of human efforts, that we glimpse most clearly an intimation of the absolute.

Jurisprudence in context

The liberal separation of politics from truth is not a complete separation. Truth is no longer the goal of politics, but politics does not escape all involvement in the attempt to uncover truth. Liberals were wise enough to understand that political creeds do not deserve to be made absolute. All are flawed or harmful in some way. Injustice will never be permanently driven from society. Jurisprudential arguments centring upon the character of justice must not be elevated to the level of truths. It is perhaps inevitable that the philosophy of *law* should encourage forms of thought which seek to entrench and defend rival positions against one another. Nor should it be surprising that perhaps the greatest of English legal philosophers, Hobbes and Bentham, were also great polemicists. Where the adversarial nature of legal argument is allowed to infect jurisprudence, it becomes harder to maintain consciousness of the limits within which human efforts (intellectual or practical) can meet with success in this world. Bentham's rhetorical brilliance is undeniable, but it is in those passages in which he is most savagely polemical that he appears both less sympathetic, and furthest from the truth. We read Bentham more often 'in context', to understand the influence of his ideas upon the current shape of juridical thought, rather than to appropriate his arguments.

Nevertheless, liberals must keep in mind the lessons to be drawn from Plato's *Republic*. Political organization is not entirely separated from the truths for which human beings seek. Justice is not to be found away from the city, in a far-off realm of the imagination. Truth is not a private vision. But neither should philosophers absolutize the city, identifying truth or justice with extant political organization. One must resist the temptation to identify truth with the idealized projection of some political creed. Philosophers need to cultivate the sense that their arguments address an intermediate order. The world is not entirely devoid of justice, but true justice will never be wholly realized within it. They must not celebrate their arguments too much. In opposing one another they do not gain any final victory. The ambition of jurisprudence must be irenic.

Political philosophers confront a social order that has ramifications beyond the domain of social fact. Viewed in one way, politics cannot be separated forever from ultimate questions. From another perspective, the significance of social order is not permanent; it does not reach beyond itself. What is the difference between these perspectives? One might say that when the domain of 'politics' is placed in context, its significance is not isolated from wider questions of the human condition. Human beings are social animals. Their political efforts are an ineliminable dimension of their attempt to live the good life. When politics is considered on its own terms (without its broader context), the significance of political achievements, of goals and credos, is relative in being confined to the material fate of present life. The hope of liberalism is that politics can be made intelligible whilst remaining agnostic about the broader contextual questions. Pursuing this hope, liberals are mistaken about the extent to which their understandings can render social life *fully* intelligible. Thinkers on law and politics must constantly guard against the tendency to absolutize their positions by forgetting the broader context. I do not believe that liberal writers have even begun to explore this dilemma. In the following two chapters, I indicate some of its complexities.

3

On the 'Protestant' inheritance
of juridical thought

Modern jurisprudential writers like to argue about the competing merits of two opposing theses: (1) given the importance and characteristics of the condition of liberal freedom ('individual autonomy'), the central political question of our time concerns the form of society implied by this condition; (2) the existence of liberal freedom, in putting the form of society into human hands, implies no single form, so that one may only seek to explain and analyze complex social and political institutions which may take many different forms. Focusing attention upon these theses, modern jurists have largely ceased to ask a larger question that was traditionally at the heart of political philosophy: that of the possibility and significance of living in an organized community. Exploring the implications of liberal autonomy, they no longer concern themselves with its origins and whether it has a meaning beyond the self-contained debates of a liberal society.

I would like to assert that the idea of liberal autonomy is not self-contained. The arguments which presently surround its implications derive from a specifically Protestant view of the world that is currently articulated as a form of secular liberalism. Secular liberalism makes possible a separation between law and religious or metaphysical ideas, but though it can effect the suppression of such connections, modern thinking cannot finally eliminate them. I therefore conclude that secular liberal interpretations of law must be given up, and I hope to indicate the limits of the Protestant world-view as an underpinning for legal and political thought.

A dualism

'Modern' legal thought can trace its origins to a turbulent period in European history which marks an important turning point in Western politics. The erosion of settled beliefs and values consequent upon the disintegration of Europe's religious heritage led to new modes of understanding which divided the scholastic, feudal political thought of the medieval period from the structures of individualistic and juridical thought that were beginning to find expression in the seventeenth century. Within medieval thought, politics was conceived as an essential component of 'the good life', for the simple reason that such a life was held to be social in nature. Relying upon conditions of mutuality for its fulfilment, the nature of the good life was believed to be reflected in the character and history of the social institutions and arrangements responsible for those conditions. Divisions of rank and social standing embodied within the community were interpreted as natural variations in the character and temperament of men, and therefore necessary features of the well-ordered society. In this way, politics addressed a finally coherent and unified good, one that could be realized only in common.

This picture did not remain forever. The political thought of the post-Reformation era confronted a world in which the shared values and institutions which underpinned this commonality were in the process of violent fragmentation. In these changed conditions, politics could no longer be regarded as belonging to the realm of ethical insight, directing human behaviour towards a convergent and unified vision of 'the good life'. Rather, politics came to be viewed as a regrettably necessary framework of rules that allow for the simultaneous pursuit by individuals of variant and conflicting notions of 'the good', and hence as belonging to the realm, not of ethics, but of juridical ideas. Whereas the feudal order had identified a person largely in terms of their social persona (the farmer, the cleric, the aristocrat and so on), the emergent framework of 'modern' political thought increasingly conceived of the human person as a distinct and autonomous 'individual'. Each individual formed an independent centre of impulses, thoughts and energies. The relationships which bound an individual to his fellow citizens were not those of shared interest in a common life, but rather liberties, powers, and protective rights and duties which placed each person at arm's length. The nature of society came to resemble, not an ethical domain of collective endeavour, but a system of jural relations structuring the interaction between autonomous domains that project in different directions. Conceived in this way, law served the good only in an attenuated sense: by maintaining order and stability amid divisions which threatened that order, and by preserving its 'neutrality' vis-à-vis the more specific conceptions of 'the good life' that might motivate the actions of different individuals.

This shift in thinking betokened a broader intellectual movement toward a Protestant world-view and a simultaneous retreat from the Aristotelian doctrines of the past. For Aristotle, the nature of the human good was to be found within the social arrangements and institutions that underpinned and solidified the essential commonalities which bound people together. Reflection upon the good was inseparable from the experience of pursuing it. Centring upon collective efforts to secure a common condition, the character of ethical thought was considered to be essentially historical. Ethical understanding derived not from some other-worldly set of 'norms' but from contemplation of a good that is already (though not fully) instantiated in the conditions of the here-and-now. Such conditions, in turn, are never pure products of the will, but are instead the latest expressions of historical practices that are 'old, hoary, encrusted with mutations, split and penetrated by regulatory intrusions'.[1]

In contrast to this picture, modern thought addressed a context in which the traditional anchors of the ethical life – a universal Church, fixed social traditions, static hierarchies and so on – had undergone considerable disintegration, and thus no longer afforded a stable institutional basis upon which ethical understandings could converge. The resultant framework of thought was essentially Protestant, in that the human condition was no longer deemed to be informed by a single, unified object of ethical contemplation ('the good'), but instead resembled a predicament wherein each person seeks to navigate a course through life according to their own notions of what is 'good' for them. Against this background of competing moral viewpoints, a person's ethical understandings could not be thought to derive from historical reflection upon the human condition, but must instead owe their source to an autonomous domain of 'norms' that is contemplated separately from understandings of 'the world'. The earlier Aristotelian approaches to ethics were thought to embody the error of attempting to derive values from facts, an 'ought' from an 'is'. Lying outside the category of 'what is', ethical values came to be viewed as products of the inner mental life of rational 'agents', stemming ultimately from the will.[2] This resulted in an especially potent form of moral voluntarism of which the jurisprudential and ethical thought of the present day is a direct descendant. Its clearest expression can be found in Kant's conception of morality as that which

---

[1] NE Simmonds, 'Between Positivism and Idealism', *Cambridge LJ*, 50 (1991), 308–29 at 329.

[2] For a detailed discussion see S Coyle, *From Positivism to Idealism* (Dartmouth, Ashgate, 2007), ch 2.

'can rise above the emotional impulses of human nature through the purifying processes of choice': a choice which is 'free' in that it 'involves an act of independent will rather than a mere acquiescence in a goal set by nature . . . Reason paradoxically becomes practical by subjecting every maxim to the purely formal test of whether it can be re-described as a universal law.'[3]

The resultant duality of 'the world' against the body of norms which stand over it in judgment, is one of the defining characteristics of the modern point of view. That a tradition of thought owing its origins to the Reformation should give rise to a dualism of this kind is not surprising. The Christian message in virtually all its forms stands as a warning against the dangers of too close an identification of human purposes with the divine. History is not normative for the Christian because the accumulated achievements of a sinful world are not to be mistaken for the norms of a collective Christian life.[4] Neither Hobbes's observation that men naturally stand toward one another in attitudes of mutual hostility, nor Locke's belief that all are by nature juridically equal (even if empirically true) can serve as the basis for a Christian ethic. The limitations of the historical method are intimated in the belief that the world is a vale of tears in which the law of God has never been perfectly kept, even where it has been understood. But if Protestantism exhibited a keen sensitivity to these limits, the subsequent tradition of Protestant political thought nevertheless displayed too hasty a willingness to abandon the insights of the Aristotelian approach. It would be this attitude of dismissiveness towards the historical disposition that, in a typical irony, would pave the way for a secular vision of law and society.

Is the explanatory basis of this secular vision coherent? I shall suggest that in fact neither the dualistic separation of fact and value, nor the monist assumptions of pure historicism, provide an underpinning for a view of law that is ultimately satisfactory. The only scale of values that

---

[3] TJ Hochstrasser, *Natural Law Theories in the Early Enlightenment* (Cambridge University Press, 2000), 198. See also Kant, *Groundwork of the Metaphysics of Morals*, HJ Paton (trans.) (New York, Harper, 1964), 80: 'Everything in nature works in accordance with laws. Only a rational being has the power to act in accordance with his idea of laws . . . and only so has he a will. Since reason is required to derive actions from laws, the will is nothing but practical reason.'

[4] See R Niebuhr, 'The Christian Church in a Secular Age', in R McAfee Brown (ed.), *The Essential Reinhold Niebuhr: Selected Essays and Addresses* (New Haven CT, Yale University Press, 1986), ch 7 at 86.

can offer such an explanatory underpinning is one that transcends the intellectual categories of Protestant thought.

Protestant jurisprudence and secular liberal thought

Owen Chadwick in his Gifford Lectures of 1973–4 pointed out a difficulty that affects the historian's attempt to describe large processes, such as the rise of secularism. We must begin with some idea of what life and society were like before the process began, an idea that is based on an assumption that conditions prior to the instigation of the process embodied a plain and coherent whole.[5] The march of secularism implies a settled body of belief and dogma which pre-dated it, and it further implies that at some crucial point, a balance point was reached beyond which the coherence and intelligibility broke down. Both the implication of prior coherence and that of the processes of change in history are problematic. In order to be visible to history, such movements of thought must find expression in the literature of the civilization that is under investigation. General shifts in thought or belief must be understood to begin with the ideas of clever and freethinking men, ideas that are gradually disseminated and accepted until the attitude of the society has changed. As with Luther's nailing of the Ninety-Five Theses to the Wittenberg church door, so all historical processes are portrayed as the result of an intellectual catalyst. In this way, 'secularism' is often described as a product of 'Enlightenment' thinking. But, as another historian (and subsequent Gifford lecturer) pointed out, intellectual processes are not typically the cause of social processes. Intellectual developments (such as the Enlightenment) are of the elite few, whereas social movement is of the many.[6] It is extremely problematic to explain the general movement of minds by reference to the formally articulated propositions of the outstanding thinkers of the age:

> Everyone knows how impossible the autobiographer finds it to describe, intelligibly to others, what moved his mind at its deepest well. St Augustine beautifully if misleadingly explained the course of his mental and devotional history until the moment of conversion. In that moment we have only beauty and no more explanation. Newman eloquently justified his past against Kingsley's attack and left the decision to become a Roman

---

[5] O Chadwick, *The Secularization of the European Mind in the 19th Century* (Cambridge University Press, 1975), 2–3.

[6] See A MacIntyre, *Secularization and Moral Change* (Oxford University Press, 1967).

> Catholic almost as intellectually mysterious as when he began ... These
> inward movements are too profound for those who experience them to
> articulate successfully.[7]

Blind to this fact, the social architects of the present day optimistically
assert that the path to a higher form of collective life lies in the perfection
of social and political institutions, rather than a personal moral transformation. This can be seen, for example, in Rawls's attitude toward the
'law of peoples':

> Two ideas motivate the Law of Peoples. The first is that the great evils of
> human history – unjust war, oppression, religious persecution, slavery,
> and the rest – result from political injustice, with its cruelties and callous-
> ness. The second is that once political injustice has been eliminated by
> following just (or at least decent) social policies and establishing just (or at
> least decent) basic institutions, these great evils will eventually disappear.[8]

Rawls's faith in the power of ideas is considerable. It is necessary to
remind ourselves that it is not ideas and rational processes that drive
historical transformations, but deeper, less visible processes. 'Enlightenment' cannot bring about 'secularism' precisely because the heart of the
religious faith that preceded it was not exhausted by claims of reason.
Neither could 'rational' doctrines destroy that faith.

When thinking about the character of secular politics, it helps to
understand secularism not as a dogma (like atheism) but as a general
standpoint on the world. Just as, for the devout mind, religion permeates
life in all its aspects and does not simply rest on top of everyday experience as a set of propositions, so the ebbing of the sacred from the
mundane social world is not brought about by the replacement of one
set of propositions by another set. The question to be asked is not how
the diverse populations of the West were persuaded out of their previous
beliefs by the lights of science and reason, but why they gradually
abandoned ritual, prayer, church attendance, etc., which had previously
formed part of the habit of existence. It is necessary to know how these
cultural changes led to (or followed on from) a general re-imagining of
the institutional arrangements of the state to the point where they ceased
to be components of a religious world-view. Even this question is problematic: is it correct to assume that the 'secular' society is characterized

---

[7] Chadwick (above n 5), 13.
[8] J Rawls, *The Law of Peoples*, new edn (New Haven CT, Harvard University Press, 2001), 126.

by popular avoidance of, or disinterest in, religious rite and practice? By what evidence can it be confidently asserted that levels of church attendance amongst (say) the middle or lower classes in the sixteenth century were markedly different to those of the general population today? With what authority can we claim the religious form of public acts (such as coronations, investitures and oaths sworn in court) was any more sincerely held, central to meaning, less a matter of 'outward' convention, than is true of the present? I raise these questions not in order to suggest that the problem of historical evidence is insoluble, but to emphasize the propensity for easy error in musings on secularity.

A general connection can nevertheless be posited between Protestant political thought and the emergence of a secular liberal politics. Protestantism was above all a reforming movement which sought to limit the authority of tradition and ecclesiastical interpretation of scripture, and to emphasize scripture itself as the source of revealed truth (*sola scriptura*). Its doctrines placed particular significance upon the individual as the object of God's grace and ultimate salvation (*sola fide, sola gratia*). By its doctrine of personal salvation, Protestantism encouraged the rejection of Aristotelian ideas of 'the good' in favour of a viewpoint from which each individual, faithfully reading the Bible, must bear the ultimate responsibility for their own notions of 'the good life'. The *sola scriptura* made the Bible, not historical reflection, the only possible source of moral enlightenment and salvation, thus severing the immediate connection of moral value with the sublunar world. Henceforward there would be, on the one hand, the world, and on the other, a Christian moral judgment of that world which would enable each of the faithful to maintain a degree of autonomy or apartness from its snares and seductions. Under the influence of this dualistic vision and the language of autonomy and individual responsibility, the notion of 'the good' underwent a transformation whereby the highest good or end ceased to refer to a specifically desirable form of living in the here-and-now, and was instead thought to concern salvation in the afterlife. But if present choices or ways of living derive their value from their tendency to realize that far-off goal, bestowed by faith, then it would seem that the nature of 'the just society' cannot involve the realization of a shared idea of the *summum bonum*. A conception of justice can only hope to stabilize coexistent forms of life, offering a level of protection to each without preferring any particular one.

A state which aimed to be just would have to tolerate a plurality of religious beliefs. In order to do this, the state must detach its politics from religion. The secular state was produced not by the erosion of belief but by the inner logic of the Protestant world-view as applied to the political context of the state.

Throwing off the shackles of feudalism and religion, politics became an enterprise for the governance of free 'individuals'. The relations governing their interaction must therefore be determined by reference to a 'neutral' framework of articulated rules rather than a legacy of customary biases. Law was thus the cornerstone of the liberal society. Rationally constructed rules would replace tradition and superstition.[9] It is not difficult to see why religious ideas of duty and redemption were construed as part of the cultural debris to be cleared away. Autonomy itself could not be given a religious meaning. Once the 'fact' of individual autonomy had been established, toleration of divergent religious view-points became inevitable. A government might exercise control over the outward forms of religious devotion but it could never control belief. 'Liberal' politics grew out of the political necessities of toleration. By a gradual process of transformation, the idea of religious belief itself came to be interpreted as a matter for 'personal preferences', belonging to the realm of individual freedom rather than of law.

The emergence of 'secular liberalism' was not a consequence of the erosion of a shared religious consciousness, but the progressive dismantling of the constitution that had previously protected it.[10] Its emergence was preceded by a protracted and especially brutal search by the European powers for a domestic religious settlement. The eventual success of these efforts resulted in the exiling of religious ideas to the realm of private conscience. But this process could not be entirely completed, if only because Catholics (amongst others) continued to interpret their doctrines as a matter of social fact and not of personal faith. Insofar as the state settled political thought on Protestant assumptions, it could not avoid imputing a broader significance to many of its central ideas.

It is easy to overlook the fact that the emancipatory vision at the heart of liberalism (indeed of any political movement) embodies a specific view of human redemption. Celebration of the 'autonomous individual' as the central archetype of the political persona is unavoidably a rejection of the Christian doctrine of the inherent sinfulness of mankind. The line of thought extending from Hobbes to Kant and beyond regards the

---

[9] Bentham and Kant, who put forward opposing versions of this view, offer particularly strong examples.

[10] See Chadwick (above n 5), 28.

unlimited self-interest of the individual – that essential motivator – as being subject to the governance of prudence. Immediate wants and desires are checked by the longer-term interest in a stable and peaceful environment in which to enjoy the fruits of one's labour. Immediate self-interest is conditioned and bounded by long-term self-interest.[11] In this way, egotistical impulses which 'cause' actual behaviour (and which may thus be presumed to have survived this winnowing process) will be demonstrated over the long term to be benign and rational. The apparent selfishness of human nature will be transmuted by history into a higher social harmony.[12] Secular liberalism did not eradicate the very idea of redemption from politics, but exactly transmuted it into a historical and political process. It altered the conception of what it means to be redeemed. At the root of this conception lies an understanding of human redemption as a journey from ignorance and primitiveness toward a condition of enlightenment and knowledge: of ideal order and just society. Redemption, accordingly, is viewed as a historical process in which the will, in becoming free, achieves maturity.

The tendency has been for philosophy to congratulate itself on its 'enlightenment' in becoming free of religious dogma. We might wonder whether there was not something fundamentally important in the Christian idea of redemption, and something fundamentally dangerous in its abandonment. It is not ignorance of the will that is (in Christian terms) the source of sinfulness, but its corruption. By placing freedom of the will at the heart of liberal political values, do we reduce possible occasions of evil in human affairs, or multiply them?

Amongst political thinkers of the 'modern' period, it is perhaps Hobbes who most clearly discerned this fact. A state of total freedom is one of continual universal warfare in which the adoption of hawkish postures toward one another is an immediate necessity which seemingly precludes the possibility of meaningful forms of social interaction.[13] Recognizing this, philosophers (beginning with Kant) presented law as

---

[11] The natural law writers of the seventeenth and eighteenth centuries had different ways of exploring the relationship of short- and long-term self-interest. For some discussion, see S Coyle and K Morrow, *The Philosophical Foundations of Environmental Law* (Oxford, Hart, 2004), chs 2–3.

[12] See Niebuhr (above n 4), 93.

[13] The rhetoric of freedom, so evident in recent international politics, therefore obscures the essential question of what happy condition is meant to emerge after the grand prize of global freedom has been won. Why, for example, would such a world be more stable, or peaceful?

defining a system of freedoms that are jointly or simultaneously exercisable. Law operates to restrict freedom, but (in Kant's view) should only do so when such restrictions maximize each person's freedom overall. Hence, law embodies a systematic ordering of equal freedoms which are, in this sense, compossible.[14] It was hoped that an ideal point could be discovered where optimal levels of freedom are at once associated with conditions of justice and political maturity. Much of the subsequent history of Western political thought can be read as a series of attempts to come to terms with what must occur when that ideal point stubbornly fails to manifest itself in real life.

A self-contained politics?

Having detached morality from its traditional religious bases, modern jurisprudential thought ceased to contemplate questions of metaphysics or ultimate realities. This came about not as an intellectual consequence of Protestantism, but as a historical consequence. The central concepts of 'political morality', those of liberty, equality, justice and right, did not gain their centrality by supplanting a religious framework of ideas, but became the focus of political thought because they offered a framework *within* which post-Reformation religiosity could be politically accommodated. The values of liberty, right, etc. grew out of a spirit of toleration that was not at first cosmopolitan in outlook, but which was reflective of urgent political necessities. The ascendency of liberal values, and those of cosmopolitanism, was first and foremost the product of a method of social ordering in which church and constitution were separated for their mutual survival. They were not, in the beginning, wellsprings of anti-religion. In the long term, however, exactly the same values that were needed as a means of preserving the spiritual dimension of life (by avoiding a renewal of sectarian war) also led to the progressive irrelevance of religion to the moral and political life of the state.

The juridical thought of the twentieth century and beyond is distinctive for its sublimation of the central liberal values. To a great extent, such values are no longer perceived as attempts to give structure and meaning to a particular set of historical social conditions. Instead, reflection upon

---

[14] For a recent attempt to resurrect a Kantian approach to rights, see H Steiner, *An Essay on Rights* (Oxford, Blackwell, 1994); see also Steiner, 'Working Rights', in MH Kramer, NE Simmonds and H Steiner, *A Debate Over Rights: Philosophical Inquiries* (Oxford University Press, 1998).

a systematic structure of liberal principles of justice, equality, right and so on is *itself* the context of thought within which jurisprudential questions are posed and responded to. John Gray pointed out the tendency for liberalism to distort itself into 'a model of society that in its rationalistic utopianism and its hubristic doctrine of global convergence' on universal values, becomes 'the project of transcending the contingencies of history and cultural difference and founding a universal civilization that is qualitatively different from any that has ever before existed'.[15] This leaves us with a problem, however. For the origins of the concepts of equality, justice and personal right that are central to this vision lie specifically in religious arguments advanced by seventeenth-century writers on natural law. How is one therefore to explain the fundamentality of such values, if not by reference to this theological framework?

Numerous starting points can be taken in explanation of this issue. Two are especially relevant to an understanding of the character of modern juridical thought. On the first, the central political ideas (justice, equality, etc.) are fundamental because they constitute the framework of background understandings presupposed by the various individual conceptions of morality and the good. The very recognition of personal moral autonomy depends upon the existence and enforcement of protected domains of personal choice. Rules must permit but also restrict interference. This in turn rests upon certain assumptions of formal equality. The familiarity of the central political ideas can disguise how remarkable and contingent is the situation described in this viewpoint. Why should not the inhabitants of liberal societies evolve and develop expressions of their autonomy sufficiently diverse as to destroy all but the most pragmatic commonalities? Kant himself worries that in any community, human beings will 'corrupt each other's moral disposition and make one another evil'.[16] On the other hand, the lot of man can be compared to trees in a forest: 'just because each one strives to deprive the other of air and sun, they compel each other to seek both above, and thus they grow tall and straight. Whereas those that, in freedom and isolation from one another, shoot out their branches at will, grow stunted and crooked and awry.'[17] Human beings will not flourish under conditions of

---

[15] J Gray, *Enlightenment's Wake* (London, Routledge, 1995), 151.

[16] Kant, *Anthropology from a Pragmatic Point of View*, R Louden (trans.) (Cambridge University Press, 2006), 6:93–4.

[17] Kant, 'Idea for a Universal History from a Cosmopolitan Point of View', in L Beck (trans.), *Philosophical Writings* (New York, Continuum, 1986), 249–62, proposition 5.

despotism, but neither will they make progress if left to fend for themselves, given complete freedom. Not only autonomy but society is needed. Mutual competition will be both the consequence of autonomy and the phenomenon which keeps human beings on the straight and narrow. But even here, men will corrupt one another. Enthusiasm for autonomy is not self-contained. Autonomy is necessary because of our moral shortcomings, but it is also dangerous and can proliferate evils if allowed to consume all other principles.

The second possible starting point is that of Rawls. For Rawls, the fundamentality of the central political ideas derives from the 'original position'. The full meaning of the human situation is not discovered in contemplation of social or historical processes that exist 'outside' the person, but in the internal properties of the person. Idealized agents in this position can, as it were, see beyond themselves precisely on the basis of what they *cannot* see. Rational commitments are unpolluted and unrestricted by personal desires and attachments, for all concrete identities, historical and social circumstances have been excluded. Does this adequately explain the fundamentality of what such agents imagine? Consider the response of Raymond Geuss:

> One main question is why we would have any reason to suppose that agents in such a situation would *agree* on anything at all. No matter how long they discussed matters, there might remain at the end different groups with different views. A second question is why, even if they did agree, this decision should have any relevance whatever to us, who do have concrete 'identities', parts of which sometimes can be important to us, and who live in a concrete situation in a complex real world, *not* in the idealized world of the original position. This type of theory appeals to [a] traditional prejudice among philosophers in favour of purity, autonomy, formalism and abstractness. The theory certainly purports to be pure of contamination by the facts of history, psychology, economics, sociology and political science, but it is highly questionable whether *this* type of abstractness is conducive to real understanding of the world we live in, and at least equally questionable whether we can have a useful practical philosophy, or even a useful set of normative rules, without such grounded understanding.[18]

For discussion see A Perreau-Saussine, 'Immanuel Kant on International Law', in J Tasioulas and S Besson (eds.), *The Philosophy of International Law* (Oxford University Press, 2008).

[18] R Geuss, *Outside Ethics* (Princeton University Press, 2005), 32–3.

Agency alone cannot explain a hypothetical convergence in judgments. Would such agents even recognize their own 'autonomy'? Might not their joint labours impart to them an overwhelming sense of their own nature as social beings? They are jointly responsible, not free agents! It is reasonable to assume that Rawlsian agents would only create a society appropriate to the autonomous liberal subject if they valued this condition above all things. What is it about the condition of autonomy that would lead idealized social architects to consider it 'proper', a condition to be nurtured and encouraged rather than tempered or suppressed? Autonomy has not one but many potentialities. It produces alike the image of the self-standing responsible reasoner who takes the moral law into his heart, and that of the self-made, self-promoting entrepreneur whose concern is with status and personal wealth regardless of the damage done to others. Unless the more savoury of its possible expressions are regarded as intrinsic to it, why should the image of idealized agency be taken to define the central wellspring of moral insight? The original position, the one intellectual device that can treat the liberal idea of freedom as a self-contained idea, can in consequence offer us no reasons for valuing that idea.

The limits of Protestant political theory

The idealized image of human agency depicted in Rawls's 'original position' is not, as may first appear, a neutral idea, but one that grew out of a distinctively Protestant view of the world. It is not truly self-contained. Despite Rawls's own assertions, it is clear that the idealized situation of the original position is far from being uncontaminated by historical, social and cultural ideas. One obvious instance of this is the language in which the 'debate' is conducted. Language is by its nature a social phenomenon. The structures of linguistic meaning contained within it directly reflect the patterns of thought and understanding that have arisen within the culture and history of a community. The evolution of (as Hart puts it) a distinctive technical vocabulary of normative terms is but one facet of this. Debate can proceed only in the presence of linguistic and cultural commonalities which render us intelligible to one another. The 'purity' of cultural ignorance envisaged in the original position is thus selective. In being selective, it prefigures its own conclusions.

Collingwood observed that liberal philosophies have tended to concern 'the idea of a community as governing itself by fostering the free expression of all political opinions that take shape within it, and finding some means of reducing this multiplicity of opinions to a unity'.[19] The notion of an 'original position' is but one expression given to the idea, prevalent since the seventeenth century, that individuals in municipal politics are the domestic analogues of the sovereign and independent states which are the subject of international relations.[20] Intrinsic to the idea is that of a person's thoughts and actions as their own, arising out of their own personality. This is not true of a person at birth. Independence is achieved only gradually and by degrees. In between the two stages (of complete reliance and mature independence) is a long process of learning and socialization, both of which involve the reception of that which already exists and belongs to a community. At no point does the image of the 'idealized agent' or 'sovereign individual' capture the nature of the person understood in this way. Consequently neither image can offer any insight into the conditions inhabited by such persons. The relevant starting point for moral and political reflection is not the assumption of irreducible autonomy which must *then* be conditioned by collective rules, nor the image of initial multiplicity being reduced to unity. Multiplicity can develop only within broader conditions already characterized by high levels of unity.

In another essay, Collingwood recounts a visit he undertook with some of his students to a Greek monastery.[21] The students were initially sceptical of the value of the monastic life (whilst admiring and enjoying its way of life) due to a 'Protestant' prejudice that monks 'were at worst idle, indulgent and corrupt; at best selfishly wrapped up in a wrong-headed endeavour to save their own souls by forsaking the world and cultivating a fugitive and cloistered virtue'.[22] This attitude stood in contrast to that of the local community of which the monastery was part, who valued its presence even though they may see little of the benevolent life carried on there. Is the community's judgment, asks Collingwood, to be dismissed as 'superstition', and the monastery's support by the local community but a form of insidious parasitism? Ultimately, Collingwood suggests, it is not. Our own societies fund and encourage (or tolerate) the

---

[19] RG Collingwood, *Essays in Political Philosophy*, D Boucher (ed.) (Oxford, Clarendon Press, 1989), 177.

[20] See especially R Tuck, *The Rights of War and Peace: Political Thought and the International Order from Grotius to Kant* (Cambridge University Press, 2001).

[21] Collingwood, 'Monks and Morals', in *Essays in Political Philosophy* (above n 19), 144–9.

[22] Ibid., 144.

pursuit of research into pure mathematics. They do this in the knowledge that publication of works on pure mathematics has in general the only positive result that more people may become interested in becoming pure mathematicians. But if it is good that society has pure mathematicians, this is only because the mere existence of pure mathematicians in society (whom few know or understand) is of intrinsic value, irrespective of questions of social utility. In the same way, Collingwood suggests that the presence of the monastery was treasured by the people of the community he visited, no matter whether the spiritual fulfilment of the monks should be felt outside the monastery walls. 'There is', Collingwood says, 'something which we may call the Santorin way of life. It is not a mere aggregate of disconnected units; it is one pattern into which the monks and the children who gave us grapes and the girls who gave us water and the unknown person who painted the words of welcome at Pyrgos all fit as parts'.[23]

Collingwood's observation that community is more than 'a mere aggregate of units' points to a truth that is excluded by the implications of Protestantism. It suggests that the value of things (and of the human person, for example) is realized neither within their own being or interior states, nor in the consequences that may be attributed to such being, but rather in their connections to a wider world. It is difficult to exaggerate the incompatibility (which may not at first seem *very* great) of this standpoint with the world-view that is the legacy of Protestant thought. The Protestant world-view proceeds from certain assumptions about the nature of the relationship between man and God. It is necessary to explore some of these assumptions in order to contextualize the notion of liberal autonomy, which is not finally self-contained.

Proposition 34 of Luther's 'Theses Against Scholastic Theology' asserts that human nature has neither good precepts nor good will.[24] On this basis, proposition 48 states that syllogistic methods (i.e. philosophy) are inapplicable to divine ideas. One who uses the philosophical method to gain insight into the mystery of the Trinity will destroy their belief in it (proposition 49). Philosophy and human reason are for the world, not the heavens. In so saying, Luther divides the two realms, the natural and the supernatural, from one another absolutely. Knowledge of the world, or of oneself, can tell one nothing about divine matters, for both nature and human reason are irredeemably corrupt: 'Without the grace of God

---

[23] Ibid., 148.
[24] Luther, *Martin Luther's Werke*, vol. I (Weimar, Hermann Bohlaus & Co, 1883).

[reads proposition 7] the will produces an act that is perverse and evil.' Nothing could be further from Aristotle's approach to moral questions in the *Ethics*, and it is no surprise to see Luther dismissing the Aristotelian philosophy as 'the worst enemy of grace': 'I cannot help believing', Luther wrote elsewhere, 'that the Evil One introduced the study of Aristotle'.[25]

The depravity of human reason, the irrelevance of good works in securing salvation, can be understood to mean that:

> *all forms of human self-affirmation* – all human motives, all cares of which we are the object – are contrary to God. Including, in particular, the desire for redemption, if it stops at the hope of eternal happiness as the ultimate goal: for then it, too, is a private sin, a form of self-interest unbefitting the true Christian, who should be thinking about the glory of God for its own sake.[26]

On the basis of Luther's initial premise, therefore, 'all that gives man his uniqueness as a being, preserves his distinctness and maintains his activity ... is an evil. Consequently, all individual existence is an evil, and the true fulfilment of human destiny must be loss of individuality and oneness with divinity'.[27] The Lutheran act of faith begins with an act of self-abasement, a recognition of sinfulness and realization that one's own nature provides no path to God. Only divine grace can guarantee salvation.

Despite Luther's hostility to the metaphysical speculations of the philosophers, the image in which each individual stands alone before God became the basis for Kant's moral philosophy. Kant's position represents the secular manifestation of Luther's theological opposition to the location of moral qualities in good works. One must look neither to history nor to the world of human actions, but to the pure inner will itself as the only source of moral guidance. It is precisely here, however, that the Protestant world-view fails to provide a basis for law. The Lutheran ideal of justification through faith alone is at once opposed to justification through deeds *and* justification through doctrine.[28] True Christianity was not an extension or perfection of human nature, but the process of overcoming it. But at the same time, neither could true Christianity be *knowledge* of God. The true Christian must therefore also overcome doctrines and orthodoxies. These, like works, must be empty

---

[25] Luther, in *Martin Luther: Selections from his Writings*, J Dillenberger (ed.) (New York, Doubleday, 1961), 470.

[26] L Kolakowski, *The Two Eyes of Spinoza* (South Bend, IN, St Augustine's Press, 2004), 151–2.

[27] Ibid., 152.   [28] Ibid., 154–5.

and irrelevant. Human reason cannot grasp the divine, and ecclesiastical doctrine can play no part in the essential process of self-transformation and regeneration. How is the Christian message to be transmitted? Does not Luther's message itself invariably become hardened into a doctrine, and become *Lutheranism*? Whilst not undermining the intelligibility of its spiritual core, we might come to question Lutheranism's basis as a foundation for a view of the world:

> Indeed, Christianity conceived as a purely 'internal' value, with no possible support in any visible reality, cannot be the basis of a congregation; by its very nature, it cannot create a collectivity. In faith, human individuals are unreckonable: they cannot be totted up into the sum of them all. Each stands alone before God, and their combined faith does not produce any doctrinal unity or organized collective. Thus, the whole *raison d'être* of the visible Church is put in question ... So it seems natural that the idea of faith as the non-transferable property of the individual soul, closed to the world and visible only to God, had to yield to collective forms of Christian life which could be passed on and proclaimed.[29]

The Protestant vision could survive only by transcending itself: by becoming (as in the eyes of many Reformation theologians after Luther) corrupted into a version of the very thing which had been the object of Luther's initial rebellion.

Analogously, we can consider the position of morality within the context of Kantian autonomous agents reflecting upon universal standards for the governance of human behaviour. Might we not similarly conclude that the possibility of convergence in judgment on general laws (such as could ground a community) involves precisely the transcendence of Kant's Protestant assumptions? Does the achievement of 'freedom' of the will not itself suggest a shared background of understandings against which individual wills are constituted and rendered mutually intelligible? The obvious danger of nihilism, subsequently explored by Nietzsche amongst others, that is present within the most pure forms of Protestant mysticism may therefore send us back in the direction of Aristotle. But if Protestant forms of ethical thought are revealed as resting upon an unsustainable dualism between the natural and supernatural, the actual and the normative, it may seem that Aristotle's *Ethics* is grounded in exactly those historicist assumptions and affirmations of self that prompted the development of Lutheranism, and which are themselves unsustainable.

[29] Ibid., 155.

There are interpretations of Aristotle in which historical tradition itself becomes normative for the *phronimos*, so as to threaten the extinction of the gap between what is moral or right, and what we 'happen to do around here'. But interpretations of this kind ignore the background of metaphysical ideas against which the doctrines of the *Ethics* are propounded. Aristotle's *Ethics* is addressed to a particular type of person, the *phronimos* or man of wisdom and good intentions who wishes to be virtuous. This is not the barren rationality of the Kantian agent, for Aristotle had himself provided an extensive psychological underpinning for human nature as essentially benign.[30] He is therefore able to treat the historical nexus of human practices and forms of association which reflect and embody that benign nature as providing a possible source of insight into the nature of the good. Aristotle does not *assume* that the good is present in human history to some degree. He *concludes* that it is, as a consequence of a view in which human history is part of a broader, rationally intelligible cosmos. Human beings situated within this cosmos do not resemble the free-floating individuals of the Kantian philosophy, but are possessed of definite character types and rich psychologies that are the subject of deep exploration by Aristotle, and considered as an integral part of the human *telos*.

It is not essential to adopt Aristotle's cosmology. The relevant lesson to be drawn from Aristotle's philosophy is that it is the cosmology which allows Aristotle to transcend the limits of pure historicism without thereby engaging in the dualistic assumptions that were to underpin Protestant forms of thought. It is only against a broader framework of ideas that history can be said to possess meaning and significance. It is this historical and worldly connectivity that illuminates the moral experience of the 'individual'. The image that is most appropriate to this experience is one wherein the context of social and historical commonalities completes the meaning of 'the individual', rather than the image of individuals being defined in opposition to whatever external connections they have become enmeshed in. The relentless focus within modern philosophy upon individual agency had done much to obscure the vital significance of notions of congregation and community for the explanation of moral and legal bonds.

Protestant views of law tend to emphasize the idea of rights, duties, liberties and so forth, as instruments which define spheres of autonomy

---

[30] See Aristotle, *De Anima*, DW Hamlyn (ed.) (Oxford, Clarendon Press, 1993), and elsewhere.

by keeping one another at arm's length. It is less often noticed that those same instruments variously form and express the very bonds which prevent individuals becoming separated by more than an arm's length. This dual aspect of law needs to be much more deeply appreciated if we are fully to understand the character of modern political life under the rule of law. This will not happen until liberals in the Anglo-American tradition confront the broader implications of their secular standpoint. I shall say more on this in the following chapter, which examines the standpoints of two modern liberals, Hart and Rawls, who in different ways exhibit the tendency outlined above. I will try to show that an understanding of what divides them is only fully revealed when their arguments are considered from the broader perspectives I am suggesting.

4

The form and direction of Anglo-American jurisprudence

How are we to understand the arguments between liberal philosophers of law? HLA Hart offers one understanding of liberal legal order. His general concern with the 'separation of law and morals' is itself distinctively liberal, or can be easily given a liberal meaning: the legal enforcement of morality. Should the law of the modern state impose a specific conception of morality?[1] The writings of the philosopher John Rawls are preoccupied with a different issue: the vision of justice appropriate to a liberal society. In an essay on Rawls, Hart expresses his great admiration for the achievement of *A Theory of Justice*: 'No book of political philosophy since I read the great classics of the subject has stirred my thoughts as deeply.'[2] Rawls's response is no less complimentary. The preface to the revised edition credits Hart with identifying 'one of the most serious weaknesses' of the original text.[3] Yet there is otherwise relatively little direct engagement between the two major liberal thinkers. Hart is ultimately unpersuaded by Rawls's conclusions. He wishes to draw back from 'the apparently dogmatic course of Rawls's argument'.[4] Where Rawls asserts the priority of liberty over other goods, Hart suggests the need for the state to strike a balance between various kinds of goods. Where Rawls imputes a 'latent ideal' to the law and justice of liberal order, Hart wishes to maintain the law's neutrality before a plurality of ideals. Whereas Rawls maintains that 'autonomous' agents will prioritize liberty, Hart is not sure what they will prefer.[5]

[1] See HLA Hart, *Law, Liberty and Morality* (Stanford University Press, 1963), Parts I and II; 'Social Solidarity and the Enforcement of Morality', in *Essays in Jurisprudence and Philosophy* (Oxford, Clarendon Press, 1983), Essay 11.

[2] Hart, 'Rawls on Liberty and its Priority', in *Essays*, ibid., Essay 10, 223.

[3] J Rawls, *A Theory of Justice*, revised edn (Cambridge MA, Harvard University Press, 1999), xii.

[4] Hart (above n 2), 247.

[5] Ibid., 246: 'When the veil of ignorance is lifted some will prefer A to B and others B to A.'

The heart of the issue between Hart and Rawls is whether the condition of liberal autonomy implies any specific form of society, or an open-ended diversity of forms. Why did not this issue become *the* concern of modern jurisprudence? The answer is tied up with the form and identity of Anglo-American jurisprudence. Liberal freedom is no less a self-contained idea for Hart than for Rawls's 'original position'. The liberal subject is free precisely in being free of larger contextual orders against which his character can be understood. Philosophy is a process of clarifying understandings that the liberal subject already has, 'intensively investigating a small, circumscribed range of philosophical issues while holding broader, systematic questions in abeyance'.[6] If Rawls identifies a specific ideal grounded in the formal characteristics of autonomy, it can only be because he is pursuing a 'normative' agenda rather than a 'descriptive' one.

Hart and Rawls are both liberals. But they are very different liberals. One might suspect that the differences between them are more significant than a preference for pursuing distinct 'projects'. Liberals can articulate these differences only with great difficulty because they pertain to the ultimate significance and direction of liberal legal order: a question that liberalism, in cultivating its secular identity, cannot easily confront. I suggest that the meaning of liberalism's greatest achievement, religious settlement, is different on either side of the Atlantic. Until they explore the full significance of liberalism's Protestant inheritance, liberal writers will not completely understand the differences that underpin their disagreements.

Hart and Oxford philosophy

University courses on 'Anglo-American jurisprudence' typically include consideration of HLA Hart's classic work, *The Concept of Law*. This was a work very much steeped in the 'ordinary language philosophy' prevalent at the Oxford of the time, and with certain connections to the linguistic philosophy of Ludwig Wittgenstein.[7] In this respect, Hart's principal theories about the law (theories he later defended toward the

---

[6] S Soames, *Philosophical Analysis in the Twentieth Century*, vol. I (Princeton University Press, 2003), xv.

[7] See e.g. N Lacey, *A Life of HLA Hart: The Nightmare and the Noble Dream* (Oxford University Press, 2004), and A Perreau-Saussine, 'An Outsider on the Inside: Hart's Limits on Jurisprudence', 56 *University of Toronto LJ* (2006), 371.

end of his life) are a typical example of the conceptual analytic approach to philosophical questions. Questions about the nature of social phenomena are interpreted as questions concerning the linguistic and social practices which surround those phenomena. Philosophy cannot draw its understandings from the facts. The philosopher's question about the inner 'nature' of the institutions is not at bottom one that can be resolved by the mere reporting of facts. The philosopher's enquiry seems to presuppose some critical detachment from the facts upon which judgment must be made. But neither can the answer lie in mysterious metaphysical properties supposedly attaching to such facts, for it would seem that we can have no knowledge of such properties. Instead, attention must be directed to questions about the *meanings* and *concepts* in terms of which understandings of the facts are interpreted and organized. The philosopher seeks to clarify concepts as a way of rendering more perspicuous the intellectual commitments of our own reports and representations.

But when Hart came to write down his views on the American way of thinking about law and government it was with a certain coolness and misgiving, not unrestrained admiration, that he chose to express himself. This is true not only of his engagements with Rawls. In his critical responses to Dworkin, something of the same lukewarmness lay behind the errors and concerns he found there. It is easy to perceive the Hart/Dworkin debate as an instance of disputes which originate *within* analytical legal philosophy. Conducted within certain conventional bounds and understandings, it appears as a dispute of Anglo-American jurisprudence. Is the disagreement so easily defined? Does it raise no more fundamental questions than the presence of necessary connections between law and morals; whether the legal order is better understood as a body of rules or as a system of rights; or whether or not jurisprudence can be descriptive without also being evaluative?

Hart's initial sojourn in the world of Oxonian philosophy, as an undergraduate and later as a fellow, saw him steeped in the values and methods of the 'Greats' tradition. To Greats scholars, philosophy embodied a process of speculation on permanent questions of the universe and of the human condition. Questions were to be considered through an enquiry rooted in the writings of Plato and Aristotle, as well as later writers ('modern greats') such as Berkeley, Kant, Hegel. The sense that the central questions of philosophy are unchanging and require steady contemplation cultivates an intellectual disposition that is intensely interested in roots and beginnings. It is aligned with an idea of progress concerned not with the discovery of new truths, but with the development and improvement of the philosopher's character as he contemplates old ones. To one of such a temperament, the pragmatic flavour of American philosophy, its confident emphasis on *changing* the world, transforming social arrangements in accordance with new principles of morality and knowledge, would appear both dangerous and rash. In a book published over a decade after Hart's death, Dworkin wrote in praise of his 'country's most fundamental contribution to political morality. We have been envied for our adventure and we are now increasingly copied all over the world, from Strasbourg to Capetown, from Budapest to Delhi. Let's not lose our nerve, when all around the world other people, following our example, are gaining theirs.'[8] It is not difficult to imagine the instinctive response of someone of Hart's intellectual disposition, distrustful of Rawls's 'latent idealism', when confronted with statements of this kind. He would want above all to detach permanent questions of the nature of law and of governance by rules from the expression of these shifting conceptions of moral value; would wish to separate its status as a feature of human societies whose nature must be contemplated from the ever-changing values governments may require it to serve.

The extent to which Hart departed in his later work from this Greats tradition has perhaps been exaggerated. Upon Hart's return, those at Oxford had hoped that he would defend the Greats tradition *against* the new methods of the linguistic philosophers of the analytic tradition, Ryle, JL Austin and Wittgenstein.[9] In common with many of his generation, Hart found in these new methods a powerful and original way of posing and responding to philosophical problems. But it must be remembered that Wittgenstein himself, at least, was to be subsequently recognized as a 'Great', and the themes and concerns to be found in Hart's later work, overlain as they are by analytic methodology, continue in important ways to reflect the older tradition of the contemplation of fundamental and permanent ideas.

Similar connections to an older tradition of thought are also present in American jurisprudence. These connections have been forgotten to some extent in virtue of the dominance in the law schools of the late nineteenth

---

[8] R Dworkin, *Justice in Robes* (Cambridge MA, Belknap Press, 2006), 138–9.
[9] See Lacey (above n 7), 113.

century of the standpoints of 'formalism' and 'realism'.[10] American jurisprudential theories of the mid-twentieth century, of the kind which concerned Hart, were most immediately intelligible as idealistic critical responses to *both* formalism *and* realism. Thus, Hart observes that American jurisprudence 'is marked by a concentration, almost to the point of obsession, on the judicial process'.[11] The immediate reason for this myopic concentration, Hart thought, is the constitutional importance of the United States Supreme Court. But, citing some words of de Tocqueville, Hart straightaway hints at a deeper truth: 'scarcely any political question arises in the United States that is not resolved, sooner or later, into a judicial question'.[12]

I would like to suggest that the source of Hart's uneasiness lies in his immersion within a jurisprudential tradition that is focused upon the idea of the pursuit of 'the good', whereas American jurisprudence belongs to a tradition that attempts to *free* politics (through the law) from its Aristotelian conception as a form of governance which seeks to realize the moral nature of human persons or their communities. This 'civic' politics manifests itself in complicated ways in the principal writings of twentieth-century American jurisprudence. One may glimpse it, for example, in Rawls's prioritization of 'the right' over 'the good', and in the emphasis placed upon 'process' in American law and legal writing. These ideas may be thought to imply no more than an incident of the 'Protestant' political culture inherited from Europe, and as suggesting no great ideological division. If there is not one good, but many, must not society be inevitably concerned with the procedures and instruments by which the pursuit of these goods is to be regulated? In fact, American political culture embodies an ideal other than that of achieving a reasonable ordering between fragmented moral communities that are to a large degree in competition with one another. Its 'civic' character lies in the separation of state and government from questions of moral progress. It lies in the absence of an ambition on the part of the state to enforce a moral community (even a deeply fragmented one), and the concomitant

---

[10] For a classic study see MJ Horwitz, *The Transformation of American Law 1780–1860* (Cambridge MA, Harvard University Press, 1977). See also N Duxbury, *Patterns of American Jurisprudence* (Oxford University Press, 1995); W Twining, *Karl Llewellyn and the Realist Movement* (London, Weidenfeld & Nicholson, 1973).

[11] Hart, 'American Jurisprudence Through English Eyes: The Nightmare and the Noble Dream', in Hart, *Essays* (above n 1), 123.

[12] Ibid., 124 (citing de Tocqueville's *Democracy in America*, 280).

restriction of the state's power to ensuring the security of potentially fratricidal groupings within its borders.

Rawls and American political thought

In June 1826, shortly before his death, Thomas Jefferson wrote of the Declaration of Independence in the following terms: 'May it be to the world, what I believe it will be, (to some parts sooner, to others later, but finally to all,) the signal of arousing men to burst the chains, under which monkish ignorance and superstition had persuaded them to bind themselves, and to assume the blessings and security of self-government.'[13] The reference to 'self-government' might suggest a reading of the Declaration as belonging to an Enlightenment history of political rationalism and secularization. The reference to the dissolution of political bonds, and to truths that are 'self-evident' rather than revealed, appear to belong to a Kantian tradition in which progress is made through the achievement, collective in this case, of autonomous agency. No longer would political doctrines and processes be determined by the superstitions or decisions of the past. Maturity would replace devotion to elect masters on the basis of some supposedly privileged intellection. 'Even the Holy One of the Gospel', Kant had written, 'must be compared with our ideal of moral perfection before He is cognized as such'. It is this reading of the Declaration, and of the US Constitution's similarly evocative aspiration for the creation of 'a more perfect Union', which form the basis of Hart's characterization of the 'Noble Dream': a forward-looking optimism concerned with the realization of the ideal society.

Despite these associations, the sense and flavour of the document have perhaps more in common with civic philosophers, such as Christian Thomasius and Johannes Althusius, than with Kant. The civic philosophers were also concerned with independence, but in their case the independence sought was of the realm of law and politics from that of religion and theology. To civic philosophers, perhaps the great disaster of Western intellectual development was the acceptance by the Emperor Constantine of the Christian religion. For it was exactly this convergence of political authority and spiritual enlightenment that created the situation in which the government of a state could purport to govern those subject to its authority on the basis of its access to a domain of

---

[13] Thomas Jefferson, Letter of June 1826, quoted in D Armitage, *The Declaration of Independence: A Global History* (Cambridge MA, Harvard University Press, 2007), 2.

intellection that is in some way privileged, and closed to the common stock.[14] Government must be exercised, not only for the security and preservation of its people, but for their salvation as well. It concerns the regulation not only of the political circumstances of the civil community, but the spiritual wellbeing of a moral community.

In modern times, the idea of 'community' has developed in ways which obscure the presence of a significant gap between a political community and a moral one. Both appear to be characterized by the presence and need for a certain degree of cohesiveness that is secured through institutions and mechanisms of social justice. In fact this is not the case. Whereas the notion of a political community need concern no more than its ongoing existence and stability (and hence the maintenance of peaceful relations between its members), the idea of a moral community implies a dynamic that is absent from those which are productive of mere subsistence: *regeneration*. It is not stability or long-term survival that is central to the idea of a moral community, but its *impermanence*, the need for constant transformation of its forms. In his foreword to Grotius's *De Iure Belli ac Pacis*,[15] Thomasius places the responsibility for this transformational conception of society at the door of those scholastic metaphysicians who blended an inherited pagan philosophy of nature with the Christian conception of Creation. The result of this marriage was a notion of social reality divided into visible and invisible worlds. Perceived only by the elect establishment (the clerisy), the invisible world consisted in norms which transcended the 'mere' visible realm of earthly politics. 'Through heresy-hunting and the coercion of conscience', wrote Thomasius, 'one forced these [erroneous norms and doctrines] on the people as necessary articles of faith'.[16]

This mode of thought was antithetical to the very idea of a Greats tradition. The metaphysical systems of Aristotle and Plato were considered by Thomasius as amounting to a 'secret theology' corrupting the natural law doctrines of both Catholics and Protestants alike.[17] Within the Artistotelian conception, politics was regarded as an exercise directed towards the realization of man's moral nature. Because man's nature was essentially social, human flourishing demanded a context of collective institutions and practices that were themselves promotive and exemplary

---

[14] See I Hunter, *Rival Enlightenments* (Cambridge University Press, 2001), 88.
[15] Thomasius, 'Foreword', in Grotius, *De Iure Belli ac Pacis* (Tubingen, JCB Mohr, 1950), 1–28. (I am indebted to Hunter's translations: see Hunter, above n 14.)
[16] Ibid., 8.   [17] Ibid., 24: see Hunter (above n 14), 87.

of moral excellence. Christian theology added to this image the idea that such virtues were salvific in character, so that the whole edifice of government could be seen as a manifestation (albeit partial) of God's operative grace. The prince or head of state was God's own instrument. Princely law-making partakes of the divine order of eternal truth. The classical doctrine of the natural lawyers arose directly from this supposition:

> For there is no civil law, nor can there be any, in which something of natural and divine immutable equity has not been mixed. If it departs entirely from the judgment of natural and divine law (*ius naturale et divinum*), it is not to be called law (*lex*). It is entirely unworthy of this name, and can obligate no one against natural and divine equity.[18]

Politics resembled the continual transformation of society so as to bring it ever closer to an archetype defined by the Christian virtues.

The Platonic inheritance supplied an alternative cosmology for Christian beliefs. Plato's image of the cave of conventional understandings, from which the philosopher desires escape, allowed for the differentiation of two modes of being: one in which man is viewed as a sensual creature, rooted both emotionally and intellectually in the visible world; the other in which he is viewed as God's Creation, a supernatural rather than merely natural animal, which allows him to transcend the bounds of the world and contemplate what is eternal and invisible. Whereas for Aristotle evil represented a privation, or failure to achieve the good, Plato located evil in the corrupting influence of man's concrete fleshly existence upon his rational soul and his intellect. The Platonic metaphysics translated also into Augustine's vision of the two cities, the one earthly and the other heavenly, of which the Christian man is a citizen. The earthly, imperfect city is the domain of the corrupted and sinful civic community, of which life makes us a member. But the heavenly city is also on pilgrimage in the world, being the fraternal spiritual community of Christian believers united under the Church.[19] Government could not confine itself only to the salvation of the body, but must equally concern the redemption of the soul. The transformative virtues required for the development of a redemptive character could be realized only in common, as part of the full realization of man's *social* nature.

---

[18] J Althusius, *Politica*, ch IX. Elsewhere, Althusius observes that the 'right of the realm' (*ius regni*), or princely sovereignty, 'is two-fold. It pertains both to the welfare of the soul and to the care of the body' (ibid.).

[19] See Augustine, *De Civitate Dei*, IV and XIX.

This conception of government could not survive unaltered the fragmentation of the West's confessional inheritance. No longer was there a single moral community whose regeneration it was the purpose of politics to bring about, but a number of distinct schismatic communities fundamentally at variance with one another over the meaning and form to be given to regenerative efforts. Political involvement in the pursuit of redemption would inevitably constitute a 'coercion of conscience'. Many of these communities were doctrinally committed to the notion that the will of God was itself inscrutable, beyond all human reason, and thus incapable of receiving expression through the legislative efforts of the prince (or indeed the credal formulations of the Church). Salvation became a matter not of civic forms but of metaphysical contemplation. Those wishing to be saved must cultivate a personal relationship to a transcendent truth that is to be attained not through teachings, but through private devotions. The realities of sustained politico-religious conflict in Europe had brought home the inadequacies of inherited patterns of thought and practice to deal with the regulation of schismatically divided communities. The civic philosophers responded to this divisive situation by detaching the realm of law and politics from questions of the highest good (that is, religious questions pertaining to ultimate salvation and moral transformation). Henceforward, politics was to be thought of as an enterprise aimed at the material security of peoples, not the safeguarding of their immortal souls. Politics was an enterprise to be placed in the hands of professional jurists and statesmen, not clerics or religious ideologues.[20] This was a pattern of thought which drew encouragement from, and in turn served to reinforce, the voluntarist theology at the heart of the major Protestant creeds. 'It is not Wisdom', Hobbes wrote, 'but Authority that makes a Law'.[21]

Within the new 'civil' jurisprudence, political power could no longer be assumed to derive from a general view of the world as possessing a created or cosmic order of governance. The basis of political power must be a *social* basis. The various theories of 'social contract' which arose in the seventeenth century and beyond were in essence an attempt to explain how political power can come to be transferred from an

---

[20] This is seen for example in the insistence of Hobbes and Pufendorf that the natural law is in effect given expression solely through the commands of a sovereign: Hobbes, *Leviathan*, ch 16 (and elsewhere); Pufendorf, *De Iure Naturae et Gentium*, 8.i.5.

[21] Hobbes, *A Dialogue Between a Philosopher and a Student, of the Common Laws of England* (University of Chicago Press, 1971), 55.

undifferentiated social context of individual actors, to a single sovereign power presiding over an *ordered* community. It was at the level of the individual, and not the community, that analyses of politics and government must begin. Pufendorf, for example, argued that,

> Therefore it is held that no more power was voluntarily bestowed upon that prince than what a man of reason may judge to make to [the end of his security]; although what may at any particular moment work to that end is a matter for decision not for those who do the transferring, but by him on whom that power was transferred. Therefore, the supreme sovereign can rightfully force citizens to all things which he judges to be of any advantage to the public good.[22]

The notion of 'the public good' was essentially that of public *security*. As a limit on the sovereign power, public security entailed the creation and enforcement of laws both against extra-territorial threats, and against internal disruptions to order. This process of de-sacralizing law and politics by detaching them from questions of ultimate good amounted to a juridification of politics. It lead to an equally pronounced but in some ways opposed tendency: the idealization of politics. This tendency is encountered in the language of the Declaration of Independence, and quite starkly in the method of Rawls. It arises, perhaps, because of the acknowledged proclivity of authoritarian systems of politics such as that of Hobbes (and of Pufendorf or even Grotius) to produce tyranny. Many of the social contractarian philosophies were open to the charge of being Janus-faced in nature, absolutizing political power in the sovereign on the one hand whilst implying a theoretical 'right of resistance' on the other where the terms of the 'contract' are 'breached'.[23] The character to be cultivated by the subject was one of private piety and public obedience.[24] But he was at the same time the theoretical *source* of the sovereign power. Politics itself therefore came to be regarded as a safeguard on the exercise of power, a domain of value and intellection distinct both from religious morality *and* from tyrannic civic rule. The 'more perfect Union' desired by the founders of the United States referred neither to the moral regeneration of the inhabitants, nor to the excellence of its political ideals,

---

[22] Pufendorf (above n 20), 7.vi.13.

[23] Richard Tuck famously levels this charge at the Grotian rights theory, which 'speaks the language of both absolutism and liberty': see Tuck, *Natural Rights Theories: Their Origin and Development* (Cambridge University Press, 1979), 79. See also L Ward, *The Politics of Liberty in England and Revolutionary America* (Cambridge University Press, 2004).

[24] See Hunter (above n 14), ch 4.

but to the framework of political order itself, at once free of tyranny and of the destabilizing effects of internal fratricidal discord.

Rawls's *A Theory of Justice* supplies a vivid illustration of this transformation. It is made clear from the beginning that the political system is itself the focus: 'Justice is the first virtue of social *institutions*', Rawls writes, 'as truth is of systems of thought'.[25] For these institutions preside over a form of association that is 'a cooperative venture for mutual advantage [though at the same time] it is typically marked by a conflict as well as by an identity of interests'.[26] In outlining a set of principles 'for assigning basic rights and duties and for determining what they take to be the proper distribution of the benefits and burdens of social cooperation', justice 'establishes the bonds of *civic* friendship'.[27] It is a value, to reverse Michael Oakeshott's expression, which pertains more to bodies in proximity rather than to minds in relation. This is essentially a question of well-ordering:

> In the absence of a certain measure of agreement on what is just and unjust, it is clearly more difficult for individuals to coordinate their plans efficiently in order to ensure that mutually beneficial arrangements are maintained. Distrust and resentment corrode the ties of civility, and suspicion and hostility tempt men to act in ways they would otherwise avoid. So while the distinctive role of conceptions of justice is to specify basic rights and duties and to determine the appropriate distributive shares, the way in which a conception does this is bound to affect the problems of efficiency, coordination and stability.[28]

For Rawls, politics is concerned with what is right rather than what is good. Rawls in fact seeks explicitly to detach political arrangements from questions of the good. Those in the 'original position', choosing the form of their society (one thinks again of Jefferson) from behind a 'veil of ignorance' are deprived even of 'their conceptions of the good'.[29]

Rawls explicitly considers the relationship of this 'civic' theorizing to the traditional philosophical discussion of justice. Though his approach 'may not seem to tally with tradition', considered reflection will reveal a

---

[25] Rawls (above n 3), 3 (my emphasis). The 'civic' philosophy which inspires it is evident in Rawls's assumption, as Raymond Geuss observes, 'that the agents [under the veil of ignorance] can be said to be choosing "principles" – rather than, for instance, simply designating someone as Head Man, Big Chief, *Pater Patriae*, Grand Dragon or what have you, and doing whatever this person says'. R Geuss, *Philosophy and Real Politics* (Princeton University Press, 2008), 72.

[26] Rawls (above n 3), 4. [27] Ibid., 5 (my emphasis).

[28] Ibid., 6. [29] Ibid., 12.

deeper continuity.[30] Whereas Aristotle operates with a more specific conception of justice, which is that of refraining from *pleonexia* (or gaining advantage for oneself by taking that which belongs to another, or denying him his due), Rawls is concerned with a question that is presupposed by Aristotle's discussion: 'an account of what properly belongs to a person and of what is due to him'. Aristotle's question is concerned with action. Rawls's concerns 'social institutions and the legitimate expectations to which they give rise'.[31] Hence, '[t]here is no conflict with the traditional notion'.[32]

Whether the two conceptions are indeed continuous is open to question. The Aristotelian conception and the tradition that followed it did indeed raise questions of what is due to one, as is reflected in the usage of the word '*ius*' in the Roman jurisprudence. The term carried the sense both of a private, bilateral relationship based upon conceptions of how two disputants should behave toward one another (i.e. right), and that of what is objectively just or right (i.e. law).[33] The adjudicative context therefore forced an elusive distinction upon the Roman jurists, which they were never fully able to formulate clearly as long as law texts were composed in Latin. This elusiveness demonstrates the connection between Aristotle's questions. The general notion of a 'right' signified that which is the right thing for a just man to do. But the structure of Roman pleading gave to the idea of 'right' the suggestion that 'right belongs to the recipient of the action. It is *his* right, *suum ius*'.[34] Hence, the question of what is due to one is not, in the Aristotelian tradition of which Rawls writes, finally separable from an investigation into the nature of the just, wise or virtuous character which represents the highest good of the human being. By making his hypothetical administrators ignorant of their own views on the question of the good, Rawls seeks to emancipate the discussion of justice (one's due) from questions of moral regeneration (what is good for one). Whether or not it is possible to maintain such a separation, this effort places Rawls in opposition with the Aristotelian tradition.

---

[30] Ibid., 10.   [31] Ibid.   [32] Ibid., 11.

[33] In *The Digest of Justinian*, for example, the term *ius* is applied to both sides of the bilateral relationship, so that one can refer to the *ius* of refraining from building on one's land in such a way as to interfere with another's light. Thus, *ius* could approximate to the modern sense of 'duty' as much as to 'right': see A Watson (ed.) *The Digest of Justinian* (University of Pennsylvania Press, 1997), VII.ii.2.

[34] See A Brett, *Liberty, Right and Nature: Individual Rights in Later Scholastic Thought* (Cambridge University Press, 1997), 92.

The treatment of politics as concerned with questions, not of the good, but of distribution, liberty, equality, right and process, equals the juridification of politics. But politics nevertheless requires ideals for its guidance. It is more than a mere commentary on existing arrangements. Politics is driven by a vision of well-ordering, of a 'more perfect Union' in which circumstances of schismatic destabilization are controlled and reduced. Therefore, it is also a moral vision. But it is a moral vision that concerns only free-standing social virtues (justice, fairness and equality), and not questions of the human good, or the flourishing life. For this reason, Raymond Geuss's assertion that Rawls's 'liberalism' presided over 'a re-moralization of political philosophy'[35] is capable of being misread. We should instead think in terms of 'the idealization of politics'. Geuss's analysis of the situation nevertheless describes exactly the form that the idealism takes:

> the multiple forms of life which liberalism recognizes are always assumed to be embedded in an overriding consensus that has latent moral significance. What is distinctive about liberalism isn't, therefore, so much its openness to pluralism as its view that all societies should be seen as capable of attaining consensus, despite a lack of homogeneity in the manners, beliefs, and habits of their members.[36]

The juridical form of this civil philosophy makes it difficult to separate law from the political ideals which lie at the heart of the liberal vision. For it will seem that the law, at least of a mature market society, must be understood as serving precisely those ideals. 'Law', or legal practices, do not arise as a quite distinct area of cultural endeavour to that of politics. We might say that there are no facts (and therefore interpretations of the facts) about law that do not belong to that wider political context. It is this standpoint on politics that produces Dworkin's characteristic insistence upon the interpretative quality of legal concepts:

> In fact, we have no difficulty identifying collectively the practices that count as legal practices in our own culture ... It would be a mistake [however] ... to think that we identify these institutions through some shared and intellectually satisfying definition of what a legal system necessarily is and what institutions necessarily make it up. Our culture presents us with legal institutions and with the idea that they form a

---

[35] Geuss, *Outside Ethics* (Princeton University Press, 2005), 16.   [36] Ibid., 17.

system. The question which features they have, in virtue of which they combine as a distinctly legal system, is part of the interpretive problem.[37]

To one steeped in a civil approach to politics, the question of law is of interpretative significance precisely because the domain of politics and law must remain detached from ethical questions concerning 'the good'. It is the firmness of this distinction which constitutes the noble dream: the ideal of a society in which collisions between citizens, pursuing different projects and ideals, are regulated by established rights that are identifiable without recourse to arguments centring on the merits of the courses being pursued.[38] The Nightmare is the image of the wall dividing the two realms, the agreed domain of politics and the schismatic realm of ethics, crashing down in ruin.

Hart's English liberalism

How might Hart, as a product of the Oxonian Greats tradition, be expected to respond to such a vision? Certainly his thoughts were stirred very deeply.[39] But he goes on to say: 'I am very conscious that I may have failed to keep constantly in view or in proper perspective all the arguments which Rawls, at different places in this long and complex work, concentrates on the points which I find unconvincing.'[40] Hart's assessment of the book as 'stirring', and the difficulty he experienced in keeping the relevant points and objections in view, are perhaps symptoms of his engagement with a work that lies outside the Greats tradition in which a central place is accorded to reflection upon the nature of the good life. Something of the same sort is detectable in certain passages in Hart's longest and most systematic response to Dworkin's criticisms of his theory, his 'Postscript' to *The Concept of Law*. For example, Hart says: 'It is not obvious why there should be or indeed could be any significant conflict between enterprises so different as my own and Dworkin's

---

[37] Dworkin, *Law's Empire* (London, Fontana, 1986), 91. The 'civil' quality of Dworkin's ideas is also seen in his exclusion of 'external preferences' from questions of the extent of individual rights: such rights are not to be delineated by reference to ideas concerning the general form of life that it is good for people to lead, but on the basis of weighing 'personal preferences'. See e.g. Dworkin, *Taking Rights Seriously* (London, Duckworth, 1978), 235.

[38] See Hart's characterization, borrowed from Lord Radcliffe, of the 'objective, impartial, erudite, and experienced declarer of the law' which must not be 'confused with the very different image of the legislator': Hart (above n 11), 126.

[39] See n 2 above.   [40] Ibid.

conceptions of legal theory.'[41] These somewhat cautious remarks can be contrasted with the more confident tone of his essay, 'Social Solidarity and the Enforcement of Morality', which opposes Lord Devlin's conservative agenda.[42] This essay begins by placing the theme upon which he wishes to enlarge firmly within the Greats tradition. The starting point taken is that of Plato's *Republic* and *Laws*, and Aristotle's *Ethics* and *Politics*.

Hart's biographer recalls how, in the early years of his fellowship at Oxford after his return from war work, Hart was expected, and had planned, to write a book on Plato.[43] The book never materialized, and Hart instead went on to hold the Chair in Jurisprudence, 'and to become the founder of modern analytical jurisprudence'.[44] When we think of Hart, it is often as one engaged in applying the insights of modern linguistic philosophy (especially that of JL Austin and Wittgenstein) to the area of law. But the purpose of a classical Greats education was not simply to bind the student to certain philosophical doctrines, or to raise an awareness in him of the subtleties of the positions of Plato and Aristotle. It was intended to produce, through contemplation of the classics, a sound and proper *way* of thinking and responding to problems. The Greats tradition concerned not the amassing of a body of classical knowledge, but its assimilation into a sound and wise character appropriate to one engaged with difficult social or intellectual problems. No matter how deeply impressed he may have become with linguistic philosophy, can we think of Hart as having shrugged off such a character? Or should we think of him as having adopted a series of insights, vocabularies and methodologies which, in some way, crystalized on top of entrenched patterns of thought (or perhaps, a way of perceiving the world): influencing and reshaping his intellectual commitments no doubt, but not utterly annihilating his former character? It is possible to suggest 'that Hart himself may have retained an understanding of morality influenced by Plato – not an idealist Plato, but one tentative or even sceptical about whether his very real ambitions for moral philosophy could ever be realized'.[45]

Hart's jurisprudence belongs to the English liberal tradition. It is ultimately structured around questions pertaining to the nature of the

---

[41] Hart, *The Concept of Law*, 2nd edn (Oxford, Clarendon Press, 1994), 241. On page 1, he says that he 'find[s] it hard to follow Dworkin's precise reasons for rejecting descriptive legal theory or "jurisprudence" as he often calls it'.
[42] In Hart (above n 1), 248.   [43] See Lacey (above n 7), 113ff.
[44] See A Perreau-Saussine (above n 7), 373.   [45] Ibid.

good life, and of the role that law must play in relation to that life. Despite superficial appearances to the contrary, Hart's perspective is intrinsically bound up with larger questions of the human condition that cannot be contemplated by 'intensively investigating a small, circumscribed range of philosophical issues' whilst 'holding broader, systematic questions in abeyance':[46] questions which come crashing back in chapter IX of *The Concept of Law*. But Hart remains despondent about whether efforts to confront these questions 'could ever be realized'.[47] He rests content to embrace narrow, empiricist assumptions. What is to be made of Hart's treatment of these issues in chapter IX?

In his 'Postscript' to *The Concept of Law*, Hart wrote that 'I think it quite vain to seek any more specific purpose which law as such serves beyond providing guides to human conduct and standards of criticism of that conduct.'[48] It is law 'as such' that interests Hart, not what is true of particular instances of legal order, where more specific purposes may indeed be evident. Elsewhere, Hart observes that 'the existence and content of the law can be identified by reference to the social sources of the law (e.g. legislation, judicial decisions, social customs) without reference to morality except where the law thus identified has itself incorporated moral criteria for identification of law'.[49] The connection between these quotations might seem to consist in Hart's insistence that the concept of 'law' must be based upon an analysis of its social context: that it is to be identified by reference to practices, and that it must itself be understood as a general *kind* of practice, offering an abstract structure of guidance and criticism to the context of more specific practices in which it exists. But Hart may have meant the connection in another way. At first, the reference to 'human conduct' in the first quotation may seem innocuous, the qualifier 'human' serving to do no more than identify the particular kind of animal whose conduct is in issue. But equally, it might refer to a particular kind of *conduct*, in terms of a quality which distinguishes it from animal or inhuman conduct. The reference in the second quotation to 'social sources' and 'social customs' lends support to this interpretation, for here Hart is concerned to identify the context which makes sense of the concept of 'law'. If law is to be understood on the basis of social practices, how in turn must such practices be understood?

At various points Hart is at pains to point out that the concepts he is seeking to elucidate 'must rest on a specific conception of the human

---

[46] See Soames (above n 6).   [47] See above n 44.
[48] Hart (above n 41), 249.   [49] Ibid., 269.

person and of what is needed for the exercise and development of distinctive human powers'.[50] It seems clear that Hart intended to denote the quality of the 'powers' in issue (their humanity), not simply their authorship. Famously, in chapter IX Hart argues that social practices assume only a minimal set of 'truisms' about human nature, which do not require extensive reflection upon moral philosophy. These include approximate equality, limited altruism, vulnerability to harm, etc. The truisms are not, in his view, to be understood as defining a specific end or *telos* of human beings. Philosophers are inclined, Hart thinks, to adopt a metaphysical interpretation of mundane facts and processes: for example, that the proper end of human activity is survival. But in fact 'this rests on the contingent fact that most men most of the time wish to continue in existence',[51] and 'we may mean nothing more by calling survival a human goal or end than that men do desire it'.[52] Our propensity to read into this a broader metaphysical significance is born of the appearance of necessity, that such desires are 'reflected in whole structures of our thought and language, in terms of which we describe the world and each other'. But these assumptions, or basic truths about human beings, nevertheless belong to our conceptions of law, right and social control for '[w]e could not subtract the general wish to live and leave intact [these] concepts'.[53] In other words, Hart argues that our conceptions of law, politics and society cannot be disconnected from 'elementary truths concerning human beings', but at the same time wishes to represent these truths as belonging to 'whole structures of thought and language' that are, in some sense, disposable and therefore capable of description whilst maintaining a certain philosophical detachment.

It appears as if Hart was willing to locate legal and political understandings within a conception of the human condition (as this is present in the structures of thought and language), but unwilling to situate *this* conception within further structures of judgment and analysis. We simply have them for 'as long as they hold good', and that is that.[54] Hart's 'positivism' can be regarded as a consequence of this agnosticism about the significance of the human condition (or more precisely, whether it can be said to possess any significance). Unlike the civil philosophy that is characteristic of the American approach to law and politics, which specifically separates the realm of politics and legality

---

[50] Hart (above n 11), 17. Perreau-Saussine demonstrates that this is not simply a careless remark of Hart's, but one he repeated in other essays at different times (above n 7), 385.
[51] Hart (above n 41), 191.　　[52] Ibid., 192.　　[53] Ibid.　　[54] Ibid., 193.

from broader conceptions of the human person and the 'development of human powers', Hart firmly roots understanding in such questions. But having done so, he draws back from any judgments about the significance of such conceptions, as being 'too metaphysical for modern minds',[55] seeking instead to lay down his pen once such conceptions have been merely *described*. It is likely that this agnostic attitude is a consequence of Hart's deep attachment to liberal ideals,[56] and perception of a definitive moral conception of the human person as being in conflict with these ideals. Morality, on Hart's view, has as its end 'some ideal development of human capacities which is taken to be of ultimate value in the conduct of life'.[57] This is an understanding of morality, not as a set of civic political ideals, but rather a transformational process of human regeneration. One can immediately see the effect that a Rawlsian or Dworkinian philosophy of law would have had on Hart's core beliefs. A philosophy that seeks not to *separate* the domains of law and morality, but instead specifically locates morality *within* the legal-political domain, would probably have been connected in Hart's mind with the illiberal 'classical thesis', to be found in Plato, that 'the law of the city-state exists not merely to secure that men have the opportunity to lead a morally good life, but to see that they do'.[58]

Hart's engagement with writers within the American tradition (such as Rawls and Dworkin)[59] throws up questions both more complex and more elusive than are explored by 'analytical' writers seeking to understand whether positivism has or has not been refuted. The oft-repeated suggestion that Hart and Dworkin are in fact 'talking past one another' testifies to this sense of elusiveness. But one should not lazily assume that there has been a failure of genuine engagement. It is necessary to acknowledge that what we are dealing with is a disagreement that is broader and deeper than we have supposed it to be. It is one based on a conflict not only of *ideas*, but also of *mentalities*.

Hart is undoubtedly correct when he says that 'modern minds' are resistant to the pursuit of metaphysical ideas. English jurisprudence has itself been shaped by this agnostic attitude, born of adherence to the 'classical' conception of morality as a personally transformative and possibly redemptive body of norms, and the simultaneous resistance to

---

[55] Ibid., 192.   [56] See e.g. Lacey (above n 7), 209ff.

[57] See Hart, *Essays* (above n 1), 351.

[58] Ibid., 248. The connection is explored in A Perreau-Saussine (above n 7), 386.

[59] I exclude Fuller here, for his thought drew much of its inspiration from Aristotelian philosophical conceptions.

explore the metaphysical and soteriological questions that such a conception generates. This tension has resulted in the cultivation of a broadly sceptical attitude in philosophy, marked by frequent and sometimes ambivalent tendencies towards relativism, and an abiding attraction to empiricism. It is an attitude that receives an early expression in the work of Francis Bacon:

> Those who have handled sciences have been either men of experiment or men of dogmas. The men of experiment are like the ant; they collect and use; the reasoners resemble spiders, who make cobwebs out of their substance.[60]

The mentality of the ant has dominated English jurisprudence and philosophy. It is a way of thought in which the character of the thing to be analyzed is 'collected' from the experiential contexts in which it appears. Both Locke and Hume had emphasized, in different ways, the groundedness of knowledge in experience. Discussing his famous 'problem of induction', Hume argued that, whereas our ability to conceive of things goes beyond experience, the limits of our knowledge do not go beyond 'the present testimony of our senses, and the records of our memory'.[61] Locke's epistemology is one in which both knowledge and understanding derive from cumulative experience, or learning.[62] In his own, somewhat scattered, account of his intellectual development, Bentham frequently mentions both Hume and Locke.[63] When discussing abstract geometrical figures, he asserted that not only could a figure, such as a cube, not be shown to exist without possessing size, quantity and occupying a certain space, it could not even be conceived to exist: 'But even suppose one could conceive such a thing to exist as a line without breadth or a point without parts, of what use would it be?'[64] Bentham applied this principle to his jurisprudence. In his account in the *Fragment on Government*, the principle of utility was not to be defined by enquiry into 'the good', but rather collected from the character of the relationship of the human mind to sensations of pleasure and pain. In much the same way, Austin later took 'the appropriate matter of jurisprudence' to be the

---

[60] Francis Bacon, *The New Organon* [1620], Aphorism 95.
[61] Hume, *Enquiry Concerning Human Understanding*, LA Selby-Bigge (ed.) (Oxford, Clarendon Press, 1975), 108.
[62] See Chapter 1 above.
[63] See P Schofield, *Utility and Democracy: The Political Thought of Jeremy Bentham* (Oxford University Press, 2007), 3.
[64] Bentham, unpublished fragment, in Schofield (above n 63), 8.

outward characteristics of 'laws or rules set by men to men'.[65] A similar attitude is present in descriptions of the ethos of the common law, throughout its existence, from Sir Edward Coke's observation that the reason of the law is not natural reason, inaccessible to ordinary faculties, but artificial 'reason, gotten by long study, observation, and experience',[66] to Holmes's famous dictum, 'The life of the law has not been logic: it has been experience.'[67]

The temperament of English jurisprudence has assisted in obscuring the very different suppositions which have underpinned English and American legal philosophy. Insofar as one may generalize, one may find in these general systems of thought two distinct cultural artefacts, both born of seventeenth-century Protestant natural law. The English attitude is coloured by a political world-view that took its form from the religious settlement. There is the Establishment (with its values, its priorities and its Church), and the kaleidoscopic variety of opposing interests which must be tolerated. It is the classic liberal society composed of 'outsiders on the inside'.[68] To one of Hart's mentality, it is a form of society which gives shape to a grave intellectual doubt. Ideals of tolerance (or of 'standards of criticism') are not value-neutral. They involve but do not suspend judgment, and therefore represent a cultural attitude that is (at least in its origins) peculiar to European civilization.[69] So long as they are internally consistent, value systems are notoriously immune to empirical or logical confirmation or disproof, and in this respect may be said to be equal. But it is impossible, at the same time, to avoid having a preference in such matters. Such systems are indeed in contradiction with one another and cannot 'coexist in mutual indifference'.[70] As Hart's own situation ought to have made clear, one's ability to judge foreign practices is not defeated simply by virtue of being an 'outsider'. But Hart's ant-like temperament similarly prevented him from grounding such judgments or preferences in universals. Universals would have to consist in supra-historical rules (like those of mathematics) that cannot be 'collected' from

---

[65] J Austin, *The Province of Jurisprudence Determined* (London, John Murray, 1832), viii and Lecture 1. See also, on the general empiricist character of English philosophy, GJ Warnock, *English Philosophy Since 1900* (London, Oxford University Press, 1958).

[66] E Coke, *The First Part of the Institutes of the Laws of England (Coke upon Littleton)* (New York, Legal Classics Library, 1823), s.97b.

[67] O Wendell Holmes Jr, *The Common Law* (Boston, 1881), 1.

[68] See A Perreau-Saussine (above n 7).

[69] See L Kolakowski, *Modernity on Endless Trial* (University of Chicago Press, 1990), 19.

[70] Ibid., 21. See also M Midgley, *Heart and Mind* (London, Routledge, 1981), ch 5.

historical experience. How could such universals be imposed peacefully, therefore? In virtue of its groundedness in classical philosophical conceptions, Hart's is a liberalism of doubt and uncertainty.

The liberalism of the American jural philosophers was born of no religious settlement, but a civic agreement in which credal religious questions played no part. It is a liberalism of certainty: a 'fundamental contribution to political morality', an ideally fair basis for society which deserves to be 'copied all over the world'.[71] This difference in attitudes is no peripheral matter but is central to a proper understanding of the nature and significance of current jurisprudential debates within the Anglo-American tradition.

[71] See Dworkin (above n 8).

5

Three approaches to jurisprudence

I would like to consider some further dimensions to the subject of jurisprudence. Like any branch of philosophy, jurisprudence is marked by division into discrete categories as the means by which it may be reduced to an organized understanding: analytical jurisprudence, normative jurisprudence, legal positivism, natural law, legal realism, etc. These categories supply the intellectual framework in terms of which jurisprudence is approached and thought about. Jurisprudential writers recognize that such schematic divisions disguise as well as illuminate the intricate realities of substantive positions which must sooner or later be addressed in their full and nuanced complexity. Philosophical biases may intrude at numerous points. There is no 'neutral' view of the subject.

Systematic divisions are an inevitable part of jurisprudential thinking. But they are not an impartial element of that thinking. Any set of conceptual understandings will tend to raise or exaggerate the centrality of certain questions whilst at the same time suppressing and perhaps distorting others. It is therefore possible to attempt to reconstruct jurisprudential debate in terms that allow for the formulation and consideration of questions that are neglected or obscured by the present understandings. Three categories in particular ought to command the attention of jurisprudential thinkers: (1) conservatism, (2) scepticism, (3) idealism.

In exploring these categories, one who is deeply impressed by the starting points of the present debates may conceivably find various resonances with familiar conceptual distinctions (natural law vs. positivism, for example). But it would be a mistake to think that they faithfully reproduce the assumptions which underlie the familiar distinctions. Nor do the categories I am proposing echo the concerns that animate present jurisprudential debates. I have pointed already to the polemical tendency of jurisprudential arguments.[1] It is often felt to be an important feature of

---

[1] See Chapter 2 above.

present intellectual categories such as 'positivism', that they do not elide or collapse into perceived rivals. Such an occurrence is often taken as a sign that the dogma underlying the position has been compromised, or refuted. The intellectual categories I am proposing do not possess this sense of exclusivity. They resemble variant approaches to jurisprudential reflection that may blur and combine so that it is possible to exhibit (for example) a sceptical conservatism, or a conservative idealism, in jurisprudential thought.[2] For the purposes of the present chapter I do not intend to dwell much upon possible combinations of these attitudes, except where necessary for their intelligibility. I shall instead largely confine myself to elucidating each in turn.

Conservatism

It might seem that law is both an instrument of conservatism *and* an agent of change. The relationship of law to governance implies the coexistence within law of both these forces. It is often thought that one purpose of government consists in advancing society in the direction of certain political goals, using law as its instrument. But law is also considered to form a layer of *control* on the exercise and extent of governmental powers to bring about changes to the extant situation. This dual aspect of law might be viewed as a property of all law, or as being intrinsic to the very idea of law, so that it is impossible to distinguish areas or types of law that are progressive from those which seek to rein in the forces of progress through the defence of the status quo. For example: we may conceive of statute law as expressing aspects of governance that are essentially forward-looking and progressive, whereas common law may appear more conservative, slow to change, preferring to explore and adapt old ideas rather than abandon them in favour of new ones. This is a mistake: it ignores the legal and constitutional nature of statute as a structured context for the exercise of governmental power, and underestimates both the reality and possibility of judicial innovation in the common law. Despite this interpenetration of conservative and

---

[2] These possibilities of combination arise because such attitudes are not self-standing. Conservative impulses will exist only where the established order is threatened by 'progressive' ideals or scepticism about the value of existing arrangements. Scepticism and idealism may be directed towards facets of established life, but they cannot seek the total obliteration of that life (and so on).

progressive attributes, it is possible to identify and isolate the specifically conservative ideas for separate examination.

Discussions of conservative ideas in jurisprudence have tended to focus upon the famous debates surrounding Lord Devlin's public arguments of the 1960s. The attention of jurists has therefore been focused upon what is in many ways an unfortunate (though genuine) association of conservatism with the enforcement of morality by the criminal law. Those who participated in the creation of the 'open' and 'permissive' society, and we who inherited it, have much less difficulty in aligning ourselves with progressive ideals than with 'reactionary' conservative standpoints. Yet the statistical predominance of conservative governments and conservatively dominated legislatures in the post-war political life of England and North America ought to serve as a reminder of the undiminished importance of conservative ideals. The very description of certain practices or movements as 'modern' testifies to the continual presence in society of conservative and anti-conservative forces. Perhaps the most perceptive of the comments on Devlin's conservatism, that of Dworkin, nevertheless shares in the regrettable tendency to assume that a conservative ethos is rooted in 'disapproval on moral principle'.[3] Reactive disapproval may indeed trigger conservative instincts, and thus transform itself into a 'conservative doctrine'. But the particularities of doctrines which, in virtue of context, are identified with a conservative standpoint do little in the end to illuminate what is specific to a conservative *disposition*.

The conservative is one who is temperamentally disposed to value what already exists over what may come to be. 'What is esteemed', as Michael Oakeshott memorably observed, 'is the present':

> and it is esteemed not on account of its connections with a remote antiquity, nor because it is recognized to be more admirable than any possible alternative, but on account of its familiarity: not, *Verweile doch, du bist so schon*, but, *Stay with me because I am attached to you*.[4]

---

[3] R Dworkin, 'Lord Devlin and the Enforcement of Morals', 75 *Yale LJ* (1966), 986. HLA Hart perhaps comes closer to the truth in concentrating upon the cohesive force of morality in society. But he too wonders whether this understanding of conservatism does not collapse into one concerning attachment to a specific morality: see Hart, 'Social Solidarity and the Enforcement of Morality', in Hart, *Essays in Jurisprudence and Philosophy* (Oxford, Clarendon Press, 1983), 249n.

[4] M Oakeshott, 'On Being Conservative', in *Rationalism in Politics*, revised edn (Indianapolis IN, Liberty Fund, 1991), 408.

This attitude of mind is defined not by the denial of change or refusal to submit to it, but by a particular manner of accommodating to change. 'The present condition of things' is not to be thought of as a stone turret into which one may retreat, but as the latest of a series of historical contingencies. Yet it is through such successive states of contingency, and specifically in their historical extension, that the identity of a community (and that of its members) is grounded. Such identities are founded not upon aspects of life that have been somehow isolated from historical change, but upon the continuous nature of historical experience. This explains the conservative's estimation of what is familiar: each aspect of 'the present condition of things' is significant, and therefore valuable, in terms of its familiarity, its unbroken connection with the experiences of the past. Within such familiarity is the essence of identity and self-knowledge. By contrast, revolution signals a break with the past, and thus with what is familiar. The post-revolutionary order of things, irrespective of its ethical nature or degree of 'advancement', is bound to be disorientating and uncomfortable precisely *because* it imposes on both society and the individual an unfamiliar and alien identity. The conservative's preference is for continuity with the past. This is a position from which every change will appear to constitute a threat to established identity. Thus, a conservative attitude is one which accommodates change by preserving and emphasizing those familiarities that are *not* immediately threatened, and by assimilating whatever is new to these recognizable forms. For the conservative,

> Innovating is always an equivocal enterprise, in which gain and loss (even excluding the loss of familiarity) are so closely interwoven that it is exceedingly difficult to forecast the final upshot: there is no such thing as an unqualified improvement. For, innovating is an activity which generates not only the 'improvement' sought, but a new and complex situation of which this is only one of the components. The total change is always more extensive than the change designed; and the whole of what is entailed can neither be foreseen nor circumscribed.[5]

Conservatism has a twofold claim on the attention of the jurisprudential thinker. In the first place, it is connected with a particular conception of government that is easily and often overlooked. Secondly, conservatism of the character described is an *intrinsic* aspect of legality. It is obvious that the dissolution of conservative forces within society would lead to

---

[5] Ibid., 411. See also 410.

the dissolution of law (and probably of society) itself. It would mean the collapse of all structure in the exercise of power. The removal of all limits to power. A society in which all limits to change have been discarded leaves no room for a key feature of legality, that of the existence of protected domains in which a person remains free from the will of others. In a society devoid of limits to power, each person would remain subject to a continual and open-ended transformation of their situation, over which they retain no final control.[6]

Can one identify the underlying conception of government implied by conservatism? It is tempting to regard the purpose of politics (and therefore of law) as the pursuit of valuable ideals, particularly those of the equal, fair or just society. That one should express attachment to present social arrangements *whatever* their ethical character might be, is an attitude that is not immediately intelligible to current jurisprudential doctrines. To exhibit distain towards the attempt to improve upon the ethics of present arrangements can appear as a complacent willingness to live with the fruits of *injustice*. Much of the intellectual inspiration for these developments comes from the publication in 1971 of Rawls's *A Theory of Justice*.[7] Rawls's work marked a watershed in Anglo-American political thought. The political project of the current age was transformed into the pursuit of a theory of justice aimed specifically at restructuring the institutions of society.[8] Politics must be judged on the basis of its achievements in effecting this restructuring.

Conservatives do not seek to subordinate the value of governance to a superior value, such as justice or the good. Governance itself is understood to embody a fundamental value. The maintenance of order is an achievement without which no other collective good, such as social justice, is imaginable. From the perspective of modern jurisprudence this assertion will be regarded as involving an elementary error. Might not

---

[6] On the importance of such protective domains for the idea of legality see NE Simmonds, *Law as a Moral Idea* (Oxford University Press, 2007), 141–3. The presence of conservative forces also seems to be implicit in Lon Fuller's 'eight desiderata' for the existence of law: L Fuller, *The Morality of Law*, revised edn (New Haven CT, Yale University Press, 1964), ch 2. Removal of law implies not only limitless exercise of power by government, but also by *anyone*. The situation I have described would thus be likely to deteriorate into the 'state of nature' depicted by Hobbes: see Hobbes, *Leviathan*, R Tuck (ed.) (Cambridge University Press, 1991), ch 14. Indeed, the Hobbesian state of nature might itself be described as a situation in which all conservative forces are absent.

[7] J Rawls, *A Theory of Justice* (Cambridge MA, Harvard University Press, 1971).

[8] See Chapter 1, above.

these observations be taken to reveal the maintenance of order as a *necessary* condition for the realization of collective values, whilst denying its *sufficiency*? The achievement of social order is but a preliminary step in the direction of collective values from which further movement is ethically necessary. To insist upon the presence of order as a fundamental value will seem to involve problematic reliance on a Hobbesian 'minimalism' concerning government.[9] Liberalism, for example, views the state as a necessary means to the higher end of individual freedom. Indeed the thought that general laws are required for the creation and maintenance of protected domains of autonomy (freedom from the will of others) is one that extends beyond liberal positions.[10] It may seem that governance serves a further end, the value of which is independent of 'imposed order'.

One might wonder whether it is possible to treat 'imposed order' as an idea that is separable from the context of institutional realities in which the community is manifested. Hobbes in the first part of *Leviathan* appears to discuss the need for social order as a distinct aspect of community, irrespective of whatever else may come to pass in it. Conservatives think differently. They regard governance as belonging to the nature of society not as a feature intellectually separable from the fabric of society, but as itself constituting the fabric of society. One cannot divide attention between the existence of an ordered society *and then* its particular character or identity. The identity and significance of a society is an expression of its governance. There is no freedom that does not presuppose the more fundamental value of social order.[11] Only through an existing context of concepts, values and perceptions can the value of liberty (or any other value) be represented as desirable: 'Naturally, one's neighbours may interfere with one, to a greater or lesser extent, but until we are given some concrete description of the social and political arrangement, it is impossible to say whether more or less of this interference is desirable.'[12] Dismissing the context of a concrete form of life, it is impossible to say whether the self-chosen aspects of one's situation are more valuable than those that are chosen for one. One cannot say

---

[9] See Hobbes (above n 6), chs 13–15. There are in fact serious problems with treating Hobbes as a conservative of the kind explored here. To pursue this point would however involve too great a digression from the line of argument I wish to advance.

[10] See for example Simmonds (above n 6).

[11] See R Scruton, *The Meaning of Conservatism*, 3rd edn (London, Palgrave, 2001), 66.

[12] Ibid., 39.

whether a greater degree of autonomous decision is itself a valuable end. Each occasion of autonomous choice is a starting point for consequences that reach beyond oneself and therefore potentially 'interfere' with others. Conservatives understand that government must itself form an end, in the light of which any further ends that a society might be taken to serve are incapable of independent description.

In the eyes of conservatives, government does not consist in institutional structures which may be adapted towards the service of various ends or goals. They regard with suspicion the tendencies in modern political theory and 'normative' jurisprudence which seek the progressive transformation of social institutions so as to bring about their closer conformity to imagined ideals of social justice. Such aversion is not a hatred of justice, but a sense that social institutions do not enjoy an autonomous existence apart from the social milieu into which they fit, that they may be freely adapted in this way. Belief in the open-ended possibilities of institutional transformation equals the treatment of those institutions as *sui generis* aspects of society. Conservatives perceive that the effect of such treatment is to sever the vital connection between institutions and the cultural communities from which they took their shape and significance. Social institutions are not to be thought of as abstract 'models' that may be applied to any cultural context. They function properly and possess stability only when they remain embedded within common cultures from which they emerged.

The voice of one conservative – that of John Gray – has given particularly powerful expression to the worry which underlies this modern tendency. '[W]hen they are disembedded from any context of common life, and emancipated from political constraints,' social forms, '– especially when they are global – work to unsettle communities and delegitimize traditional institutions' that such forms existed originally to nurture and protect.[13] As long as they are embedded within settled communities, traditional institutions (political and governmental organs, the market, etc.) derive their legitimation from their presence as mediating structures and as forces of cultural renewal. They are the primary means of upholding and smoothing established patterns of social concourse and cementing the sense of 'the way things are done around here'. From whence will social institutions derive legitimacy once they are given an identity that is separate from established cultural traditions? Gray

---

[13] J Gray, 'The Undoing of Conservatism', in *Enlightenment's Wake* (London, Routledge, 1995), 134.

suggests that such institutions become elements of the global market, legitimated to the extent that they are capable of delivering 'goods' which come to be expected of them. In these circumstances, 'liberal civilization itself may be imperiled, insofar as its legitimacy has been linked with the utopia of perpetual growth'.[14]

Gray's point can easily be underestimated. One might be tempted to confine its significance to the institution of the market, re-imagined as 'unrestrained market forces'. The sublimation of market forces does indeed lead to the obsession with perpetual growth that Gray identifies. But political thinkers are less ready to notice that a similar transformation is undergone by *all* aspects of governance when sublimated in this way. These too will come to be associated not with the maintenance and renewal of common forms of life, but with the pursuit and attainment of absent (or partially present) goods. These goods extend beyond 'wealth', to include ideas of greater equality, greater liberty, enhanced choice and others. In each of these metrics and others besides, the modern liberal theorist wishes above all to achieve 'growth'.

Have liberals properly come to terms with what they are doing? Major liberal philosophies of the present day (for example, those of Rawls and Dworkin) are notable because they purport to be grounded in the value of 'community'. The fuller realization of this value is thought to depend upon growth in fundamental ideals of equality, fairness and so on. Is not the treatment of social and governmental institutions in terms of such an acquisitive ethic in reality destructive of communal ties, weakening common bonds born out of tradition? It has been, perhaps unsurprisingly, the 'ordinary man' and the pundit (and arguably most of all the parish priest), rather than the professional moral philosopher, who has more clearly perceived the symptoms of this decline, and offered the correct diagnosis. Essentially the same economic and governmental processes which led to the introduction and extension of competition, which deregulated Sunday trading, encouraged the aspirations of the lowest in society by 'empowering' them with choice (etc.), are *also* the processes that are viewed as being the cause of the 'erosion of moral standards', the loss of spirituality, rises in crime and the abolition of the sense of community. It is those same processes which remade 'the market' as a free-standing entity that are indicted as having forced consumers to deal with faceless corporations whose very size excludes all but the most

---

[14] Ibid., 133.

tenacious pursuit of grievances, rather than with local producers who enjoy a greater dependency upon their local reputation for fair dealing, and whose wealth is also local.

This inherent tendency of the pursuit of 'free trade' to increase service income for the multinational institutions of 'the City' whilst steadily eroding the productive sectors, was remarked upon as early as 1907 by that most forgotten of Conservative Prime Ministers, Arthur Balfour. Concerned that the separation of economic phenomena from their cultural context produced 'artificial simplifications' which diminished the importance of productive wealth as the basis of national prosperity, he penned a treatise (never finished or published) in which he observed that

> some economists have been haunted by the notion that the infinite variety of economic effect exhibited in different stages of culture, display the workings of a single set of eternal and unchanging principles, which it was their business to disengage from their temporary setting. ... For my own part ... I doubt whether much is gained in any branch of sociology by searching after laws of universal validity. The field of economic validity, at least, is no regime of unalterable outline, retaining its identity through every stage of social development. It depends for its content upon such variable elements as custom, law, knowledge, social organisation; nay on human nature itself which ... is not necessarily the same from generation to generation. ... Every phase of civilization requires its own political economy.[15]

Balfour was presciently attuned to the destructive effects of free-standing institutional structures upon established communities. The result, as Balfour understood, is the treatment of wealth as something distinct from the material arrangements of actual communities, and the fulfilment of Adam Smith's idea that 'the merchant has no country'.[16]

Conservatives understand that law cannot be comprehended apart from its embeddedness within communities, and in isolation from its role as a force of cultural renewal. Regarded from a conservative standpoint, the purpose of law is essentially managerial, structured by ideals that are understood through their concrete presence and historical extension within living forms of association. It should not be understood through the contemplation of abstract principles serving to transform a

---

[15] AJ Balfour, unpublished draft MS, Balfour papers, Add. MSS 49950, fos. 10–14. Quoted in EHH Green, *Ideologies of Conservatism* (Oxford University Press, 2002), 26.
[16] Ibid., 29.

'living science' into a 'petrified [and] unchanging creed'.[17] Conservative jurisprudence stands against the *idée fixe* of the modern age, 'that envy, vanity, greed, and aggression are all caused by the deficiencies of social institutions and that they will be swept away once these institutions are reformed'.[18] The conservative will ask, 'How on earth did all these institutions arise if they were so contrary to the nature of man? To hope that we can institutionalize brotherhood, love and altruism is already to have a reliable blueprint for despotism.'[19]

Scepticism

It is sometimes difficult to tell whether conservatives are also, or perhaps even entirely, sceptics. Michael Oakeshott, often considered as a leading philosophical conservative, is sometimes portrayed as an important figure in modern sceptical philosophy.[20] This uncertainty over the deepest philosophical motivations of his work is not entirely surprising. Challenging what he identified as the fundamental orthodoxy of modern political thought (which he describes as 'rationalism'), Oakeshott's own conservatism stands in a sceptical posture toward the dominant aspirations of modern thinking. This dimension of Oakeshott's work is indicative of a deeper connection between conservative and sceptical viewpoints. To be doubtful of change is to exhibit belief in the value of present things. All things are imperfect! True value is only ever partially realized in daily associations. The conservative is the archetypal doubter because he also has the wisdom to accept that man's capacity for goodness is all around him. There is no 'delayed' capacity for good works, awaiting the right ideals to bring it forth. He is innately suspicious of ideals. Balfour, who before his ascendency to the leadership of the Conservative Party wrote a treatise entitled *A Defence on Philosophic Doubt*, was *also* the author of a book on *The Foundations of Belief*.

---

[17] Balfour, 'Politics and Political Economy', *National Review* (May 1885), reprinted in Balfour, *Essays and Addresses* (1893), 232.
[18] L Kolakowski, *Modernity on Endless Trial* (University of Chicago Press, 1990), 225.
[19] Ibid., 226.
[20] See for instance, SA Gerencser, *The Skeptic's Oakeshott* (New York, St Martin's Press, 1990); R Tseng, *The Sceptical Idealist: Michael Oakeshott as a Critic of the Enlightenment* (London, Imprint Academic, 2003); R Devigne, *Recasting Conservatism: Oakeshott, Strauss and the Response to Postmodernism* (New Haven CT, Yale University Press, 1994); A Farr, *Sartre's Radicalism and Oakeshott's Conservatism: The Duplicity of Freedom* (London, Palgrave, 1998).

Balfour's scepticism was to play an important part in his career as prime minister. His anti-dogmatic, cautious stance towards the vexed question of tariff reform led to a popular perception of him as indecisive and indifferent. Yet it is precisely in his possession of a sceptical temperament and his distrust of commitment to broad ideals that he resembles the man of conservative disposition: 'Balfour's very scepticism could, if one accepts the notion of "intellectual imperfection" as a central aspect of the creed, be regarded as an essential part of his adherence to Conservative ideology.'[21]

Scepticism has a number of affinities *and* dissimilarities with conservatism. (One can after all be sceptical about conservative beliefs.) What is distinctive about the sceptical point of view? A sceptic is prepared to doubt or at least to question the value of things, therefore including the things that are most dearly valued by the conservative. Sceptics like to remind other thinkers that a primary function of philosophy is to question everything. The more something appears to be true, the greater the urgency with which it needs to be subjected to question. Scepticism and conservatism are both anti-dogmatic positions, but in different ways. The sceptic's anti-dogmatic posture is directed not specifically at 'rationalism' but to ideas and ideologies of all kinds.

Scepticism is of perennial importance to jurisprudence. Successive eras of philosophical thought have accentuated or centralized certain questions, whilst neglecting or excluding others. This is a natural consequence of any intellectual framework. Knowledge and understanding must be organized in some way. Being a self-reflective subject, philosophical speculation invites conscious engagement with the nature of the questions being pursued, and with the aims, methods and assumptions involved in this pursuit. The conceptions are then reflected back into the structure of categories and background assumptions, until they cease to be objects of direct contemplation and become implicit and forgotten. On occasion, processes of this kind are reinforced by specific doctrinal positions within philosophy which demand the deliberate exclusion of certain questions or ideas. In the first decades of the twentieth century, rapid advances in the philosophy of language had suggested the possibility of reducing problematic metaphysical questions to analyses of linguistic usage and the properties of 'concepts'.[22] Buoyed by a sense of 'new

---

[21] Green (above n 15), 23.

[22] See for example Quine's famous remark that 'Meaning is what essence becomes when it is divorced from the object of reference and wedded to the word': WVO Quine, 'Two

beginnings', jurisprudential writers came to endorse the view that questions about 'the nature of law' should not be thought of as concerning the identification of mysterious 'essences', but demand careful analysis and clarification of the *concept* of 'law'.[23] Such was the perceived power of the new method that subsequent challenges to the substance of Hart's position did not question the rejection of metaphysical perspectives.

It is not simply that the sceptic is willing to challenge orthodoxies, or to resist the narrowing of focus that is consequent upon the construction and defence of entrenched positions. Aware of the absurdities of dogmatic positions, sceptics understand more clearly the nature of belief. Scepticism is unimaginable without a more encompassing faith. Doubt is possible only when preceded by an anterior certainty. It requires a body of accepted ideas with which the thing that is doubted is incongruous. Without a bedrock of certainty, doubt becomes impossible so that the only conceivable mental attitude is one, not of 'universal scepticism', but of unthinking acceptance. Descartes's method of doubt proceeds from such a bedrock (*cogito ergo sum*). Equally, the doubt of Thomas the Apostle is produced when his world-view is shaken by paradox. *Both*: the dead do not arise, *and*: the basis of knowledge is sensation.[24] Universal scepticism does not involve the simultaneous denial of everything. It is an attitude rather than a state of knowledge. Willing to question all beliefs, assumptions and understandings, the sceptic cannot move freely from one platform to the next, doubting all but the ground he currently stands on, then shifting position so as to subject his last standing-place to doubt also. One cannot accept one's certainties 'for the sake of argument' alone. One may truly doubt one's present position only by shifting the basis of one's certainties elsewhere. If the new basis is held merely 'for the sake of argument', one would lack the conviction necessary to reject one's previous position as erroneous. Retaining belief in one's present position, the process of questioning those beliefs produces not doubt, but renewed commitment.

Unkind to the idea of faith, modern philosophy marched with confidence toward the 'certainties' offered by linguistic and conceptual analysis. Metaphysics was to be rejected, as presupposing mysterious 'essences'

Dogmas of Empiricism', in *From a Logical Point of View*, new edn (Cambridge MA, Harvard University Press, 1980), 22.

[23] See e.g. Hart, 'Definition and Theory in Jurisprudence', in *Essays in Jurisprudence and Philosophy* (Oxford, Clarendon Press, 1983), 21–48.

[24] John 20:24–9.

or unknowable entities. The emergence of the 'secular state' suggested the existence of a secular morality. Underpinning a society of numerous faiths, secular morality required the truth of none of them. These standpoints led naturally to a situation in which faith is distrusted, for it will seem to be germane neither to the substance nor to the method of juridical and political philosophy. Confident of their new methods, philosophers appeared to forget that such an anti-metaphysical viewpoint is itself a way of looking at the world. Must it not in turn be sustained by belief as to its correctness? Must a philosophy grounded in 'scientific naturalism' only appeal to this congruence as proof of its validity?

Impressed by science, philosophers sometimes believe that science is not an imaginative vision of the world, but a neutral source of knowledge of the world. A philosophy which confines its speculations to what is scientifically known will be on firmer ground than one which relies upon postulated entities. We should refuse this image. Science is not merely a neutral body of facts, but frequently also a source of judgments. How else can scientific naturalism ground philosophical efforts if not as a specific conception of the way in which the world *should* be viewed? The suggestion that scientific naturalism defines the limits of possible knowledge cannot itself be based on *knowledge* of those limits. The decision to believe only in what can be shown (or what can be derived therefrom) is perhaps an easier faith than any other. But it is nonetheless a belief rather than knowledge. To those who announced the 'death' of metaphysics,[25] Mary Midgley advised: 'such large-scale items don't suddenly vanish. Prominent ideas cannot die until the problems that arise within them have been resolved. ... Instead of dying, they transform themselves gradually into something different, something that is often hard to recognize and to understand.'[26]

The faith that lay at the centre of medieval and early-modern political philosophy was essentially religious. That of the Enlightenment consisted in the primary place given to reason.[27] Political and jurisprudential philosophy at the present day is formed from an outlook structured by scientific naturalism and the method of conceptual analysis. These are no

---

[25] See e.g. P Laslett (ed.) *Philosophy, Politics and Society* (Oxford University Press, 1956), vii.

[26] M Midgley, *The Myths We Live By* (London, Routledge, 2004), 4–5. See further Kolakowski, *The Presence of Myth* (University of Chicago Press, 1989).

[27] See FC Beiser, *The Fate of Reason: German Philosophy from Kant to Fichte* (Cambridge MA, Harvard University Press, 1987).

less 'objects of faith'. The ultimate nature of belief remains mysterious. There is no end to the activity of speculating upon the mysteries. Sceptics understand this. Scepticism is not a sustainable state of knowledge but an intellectual attitude. Leszek Kolakowski is wrong in his ironic suggestion that the perfectly consistent sceptic is obliged to remain silent, so that we shall never know the names of the great sceptics, as they never said anything.[28] Scepticism cannot be separated from belief. An honest sceptic must sooner or later decide upon what he is prepared or obliged to believe in. Catholics venerate the saint known as Doubting Thomas but they also know him as Thomas the Believer. Sceptics are never complacent about the truth precisely because they value it so highly.

Humble in their belief, sceptics are more willing to question established doctrines and positions than to entrench them. Perceiving error in all positions, the sceptic will be more interested in the assumptions which structure and inform the opposing sides of argument. The voice of the sceptic is never a popular voice. It is one full of warnings rather than persuasion. The sceptic has no great reason to be conservative. It is because present intellectual conditions favour ideals that are essentially anti-conservative that the sceptical positions of the present day tend to find some resonance with conservative outlooks. Scepticism will focus on many of the same targets that are identified as unsatisfactory by the conservative: the promotion of 'free-standing' institutions of the market, human rights, global democracy, universal liberalism, and so on. But conservatism is not the natural or final resting place of the sceptic. In conservatism too the sceptic will find intellectual commitments that are problematic: an implicit tendency towards fatalistic acceptance of injustices and imperfections, for example.[29] Like the idealist, the sceptic cannot find the truth manifested in present arrangements. Like the idealist, he believes the truth lies elsewhere.

Idealism

Can a society survive which has given up altogether the pursuit of ideals? A society faces extinction through stagnation if it abandons all aim and direction, just as it must invite destruction through its negation if all anchors to its established identity are removed. Led by these reflections, it

---

[28] See Kolakowski (above n 18), 22.
[29] See S Coyle, 'The Reality of the Enlightenment', 17 *British Journal for the History of Philosophy* (2009), 849–58.

might be suggested that every society must be sustained by a mixture of conservative and transformative forces, each tempering the other so as to avoid the suicidal situation consequent upon one or other of these forces being unleashed and pursued to the uttermost. But what is the nature of specifically idealistic forces within society? What is idealism's own ideal form?

One might hope to discover the nature of idealism as a negation of conservative thinking. The conservative's suspicion of ideals and general posture of resistance to emblematic slogans of progressive transformation, clearly embody the antithesis of idealistic sentiments. But since conservatives might also be said to possess an ideology, the basis of idealism cannot be said in any straightforward sense to consist in the *rejection* of conservative modes of thought.[30] Taking a more general perspective, we might attempt to capture the notion of an ideal by the suggestion that pursuit of an ideal involves the effort to move society further along the road in some particular direction, by deepening the emphasis upon an already-present feature of the society's common heritage. In doing so, one might put some distance between the notion of idealism and that of revolution, and allow room for the possibility of furthering a society's commitment to a distinctively *conservative* ideology.

The essential characteristic of an ideal is its universality. In pursuing an ideal, a society points beyond itself. It attempts to reach beyond its own identity and custom. The description of any ideal involves the attempt to give expression to a value in a way that is transcendent of its particular manifestations in the concrete circumstances of the world. Ideals do not inevitably have to point towards an unknown future: in seeking to give further depth to a dimension of meaning that is *already* present within a historically extended cultural tradition, the ambition may not be to move forward into hitherto untraversed territory, but to journey back toward a real, or an imagined past. The idea of an ancient condition or 'Golden age' of the world, in which natural abundance was greater, mountains taller, colours brighter, is one that has a grip on the imagination equally fundamental to that of future perfectibility.[31]

---

[30] One is reminded of Arthur Balfour's espousal of conservative ideology in connection with scepticism, quoted above.

[31] Romantic attitudes towards the past do not, of course, have to take this extreme form. On the powerful influence on modern thinking of nostalgia for 'the good old days', see Kolakowski (above n 18), 3–13.

Idealism is compatible with a conservative outlook precisely insofar as one may conceive a desire to halt the progress of society away from its idyllic past, and to preserve and protect those dimensions of present experience which are the faded echoes of ancient majestic forms. (One may do this without any hope or ambition of being able to *reverse* the loss of majesty.)

The pursuit of ideals begins from a sense of dissatisfaction with current conditions. The meaning that is manifested by present arrangements is the wrong meaning. Something demands to be done! The attitude of the idealist is distinctive in taking as the starting point for reflection the idealized meaning, and attempting to draw the actual conditions towards *it*, rather than beginning with concrete arrangements and pursuing the ideal within them. It might be supposed that idealism demands an absolute distinction between fact and value. Confronting a corrupted world, we can learn nothing of true goodness. Insight must be derived from an autonomous domain of moral 'principles'. Idealism cannot *necessarily* presuppose this division. Distinctly conservative ideologies would become virtually impossible. Valuing their ideology, conservatives could only believe that the conditions of the present pleasingly happen to coincide with the tenets of a wholly free-floating moral ideology. This is a considerable distortion of what conservatives think. Contemplation of social conditions would be impossible if social arrangements did not bear certain meanings. Is meaning imposed upon the world of 'facts' by the human will? Or is human understanding of the world based upon the perception or intellection of meaning?[32] Leaving open these possibilities, idealism can be thought of in different terms. Idealism is manifested at the point that the focus of attention shifts to the contemplation of the body of meanings itself, in terms of its own desirability and coherence considered independently of its present manifestation within the social world. 'Values' need not appear in separation from the factual world, but as an idealized projection of present arrangements considered as a source of value.

One may again bring to mind certain features of Rawls's position in this connection. Rawls's theory of justice purports to be grounded in 'intuitions' of the value of things developed from beneath a 'veil of ignorance'. Proceeding from this starting point, Rawls's theory 'eventuates in a constitutional structure that is a virtual replica ... of the

---

[32] For criticism of voluntarist positions in ethics, see S Coyle, *From Positivism to Idealism* (Dartmouth, Ashgate, 2007), ch 3.

arrangements that exist in the United States', a conclusion which is in Raymond Geuss's view 'extremely striking, not to say astounding'.[33] It is not the plausibility of such idealized projections that is remarkable, but the extent to which meaning has become predominant over actual arrangements as the focus for moral and political reflection. All reflection requires a certain degree of abstraction in one's thinking. The idealist temperament is marked by a certain obsessiveness with abstracted forms. What drives this obsession?

Many of the causes of idealism are prosaic. It is easy to become infatuated with ideas. Politics needs readily identifiable positions around which large numbers of people can rally. But the idealism one encounters in jurisprudence and political philosophy is of a different nature. Where the pursuit of ideals is the product of more than merely an 'alienated conscience' (in Aurel Kolnai's term),[34] its source might be said to lie in the desire to simplify thought by reducing explanatory phenomena to a single, internally consistent system. One might say that it reflects the difference between 'thinking philosophically' and constructing 'a philosophy'. Borrowing Berlin's famous image, it is tempting to say that the idealist is marked by his adoption of the hedgehog's position over that of the fox ('the fox knows many things, but the hedgehog knows one big thing').[35] This is not an entirely fortuitous comparison. Implying a bipartite contrast between idealism and a bleak moral scepticism, no room is left for the distinctive ethos of the conservative. Nevertheless, some aspects of the hedgehog's position reflect the idealist's motivation. The aim is to discover (or construct) a coherent set of principles for the guidance of moral understanding. When confronted with 'good' circumstances as well as 'bad' ones, idealists (like the hedgehog) try to identify some general and transcendent principle of justice, that we may be released from the influence of bad customs.

Idealism reflects an absolute distinction between good and evil. Good and evil are not 'anthropological' values. They do not derive from questions of human advantage or disadvantage. They are properly transcendent. Like Kant, the idealist asks: 'can our civilization actually survive

---

[33] R Geuss, *Outside Ethics* (Princeton University Press, 2005), 22.

[34] A Kolnai, 'Erroneous Conscience', reprinted in Z Balazs and F Dunlop (eds.), *Exploring the World of Human Practice: Readings In and About the Writings of Aurel Kolnai* (Budapest, CEU Press, 2004), 66. Alienated conscience occurs in the individual whose moral outlook becomes focused upon the demands of some particular person or scale of values, to the suppression of his own critical inner voice.

[35] Originally attributed to the classical poet Archilochus.

without the belief that the distinction between good and evil, between the prohibited and the mandatory, does not depend on our respective decisions and thus that it does not coincide with the distinction between the advantageous and the disadvantageous?'[36] Is the hedgehog's outlook capable of sustaining this distinction? Adopting the position of the hedgehog, Dworkin suggests that the first aim of political thinking is 'to construct conceptions or interpretations of each of these values that reinforce the others', for '[u]ntil we can see how our ethical values hang together [in that mutually supportive way], we do not understand any of them'.[37] Is this any different from the fox's reliance on political concepts which directly oppose one another? Regarding moral issues as matters of ungrounded choice, the fox's mutual opposition of political concepts depends upon supplying them with rigid identities that are 'invulnerable to the twists and turns [they] can receive in ordinary human discourse'.[38] It is an outlook that 'is not really separable from the idea that philosophy can and should concern itself with "conceptual clarification" rather than substantive moral reflection'.[39] Adopting fixed definitions of central political ideas (such as 'freedom'), we are driven to conclude that politics is finally a matter of ungrounded choice between opposing values. Are the hedgehog's confident proclamations concerning mutually supporting values any different? Must he not engage in the same search for definitional shortcuts? He must define the same political concepts in ways that exclude the possibility of ultimate conflicts. Can these definitions appear as anything other than convenient and unreal?

Both the hedgehog's position *and* that of the fox must be distinguished from a reflective understanding, born of a submissiveness towards the kaleidoscopic nature of moral experience, which will 'reveal complex relationships of mutual support between seemingly distinct values, while also resisting the temptation to regard all sound values as realizable without significant moral cost'.[40] We may then come to recognize that 'there are various complex ways in which values can be interdependent yet nevertheless capable of conflict'. Subliming certain values, the idealist will inevitably erode commitment to other dimensions of value, even if the latter depend in some measure upon the realization (to some degree) of the former. When applied to the sublimation of social institutions, idealistic thinking causes political theories to function as 'compensatory

---

[36] Kolakowski (above n 18), 45.
[37] Dworkin, *Justice in Robes* (Cambridge MA, Belknap Press, 2006), 161.   [38] Ibid., 180.
[39] See Simmonds (above n 6), 179.   [40] Ibid.

fantasies'[41] exhibiting that same dualistic quality identified by Kolakowski: the tendency to assume that the further extension of the values of the present will overcome entrenched inequalities, hatreds and unjust impulses, whilst forgetting the extent to which present institutions, and the values they serve, are products of human endeavour to which such attitudes are native.

Idealists must turn away from the perfection of social arrangements. They must resist the identification of ideals with the ideal society. Certain aspects of Western Christianity illuminate what is indispensable in idealism. Transcendent notions of morality and moral duty intrinsically concern processes of transformation. Christians understand that 'the transformative power of Christian faith does not entail a radical transformation of the world as it now is, but rather induces a radical transformation in our understanding of the significance, or insignificance, of the present world'.[42] Ideals give encouragement to a *personal*, rather than social, transformation. An idealistic standpoint resonates strongly with the advice of Augustine that the religious man inhabits the earthly city yet also enjoys membership of the City of God. His responsibility is not to seek to transform the earthly city so as to resemble the divine (for this is impossible). He must instead live and act as a citizen of both cities simultaneously, striving to embody the qualities and virtues of the Godly citizen in his engagement with and response to the sublunar world.[43] There is no value to be found in pursuing the 'ideal society' or the 'ideal human being'. No such types exist. One must seek to embody ideals of conduct in one's own life, whatever the external circumstances might be. There is some correspondence between this image of human morality and the picture of the *spoudaios* (those who realize the need to live well, and correctly) of Aristotle. The Augustinian conception of the man of moral ideals identifies the necessary form of idealism.

The idea of law implicit in this form of idealist thought is not unrelated to the standpoint of Hobbes. Hobbes thinks of law as offering an escape from the chaotic and terrible conditions of the state of nature. In the natural condition, man is as a wolf to his fellow man. Lacking a common basis for the communication of intentions, the individual is rationally obliged to use pre-emptive attack as the most secure form of defence.[44]

---

[41] Geuss (above n 33), 34.

[42] T Fuller, 'Introduction', Oakeshott, *Religion, Politics and the Moral Life* (New Haven CT, Yale University Press, 1993), 21.

[43] Augustine, *De Civitate Dei*, Bk X.   [44] Hobbes (above n 6), ch 13.

The human condition without law is one in which human beings, having complete freedom of action, paradoxically lack free will. Hoping to survive, men are forced to do evil by the evil of others. Law changes such conditions. In stabilizing social conditions, law allows each person to exercise a meaningful choice in their interactions with others of their kind: the choice whether to act well, or badly. (Such choices are 'meaningful' because the exercise of either option does not result, or threaten to result, in death.) Despite many and obvious differences between Hobbes's outlook and the Augustinian and Aristotelian traditions, they would seem to have at least this in common: law fosters conditions in which the human being can learn to be good, through acting well.

The categorical context

Liberals live under a constantly shifting combination of these attitudes. Sceptical of attempts to direct society toward unifying ideals, they insist upon the 'open' nature of society. Burning with certainty over the superiority of the open society, they advance liberalism itself as an ideal. Despite a certain hostility toward tradition, liberals in the United Kingdom and North America consistently return Conservative governments to power. Is this restlessness a symptom of liberal culture or of modern man himself? The first moderns who attempted to come to terms with 'modern' conditions all pointed to this restlessness. Hobbes diagnosed in man a relentless desire for power, a constant motion of thought which terminates only in death. In Locke, man becomes the tireless labourer, forever bestirring himself and society in a 'constant succession of uneasinesses'.[45] For Adam Smith, he is the archetypal consumer, moving all the time between trinkets and novelties with which he quickly becomes bored.

Locke's diagnosis in particular should capture the attention of liberals. Man is not moved by 'the good' but by evil. Man's desire is not orientated to future goods and noble ends, but to fleeing the evils of his present experience.[46] Liberalism has not abolished evil, but no better solution exists to the problem of collective living.[47] Evil cannot be confronted but only channelled into more harmless forms: the covetousness of the capitalist society. It is wrong to think that individuals can be contented, or that liberal law and politics can produce their contentment. Modern

---

[45] Locke, *Essay Concerning Human Understanding*, II.XXI.   [46] Ibid.

[47] F Fukuyama, *The End of History and the Last Man* (London, Penguin, 1993).

man is inherently 'unsettled'. Despairing of finding a solution, liberal society leaves man to his own devices. He must find his own meanings. Naturally, he will be drawn toward ideals. Anywhere but here! But he will also be conservative, clinging to the devil we know. Finally, the imperfection of both society and his ideals will produce in man a profoundly sceptical outlook.

Theorists of the legal order must come to terms with these dimensions of experience. Confining attention to 'positivism' and its rivals, they will only scratch the surface of the problem. Positivists are correct to insist that the law of a liberal society does not have a specific ideological meaning. But its meaning cannot be understood in a 'neutral' way. The law cannot fail to embody ideals. The openness of the liberal order is itself structured. However much he values freedom, the liberal individual recognizes the need for something greater than himself to confront the deepest problems of his existence. Society must be led by visible hands as well as invisible ones. The fate of material life is too important to be left entirely to the market. As well as freedom, there must be justice. A sense of direction to set alongside the very desire for a lack of direction. By concentrating on the law's open or 'neutral' character, positivists do little to illuminate this dilemma. They effectively absolutize one of its relative characteristics. Too quick to oppose positivism, anti-positivists are too ready to ascribe to the law a specific ideological meaning. They absolutize the structure of liberal society by paying insufficient attention to its openness. One must place these tendencies of thought 'in context'. The intellectual categories I have proposed offer a perspective from which the distinctive tensions and problems of the modern age can be understood in a new way. As these dimensions of experience converge, overlap and separate to produce its characteristic tensions, how are we to understand the present?

PART II

Understanding the present

6

Authority and tradition: visions of law and politics

Jurisprudence addresses institutions and practices of law that owe their existence to the flow of historical events. These institutions are not the product of conscious design or of 'world-building'. They do not emerge from sources of insight into the disordered practices over which they preside. It is necessary to perceive them as already present and operative before they are revealed to the understanding as separate and identifiable aspects of collective experience. The present form of political and legal institutions should not be considered as an expression of consciously adopted political ideals. Governance through law has survived in unbroken tradition through innumerable historical watersheds and reversals that have come down to us in the West. Legal and political order is a complex inheritance of which no single coherent interpretation is possible. It exists as a set of practices which are 'old, hoary, encrusted with mutations, split and penetrated by regulatory intrusions'.[1] Interpretations of the modern political community are partial regimentations of a broader whole which can be understood in diverse ways. Interpretations of this order will tend to convey particular implications for the self-understanding of the political community. One may accordingly regard them as simultaneously clarifying the characteristics of the beings to whom the practices are addressed. A vision of law as the reflection of liberal values of mutual toleration and individual freedom will have as its corollary an understanding of the citizens of a liberal society as autonomous and individualistically minded beings of whom such an order is the expression.

Wishing to examine the deepest implications of current liberal ideologies, we must proceed not by undertaking delicate analyses of the system of values being pursued, but by considering the underlying image of the citizen that informs them. Belonging to a complex tradition of thought,

---

[1] See NE Simmonds, 'Between Positivism and Idealism', *Cambridge LJ*, 50 (1991), 308–29, 329.

liberal ideologies are correctly understood not as the culmination of Western political thinking, but as the latest expression of a tradition that exhibits a degree of internal tension. The image of the citizen that lies at the heart of politics is also the product of opposing forces and discontinuous ideas. We limit our horizons if we explore the idea of 'man' from the perspective of the particular system of values by which he is currently supposed to live. The concept of the citizen too is old, split and penetrated, and 'encrusted with mutations'.

It is also true that the concepts of man and citizen cannot genuinely inform political understandings if they are abandoned to a final incoherence. Intellectual histories of politics display 'man' and 'citizen' in all of their wondrous and often terrible contradictions. But the goal of philosophical understanding cannot terminate with the effort to bring into focus the manifold lineaments of historical man. Philosophy requires an irenic search for the truth of *homo philosophicus*: man and citizen as historical beings understood under the aspect, not of history, but of eternity. If governance through politics and law is not finally to be deemed arbitrary, then it must find expression in features of the human condition that are enduring and permanent. Within modern jurisprudence, it is HLA Hart who most clearly perceives this fact. In chapter IX of *The Concept of Law*, he suggests that legal order depends upon certain 'truisms' about the human condition that must find expression in law, truisms involving (for example) the need for protective instruments and punitive structures, and the establishment of a system of property. But Hart ultimately wrestles with the idea that such modes of governance are indeed permanent. He thinks these features of law are necessary because of the overarching goal of human survival. Yet survival is not an antecedently fixed goal. It is one we are committed to only because our concern happens to be 'with social arrangements for continued existence, not with those of a suicide club'.[2] The possibility of a genuinely philosophical understanding of the human being is something that is not clear at the outset. Philosophy must nevertheless proceed with the faith that this understanding *is* possible, or else the enquiry must annihilate itself.

The final understanding of the liberal citizen is dependent upon images of the human being which impinge upon the deepest questions of philosophy. Philosophical questions are without a determinate end. They admit of consideration but not of resolution. Philosophers are

---

[2] HLA Hart, *The Concept of Law*, 2nd edn (Oxford, Clarendon Press, 1994), ch IX.

condemned forever to start in the middle, never reaching the beginning or the end. The mode of approach to such questions is dictated by no set of 'given' criteria, no standard set of assumptions, and no uncontestable starting points. It is consequently necessary to structure knowledge and understanding of such questions by reference to authority. Philosophy does not require the philosopher to hold certain opinions, or display willingness to cleave to specified 'truths'; but the infinite nature of its problems unavoidably necessitates the guidance of thought along established 'channels of conceptualization'.[3] Reverence or devotion of an absolute kind toward philosophical 'systems' is to be avoided, but the selection of the primary authority is obviously vastly important and not a random matter. The encyclical *Aeterni Patris* of 1874 recognizes this: in it, Pope Leo XIII famously enjoins Catholic philosophers to think and study through engagement with the works of Aquinas above all others.[4] It is the wisdom, sanity and subtlety of the 'angelic doctor' which shape this judgment. By contrast, as Raymond Geuss has observed, the autonomous character of the citizens of a liberal community, and the individualistic nature of their outlook and practices, have in modern times received expression through jurisprudential philosophies and political theories that are broadly Kantian.[5]

For what reasons have modern moral, legal and political philosophers dethroned Thomas in favour of Kant? Have philosophers fully understood the significance of this shift? I limit myself to a consideration of Kant's picture of the human being, as it has been absorbed into Western thinking, and to the contrast between this image and two rival images which have exerted a significant influence upon modern political thought: that of Thomas Hobbes, and that of another philosopher who is spoken of with high praise in *Aeterni Patris*, Augustine.[6] One is faced with a problem, however: for as Leszek Kolakowski (and others) have pointed out, Kant's teachings on morality are really transcendental, not anthropological.[7] Nevertheless, a general 'picture of the human being' can be extracted from Kant's treatment of the subject of morality.

---

[3] See A Kolnai, *Political Memoirs*, F Murphy (ed.) (Lanham MD, Lexington Books, 1999), 242.

[4] *Aeterni Patris*, s.26.

[5] R Geuss, *Philosophy and Real Politics* (Princeton University Press, 2008), 1.

[6] *Aeterni Patris*, s.13.

[7] See L Kolakowski, *Modernity on Endless Trial* (Chicago, University of Chicago Press, 1991), 44.

It is upon this Kantian picture that I intend to dwell at greatest length. My concern is to uncover this picture and to relate it to the vision of law and politics it suggests. I hope to show that the deep questions that it raises are incapable of resolution within the Kantian framework. One must explore their implications by looking elsewhere: toward Augustine, or in the direction of Hobbes.

One vision of politics: Kant

The vision of politics that has dominated legal and political thought for the last generation of Western philosophers is one which centres upon the realization of a broadly Kantian theory of justice. It was above all through the influence exerted by Rawls's work upon the modern intellectual scene that Kant came to be fashionable again. Prior to the publication of *A Theory of Justice* in 1971, there seemed to be two alternative ways of reflecting upon the nature of morality and its implementation at the level of law and politics. On the one hand were those utilitarian theories which placed conceptions of wellbeing or happiness at the heart of moral understandings. Such theories tended to represent human beings as subject to the pull of more or less equally valid desires and preferences, and the vision of politics that resulted could therefore offer little greater hope than the achievement of some maximal accommodation or averaging of these preferences. On the other lay intuitionism, which discovered in moral thinking no single or certain ground of belief, but a body of moral ideas grounded in intuitions which may come into conflict with one another. This understanding left even less to politics: politics promised to resemble an arena of endless disagreement to which no distinctive or final order could be given. If utilitarianism frequently and infamously took politics in the wrong direction, intuitionism threatened to take it in no direction at all.

The rediscovery of Kant suggested a fundamentally different view of the nature of politics. This was a vision of politics as the attempt to improve the human lot by bringing social arrangements more closely into line with an overarching moral theory (a theory of justice). Viewed under its most noble aspect, politics is intrinsically connected with the desire to make the world a better place. But if this is sometimes its motivating force, what sustains the underpinning belief that human powers would avail in such an endeavour? Amongst the philosophies of the past, it is possible to find entirely depressing answers to this question.

It was not only Christians, embracing the doctrine of the Fall, who depicted human history as a gradual decline from earlier greatness, or as a series of moral disasters wrought by men who, seeking to avoid descent into ruin and darkness, actually bring it about.[8] Lying in human hands, change is always for the worse. Equal in sadness, others viewed social and political change as genuinely measurable only at the level of the species, across vast distances of time.[9] Change does not lie in human hands. Humans are at the mercy of the inscrutable processes of history itself.

The vision implicit in modern politics of steady growth and improvement requires a very different estimation of the transformational powers of human beings. Kant's ideas concerning human autonomy seemed to offer an underpinning and a source of encouragement for transformational conceptions of politics.[10] They suggested that impediments to social progress lie not in any want of knowledge or shortness of stature, but in the quality of the will through which transformative decisions can be taken: a will, moreover, that is essentially *free*. It is not surprising that Kant's views on moral agency should be regarded as a ringing endorsement of the Enlightenment faith in human powers and human progress. His own essay on the subject defined 'enlightenment' as 'the human being's exit from its own self-incurred immaturity', for which 'nothing is required but *freedom*'.[11]

Here and elsewhere in his moral philosophy, Kant raises the general question of how the prosaic, sinful reality of human life may be reconciled with the human capacity for greatness and (apparently) limitless potentiality. Kant's answer seems obvious and optimistic: moral darkness 'lies not in lack of understanding but in lack of resolution and courage to use it without direction from another. *Sapere aude!* Have courage to

---

[8] See, for example, Hesiod, *Theogony and Works and Days* (Oxford University Press, 1999), *WD* lines 109–201; Plato, *Cratylus*, B Jowett (trans.) (Middlesex, The Echo Library, 2006). A similar view of the world is also present in the idea of *felix culpa*.

[9] I refer to theories of social evolution such as that of Adam Smith: see Smith, *Lectures on Jurisprudence*, R Meek, D Raphael and P Stein (eds.) (Oxford, Clarendon Press, 1978), A.i.27.

[10] J Rawls, *A Theory of Justice* (Cambridge MA, Harvard University Press, 1971), xviii: 'What I have attempted to do is to generalize and carry to a higher order of abstraction the traditional theory of the social contract as represented by Locke, Rousseau, and Kant ... The theory that results is highly Kantian in nature.'

[11] Kant, 'An Answer to the Question: What Is Enlightenment?', in M Gregor and AW Woods (eds.), *Practical Philosophy: The Cambridge Edition of the Works of Immanuel Kant* (Cambridge University Press, 1996), 8:35–6.

make use of your *own* understanding!'[12] Modern 'Kantians' have tended
to draw upon this aspect of the Kantian inheritance. Christine Korsgaard
(for example) argues that Kant's theories of personal and moral relations
'provide some answers' to pressing social problems, whilst making us
'more transparent to ourselves'.[13]

To what extent is the image of Kant cast by Rawls's shadow an
accurate reflection? The idea that we might through unaided efforts
'create the kingdom of ends', represents a pale echo of the gnostic
suggestion that it is possible to create a kind of heaven on earth within
history.[14] The goal suggested by such efforts 'need not be understood
very precisely; it may consist of no more than an idealization of this or
that aspect of the situation, considered valuable by the thinker'.[15] Despite
the tendency of modern-day Kantians to adopt this interpretation, the
real conception of the person to be drawn from Kant's moral philosophy
paints a somewhat darker image, closer to that of sinful man.

Kant's own position as an Enlightenment thinker seems at times to
betray a gnostic ambition. His efforts in philosophy are directed at
removing 'superstition' and 'enthusiasm' from moral and religious belief.
Superstition meant belief in the worship of saints, the use of images and
relics in prayer, and the necessity of priestly intercession to attain salvation.[16] Enthusiasm involved 'supposed inner experience' of God or the
effects of grace.[17] In seeking to restrict religion to within 'the bounds of

---

[12] Ibid., 8:35 (original emphasis). The literal translation (from Horace, *Epodes* I.2.40) is
'Dare to be wise!'

[13] C Korsgaard, *Creating the Kingdom of Ends* (Cambridge University Press, 1996), 188
and 197.

[14] See, especially, E Voegelin, 'Science, Politics and Gnosticism: Two Essays', in *Modernity
Without Restraint: The Collected Works of Eric Voegelin*, vol. V (Columbia, University of
Missouri Press, 2000), 243–313. 'According to the Kantian idea of progress,' Voegelin
wrote, 'humanity is moving in an unending approach toward the goal of a perfect,
rational existence in a cosmopolitan society – though to Kant's credit, it must be said
that he was able to find in the unending progress of mankind no salvation for the
individual man, and the relevance of progress for the fulfillment of the person therefore
seemed doubtful to him' (ibid., 299).

[15] Ibid.

[16] JB Schneewind, 'Kant and the Sources of Darkness', in Schneewind, *Essays on the History
of Moral Philosophy* (Cambridge University Press, 2010), 299. For Kant's remarks on
'superstition' see P Guyer (ed.), *Critique of the Power of Judgment: The Cambridge Edition
of the Works of Immanuel Kant* (Cambridge University Press, 2001), 5:294.

[17] Kant, 'Religion Within the Boundaries of Mere Reason', in AW Wood (ed.), *Religion and
Rational Theology: The Cambridge Edition of the Works of Immanuel Kant* (Cambridge
University Press, 1996), 6:53.

mere reason', and by defining the will as nothing but practical reason, Kant appears to be making those moves that will pave the way for a modern conception of politics (the removal of grace from the world, the notion of a good that is both transparently understood and to be achieved through human powers unaided, etc.). Man, and not God, would henceforth be a source of light in the world.

Is this an accurate image of Kant's doctrine? By lodging good and evil in the *will*, Kant gestures not only towards the capacity for greatness in the human spirit, but also to its Fallen, sinful character. In the *Enchiridion*, Augustine had depicted evil as 'but the absence of good'. Augustine explains that what are called 'vices in the soul are nothing but privations of natural good', in the same way that

> disease and wounds mean nothing but the absence of health; for when a cure is effected, that does not mean that the evils which were present . . . go away from the body and dwell elsewhere: they altogether cease to exist; for the wound or disease is not a substance, but a defect in the fleshly substance – the flesh itself being a substance, and therefore something good, of which those evils – that is, privations of the good which we call health – are accidents.[18]

For Kant, by contrast, evil represents not a privation, but a choice.

The first proposition of the *Groundwork of the Metaphysics of Morals* runs as follows: 'It is impossible to think of anything at all in the world, or even beyond it, that could be considered good without limitation except a *good will*.'[19] Understanding; judgment; courage; honour. These qualities of mind are good for many purposes, but they are also capable of being useful for evil, 'unless a good will is present which corrects the influence of these on the mind and, in so doing, also corrects the whole principle of action and brings it into conformity with universal ends'.[20] The good will 'corrects the whole principle of action'; but it is 'not good because of what it effects or accomplishes . . . but only because of its volition'.[21] The source of goodness resides not in what is known or understood (nor evil in the want of it), but in volition itself.

In connecting evil with choice rather than ignorance, Kant emphasizes the corrupted and sinful character of human actions. The potentiality for

---

[18] Augustine, *The Enchiridion on Faith, Hope and Love* (Washington DC, Regnery Publishing, 1961), XI, 11–12.

[19] Kant, Groundwork of the Metaphysics of Morals, in *Practical Philosophy* (above n 11), 4:393.

[20] Ibid.   [21] Ibid., 4:394.

greatness is a part of our sinfulness, for the 'good will' is not absent from human life. A good will 'already dwells in natural and sound understanding and needs not so much to be taught as only to be clarified'.[22] The good will is both needed *and* present amongst human capacities. It is perhaps impossible to think of a process of moral improvement as beginning with a will that is wholly untouched by the understanding it seeks. Why would such a will ever discover or seek to embark upon the road to enlightenment? Just as the prosaic, sinful character of human beings cannot signify the utter remoteness of such beings from God's light and grace (for what would then grace avail?), it is possible that we must think of the 'good will', not as the superaddition of a radically new quality to a pre-existing substance, but as an explicable transformation of a given *kind* of substance into its fullest potentiality. One must 'clarify' the will in the same way that one must purify silver: by cleansing it of impurities, picked up in the course of its worldly sojourn, that are foreign to its nature.[23] This process of clarification is precisely a withdrawal from worldly snares: 'I do not ... need any penetrating acuteness to see what I have to do in order that my volition be morally good. Inexperienced in the course of the world, incapable of being prepared for whatever might come to pass in it, I ask myself only: can you also will that your maxim become a universal law?'[24]

Seizing upon Kant's idea that moral enlightenment might come from a process of *withdrawal* from the world, it has appeared to many writers that Kant's moral philosophy signals a radical departure from the older, Aristotelian tradition of reflection upon ethics. One could not 'give worse advice to morality', Kant writes, 'than by wanting to derive it from examples'.[25] Consider Aristotle's Doctrine of the Mean.[26] The *spoudaios*, concerned with moral improvement, realizes that the worldly examples of virtue with which he must educate his character contain but pale and corrupted echoes of the virtues of which he seeks knowledge. Each represents a situation in which the required virtue is imperfectly embodied, and partially absent through its corruption into other forms. Reflecting upon courage, we encounter only examples in which it is

---

[22] Ibid., 4:396.
[23] It is possible to think in these terms of Kant as basing his moral philosophy on a conception of the will that is ultimately Thomist rather than Platonic.
[24] Kant, *Groundwork* (above n 11), 4:403.   [25] Ibid., 4:408.
[26] See Aristotle, *Nicomachean Ethics*, R Crisp (ed.) (Cambridge University Press, 2000).

admixed with foolhardiness (on the one hand) or cowardice (on the other). The wise man realizes that the absent virtue lies somewhere in between these actual instances. The more examples we contemplate, the more precise becomes our focus upon that which is missing. Yet our understanding never becomes completely determinate. Our perception of what is good is clarified as we pierce through the mists of ambiguity and deceit that surround what is sought.

Kant's departure from this picture of ethical understanding has perhaps been exaggerated. 'There is something splendid about innocence [he writes], but what is bad about it ... is that it cannot protect itself very well and is easily seduced.'[27] Therefore, 'even wisdom' requires a (moral) science, 'not in order to learn from it but in order to provide access and durability for its precepts'.[28] It is possible to think of Kant as intending only a more limited departure from Aristotle. Wisdom is required, for without it we fall prey to the seductions of the world. But the science of moral principles that Kant is proposing must serve as the logical ground of that wisdom. In Aristotle too, wisdom has a logical ground. The world is not to be thought of as a 'brute' phenomenon, but a teleologically ordered universe. Kant explains in a footnote the more modest nature of his departure from this framework: 'Teleology considers nature as a kingdom of ends; morals considers a possible kingdom of ends as a kingdom of nature. In the former, the kingdom of ends is a *theoretical* idea for explaining what *exists*. In the latter, it is a *practical* idea for the sake of bringing about, in conformity with this very idea, *that which does not exist*, but which *can* become real by means of our conduct.'[29] What Kant is proposing is something less than a total withdrawal from the world.

The good will (the particular kind of will that is the source of moral knowledge) is characterized not by the ends which it has in view, but by the nature of its volitions. Being a creature of intellect and of reason, the human being is capable of representing to itself considerations of an abstract and general nature, apart from the particular circumstances of the world. But the human being is *also* a creature of sense, inhabiting a world which demands certain responses to its varying circumstances. This dualistic nature of man is essential to Kant's moral theory. Lacking the rational aspect which holds us apart from the world, a man would be

---

[27] Kant, *Groundwork* (above n 11), 4:405.   [28] Ibid.
[29] Ibid., 4:436 ftn (emphasis added).

capable of representation 'only as subject to the natural law of his needs'.[30] Subjection of this kind amounts to slavery to one's animalistic, worldly nature. Consequently, Kant is led to say that the 'good will' is one that is 'free': that is, free of subjection to its worldly associations.

It is possible to think of the world as an endless source of influences upon the mind's determinations, as responses are constantly demanded to stimuli from outside the person. By the 'unfree' will, Kant has in mind a will that takes its *principles* of action from these outside sources. Such influences, 'as sources of needs, are so far from having an absolute worth ... that it must be the universal wish of every rational being to be altogether free of them'.[31] The free or autonomous will is one that gives to itself its own laws. But the will that suffers its volitions to be determined by its reactions to the world is one belonging to the man who is 'subject to the natural law of his needs'.

> The will in that case does not give *itself* the law; instead the object, by means of its relation to the will, gives the law to it. This relation, whether it rests upon inclination or upon representations of reason, lets only hypothetical imperatives become possible: I ought to do something *because I will something else*.[32]

Freeing itself from these snares, the will becomes truly self-determining. Then, its only guide in moral matters will be pure reason. I ask only, can my maxim stand as a universal law, one that is not conditional upon inclinations, needs, or any context of reaction to the circumstances of the world. An action that can coexist with this autonomy of the will, Kant defines as morally permissible. One that does not accord with it is forbidden.[33] Thus, we arrive at a conception of the will that is ideally good: one whose maxims (volitions) *necessarily* harmonize with the laws of autonomy. This, Kant says, is 'a *holy*, absolutely good will'.

Moral understanding does not require a will that is absolutely good. Indeed, it is in the very gap between inclination and what is necessarily good that one finds the essence of morality: 'The dependence upon the principle of autonomy of a will that is not absolutely good (moral necessitation) is *obligation*.'[34] It is this aspect of Kant's moral thought that has presented the main challenge to philosophers. For it demands that one must perform moral actions 'not from inclination but from

---

[30] Ibid., 4:439.   [31] Ibid., 4:428.   [32] Ibid., 4:441 (some emphasis added).
[33] Ibid., 4:439.   [34] Ibid.

duty.[35] Howsoever an action might conform to what is required, if it is admixed with volitions formed from inclination (and be the inclination ever so praiseworthy), it 'has nevertheless no true moral worth'. This is the reason why Kant suggests that there has been 'no true example' of moral action in the world. Moral action can occur only 'where every material principle has been withdrawn from it'.[36] We, who inhabit the world of sense, to which reactions are inevitable, may for this reason find the possibility of such actions impracticable.[37]

Kant's assertion that the world has not seen an uncorrupted example of moral action is not as startling as some have interpreted it to be. The purpose is to *contrast* the 'good will' of the rational being with that of the 'holy will' of the supreme being. Kant's maintenance of this distinction places him firmly within the tradition of Christian philosophers reflecting upon the situation of mankind's fallen state. To remove the distinction is to eliminate any room for operative grace, and do precisely that which Kant's contemporary detractors accused him of doing: of elevating man to the level whereat he 'finds the only source of value within himself and believes that what he wills to be right is right – and just because he wills it. [In doing so, he] becomes such an egomaniac that he is convinced that he is God'.[38] Kant is therefore careful to suggest that the upward potentialities of the human spirit, though they are limitless, nevertheless fall short of perfection. The perfectibility of human nature is not to be confused with *moral* perfection, and is thus not a useful target for rational reflection.[39]

Knowing that, as a creature of sense, it is impossible for a human will to escape these 'foreign' impulses, Kant is able to maintain that 'the ground of obligation must not be sought in the nature of a human being or in the circumstances of the world in which he is placed', for although morality 'is applied to the human being, it does not borrow the least thing

---

[35] Ibid., 4:398. We therefore confront the seeming paradox that the person of good character, who is inclined to do good, and who takes fulfilment from it, is less moral than one who, doing the right thing, takes no delight in it.

[36] Ibid., 4:400.   [37] Ibid., 4:408.

[38] See FC Beiser, *The Fate of Reason* (Cambridge MA, Harvard University Press, 1987), 83 (discussing the views of FH Jacobi).

[39] Kant, *Groundwork* (above n 11), 4:443. This is 'not merely because we cannot intuit the perfection of [God's] will but can only derive it from our concepts, among which that of morality is foremost, but because ... the concept of His will still left to us, made up of the attributes of desire for glory and dominion combined with dreadful representations of power and vengefulness, would have to be the foundation for a system of morals that would be directly opposed to morality'.

from acquaintance with him'.[40] But moral laws 'no doubt still require a judgment sharpened by experience, partly to distinguish in what cases they are applicable and partly to provide them with access to the will of the human being and efficacy for his fulfillment of them'.[41] Although it is corrupted, the world and human nature are not so utterly remote from goodness and the divine will as to contain nothing except obstacles to moral understanding. If human misery clouds our sight, nevertheless the potentialities of human nature ensure that we are not completely blinded.

Kant's account of moral knowledge sheds light upon the reality of human beings as sinful and corrupted, as well as potentially great. Human efforts, which are the stuff of politics, arise from the volitions of a divided creature. A political vision dominated by the image of human beings as sinful wretches points in the direction of a politics that is essentially tragic: it is a ship of fools, mired in the darkness and lies of men of 'enthusiasm', extinguishing the light of God's Word in man. It calls attention to features of the human condition that frustrate and limit endeavours to bring about a tolerable and genuinely virtuous form of life. Here, Kant points in the direction of Hobbes:[42] the achievement of politics is not enlightenment, but peace; not progress, but survival. But a vision of politics in which there is too enthusiastic a fixation upon mankind's upward potentialities encourages a form of moral hubrism. Left unchecked, the image of the rational agent in the *Groundwork* lends itself to the Pelagian view of human powers to transform the world that was challenged by Augustine. Though the world has seen no uncorrupted example of it, human autonomy (in the form of the 'good will') serves to align the agent to the moral law through the act of self-legislation. It is this renewed confidence in human judgment that underpins those political philosophies of the present day which regard as a genuine possibility (or at least as a useful target for thought) the creation of the 'just society' or realization on earth of a 'kingdom of ends'.[43]

But Kant is less sure. In his late work, 'Religion Within the Boundaries of Mere Reason',[44] Kant appears to cast doubt upon the ability of human

---

[40] Ibid., 4:389.   [41] Ibid.

[42] Instructive comparisons are possible in this respect between Kant's 'Enlightenment' essay (above n 11) and Hobbes's remarks in Part IV of *Leviathan*: 'Of the Kingdom of Darkness'. See Hobbes, *Leviathan*, R Tuck (ed.) (Cambridge University Press, 1991), chs 44–7.

[43] See Rawls (above n 10), ch 1; Korsgaard (above n 13), 40.

[44] Kant, 'Religion Within the Boundaries of Mere Reason' (above n 17), 39–216. It has been described as a 'pioneering attemp[t] to consider religion philosophically, tolerantly, and

beings to rescue themselves from their own subjectivity. In it, Kant considers a problem for autonomy that seems, on the face of it, most un-Kantian: the ability of men to save themselves from evil and darkness – to become enlightened – without outside (divine) assistance. Moral evil arises from the will's production of bad rather than good maxims as grounds for action. Evil is defeated where the will selects good maxims, and yet the evil that human beings must ultimately face is a 'radical' evil, because:

> it corrupts the grounds of *all* maxims; it is, moreover, as a natural propensity, *inextirpable* by human powers, since extirpation could occur only through good maxims, and cannot take place when the ultimate subjective ground of all maxims is postulated as corrupt.[45]

It is made clear by the editor of Rawls's *Lectures on the History of Moral Philosophy* that it was only in the mid-1980s, long after the publication of *A Theory of Justice*, that Rawls revised his lectures on Kant to correct their 'too intense' focus upon the *Groundwork* by considering the 'Religion Within the Boundaries of Mere Reason'.[46] The scale of Rawls's error could scarcely be clearer: we inherit from Kant the thought that normative politics is possible because our self-chosen decisions, policies and goals are those of beings who can identify the good, and pursue choices that are transparent in their direction and motivation. But in the *Religion*, we find Kant following a different thought: the Pauline realization that 'I do not understand my own actions. For I do not do what I want, but I do the very thing I hate.'[47] 'The deeps of the heart', Kant says, 'are inscrutable': they are inscrutable because freedom, if genuine, is itself inscrutable.

These aspects of the Kantian legacy have not been sufficiently explored in modern theories of law and politics. The deep mysteries of freedom are glossed over by the deep attachment to individual autonomy as a more or less self-standing end of liberal ideology.[48] Kant's own thoughts on the

---

positively, within the acknowledged limits of reason': VA McCarthy, *Quest for a Philosophical Jesus: Christianity and Philosophy in Rousseau, Kant, Hegel and Schelling* (Macon GA, Mercer University Press, 1986), 215.

[45] Kant (above n 17), 6:51.

[46] See Rawls, *Lectures on the History of Moral Philosophy*, B Herman (ed.) (Cambridge MA, Harvard University Press, 2000), xiii–xiv.

[47] Romans 7:15.

[48] See e.g. Rawls (above n 10), ch 1. The 'thin theory of the good' famously gives encouragement to expressions of moral ideas in terms of 'right' rather than 'duty': it causes focal awareness to shift to the definition of the circumstances in which I am free to pursue my

subject provide no clear escape from the predicament. He speaks of the 'predisposition to be good' but of an innate 'propensity to evil'.[49] He is 'driven to believe in the cooperation or the management of a moral ruler of the world' as the sole path to moral goodness,[50] but seems to suggest that man must overcome moral weakness on his own: 'Rather must man proceed as though everything depended upon him; only on this condition dare he hope that higher wisdom will grant the completion of his well-intentioned endeavours.' What of such endeavours as present in politics? Is politics ultimately redemptive or irreducibly corrupted? Can good be achieved here on earth, or only hoped for in the next life?

Kant is right to raise these issues as central questions of politics. It is perhaps of little surprise that they should be almost completely neglected within a liberal tradition to which such questions stand as a permanent embarrassment. The Kantian framework offers little hope of resolving these questions. It leaves mysterious the means by which evil is to be overcome. The broadly Aristotelian philosophies that had come down to natural law in the writings of Aquinas placed their emphasis on the cultivation of virtue. The virtuous personality develops only gradually with long immersion within the realm of experience and practice (of the right kind). The young will generally lack practical wisdom because 'some length of time is needed to produce it'.[51] Becoming good is the work of a lifetime, not of a moment. It requires the cultivation of good instincts (the steady willingness, as Aristotle said, to become 'serious' about matters and not casually settle for the imperfection of one's actions: *spoudaios*). Anyone who has yielded to the temptation to take the quick and easy path, to give in to selfishness, will know that one's will to resist in future becomes steadily eroded. One may speak of a turning point in breaking bad habits, but the process of recovery is a long and hard one. Progress is possible, but always fragile and never unreversible. One must build strength of character. These facts are well known from experience. But Kant leaves no room for the idea of a *process* of becoming good by cultivating a specific type of personality. He speaks of a man being evil 'up to the very moment of an impending free act' through

---

self-chosen ends; I do not ask, what is it my duty absolutely to do, and why do I fall short? The ultimate goal of politics is then the maintenance of a scale of values which allow individuals to participate in justice whilst preserving their freedom to define and pursue their own ends: a position more evident in Rawls's later writing: see e.g. *Political Liberalism*, 2nd edn (New York, Columbia University Press, 2005).

[49] See Kant (above n 17), esp. 6:26–6:53.   [50] Ibid., 6:139.

[51] Aristotle, *Nicomachean Ethics*, 1142a.

which he will now 'better himself'.[52] This act can have no causal antecedents, but represents radical freedom from one's past decisions. The
'autonomous' agent is one who is able to disconnect himself from his past
efforts, precisely because *not* to do so represents heteronomous attachment to influences which lie outside one's present will.

Despite the tendency of modern liberal writers to adopt the 'Kantian'
image of the 'autonomous agent', the real conception of the person to be
drawn from Kant's moral philosophy is ultimately darker and less cele-
bratory. The implications of such an image are not fully explored or
settled within the Kantian framework. It is necessary to go beyond (or
rather behind) Kant for their assimilation to politics: to Hobbes, or to
Augustine.

An alternative vision of politics: Hobbes

It is possible to draw from Hobbes too a theory of politics centred upon a
creature of will. Hobbes's vision appears in many respects to embody the
antithesis of Kant's. Its central message is not the encouragement to will
freely, stepping out of all tradition. It is a message of subjection, the
submission of the will and judgment to the external authority of government.[53] Hobbes's 'whole concern is to establish and then to fix the city
against the flux of nature'.[54] The vision of mankind in chapter 13 of
Leviathan is one in which man is enemy both of himself and of others.
But in chapter 14, 'the civil order appears as the whole or a part of the
scheme of his salvation'.[55] For Kant there are not distinct conceptions of
'the good' which define the adopted ends of human beings, but one good
of which the world has no real example, and can therefore be encountered only in an act of truly autonomous reflection. For Hobbes, 'these
words of Good, Evil and Contemptible are ever used with relation to the
person that useth them: there being nothing simply or absolutely so'.[56]
One must abrogate one's own judgment so as to gain a 'common rule of
good and evil' from 'an arbitrator or judge, whom men disagreeing shall
by consent set up, and make his sentence the rule thereof'.[57]

---

[52] Kant (above n 17), 6:51.
[53] Hobbes, *Leviathan* (above n 42), ch 18: '... and therein to submit their Wills, every one to
his Will, and their Judgments, to his Judgment'.
[54] See A Brett, *Liberty, Right and Nature: Individual Rights in Later Scholastic Thought*
(Cambridge University Press, 1997), 205.
[55] See M Oakeshott, *Hobbes on Civil Association* (Indianapolis IN, Liberty Fund, 1975), 6.
[56] Hobbes (above n 42), ch 6.   [57] Ibid.

In another sense, Hobbes carries in a particular direction the consequences of the darker aspects of Kant's conception of the citizen. Kant's philosophy is populated by individuals aiming to manifest fully their autonomy, by aligning their wills with the moral law. But lacking this true autonomy, our knowledge of this good is ultimately not transparent to us. We confuse it always with those material and intellectual delights to which, as it appears to us, we have a right. For Kant the autonomous agent is a figure which never fully appears. One can think of Hobbes as taking thought concerning the political realities which must hold given these facts.

When Kant speaks of the will becoming 'free' in binding itself to universal laws, he is addressing the upward potentialities of the human spirit. But his account of the good, though not holy, will shows him confronting the embodied and animalistic nature of human beings. The moral person is one who acts from duty alone, feeling the pull of obligation reducing his options. Hobbes's theory similarly recognizes the need for human beings to suffer some degree of restraint upon their efforts to pursue the good, or 'felicity'. The natural condition of mankind, Hobbes says, is one of war, defined precisely as the uninhibited pursuit of felicity.[58] This lack of inhibition (or 'right of everyone to everything') extends even 'to one another's body'.[59] It is therefore above all imperative that men must give up the right to govern themselves (to be their 'own arbitrary deliberator[s]')[60] and to determine on what conditions they may pursue their chosen ends. There is some measure of truth in Annabel Brett's suggestion that Hobbes's entire theory 'rests on the idea that individuals will be so concerned to keep others off their body that they are prepared to allow them access to their will instead'.[61] But the natural competition which exists amongst men is *not* due exclusively to their sensate nature, the tendency to desire incompatible things. Though Hobbes sometimes gestures towards this explanation, the ultimate blame lies in the distortion of man's intellectual nature. It is not finally a conflict between forms of the good but the *libido dominandi* or desire for superiority which creates the scarcity that is necessary for competition.[62] Taken together, the crucial chapters (6 to 21) of the early part of *Leviathan* constitute an acknowledgement that the felicity that is pursued is of a kind obtainable only in concert with others. Both its basic and its

[58] Ibid., ch 13.   [59] Ibid. See also Hobbes, *Elements of Law*, ch 14.
[60] Brett (above n 54), 215.   [61] Ibid., 216.   [62] Hobbes (above n 42), ch 11.

deepest satisfactions are delivered in the responses and common efforts of others. Without these, there is

> no place for industry, ... no culture of the earth, no navigation nor use of commodities that may be imported by sea, no commodious building, no instruments of moving and removing such things as require much force, no knowledge of the face of the earth, no account of time, no arts, no letters, no society, and which is worst of all, continual fear and danger of violent death[63]

– constituent forms of felicity without which the life of man is unrecognizable as human, but instead 'solitary, poor, nasty, brutish and short'.

The lesson to be extracted from these passages is that the 'felicity' being pursued is not a fully *private* good of an individual. Despite the social tensions its pursuit may engender, it is in its beginning and its end appointed to a good that is shared and public. It is above all pride that causes a man to seek the fulfilment of his felicity on a basis which ignores the participation and equal priority of others.[64] Pride is corrupting because it causes a man to see the world in an ultimately solipsistic and distorted way. Its origin is the 'equality of hope' (of realizing one's ambitions) which comes from acknowledgement of the approximate equality between persons despite superficial dissimilarities. Pride is a distortion of this experience. 'For such is the nature of men that howsoever they may acknowledge many others to be more witty, or more eloquent or more learned, yet they will hardly believe there be many so wise as themselves; for they see their own wit at hand, and other men's at a distance.'[65] The result is a distortion of the hope of achieving one's ends, and the desire of every man that others 'should value him at the same rate as he sets upon himself'. It makes it appear that the good that one pursues is separable from and prior to the good of others.

Hobbes displays ambivalence about the nature of this pride. Unlike Augustine, he does not steadily regard the *libido dominandi* as a consequence of man's fallen, sinful nature. In chapter 13, he professes not to 'accuse man's nature in it. The desires, and other passions of man, are in themselves no sin'. Being in effect part of the nature of man, we must suppose it to have been present (as it were) from the beginning and not

---

[63] Ibid., ch 13.
[64] Ibid., chs 8 and 13 (and elsewhere). Hobbes sometimes elides this argument with his discussion of 'glory' or 'vainglory'.
[65] Ibid., ch 13.

as a result of a fall, or corruption of that nature.[66] But there is little doubt that Hobbes *does* perceive pride as a *defect* of human nature, one that is not (as Kant might have said) extirpable. Salvation eventually comes not through the mental act of breaking through the illusion of pride, but from its recognition. In coming to understand that pride forces upon us a wrong image of the world and of one's place in it, we begin to comprehend our predicament, and despise it. The possibility of peace lies therefore as much in the passions as in the reason.[67] But it is reason which suggests the *form* that peace must take, for it 'suggesteth convenient articles of peace upon which men may be drawn to agreement'. These, as listed in chapter 14 of *Leviathan*, crucially depend on the Gospel injunction that 'Whatsoever you require that others should do to you, that ye do to them. And that law of all men, *quod tibi fieri non vis, alteri ne feceris.*'

Though it often appears from his description of the 'natural condition' that Hobbes makes a fundamental break with the Aristotelian philosophy which depicts man as a political animal, in fact the final lesson of Hobbes's argument is that a system of politics is an inescapable dimension of the human condition as we are familiar with it.[68] Though politics is artifice, it is also 'natural'.[69] Central to this human condition is a framework of rules and arrangements which embody and preserve the collective recognition that competitive behaviour cannot be without limit. But *Leviathan* is remarkable in its insistence that it is the form, much less than the substantive shape, of these arrangements which matters. Hobbes is ultimately agnostic about the form of government. It is not in his conception (and cannot be) a representative institution.[70] Government is not an interpreter of a people's wants but the custodian of their collective will for peace.[71] The main political consideration is not *wise* rule, but *authoritative* rule.[72]

The political vision at the heart of Hobbes's writings is one in which human beings must abrogate their autonomy precisely at the point at which Kant (and Kant's modern-day interpreters) most insist that

---

[66] This is also Oakeshott's position: (above n 55), 63–4.   [67] Hobbes (above n 42), ch 13.

[68] We must contrast this with the 'brutish' condition of the natural state.

[69] See Hobbes (above n 42), ch 13: the 'articles of peace' are 'otherwise . . . called the laws of nature'.

[70] Ibid., ch 19.   [71] Oakeshott (above n 55), 44.

[72] See Hobbes, *A Dialogue Between a Philosopher and a Student, of the Common Laws of England*, in A Cromartie and Q Skinner (eds.), *Thomas Hobbes: Writings on Common Law and Hereditary Right* (Oxford, Clarendon Press, 2005), 10.

autonomy is required. 'The conditions on which felicity may be pursued' is exactly the question to which Rawls's theory of justice is a response. Recognizing the heteronomy of human minds, Kant demands: *sapere aude!* Rely upon your own convictions! But Hobbes, contemplating that same state of heteronomy (i.e. the tendency to take one's principles of action from worldly stimuli), fears that only a system of politics will serve to restrain depravity. Politics is not something that arises out of the free will of autonomous agents,[73] but precisely from the alienation of that will. Enlightenment brings, not escape from tradition and the withering away of the state (perhaps *the* underlying central motif of German philosophy), but *more* politics, more structure, and more authority. Hobbes offers an understanding of what politics *must* be like, if human beings are as they appear in Kant's ultimately gloomy moments.

A liberal society which draws its inspiration from Kant cannot afford to divert its attention from the lessons of Hobbes. The idea of civil society in Hobbes is a kind of 'middle condition'. In it, men find justice. Outside of civic bonds of law, 'justice and injustice have ... no place'.[74] Justice and the civil condition are coextensive: justice consisting in obedience to civic laws (for it involves the keeping of promises and covenants),[75] injustice involving the breach of those laws. But there is not to be found in Hobbes the sense that citizens may be 'taught' justice in such a way that they may fully embrace its demands. Though the 'righteous man' does not lose his character by a few instances of injustice, such a character is informed by 'a certain nobleness or gallantness' which is 'rarely found'.[76] Hobbes is aware that most citizens will obey the law either through fear, or through a mixture of motives that are alloyed with fear. The bonds of law, being 'artificial' are 'but weak', yet 'may nevertheless be made to hold by the danger, though not by the difficulty, of breaking them'.[77] At the same time, a condition in which obedience is secured *only* through fear is not a civil, but a natural one. Hobbes is sure that he has demonstrated, in chapter 13, that fear alone is ultimately incapable of

---

[73] See Rawls (above n 10), ch 1.   [74] Hobbes (above n 42), ch 13.

[75] Ibid., ch 15. Pierre Manent complains that 'by "politicizing" or "socializing" the virtues ... Hobbes degrades them. From ends desirable in themselves because they perfect the soul and raise it higher on the scale of being, they become mere means for protecting the physical life': see Manent, *The City of Man* (Princeton University Press, 1998), 19. For a contrary understanding of Hobbes as a virtue theorist, see RE Ewin, *Virtues and Rights: The Moral Philosophy of Thomas Hobbes* (Boulder CO, Westview Press, 1991).

[76] Ibid.

[77] Ibid., ch 21. See also M Goldsmith, 'Hobbes on Liberty', *Hobbes Studies*, 2 (1989), 23–39.

ensuring stable compliance of any kind. Even the strongest man has reason to fear those he has dominated.

The darkness that exists within man's character, and which (if Kant is right) cannot be eliminated wholly from it, defines him as a citizen and (finally) as a subject of political order. It is only within the political order that he may achieve in his character some measure of justice. The stability and security of the commonwealth is guaranteed only if its subjects 'can be brought to recognize that they are obliged by covenants, and on those grounds to keep them: that is, to admit themselves a restraint of their natural liberty, and thus to act justly'.[78] But this never entails the loss of man's dark and prideful characteristics. At no point do we find in Hobbes the suggestion that men may come to be lovers of justice independently of their fearful subjection to authority. There is no point at which, upon some evolution of character and manners, the powerful and imposing organs of state lose their rationale, and wither away. Hobbes shows that 'there could be no such thing as "high thought", nor ... any generous and unselfish modes of life without a fair measure of legal order with a massive power to sanction and enforce it'.[79]

A third vision of politics: Augustine

Hobbes's insistence upon political order as the only context in which justice is imaginable represents one direction of response to the problem of those who fail consistently to manifest the Kantian 'good will'. The thought of Augustine indicates another. Justice, in Hobbes's view, has no meaning outside of structures of civil order. For Augustine, justice has no place *within* such orders.

Augustine's separation of the two cities, the City of Man and the City of God, draws attention to the fact that individuals, whatever their attachment to worldly priorities (including political realities), are not exhausted by such involvement, but find completion in a moral (and, for Augustine, sacramental) community.[80] The first of these cities is centred upon the love of earthly rewards, whereas the second finds its community in the love of God. This second community achieves its highest fulfilment in the heavenly city of the afterlife, but part of it can

---

[78] Brett (above n 54), 234.
[79] See Kolnai, *Ethics, Value and Reality* (New Brunswick NJ, Transaction Publishers, 2008), 183.
[80] Augustine, *De Civitate Dei*, XIV, 28.

be found on earth, manifested in the good works and charitable acts of those who love God. Considered under their moral aspect, '[h]uman beings would belong to civil society by only one part of themselves, and not the most important part at that'.[81] Earthly communities cannot avoid instituting arrangements for the creation of wealth and its distribution. But believers must withdraw their gaze, and some of their cooperation, from this enterprise if they are to direct their love toward the correct objects.

By setting his argument on the separation of the moral horizons of human beings from the structures of civil society, Augustine points in the direction of Kant. Earthly arrangements do not exhibit justice, in the sense of true and rightly ordered relations, but only the internal and relative ordering of the criminal gang.[82] Politics does not achieve 'the good', but serves only to restrain evil.[83] Its object is not 'to embody an over-arching rational order in society, but to secure its fabric against the forces of disintegration, helping to check conflict, to minimize its disruptive power. All human order was fragile, poised over an abyss of chaos.'[84] Despite its possession of order, '[t]he society of mortals ... is nevertheless divided by each group seeking its own advantage and its own satisfaction; and as these are not the same for all, either no one or not everyone is satisfied. Thus society is divided against itself, one part, the stronger, generally oppressing the other'.[85] Augustine's diagnosis finds an obvious echo in Kant's understanding of radical evil: men fall into evil by directing their love toward inappropriate objects (earthly rewards), by taking their principles of action from worldly impulses rather than the moral law. To act justly, human beings must separate their desires and instincts from those which inevitably inform the substance of the laws and policies of their societies. They should not break the law (for only *part* of their service is to be withdrawn from Caesar), but must recognize its limitations.

Like Hobbes, Augustine offers a sustained reflection on what the characteristics of the human condition must be, if we explore deeply

---

[81] E Fortin, *Human Rights, Virtue and the Common Good: Collected Essays*, vol. III (Lanham MD, Rowman & Littlefield, 1996), 4.

[82] Augustine, *De Civitate Dei*, IV, 4.

[83] See TW Smith, 'The Glory and Tragedy of Politics', in J Doody, KL Hughes and K Paffenroth (eds.), *Augustine and Politics* (Lanham MD, Lexington Books, 2005), 187–213.

[84] RA Markus, *Saeculum: History and Society in the Theology of St Augustine* (Cambridge University Press, 1970), xi.

[85] Augustine, *De Civitate Dei*, XVIII, 2.

and seriously the implications of Kant's darker view of the human being. But Augustine has a completely different vision from Hobbes of what politics must be. The good citizen is for Augustine not one who is required to abrogate 'high thought' about his duty to morality, and dedicate himself to accommodating his activities only to the law. Reason is indeed that exercise through which we achieve greater perfection of our nature. It is 'that very quality by which [God] has raised us above the beasts'.[86] Augustine is more clear than Kant about the need for operative grace. God does not 'hate in us' the quality of reason which distinguishes us from the beasts, but the knowledge that is arrived at on the basis of reason remains insufficient. It requires the help of Revelation, and must point towards faith.[87] Faith is not a supplement to reason but its perfection or fulfilment, just as faith requires and becomes more transparent to itself through the use of reason. Augustine allows us to make sense of the idea that 'man must proceed as though everything depended upon him', whilst at the same time being 'driven to believe in the cooperation or the management of a moral ruler of the world'.[88] Human beings become good, act justly, perfect their characters, through the use of reason. But in the end 'everything good is of God'.[89]

At the centre of Augustine's vision of politics is the notion of order. Human societies represent one source or principle of ordering in the world. It is right that human beings should cleave to one another to form societies. The City of God is itself a 'city', a community in the highest sense. But whereas Hobbes and Kant regard politics through the medium of will, Augustine focuses instead upon *love*.[90] Societies are formed on the basis of a willingness to share in the objects of that love: 'the better the things, the better the people; the worse the things, the worse their agreement to share them'.[91] But the notion of 'agreement' in this case does not imply (as for Hobbes and Kant) that the objects of love are matters of deliberate choice. Gaining a measure of control over one's loves is the work of a lifetime, for love is not grounded in the open will. Love 'can take form only as a cognizance of reality', and the 'objective measure by which we may differentiate "better" from "worse" loves . . . is the adequacy of their grasp of reality'.[92] Augustine is painfully aware that

---

[86] Augustine, Letter to Consentius (120.3).   [87] See Augustine, *De Libero Arbitrio*, I.3.6.
[88] Kant (above n 17), 6:139.   [89] Augustine (above n 87), II.1.2.4.
[90] Augustine, *De Civitate Dei*, XIV, 28.   [91] Ibid., XIX, 24.
[92] O O'Donovan, *Common Objects of Love: Moral Reflection and the Shaping of Community* (Grand Rapids MI, Eerdmans Publishing Co, 2002), 23.

the love that is most often taken as the ordering principle of human communities exhibits an attachment to material goods, or to twisted spiritual realities. Rome, the most impressive civilization of Augustine's time, was itself misguided by the 'lying love' that is informed by the *libido dominandi*. Though Rome did indeed bring peace to its empire, and a measure of civility to conquered nations, the primary motivation for its wars was Rome's own earthly glory.[93] Though the Roman virtues offer 'useful examples' of virtue,[94] nevertheless the ultimate coin in which Romans receive their reward is the 'arrogance of human glory' of those who 'were on fire with unlimited lust for glory, and waged their wars of burning fury'.[95]

Here, Augustine points in the direction of a politics that is inherently corrupted. Love requires implementation. We are required to love not simply in 'thought and speech' but 'in deed and in truth'.[96] But if love is directed to the wrong objects, if it is the love of the City of Man and not the heavenly City, then it cannot be truly virtuous or truly just. The order that it creates may displace chaos, and thus restrain sin, but it can achieve nothing of good. Augustine does not suggest that politics can be avoided. Human life requires 'an earthly peace, and [politics] establishes an ordered concord of civic obedience and rule in order to secure a kind of cooperation of men's wills for the sake of attaining the things which belong to this mortal life'.[97] Justice, and reasoning about justice, require a context of civic relations. Because such relations are grounded in an agreed sense of what is loved, the moral reasoning which informs the ordering of such relations cannot be a private and individual matter, related solely to the will. It is at every stage intrinsically shared and collective in nature. But the same context of civic relations precludes the emergence of justice. The peace that is established by civic order is an 'unjust peace'.[98] Human beings must recognize that none of the fruits of their efforts in politics can be ultimately recommended. Augustine's political vision:

> points to a radicalism which will not permit any endorsement of what is, and will reject no less uncompromisingly any plan for what is to be. We can, and in Augustine's view, we must, dedicate ourselves to the pursuit of a justice we know to be unattainable here: to a quest which is doomed, and yet is an inescapable duty.[99]

---

[93] Augustine, *De Civitate Dei*, V, 17.   [94] Ibid., V, 16.   [95] Ibid., V, 17.
[96] 1 John 3:18.   [97] Augustine, *De Civitate Dei*, XIX, 17.   [98] Ibid., XIX, 12.
[99] Markus (above n 84), xx. See also Chapter 15 below.

At times, Augustine appears to share with Hobbes the belief that the principal function of politics is, not the implementation of justice, but the institution of authority. But this is not quite the case. Justice, for Augustine, remains the proper end of political endeavour, whereas authority is what we must settle for in its absence. It is this ambition which separates his thought from that of Hobbes. The dependence of fallen man upon powerful structures of political authority is a conclusion of Hobbes's argument. For Augustine, its inevitability does *not* bring to an end the obligation to pursue justice and 'the good' in one's life. Augustinian man is fatally divided. He seeks a good that is inescapably common, capable of definition and satisfaction only within the bounds of civic and political structures. But he finds the highest expression of this good only in separation from those structures: in the spiritual community of the *civitas dei* as it exists on pilgrimage here on earth, and ultimately in the celestial Jerusalem.

Closed to Augustine is the path pointed out by Kant in his 'Enlightenment' essay: to detach oneself from authority, from tradition and the opinions of others, and to reflect upon 'the good' as it becomes present to one's rational will. The path is closed not simply because Augustine has not Kant's optimism in the power of the human mind to achieve a detailed understanding of moral truth. It is closed also because Augustine recognizes the civic nature of that truth. It is a truth that belongs to a community which, although he himself belongs to it, man does not rightly understand. Because a 'community' is constituted by the relation of mind with mind, and not simply by distinct bodies existing side by side, a man cannot comprehend the ordering principles that are proper to it by contemplating it as an 'individual',[100] by detaching himself from the whole of which he is merely a part. The common structures in which he does participate, being the product of human endeavour, do not contain anything except a pale reflection of the truth that is being pursued. The greater part of the spiritual community that is the object of understanding (the heavenly City) remains invisible. Augustine thus closes the door on those tendencies within political theories which, drawing their inspiration from Kant, result in hubristic celebrations of a chosen scale of values. The values by which the liberal citizen is supposed to love are never fundamentally divorced from those by which his society actually lives. Thus:

---

[100] Augustine, *De Civitate Dei*, XIX, 13. See also Oakeshott, *Religion, Politics and the Moral Life* (New Haven CT, Yale University Press, 1993), 51, and below Chapter 15.

> The best way to see what the theory is really about is to study the systematic, long-term effects of applying it. At some level, a widely accepted theory gets the world it really wants or, at any rate, the only world that is realistically possible if people hold the theory in question and act on it. The surface appearance of Rawls's theory – its apparent egalitarian content, standing and implications – is deceptive because the world that has arisen as the theory has established itself more and more firmly is one of increasing inequality.[101]

Augustine's vision of politics is both darker and more hopeful than that of Hobbes. It is darker because Augustine is not willing to settle for a conception of 'justice' that identifies it simply with 'civil society'. Justice may not appear in the natural condition, according to Hobbes, but neither does it appear, according to Augustine, in the political state. But it is more hopeful because we are not, in Augustine's view, allowed or even doomed to settle for injustice. No matter how depraved civil society may become, it is never wholly beyond the help of grace. Civil rule is always admixed with the unlawful pride of those who would be rulers of men. 'This means that it hates the just peace of God, and loves its own peace of injustice.' Yet 'it cannot help loving peace of some kind or other. For no creature's perversion is so contrary to nature as to destroy the very last vestiges of its nature'.[102] The citizen, for Augustine, may be a tragic figure; but his identity as a political animal does not constitute (even if it may at times threaten to consume) his whole identity. He does not require perfected social institutions in order to become good, but must rather transcend them if he is to attain the full measure of goodness of which he is capable.

The lesson to be drawn from Augustine is that we must (as with Hobbes) regard politics as a 'middle condition'. But his understanding of the significance of this condition is different. It is not the condition that is *proper* to human beings, even if it is the only condition of which, through collective effort, they are capable. *Vera iusticia* lies in transcendence from concrete political arrangements. But if, unlike Kant, Augustine suggests that such transcendence means something less than stepping *outside* those arrangements (the good is not to be found outwith the bounds of community), nevertheless he holds, unlike Kant's modern

---

[101] Geuss, *Outside Ethics* (Princeton University Press, 2005), 36.

[102] Augustine, *De Civitate Dei*, XIX, 12. Compare Kant's remarks on the fallen individual's lack of 'devilishness' in 'Religion Within the Boundaries of Mere Reason' (above n 17); and see PL Quinn, 'Original Sin, Radical Evil and Moral Identity', *Faith and Philosophy*, 1 (1984), 188–202.

intellectual descendants, that the elevated condition that is sought is not to be discovered in any transformation of those arrangements. The final achievement of the social architects is not true justice, but a condition in which 'the present peace [has been] exchanged for one that suits their wishes'.[103]

The nature of the question

Seeking to shed some light on the nature of politics, I have attempted to discover something of the character of the human being as a citizen. The task of philosophy is to supply an understanding of this nature that is valid not only for a season, or for an age of the world, but which finds expression in permanent features of the human condition. This is not an easy task. The broadly Kantian political theories of the present day are premised upon an understanding of the citizen, or human being, that is somewhat removed from Kant's deepest concerns. The image of the human being as an 'autonomous rational agent' dominates present-day perspectives on politics. Differing from the image offered by Kant, the modern idea of the citizen fails to take full account of the range and depth of Kant's anxieties about the ability of human beings consistently to manifest this character.

Should one turn back to Kant? I have argued that Kant does not himself explore successfully or fully the implications of his own theory of the human being as a subject of politics. What Kant has to say is important, but it is not the final word. We must read and learn from Kant, but not seek our answers within his pages. In Hobbes and perhaps above all in Augustine, politics is elevated, and reduced, to its proper condition. But we turn to such works not for answers, but for a heightened understanding of the questions that must drive us. In each of these works, we glimpse 'the still centre of a whirlpool of ideas which has drawn into itself numberless currents of thought, contemporary and historic, and by its centripetal force has shaped and compressed them into a momentary significance before they are flung off again into the future'.[104]

Philosophical questions are indeed infinite, but the task of the philosopher is to reduce them momentarily to something finite. Knowledge of the human condition is always incomplete. Understanding is always

<hr>

[103] Augustine, *De Civitate Dei*, XIX, 12.   [104] Oakeshott (above n 55), 8.

imperfect. It is not simply the range and depth of the 'great' philosophical systems that makes them great, but the fact that they touch upon something fundamental in the condition they are attempting to understand. If a philosopher's life's work is very great, then it may display aspects of the human condition in ways that are merely incomplete, but without being distorted. (The Catholic Church believes this of Aquinas, for example.) But even in this case, the irenic ambition of philosophy will often cause us to be drawn to the writings of more than one great thinker, and to attempt to synthesize apparently disparate and sometimes contradictory considerations into a coherent picture of our own. The truth that is sought is of a kind that may be approached through numerous different sources. Both Augustine and Aquinas were aware, for example, that important dimensions of truth were revealed in the writings of Aristotle, Cicero and Plato, who did not have the Gospels. It may be glimpsed in many philosophical writings, but may be altogether absent from some, or corrupted in others, admixed with error.

The political theories of the present day take as their starting point a more limited set of questions than is encountered in the 'great' works of the Western tradition. Do they experience a greater confidence in the judgment of where one must begin the enquiry? Or perhaps it is that much that is troubling to Kant, and those who came before and after him, no longer seems to form part of the enquiry into politics. Could it be that Kant's modern-day heirs assume that the liberal citizen (if he is truly *liberal*) is naturally *good*? If so, it will appear to them that individuals will become more perfect citizens as they align themselves more closely to the political system of liberal values. Evil and injustice do not reign over human nature, but intrude upon the human condition where imperfect institutions give encouragement to passions which cause destructive competition between citizens. Liberalism will encourage individuals to confine their pursuit of their good within the 'proper' limits defined by political institutions. But it is often forgotten that 'the good' is itself defined by its power of attraction, and that its pull will always be stronger than the individual's desire for institutions of a certain kind. Consequently, he will often love justice (as defined by those institutions) less than the good that is being pursued, and will at crucial times regard those institutions, not as perfective of his nature, but as obstacles to the fulfilment of his chosen ends. No set of institutions will therefore cause the disappearance of destructive passions.

The function of liberal politics is to be enabling as much as to be constraining. But this assumes that the nature of the being who is being enabled is necessarily good, and 'evil' only insofar as his pursuit of this good accidentally causes harm to those around him. A politics appropriate to a character that was largely or wholly directed toward evil would of necessity be of an authoritarian and repressive nature. We find, in Augustine, Hobbes and Kant an understanding of the human being as a divided creature: one who, so it seems to himself, *must* be good, but is transiently as well as permanently *not*.[105] In what ways must politics be imagined to differ from the dominant conceptions of the present day, that it may make sense as the product of the efforts of such a character?

---

[105] Kolnai (above n 79), 94.

7

Legalism and modernity I: Identifying and understanding the problem

In dealing with 'modern' politics, are we addressing a set of questions that are genuinely new, appropriate only to the experience of present times? Does 'modern man' bestride the world as something fundamentally other than he was in the classical or medieval periods, or in early modernity? Should one begin to understand modern life under the rule of law as something altogether without precedent?

It is often remarked that the central problem of modern political theory concerns the possibility of legal order and political stability in a morally divided world. Law protects and nurtures the freedoms that allow individuals to formulate and pursue independent ideas about what is good or valuable in life. But law is also an impediment to independent action, placing limitations upon individual choice even as it defines the scope and availability of choice. The law of a modern society is deeply mysterious. Existing to regulate individual conceptions of the good which are in competition with one another, juridical concepts and obligations cannot at the same time be thought of as founded upon a shared understanding of the human good. How is legal order possible in a world where no other values are shared? In as much as the law structures moral choices, its capacity to offer stability to the social world would appear to be at odds with the supposition of conditions of discordance which require stabilization.

The basic problem sufficiently appears in the political thought of Hobbes. Hobbes tells us that where men stand outside the social bonds imposed by law, they stand before one another as free and equal beings. The conditions which characterize unlimited freedom and approximate equality between persons would be marked by continuous warfare of every one against every one. Lacking any common rule of good and evil, each person will deem to be 'good' that which accords with his appetites or desires, so that life becomes a permanent struggle to assert one's will over others. In reaching this conclusion, Hobbes reversed some of the intellectual priorities that had informed both ancient and medieval conceptions of legality. The classical jurists had supposed there to be an object of the understanding, 'the good life', which it is the purpose of ethics and philosophy to contemplate. Political institutions (such as law) would then play a role in fostering conditions in which such excellent lives might be pursued. The view to be encountered in Hobbes denies any independent existence to notions of good or evil. Good and evil are to be regarded as constructions *of law*:

> there being nothing [that is good or evil] simply and absolutely so; nor any common rule of good and evil, to be taken from the objects them-selves, but from the person of the man (where there is no commonwealth) or, (in a commonwealth) from the person that representeth it; or from an arbitrator or judge whom men disagreeing shall by consent set up; and make his sentence the rule thereof.[1]

In this passage we seem to uncover a different and recognizably modern point of view. No longer simply an instrument wherein some agreed conception of the human good is amplified and protected, law is inter-preted as a means of regulating and containing forces of opposition and *disagreement*. Liberals have long pondered this situation, but without fully responding to its central problem. Law emerges as a necessary means of establishing common rules or standards of right and wrong (or preventing the loss of them). But law can only appear if those subject to it *already* share values in common. If the existence of law depends upon a form of collective recognition or consensus on the part of the governed, upon what basis is such consent founded? If consensus is sufficiently achieved to allow for the development of common political institutions, in what sense is law necessary for the establishment of common rules and standards? How can law be both *reflective* and at the same time *constitutive* of social order?[2]

Confronting these problems, it is possible to identify two sets of ideas concerning the orientation of law in the modern world. Upon the one hand were theories of a broadly positivist character, which emphasized the necessity of a body of deliberately formulated standards in order to regulate the competing actions and desires of individuals. For Hobbes, all understanding is rooted in desire. A set of common rules is necessary to define conditions in which opposing desires could be peacefully pursued. It became natural to think of such conditions as lying in various points of

---

[1] Hobbes, *Leviathan* [1651], ch 6.
[2] See S Coyle, 'Positivism, Idealism and the Rule of Law', *OJLS*, 26 (2006), 257–88.

convergence or overlap between the competing conceptions of 'the good', to which the rules give authoritative expression. Legal rules have a dual status. Grounded in shared values, they also offer further refinement and extension of those values. On the other hand were theories that sought a more rational basis for legal obligations, located in permanent features of the person or of the human condition. The human being is not a locus of fleeting whims and shifting desires, but of a more stable bedrock of interests. One must attempt to identify general principles of morality and political association that could inform the understanding and interpretation of legal doctrine.[3] Theories of this kind were essentially idealistic: they regarded law not merely as a necessary instrument for addressing situations of conflict and contingency, but as a means of transforming the present form of society into a more proximate expression of certain moral values, themselves grounded already to a degree in human characteristics.

Though obviously distinctive, these traditions of thought are at a basic level dependent upon one another in virtue of deriving from a 'modern' political context. If the idealist's transformative ideal depends upon the identification of abstract ideas of equality and general norms of justice, possessing an identity beyond the textual confines of the written rule, it is nevertheless also animated by a constant drive to clarify and solidify present arrangements in a way which reveals but also perfects those norms and ideals. Law can identify or reflect interests and moral values only upon the basis of detailed rules and procedures of the kind celebrated by the classical positivist. The ability to receive and understand such ideas as they appear in their social functioning is tied to their concrete expression in explicitly formulated, authoritative propositions. At the same time, general rules are inevitably fairly blunt instruments. They possess a kind of incompleteness when applied to specific situations. It is necessary to interpret rules against a background of broader ideas. Because a shared body of rules requires a common interpretation, the ultimate mental framework for the interpretative enterprise must be understood as terminating not in variable and transient desires, but in fixed and commonly shared *interests*. The ideas at the heart of positivism

---

[3] Samantha Frost has argued that elements of this second view are also to be found in Hobbes, betraying 'a thinker whose appreciation of our embodiedness or materiality issues in a complex portrayal of our profound interdependence and a compelling account of the ways and means to peace'. See Frost, *Lessons from a Materialist Thinker: Hobbesian Reflections on Ethics and Politics* (Stanford University Press, 2008), 2.

and idealism are therefore mutually reliant: posited rules seemingly embodying fragments of more general moral ideas, but such ideas existing merely as abstract wishes when viewed apart from their concrete expression in the rules. A 'modern' political society can accordingly be expected to oscillate between these two perspectives, giving emphasis at different stages to the need for explicit and precisely formulated standards, and at other times to the broader ideas which inform the 'spirit' of the law.

For over three hundred years, jurisprudence has offered defences and refutations of positivist and idealist outlooks. Is jurisprudence correct to oppose these theses? I contend that liberals must find an alternative way of looking at the problem of modern politics. The argument proceeds in two parts. In the present chapter, I suggest that 'modernity' is not merely a relevant intellectual context for the contemplation of a specific set of problems, to which the theoretical traditions of positivism and idealism are responses. Modernity itself must be understood as the problem that requires investigation. It is undeniably in some respects a 'new' problem, reflecting a new set of assumptions about 'man' and 'citizen'. But neither modern politics nor the modern citizen are radical creations, without antecedents. They continue to reflect (and refract) perennial problems of the human condition that the oscillation of positivism and idealism often conceals. Building upon this insight, the following chapter attempts to illuminate the political landscape of modernity so as to progress beyond the intellectual categories through which it is presently understood.

The nature and source of the problem

In the first place, it is necessary to investigate the source of the problem, and its antecedents. This is not a simple matter. 'Modernity' does not admit of easy definition. How is the 'modern' age to be separated from those preceding it? As Leszek Kolakowski pointed out, no age or civilization is capable of identifying itself finally or universally.[4] One may at most discover a certain meaning in present forms of experience, but this will always amount to less than their total meaning. Thus to give to such an ephemeral idea as 'modernity' sufficient shape to enable discussion of it, is already to invite certain distortions.

---

[4] L Kolakowski, *Modernity on Endless Trial* (University of Chicago Press, 1990), 3.

Mindful of the distorting power of intellectual frameworks, we might try to locate the problem by considering the reception and mutation of the very idea of 'politics' itself, from the medieval period of European thought to the time of Hobbes and his contemporaries. The term *politicus* surfaced in medieval language in the middle of the thirteenth century, as a direct consequence of Latin translations of Aristotle's *Politics* and *Ethics*.[5] Aristotle's own use of the term had indicated a number of related meanings, all of which were linked to his discussion of the forms of constitution in which government is for the common good.[6] In Book I of the *Politics*, Aristotle is careful to distinguish between the idea of a statesman and that of a monarch or head of a household, which earlier writers such as Plato had argued were separated only by degree.[7] The fundamental difference, Aristotle suggests, lies in the fact that the statesman, unlike the monarch or master who exercises authority over slaves, rules over equals who are by nature free.[8] In his *Commentary* on the *Politics*, Aquinas adopted the same position: a regime is called 'royal' when 'one and the same person exercises authority *simpliciter* and in every respect', whereas a 'political regime' exists only when the ruler rules through the law and according to 'political discipline'.[9] But in later glosses on Aquinas's *Commentary*, a different picture begins to appear. Writing in the fifteenth century, the English judge Sir John Fortescue extended the term *politicus* to forms of monarchical rule, citing Aquinas as authority.[10] Lying in between the categories of *regimen regale* and *regimen politicum*, was a third possibility (*regimen politicum et regale*): that of the rule of a king who governs according to the laws of the land. This possibility arises where the population under regal rule constituted itself as a 'body politic'. The king as head of this body cannot change its laws 'any more than can the head of the physical body change its

---

[5] DA Callus, 'The Date of Grosseteste's Translations and Commentaries on Pseudo-Dionysius and the Nicomachean Ethics', *Recherches de Théologie Ancienne et Médiévale*, 14 (1947), 101.

[6] See Aristotle, *Politics*, Book I, 1294b1.

[7] Ibid., 1252a7–9; Plato, *Politicus*, 258a8: see N Rubenstein, 'The History of the Word *Politicus*', in A Pagden (ed.), *The Languages of Political Theory in Early-Modern Europe* (Cambridge University Press, 1997), 41–56.

[8] Aristotle, *Politics*, 1274b36. See Aquinas, *Commentary on Aristotle's Politics*, RJ Regan (ed.) (Indianapolis, Hackett Publishing, 2007), I.1.

[9] Aquinas, *Commentary* (above n 8), I.2.

[10] Sir John Fortescue, *De Laudibus Legum Angliae* [c.1470] (London, T Evans, 1776), quoted in Rubenstein (above n 7), 49. See also HG Koenigsberger, 'Monarchies and Parliaments in Early Modern Europe', 5 *Theory and Society* (1978), 191–217.

nerves'.[11] In this way, English rule was to be contrasted with the character of the French king's rule, which was *dominium regale tantum*: rule through the subjection of a people.

The difference between the two sorts of rule lay in the source of the law through which the governance of the realm was applied. Upon the one hand was the entire will-of-princes tradition, which drew constant strength throughout the late-medieval period from the considerable number of Glosses on the famous text of Justinian's *Institutes*: Marinus, for example, stating that a 'free king, who was subject to no one' could promulgate laws even against the *ius commune*.[12] On the other hand was the notion of the state as a *res publica*, arising from the actions and the history of a people. The source of these customs too formed a narrower basis than that of *ius commune*, Coke and Bracton (amongst others) contrasting the certainty and immunity from interpretation of the common law with what they had to say about the *ius commune*: 'Upon the text of the civil laws, there be so many glosses and interpretations, and again upon these so many commentaries, ... and therein so many diversities of opinions, as they rather do increase than resolve doubts and uncertainties, and the professors of that noble science say that it is like a sea full of waves.'[13]

Both of these ideas found expression in the text of Augustine's *City of God*. In Books V and XIX, he castigates the Empire because it was never truly the property of the people, stating that 'there never was a Roman commonwealth'.[14] Indeed, he suggests that there was never a Roman 'people', if by this is meant a populace bound together by a common understanding of what is right. Here, Augustine seems to be suggesting that the existence of the Roman state did not require the 'incorporation' of its 'people'. It requires only the establishment of 'an ordered concord of civic obedience and rule in order to secure the cooperation of men's wills'.[15] At the same time, Augustine believed that no state could exist without some measure of 'common agreement' amongst the populace 'as

---

[11] Fortescue, *De Laudibus*, ch 9.

[12] Francesco Calasso, *I Glossatori e la Teoria Della Sovranita*, 3rd edn (Milan, 1957), quoted in K Pennington, *The Prince and the Law 1200–1600* (Berkeley, University of California Press, 1993), 103. See also JP Canning, 'Ideas of the State in Thirteenth and Fourteenth-Century Commentators on the Roman Law', 33 *Transactions of the Royal Historical Society* (1983), 1–27.

[13] E Coke, *Second Part of the Institutes of the Laws of England* [1671] (London, E & R Brooke, 1797), conclusion to the proeme.

[14] Augustine, *De Civitate Dei*, XIX.21.   [15] Ibid., XIX.17.

to the objects of their love'.[16] If such agreement is taken to constitute a 'people', then it seems as if the integration of a community is an essential source of the state's customs and organization, even if the people's local customs and understandings are directed not toward what is right, but rather to their own glory. For Augustine therefore, neither of these sources of law (the vertically imposed order, nor the horizontally pro-duced arrangements) creates an order of governance that is legitimate, as opposed to provisional and merely necessary.[17]

Augustine's thought divides a 'city' and its 'people', whilst insisting that the city (ultimately one's citizenship of the community of the heavenly city) forms either a part or the whole of the means of man's salvation. It was entirely possible to situate this aspect of Augustine's thought within the broader context of the tradition of Western philoso-phy to which the notion of reason was a central idea. Thus, Aquinas is able in his *Commentary* on Aristotle's *Politics* to point to a vision of society which exists not simply to restrain evil, but provides the context in which life may be lived fully and properly. Man is by nature a social being, to whom the idea of community is essential: hence, *politics* must be directed at once to the ultimate fulfilment of this salvational end (and is therefore not without an eternal aspect), and more immediately to the present needs of man's earthly communities. But this very statement was also capable of being read in a different way. Augustine thinks of the earthly society as the necessary arena in which men live out their lives, and that 'community' more broadly is proper to man-kind. Earthly societies are however an expression not simply of man's nature, but of his *fallen* nature. Though a modicum of justice is required for the existence and stability of any society, this *pax civilis* should not be mistaken for the true laws which govern the heavenly city. Thus the primary achievement of earthly societies is the restraint of evil rather than the realization of true justice.[18] On this second reading, August-ine's thought belongs instead to the tradition of philosophizing of which the central idea is Will, or artifice: the *pax civilis* being the artificial product of men's wills, and therefore distinct from the *pax dei* which is their true end.

---

[16] Ibid., XIX.24.   [17] Ibid., IV, 4.

[18] For a starker contrast between Augustine and Aquinas (to my mind too stark), see RA Markus, *Saeculum: History and Society in the Theology of Saint Augustine* (Cambridge University Press, 1970), 211.

Turning to Hobbes's civil philosophy, we find this 'will and artifice' tradition being given a different meaning. Hobbes 'does not normally speak of Reason, the divine illumination of the mind that unites man with God; he speaks of *reasoning*'.[19] Even nature is simply 'the *art* whereby God has made and governs the world'.[20] The presence of laws, of arrangements and of principles, is therefore also the product of artifice. Without such artificial structures, the mind is free. Having nothing to latch onto, human 'reasoning' enjoys no terminus except in death. Hobbes is able subtly to modulate the Augustinian position. 'Justice' is coeval with the specific form of the polity. Without the polity, there exist no exact or detailed rules, no *conclusions*, but only general 'theorems' of prudence. The thought that the civil condition is a 'full' or 'proper' context for mankind, part of a salvational scheme, is retained but transformed. For Hobbes, the human mind is something that is agile and restless, whereas society is fixed and stable. One might almost say, in contemplating these opposed forces, that Hobbes wishes to fix society *against* nature.[21] It is the placement of will and artifice at the centre of thought that makes this opposition inevitable, and transformative of the idea of 'politics'. Hobbes uses the term 'civil' to describe the artificial product of more than one will.[22] Hobbes is careful about the implications of this statement. There cannot be a common understanding amongst men (still less a 'common will'). There can be only a common *object* of will, in the form of an 'arbitrator or judge' whose single will shall stand in the place of all the others.[23] The civil condition comes into being as the product of many wills, *not* because it is the fruit of a shared endeavour, but because it can be achieved and sustained only through the mutual restraint of many wills. Hobbes entrenches Augustine's division of a 'city' and its 'people' in a more extreme form: 'Neither before nor after the establishment of civil association is there any such thing as the *People*, to whom so much previous theory ascribed sovereignty.'[24]

Under Hobbes's influence, the central *political* problem came to be viewed in a new and changed light. Governance in accordance with the

---

[19] M Oakeshott, *Hobbes on Civil Association* (Indianapolis IN, Liberty Fund, 1975), 27 (emphasis added). See Hobbes, *Leviathan*, ch 5: '*reason*, in this sense, is nothing but *reckoning*'.

[20] Hobbes, *Leviathan*, introduction (emphasis added).

[21] See e.g. A Brett, *Liberty, Right and Nature: Individual Rights in Later Scholastic Thought* (Cambridge University Press, 1997), 205.

[22] See Oakeshott (above n 19), 29.   [23] Hobbes, *Leviathan*, ch 5.

[24] Oakeshott (above n 19), 65.

ars politica could no longer derive its authority from the history and legal customs of a 'people', but remains dependent upon the existence of a *pax civilis*. Its source is not a common understanding, but a particular arrangement of ever-distinct wills, regimented and to some extent coerced into a tolerable harmony. The idea of legalism came to predominate the imagination as a means of comprehending the predicament and actions of *individuals*.

The character of 'the individual', as an object of political concern, did not of course spring forth suddenly in Hobbes's writings, as a pure and complete creation of thought, and was not therefore without antecedents. Both Aristotle and Plato had given sustained consideration to the properties of the individual soul. Western Christianity added to this a tradition of reflection upon individual salvation and personal responsibility which was embodied not only in its doctrines, but also in its art, its sermons and sacraments. If the 'sinner' was a type, nevertheless it was the individual who lost her soul or daily confronted the peril of its loss. For example, Aquinas, contemplating Boethius's definition of the person ('an individual substance of a rational nature'), complains of its inadequacy precisely because it lacks the necessary singularity of a 'person'.[25] But if man, contemplated as an object of religious salvation, possessed such traits of individuality, nevertheless he did not possess them when viewed as a political figure, from the perspective of his place within civil society. There, he was identified according to his class, profession or status: as a worker, criminal, cleric, etc.

As with most of the central concepts of Western political thought, the notion of the individual as a political rather than a religious figure did not arise as the product of philosophical assertion or the conscious enumeration of necessary truths, but as a series of retrospective modifications to the structure and conditions of medieval thought. Medieval society in Europe was of a kind that did not permit the conscious expression of human individuality. The conditions of life and practice were of a nature that emphasized the inherently communal character of human endeavour, and thus of human nature. The *regimen regale* and the *regimen politicum* give no particular recognition to the individual. 'The individual' of later philosophical thought could not emerge with sufficient consistency within such conditions of life to form a basis for self-conscious understanding. The human personality was by and large

---

[25] See Aquinas, *Summa Theologiae*, I 27.1.

submerged beneath the recognition of human beings as they appeared within the various social and familial contexts that represented the circumstantially possible limits of human experience.[26] To possess self-knowledge was, in the main, to understand oneself as a member of a class (the feudal overlord, the vassal, the member of a church, a family, poet, preacher, etc.). The idea of a uniquely differentiated 'individual', merely *participating* in various communal activities in a manner and under conditions distinct from his neighbours, was not significantly identifiable.[27]

The emergence of 'the individual' did not represent the intellectual triumph of a bold philosophical doctrine, but the gradual abatement of communal ties and the corresponding emergence of opportunities for new and distinctive forms of personal engagement with the social world. Freedom represented not the ideal form of human engagement, but the generation of an alternative means of intellectualizing the sum of human experience. Within the new idiom, the human condition no longer appeared (as in the Aristotelian and Scholastic traditions) as a progressive journey towards some common end or higher plane of existence, but as an unfortunate predicament in which individuals relate to one another as separate and autonomous centres of activity.

Hobbes is a 'modern' philosopher, not because he was the first to conceive of human beings as independent centres of thought and activity, but because he offers a striking example of a politics in which such individuality appears as the central characteristic of the human condition. His boldness is the product, not of inventing new categories, but of

---

[26] See Oakeshott, *Rationalism in Politics*, revised edn (Indianapolis IN, Liberty Fund, 1991), Essay 11. There was however some recognition of the individual within the otherwise group-centric form of medieval society, to a greater extent than is acknowledged by Oakeshott: see A Black, 'The Individual and Society', in JH Burns (ed.), *The Cambridge History of Medieval Political Thought c.350–c.1450* (Cambridge University Press, 1988), 588–606.

[27] The individual only fully emerges when we see significant mobility between these states or classes, i.e. when these states come to be regarded as inessential to one's destiny and character. Medieval tales of kings disguised as peasants, or of princes forced to live the life of stable boys always reinforced the suggestion that the condition of peasantry endured by the royal person was only apparent and not 'real': a tradition which persisted into the nineteenth century. See e.g. Tolstoy, 'The Three Questions', in *Walk in the Light and Twenty-Three Tales* (Maryknoll NY, Orbis Books, 2003), 347. By contrast, Cervantes's *Don Quixote* is often regarded as the 'first' modern novel precisely because Quixote's journey involves the 'creation of oneself from nothing, without regard to existing social conditions or supposedly "natural" facts': R Geuss, *Politics and the Imagination* (Princeton University Press, 2010), 63.

giving to them a particularly potent and systematic treatment. The result was the flowering of an intellectual tradition in which will and artifice were central ideas.

This changed understanding of the human situation transformed politics. The absence of any shared end or mode of being meant that the *pax civilis*, the unifying forces which make peaceful social coexistence possible, could no longer be found in the process of pursuing a common condition, recognized as good for all. Increasingly, it was to be found in a legal order that could define a stable set of circumstances in which each person can choose their own method of determining and pursuing their preferred mode of existence.[28] In the absence of law, the condition of humanity was perceived to be one of turmoil, a relentless attempt of each person to deal with others on terms which promote his position and interests over those of others.[29] Law represented the sole means by which the activities of individuals could be regulated sufficiently so as to allow the human condition to subsist. It was in defining the circumstances of permissible choice and action, and corresponding areas of duty or obligation, that law came to occupy a central position in the development of the modern political idiom. This 'law', however, was neither finally that of the dynastic ruler (*regimen regale*), nor the collective will of the people (*regimen politicum*), but of the 'artificial man', i.e. of the *state (civitas)*.[30] It is no accident that the modern form of the 'state' began to emerge precisely at the same time as notions of individuality began to take a central position.[31] The new realities required a new conception of the state. As Quentin Skinner observed, the modern conception of the state 'has come to embody a doubly impersonal character. We distinguish the state's authority from that of the ruler or magistrates entrusted with the exercise of its powers for the time being. But we also distinguish its

---

[28] The *pax civilis*, in other words, became an entirely formal condition, or precondition, of governance, rather than a substantive body of customary agreements.

[29] See Hobbes, *Leviathan*, ch 13. Not everyone agreed with the grim picture of humankind's natural state to be found in Hobbes's writings: Grotius and, later, Locke, for example, viewed that condition as one governed already by natural laws or shared precepts of reason. But almost all writers within the Western philosophical tradition viewed life in the absence of declared and organized laws as one of inconvenience and misfortune in which the threat of conflict is ever present: see e.g. Locke, *Two Treatises of Government* [1689], P Laslett (ed.) (Cambridge University Press, 1988), chs 2–3.

[30] Hobbes, *Leviathan*, introduction.

[31] See e.g. R Tuck, *The Rights of War and Peace: Political Thought and the International Order from Grotius to Kant* (Oxford University Press, 1999), 9–10.

authority from that of the whole society or community over which its powers are exercised'.[32]

Several important consequences can be detected in this movement towards modernity. The assumption that law represents an attempt to impose rationality upon an otherwise chaotic situation encouraged a tendency within both academic law and philosophy to devalue the ideas of tradition, history and practice. Outside the bonds of imposed law, individuals would be entirely 'free'. But more important is the shift in moral thinking that led to the idea that human beings not only possess freedom (as a necessary consequence of being alive), but that human thriving specifically requires the enjoyment and exercise of freedom. Freedom increasingly represented not simply an extant condition to be analyzed and understood, but also a condition of moral welfare to be protected and advanced. It is possible to regard the history of modern legal and political thought as the transformation of the idea of freedom from a condition into an ideal. It is the recognition of freedom as an idealized state (one which of necessity *in fact* obtains, but only imperfectly) that gives rise to the problem of modernity. Outside the scope of law, the human situation is meaningless. The state of total freedom equals the absence of all structure. Only under law does the human condition possess significance. Exercising freedom in a meaningful way, individuals will flourish. Law became central to political theory, not only in virtue of forming an integral element of the analysis of the human condition, but also as a central means of more fully realizing an imperfectly established ideal.

Philosophers were not responsible for inventing the new approach of legalism. More the product of accumulated social change than as the outcome of applying a philosophical theory to the real world of politics, legalism nevertheless came to occupy a central place in philosophical reflection upon politics. The emergence of 'the individual', and thus of the idea of freedom, encouraged an altered view of the social conditions which had predominated during the medieval period. The matrix of social institutions such as the Church, the family, conditions of tenure and employment and so on, previously thought of as providing the terms in which personal identities are interpreted and constituted, came to be regarded as pressures or hindrances from which the individual must escape if he is to have latitude in which to develop his own character.

---

[32] Q Skinner, 'The State', in T Ball, J Farr and RL Hanson (eds.), *Political Innovation and Conceptual Change* (Cambridge University Press, 1989), 112.

A world in which political power is distributed throughout society, in the manner of a *regimen politicum* (that is, a world of variously intersecting and overlapping communal ties, each of which in some way determines the form of social interaction or the direction of activity), is one that inhibits self-direction: either through the suppression of choice, or by proscribing the form of available choices. A world made up of 'individuals', on the other hand, requires a concentration of political power in one place, for it is only through the existence of a single, unified centre of authority that each person can come to enjoy that freedom from the will of others that is a precondition of autonomous decision. Independence of the will requires some level of control of other wills that are external to one's own. A social condition wherein the individualist disposition is strong is most naturally interpreted as one structured by firmly fixed areas of right and duty. The establishment of such domains depends upon the existence and effectiveness of a centralized source of authority. It requires *legal* order. Hence, the disposition towards individual thought and decision (if this is taken as the central characteristic of 'modern' man) both depends upon and promotes the value of legalism.[33]

Intellectual frameworks remain distortive. This account of the emergence of legalism is only a schematic and exceedingly rough abridgement of a mass of historical experience. In common with any attempt to impose a degree of coherence upon a disparate reality of reversals, dead ends and unexpected turnings, it embodies no more than an abstraction. But it is perhaps sufficiently intelligible and familiar to be taken as a recognizable approximation to a distinctively 'modern' way of thinking. If this is granted, the following observations may be thought to cast some light on the nature of modernity, and in consequence upon the various problems associated with that condition of life.

The centrality of legalism to modern politics

Legalism does not simply denote the existence within society of a body of laws. It refers to the presence of a specifically juridical conception of the human person, interpreted as the bearer of rights and duties. To characterize legalism in this way is to attribute to law a particular *raison d'être*

---

[33] At the same time, ironically, legalism can be seen to *subvert* individuality: the concentration of power at the centre operating precisely to suppress the functioning or the existence of mediating institutions which might otherwise provide a buffer between the individual and governmental powers of direction and control.

in the socio-political world, which is best explained in contrast to certain historical antecedents. Medieval political thought had followed Aristotle in regarding social institutions and arrangements as constituent factors in the realization of the human good.[34] The moral character of man (that which made him virtuous or civilized, and capable of progress) was thought to be reflected in the arrangements he had created for the furtherance of peaceful cooperation and human endeavour, and for the general alleviation of the human condition. Social arrangements were not to be viewed merely as furnishing the external context in which each person pursues the good. They were instead part of the good that is being pursued. The human good was a complex ethical object that is realizable only through joint endeavour. In modern political thought, however, social institutions did not present themselves as elements of a common good but as necessary evils whose encroachments upon an individual's capacity for self-expression through choice must be limited as far as possible.[35] If the unique value of a person consists in what differentiates him from other people rather than in his approximation to some common ideal, then the imposition of desired conditions upon the person does not promote his wellbeing, but simply destroys his individuality, and thus his means of discovering and realizing the good that is appropriate to his own conceptions and circumstances.

Legalism naturally leads to a specific conception of the contribution of law to the general shape of society: that of the translation of traditional and informal modes of association into a system of rights and duties determined at some level of abstraction from, and independence of, the detailed actuality of social practice. Law is not just one amongst many determinants of social concourse, but the pre-eminent means of regulating the activities and interrelationships of various social units. In a world where no common condition of human flourishing unites all persons, legal order represents the only means of securing any degree of mutual accommodation. Law does not exist to unite all of society in the pursuit of a single, common endeavour, but to devise and maintain a set of standards by which individuals are able to pursue their own activities, and to reconcile those activities with the conflicting actions of others as far as possible.

[34] See e.g. Aquinas, *Summa Theologiae*, II–I 95.1.
[35] See e.g. Kant, *The Metaphysics of Morals*, in M Gregor and AW Woods (eds.), *Practical Philosophy: The Cambridge Edition of the Works of Immanuel Kant* (Cambridge University Press, 1996), Part I.

Underlying this conception of 'politics' is a view of the human condition that is at odds with the understanding to be found in the ancient and medieval writers. It was not merely society that was transformed but man himself. The classical philosophers saw human life as being directed towards a specific end (the development of a noble and virtuous disposition), and society as the necessary medium in which noble and virtuous characteristics could be exercised and developed.[36] Human life was structured by an ideal that is both external to the person (being a possible occasion of legal enforcement) and realized within the inner life of each person. The medieval writers worked around this ideal a theological framework, whereby the direction of human activity was conceived as determined by external moral *laws*, and the goal of the moral life not the pursuit of a state of perfection within the world, but salvation beyond the plane of mortality. In both cases, however, human life is interpreted according to its perceived place within a larger metaphysical order which indicates its ultimate direction.

The 'modern' view of the person depended upon an altered view of the world as something metaphysically inert, providing no external forces for the direction of human conduct but instead mere *possibilities* for self-directed action. No moral ideal is indicated by the range of possibilities available, unless it is imposed upon the world by human will and thought: 'It is as impossible for nature to discover any morality in the actions of a man without reference to a *law*', wrote Pufendorf, 'as it is for a man born blind to choose between colours.'[37] The trajectory of human life does not signal movement in any particular direction, but merely movement as opposed to its cessation.[38] In the absence of a governing ideal or *telos*, that which causes or motivates movement must spring from the agent himself, in the form of desires, wants or interests. In the absence of any fixed direction to human endeavour, such desires and wants have no terminus, because no condition of being exists that could act as the end in which they are all fulfilled.

But it is in the pages of Hobbes that these characteristics of the individual appear most potently:

> Continual success in obtaining those things which a man from time to time desireth, that is to say, continual prospering, is that men call Felicity; I mean the felicity of this life. For there is no such thing as perpetual

---

[36] See Aristotle, *Politics*, Book 1.   [37] Pufendorf, *De Iure Naturae et Gentium*, 1.2.6.
[38] Hobbes, *Leviathan*, ch 11.

tranquillity of mind while we live here; because life itself is but motion, and can never be without desire, nor without fear, no more than without sense.[39]

Several important consequences can be observed in this understanding of the individual, all of which combine to promote the value of legalism as a central determinant of modern politics. The men of Hobbes's world do not require the society of others for their completion. Each person forms a *separate* locus of desires and abilities. They require society merely to facilitate the pursuit of their wants and interests. The individual stands as a naturally complete entity apart from society, but requires a common basis of social order to ensure his continued survival and a degree of protection from the aggressive pursuit by others of their own designs and priorities.[40] Common rules are important for the creation of mutual understandings and the pursuit of mutual advantage. In the absence of such rules individuals remain fundamentally opaque to one another: 'Whatsoever is the object of any man's appetite or desire', writes Hobbes, 'that is it which he for his part calleth Good: And the object of his hate and aversion, Evil ... For these words of Good, Evil and Contemptible are ever used with relation to the person that useth them.'[41] Law is thus given a central place in the construction of social meanings and the creation of stable practices (such as trade) for the alleviation of the human condition.

One might reflect on the fact that the politics of individualism (and thus of legality) do not point in a single direction, but in at least two incompatible directions. On the one hand, it is possible to emphasize (as Hobbes does) the essentially limited character of government that is implied by this notion of the individual. Law exists not for the promotion of the human good, but merely for that of social order. The good of each person is something that can be formulated and realized only through

---

[39] Hobbes, *Leviathan*, ch 6. The modern-day 'consumer' might be said to be the heir to this conception of the individual, though other guises (such as the existential self) also bear its mark.

[40] The 'modern' individual is thus the antithesis of the human character as presented by John Donne's famous sermon: 'No man is an island entire of itself; every man is a piece of the continent, a part of the main ... Any man's death diminishes me, because I am involved in mankind; and therefore never send to know for whom the bell tolls; it tolls for thee.' Donne, *Devotions Upon Emergent Occasions* [1624], Meditation 17, in EM Simpson (ed.), *John Donne's Sermons on the Psalms and Gospels* (Berkeley CA, University of California Press, 1963), 243.

[41] Hobbes, *Leviathan*, ch 6.

individual endeavour, and cannot be *imposed* upon the person from outside. (This would be the case even where two or more individuals happened to agree upon the character of the good life, for on this conception mere 'happiness' falls short of the good precisely insofar as freedom is lacking.) To seek to promote another's good is not to furnish them with opportunities for self-improvement, but to determine in some measure the future direction of their action. Inasmuch as the political process lends itself to such well-meaning attempts to improve the lives of its subjects, the rule of law serves to insulate the individual from external interference as far as possible, by separating the world of politics from that of private life. But, on the other hand, legalism might be interpreted as seeking, not simply the emancipation of the individual from the tyranny of other wills, but to *impose* freedom upon the subject *as a condition* of the worthwhile life. Here, freedom is viewed as something possessed of a distinctive moral structure, rather than the absence of all structure.

What is one to make of this? At the root of modern politics is a notion of freedom which itself exhibits bipolarity. First, freedom is understood as an extant condition that is fully available only in the *absence* of law. But it is also fatally compromised without the existence of law. Legal order intervenes as an unfortunately necessary means for creating conditions in which freedom can be meaningfully exercised. Second, freedom is understood as a condition which obtains only *through* law, and is susceptible of degrees dependent upon the extent to which the legal order approaches the perfection of its moral form. Here, the structure of freedom is thought to depend not only upon security, but upon the imposition of various equalities (of opportunity, education, perhaps resources, etc.). One will struggle to find examples of the appearance of either conception in its pure form in the political writings of modernity (although Humboldt comes very close to the notion of freedom as absence of any externally imposed conditions).[42] This is doubtlessly in part the result of the essential instability of the respective poles. But it is not difficult to observe more or less pronounced tendencies towards these poles in the political texts that have defined modern political understandings. Even in Hobbes one encounters a view that consists of an ambiguous mixture of the two tendencies. It is this ambiguity that defines the problem of modern politics.

---

[42] See W von Humboldt, *The Limits of State Action*, JW Burrow (ed.) (Cambridge University Press, 1969), chs 2, 3 and 6.

Rooted in a conception of 'the individual' that both depends upon and promotes the value of legalism, the political thought of 'modernity' produced a situation that was not envisaged within the traditional taxonomy of political forms. How stable was this new situation? The essential condition of the individual, thought to be guaranteed by law, is ambiguous in nature, capable of being interpreted variously as an extant condition that requires *protection* through legal order, or as an idealized state which is *promoted* by law and which therefore exists imperfectly and by degrees. The theoretical traditions of positivism and idealism might be seen not as inherently *flawed* conceptions of the modern political world, but as the inevitable symptoms of the structural conditions of modernity itself. Springing from the tensions contained within modernity, they cannot be expected to overcome or otherwise finally dispose of those tensions, but can instead merely reflect them in different ways.

Can the existence of the dynamic tensions of modernity be to some extent mitigated? It is doubtful whether they can be dissolved or altogether avoided. A different intellectual framework is needed. Standing in opposition to many of the most intimate touchstones of 'modern' political and jurisprudential thought, this intellectual framework must possess its own historical pedigree if it is to be serviceable as an interpretation of current political circumstances.

8

Legalism and modernity II: Reflections upon the problem

A 'modern' political vision arises from the centrality of the character of the 'individual', generating a response of 'legalism'. The intellectual framework which results from these elements is subject to certain limitations. Upon the one hand is the idea of individual 'freedom' as a historical condition that is recognized and protected through law. Upon the other, such freedom appears on the scene as an idealized state which is only ever imperfectly instantiated and expressed in history, and which therefore promotes the idea of law itself as a partially realized ideal. Can one overcome these unsatisfactory tensions?

Habit, tradition and rule

The tensions that define the condition of modernity are produced by the character of 'the individual'.[1] Having eliminated the *summum bonum*, Hobbes gave expression to a figure that is essentially opaque. Not possessing a *telos* or pointing in a determinate direction, what can be said about the individual? Classical and Christian images of society had depicted the life of men as part of society's order, not its *disorder*. The order of society consisted in the *homonoia* of its members, who are members of society through their participation in the *Nous*, or else the Christian *Logos*.[2] As it appears in Hobbes, on the contrary, the *pax civilis* points in no direction, and at no ends:

> When men aim directly and naively at attaining the good city of virtue by law according to the best regime, they impose on themselves very harsh constraints – they 'afflict' their nature – and condemn themselves to a life

---

[1] See Chapter 7 above.

[2] See E Voegelin, 'Necessary Moral Bases for Communication in a Democracy', in E Sandoz (ed.), *Published Essays 1953–65: The Collected Works of Eric Voegelin*, vol. XI (Columbia, University of Missouri Press, 2000), 55.

of war against other men and against their own nature. The greatest good
that can befall men is the one they derive from the evil that besets them.[3]

Remarkably, Hobbes is able to suggest that the virtues of the moral life
indicate 'the means of peaceable, sociable, and comfortable living'[4] only
when they have become *detached* from the '*finis ultimus*, utmost aim' of
life. Virtues are not to be understood as ends appointed for the perfection
of the soul, but mere means of protecting the physical body when the
soul is radically free of all ends.

Appearing in this guise, man possesses freedom innately and not as an
ideal. In consequence, the primary purpose of law is that of control. Because
he does not participate in a common good, man does not possess a 'nature'
as such, but is forced by his circumstances to invent one. In place of 'the
right of everyone to everything', man must create structures which limit
his modes of operation. One might say that by erecting artificial limits to his
freedom, man determines himself. Applying the language of Aristotle to
the un-Aristotelian lessons of chapter XIII of *Leviathan*, we can say that
man discovers his character when he learns to share it with other men.
Repeatedly, Hobbes tells us that the basis for all of man's motivations is the
desire for power. In creating legal order, man does not overcome or displace
this hunger for power (he does not fundamentally change his inner being),
but places external limitations upon his freedom to pursue its forms. It will
seem that the realm of politics is one in which internally generated impulses
and motivations constantly confront external forces which must be tamed.
But each individual as a mover within the social world is not only a source
of internal impulses. As an external force acting upon others, the individual
also demands regulation and limitation. In aligning the virtues to this
incredible new role, Hobbes creates a political situation in which the truth
of society is opposed to the truth of the soul which agitates man.

At the same time, it is possible to think (as Hobbes in chapter XIII
clearly does) that when devoid of limits to power, there was something
missing from man. His freedom was fundamentally the freedom *to act* in
accord with desire, but this meant that he lacked a more important
dimension of freedom: freedom *from the will of others*. It was not difficult
therefore for Hobbes's modernist successors to move from a conception
of law as a controlling authority above all else, to one in which law
implements conditions of freedom. Man always possessed a certain

---

[3] P Manent, *The City of Man*, M Lepain (trans.) (Princeton University Press, 1998), 42.
[4] Hobbes, *Leviathan*, ch 15. (See also ch 42.)

latitude of will, but his genuine 'freedom', the freedom which allows him to put his plans into practice, depends upon the existence of irresistible social structures. Whatever his inner 'nature', man may have more or less of this freedom depending upon his external environmental conditions, and consequently freedom exists as a specifically legal ideal.

The dichotomy of 'internal' and 'external' spheres (as definitive of the individual's predicament) must be squarely confronted. Does one truly understand modern man through these terms? It is not sufficient to oppose one notion of freedom to the other. The power of will and decision is not lost when man exists in the context of social structures, but the ability to will is not at the same time unaffected by external conditions. As Maurice Barres reminds us, man in being a social animal is not the master of his own ideas. Thoughts are not 'born in us' without reference to experiences and conventions that have been shaped by others:

> Nous ne sommes pas les maîtres des pensées qui naissent en nous. Elles ne viennent pas de notre intelligence; elles sont des façons de réagir ou se traduisent de très anciennes dispositions physiologiques ... La raison humaine est enchaînée de telle sorte que nous repassons tous dans les pas de nons prédécesseurs.[5]

Equally, the power to will would exist in 'natural' man only in a rudimentary sense: our very reason is 'chained' to the steps of our predecessors. Considering these thoughts, one must already leave behind any literal commitment to the idea of 'atomic' individuals interacting with one another as 'external' centres of motion. Human relationships are never contemplated as totalities. They are always viewed from a perspective informed by particular interests or concerns. We confront one another in society not as people, but in a series of *personas*: as shopkeeper, litigant, mother, party-member, etc. The degree to which we are known by another person will therefore depend upon the range of personas through which we are related. Man is both 'stranger' and 'friend'.[6] Crucially, some

---

[5] Barres, *Scènes et Doctrines du Nationalisme* (1902), reproduced in R Girardet, *Nationalismes et Nation: Questions au XXes* (Brussels, Editions Complexe, 1996), 140.

[6] There is nothing new about the observation that 'the whole person' never fully appears in social life. The fact that each person has impulses or thoughts which are reserved from public exposure is reflected in Jacques's lines in Shakespeare's *As You Like It*: 'All the world's a stage,/ And all the men and women merely players;/ They have their exits and their entrances,/ And one man in his time plays many parts' (Act II, Scene 7). A different dimension is revealed in Sterne's *Tristram Shandy*, viz. the limits to the communication of experience, which demonstrate those 'parts' to be, not the inevitable outcome of a universal intent to deceive, but something in fact necessarily intimated in the human condition.

of these personas (e.g. 'taxpayer') are *imposed by* the social conditions in which we move, whereas others are produced organically *within* the conditions of association which make up the world of our experience. Still others are constituted by a mixture of these origins, so that it is difficult to find pure instances of either kind. If the role of a teacher is normally voluntarily adopted, and one's style and method of teaching is largely one's own, there is nevertheless usually a specific curriculum to be taught (often set out by government or by professional bodies), and there are inevitably certain rules to be followed and standards to be adopted in the course of professional teaching that spring from both formal governmental and social sources. An alternative example is provided by the persona of a 'neighbour': the meaning of this term is partly a matter of established social usage and conventional understandings (as well as physical circumstance), but it is also partially determined by the presence and operation of complex laws of property. In the same way, the role of a parent is formed by a mixture of social expectations and legal responsibilities.

The dichotomy of 'internal' versus 'external' conditions of action is rather a blunt instrument for the description of these relationships, because the personas which constitute the *relata* under consideration are not themselves the product of purely 'internal' or 'external' determination. There are not two separate stages involved in an individual's engagement with the social world: one does not first 'put on' an abstract persona *and then* explore limitless possibilities for engagement with other personas. One might say that the various personas adopted by 'the individual' in all areas of life that matter to politics simultaneously constitute *and are constituted by* the relations in which they figure. Such personas are not easily or completely demarcated from one another within an individual's character. One's identity as a 'consumer' is not unrelated to one's identity as a religious believer (or unbeliever), or as the adherent of a left- (or right-) leaning political doctrine. Each facet of identity is influenced and conditioned by the others. One's character is not typically capable of supporting the double standards necessary for an extreme compartmentalization of these personas. The nature of man may be divided but it is not radically fragmented. Subject to doubts and anxieties, man's character is nevertheless an integrated whole.[7]

---

[7] See Aquinas, *Summa Theologiae*, I 29.1, II-II 145.2. The Papal decree *Gaudium et Spes* acknowledges that man is subject to many divergent and contradictory opinions about himself, the result of which is 'doubt and anxiety'. *Gaudium et Spes*, 7 December 1965, I.I.12.

The character of 'the individual' is not to be thought of as a fully self-determining and boundless centre of potentialities, related to others (and thereby conditioned) only by virtue of legal rules. Taking shape from within the matrix of connections and historic modes of engagement in which it is enmeshed from the start, man's character is indeed social. Once this fact is grasped, the distinction between internal and external determinants on conduct is seen to be wholly inappropriate and misleading as a means of understanding social relationships. A vision of law as a set of 'external' rules within which individuals freely move can be seen as illusory. Most aspects of social life are grounded to a greater extent in habit and tradition than in rule. To bring social relationships within the scope of formal rules, the law must perform its reflective function, seeking to give more precision and stability to those modes of interaction which exist socially and independently of it. But in carrying out this important function, the law also gives definite expression and authoritative shape to those modes of interaction. In imposing a fixed (or relatively fixed) form upon the conditions of social engagement, the law inevitably supplants and modifies what it attempts to pin down.[8] Viewed in this way, the question of how law can be both reflective *and* constitutive of social order becomes more clear. Reflection, creation and modification are not *separate* processes undertaken by the legal order, but aspects of the same process.

Neglecting habit and tradition as sources of reflection, and promoting the value of legalism, the intellectual framework of modernity has had profound effects on our understanding of the condition of modern man. The freedom that arises from legal order aspires to be an equal liberty for all citizens. Which of these two terms, liberty or equality, has become more important for modern liberals? The principles of 1789 and those of 1948 are concerned with both ideas. The innate equality of mankind is declared with the same force and in the same breath as its innate freedom. Without the law that gives him his vital independence, modern liberals assert, man would be *absolutely* free. Modifying this freedom, law renders man unequal with man. In becoming civilized, man becomes sporadically free of the will of others, but left to his own devices he will

---

[8] It is 'relatively' fixed, because neither statutory rules nor (especially) those of the common law can claim to be fully determined and incapable of further refinement. What we see in the judicial application of law is the symbiosis that exists between the legally determined meaning and its wider social meaning, which can be said to exist as mutual influences. My discussion in the main text will pass over this additional complexity.

create social structures in which liberty, prestige, wealth and opportunity are unevenly distributed. Customary behaviour will create a stable society long before it achieves the just society, and perhaps at the permanent expense of justice. Only when man intervenes deliberately in the fabric of social life, only when he creates explicit structures of rule and norm, will justice stand any chance of appearing. Government must do what men collectively cannot do.

The assumptions of legalism created a dilemma for liberal political thought. Valuing man's innate freedom, liberals wondered about the extent to which law ought to occupy a neutral position as between opposing conceptions of 'the good'. Drawing upon one strand of Hobbes's thought, liberals drew attention to a social need that is prior to justice: *order*. Men require a stable order in which to exercise their freedom, but they will not agree about the kind of order that is needed. But enamoured of the 'value' of freedom, liberals will not tolerate just any order. Consequently, it often seemed as if order could not be thought of except in association with ideas of that form of order aiming at ideal social conditions. Order collides with liberty in many ways, but once the attention of liberals fell on freedom as a value, it became possible to calibrate order for the management of a system of liberty without much regard for the fate of individual liberties.

These facts go some way to explaining the ease with which it was possible for Rawls to suggest that justice is a property of a society's 'basic structure'. Justice cannot exist without order, without the systematic administration of justice. Law is, so to speak, both the administration of *justice* as well as the *administration* of justice. But just as the medieval Christian rulers, charged with the enactment of justice, too easily became tyrants, so it is necessary for philosophers to treat this idea with great caution.

Justice as a moral idea implies *control*: the power to alter or manipulate the situations to which it applies as a value. Lying beyond human control, certain situations (such as natural disasters or personal disabilities) can to an extent only be borne, whether with fortitude or resentment. But they must be accepted for what they are, lying beyond the limit to which human action can alleviate the condition endured. Justice demands the possibility of change. It requires agency. The very idiom in which life is occasionally spoken of as being unfair or unjust is one which invokes the notion of being in the play of animate forces lying beyond the scope of human determination (God, Fate, Nature). It is obviously possible, through the human action of crafting deliberate rules, to make alterations and revisions to virtually *any* aspect of social relationships and personas. Enjoying the fruit of various technological advances, governments in recent times have been able to exercise an incredible level of control over the societies over which they preside. But what technological advances have *not* produced (and could never produce), is the power to exert control over *all* aspects of society simultaneously.[9] It follows that whilst particular relationships and circumstances are always amenable to assessment as just or unjust, 'justice' and 'injustice' are not qualities that can be straightforwardly ascribed to 'society' taken as a whole.[10]

Exaggerating the range and scope of government, the value of legalism lends an impressive coherence to the idea of just government. Philosophers who are wedded to legalism as a central political idea have failed to question this sense of coherence. Society is shaped and directed not only according to deliberate rule but also by habit and tradition, which exceed the powers of governmental control. Government is an inherently limited enterprise. The justice of society's 'basic structure' is not only relative but incomplete. How must the character of government be understood in the light of its limitations?

Direction and purpose

Having framed the central question of government as the promotion of an ideal of justice, philosophers were drawn to an image of political theory as being directed towards the analysis of a form of association. The purpose of jurisprudence is to explore the role and position of law within a political society which aims at that ideal. It is above all liberalism and democracy which embody the political forms that are regarded in the West as central to the ideal. Intended as descriptions of the form of modern society, they appeared also to indicate an ideal of justice, and hence to invite description in terms of a 'theory' of justice that embodies the abstract perfection of the form of society being pursued. The context of modernism consists of a particular mixture of forces which conspire to

---

[9] For an effective criticism of the possibility of minute and total governmental control, see NE Simmonds, 'Law as a Moral Idea', *University of Toronto LJ*, 55 (2005), 61–92. Even if benign tyrannies were possible to this extent, they would instantly prove themselves incompatible with the value of individualism and would thus lie outside the bounds of modernity.

[10] Aquinas, in particular, follows the classical tradition in regarding justice to be a property of the soul: see *Summa Theologiae*, II-II 58.8. For the significance of the idea of the 'just society' as a modern category of thought, see Chapter 10 below.

place law at the centre. Through a series of suggestive intellectual trans-formations, law is understood to articulate an as-yet-imperfectly-realized liberal democratic theory of justice, and thus itself to possess a liberal democratic character.[11]

Legalism connects democracy with the question of political authority. Some of the social conditions to which individuals are subject are exter-nally imposed through rules. All social conditions are in principle capable of variation through rules. Individuals are therefore owed an explanation of the basis and justification of the power that imposes rules. This is a distinctively modernist idiom: the question of authority arises in this form as a result of the conception of an individual as an otherwise free agent subject to a set of unfortunately necessary yet externally imposed constraints. Impressed by the power of government to revise a wide variety of social conditions, habit and tradition are conceived as every-where subordinate to rule. In order to secure the 'liberal' character of society, it is thought that the mandate to exercise power must be some-how traceable back to the individuals upon whom it is subjected. (Indeed, in the less sophisticated versions of contractarian philosophy, the exercise of the vote is seen as a means of donating power from the individual to the government.)

Ideas connecting the idea of justice to the structure of the democratic and liberal regime are nourished on the same illusions that give structure and direction to Hobbes's philosophy. Political power is assumed to stem from a finite and identifiable origin, and thus to have an ultimate 'justification'. In the very passages in which Hobbes places the notion of power at the heart of political philosophy, he gestures toward an understanding in which power is endemic to the complexity of the human situation: 'The passions that most of all cause the difference of wit, are principally the more or less desire for power, of riches, of knowledge, and of honour. All of which may be reduced to the first, that is, desire of power. For riches, knowledge and honour are but several sorts of power.'[12] The very variety of the human situation is an outpour-ing of essentially the same continuous force. A desire for power runs constantly throughout the human condition. The presence of power is inherently presupposed in all forms of human association (being present in the very idea of 'association'), and does not intrude upon association, either naturally or through deliberate effort, after its establishment.

---

[11] See especially R Dworkin, *Law's Empire* (London, Fontana, 1986), chs 6 and 7.
[12] Hobbes, *Leviathan*, ch 8.

Where the power to determine conditions of interaction lies *wholly* within the individuals concerned, we have the antithesis of society, and only the hypothetical possibility of engagement. Such a condition of abstract equality would amount to the possession by each individual of a 'right of nature', each man being conceived as an *ens completum* whose every interaction is an occasion of conflict rather than of association. Within society, man is partly determined by external conditions (such as those of language) and partly by the ability to move voluntarily within the opportunities presented by those conditions. All forms of association contain loci of power that are external to individuals and which lie outside their control. Hobbes is able to identify an origin for *political* power only by insisting that men enjoy no form of association until one is specifically erected over them: 'This great Leviathan, which is called the state, is a work of art; it is an artificial man made for the protection and salvation of the natural man, to whom it is superior in grandeur and power.'[13]

It is easy to ignore the magnitude of the steps taken by Hobbes. In proposing a radically formal *pax civilis*, Hobbes sweeps away the traditional categories in which politics was understood in the classical and medieval treatments. There is no *regimen politicum*, and strictly speaking no *regimen regale*, but a new situation in which the incorporation of a 'people' occurs at the precise moment when the political order is entirely deduced from its first appearance. If we are inclined to reject the picture suggested by Hobbes's standpoint, then we may come to see that the conception of democracy as an analysis or recommendation of the bases of authority of offices of power is misconceived; for centres of power *have* no identifiable basis in that sense.

Earlier political philosophies were alive to the inevitable presence of concentrations of power within a form of association. The establishment of a *regimen* did not involve the creation of power, but its *assertion*. Not its realization, but its *organization*. But organization has its limits. Power that is manifested within social conditions can no more be brought under complete control than can the tides of the oceans. Like the tides, it is bound to be useful but it can also be uncontrollable and destructive. If human beings can know peace of mind, exercise reflective control, nevertheless it is states which most truly resemble the Hobbesian depiction of ceaseless activity, the inability to achieve an equilibrium point which does not demand further action or imply additional consequence.

[13] Hobbes, *Leviathan* (introduction to the Latin edition).

Democracy is correctly interpreted as an understanding of the manner, rather than the basis, of government.[14] If we forget this fact, a certain recklessness leads to the characterization of democracy as an integral element in a general theory of justice. Neglecting habit and tradition, the centrality of rule is exaggerated, so that a society's law becomes automatically the moral theory of its state. It is natural that this moral theory will come to regard this same law as central to the balancing of individual freedoms with the collective control required for a stable and peaceful society in which such freedoms can be meaningfully exercised. Within a legalist standpoint, the values of individualism and collectivism represent the polarities that inform attempts to establish and justify this balance. Because they constitute the mutually defined antitheses of the notion of legalism rather than fully independent visions of politics, all but the most eccentric political writings will exhibit the pull of both dispositions in the particular balance struck. Where democracy is mistaken for a value system rather than a mode of governance, one is led to a mischaracterization of the collectivist elements that are inevitably present in a legalist (i.e., 'modern') vision of politics. Not merely *directive* in character, necessary in order to keep the ship of state afloat, those elements will present themselves as of a *purposive* character, subverting the very intellectual underpinnings of individualism that gave rise to these developments.

The emergence of 'the individual' as the central character in the field of morality and politics signals the appearance of a non-purposive form of association. In a non-purposive political order, the function of law is to facilitate human endeavour rather than direct society towards a common goal. Recognition of the individual as an *ens completum*, deriving its character from the will rather than from external social forces, effectively brought to an end the idea that the human condition could be described in terms of a moral rather than a merely biological or historical, nexus. Whatever moral properties could be deduced from this condition were thought to spring precisely from the *absence* of any unifying features of 'moral man': that is to say, from a supposed basic condition of *freedom*.

---

[14] That democracy does not, strictly speaking, concern the distribution of power throughout society is reflected in the numerous forms democratic rule can take: from an elected monarchy invested with unfettered power, to a democratically established government backed up by a vast but unelected bureaucracy and judiciary, to the various levels of inclusiveness (or sphere of operation) that can be associated with the franchise (to name but a few).

The absence of a common condition of human flourishing intimated a style of politics in which the endeavour was not to seek the alignment of all individuals in a single direction, understood as improving the collective lot (or, equivalently, as the perfection of the human character or the salvation of the soul), but the maximization of opportunities for personal development along numerous and opposing trajectories.[15] This style of politics is uniquely appropriate to the human condition as it is understood by Hobbes. Human life itself is ceaseless motion, offering no possibility of tranquillity of mind in a static condition of being-in-the-world. In the absence of a *summum bonum*, the recognition of 'progress' appears not as the manifestation of united movement in any one direction, but constant movement in many different directions simultaneously.

At the same time, this style of politics has an almost inevitably self-transforming character. It has rightly been suggested that a free society requires some measure of confidence in the ability of citizens to reach tentative and tolerable adjustments between their competing interests, and on this basis to arrive at common notions of justice.[16] Too often despairing of mankind's capacity for justice, governments insist upon the *imposition* of order. The regulation of social life alone preserves its 'social' character! The capital and labour markets have been liberalized, but they have never been more controlled. Social and economic life is 'free', but its happenings demand to be given a meaning. The history of the open society must confirm and deepen the glory of its own central values.

Lacking the constant and determined act of will necessary to avoid it, Western philosophers have found it difficult to resist the impulse to move from what might be termed a politics of 'minimum duty' to a politics of 'aspiration'. A politics of minimum duty seeks to institute conditions in which individuals can formulate and pursue radically opposing projects without thereby assuring their descent into anarchy and mutual self-destruction. Its central theme is that the life of total freedom without law is the life 'solitary, poor, nasty, brutish and short', and the freedom of unrestrained competition nothing but the slavery of the individual to the play of circumstance. Philosophers drawn to this image cannot resist concluding that the life of the *Rechtsstaat* is the realization of an improved condition of humanity and not merely a

---

[15] See I Hunter, *Rival Enlightenments* (Cambridge University Press, 2001).

[16] See R Niebuhr, 'The Children of Light and the Children of Darkness', in R McAfee Brown (ed.), *The Essential Reinhold Niebuhr* (New Haven CT, Yale University Press, 1986), 160.

random alternative to the 'state of nature'. ('O, if through confidence misplaced They fail, thy saving arms, dread Power! around them cast.'[17]) Thus, an aspirational element is reintroduced into politics: for the recognition will gradually dawn on the collective political consciousness that this improvement is realized never absolutely, but is present only by degrees. A purposive concern with further refinement, perhaps unavoidably expressed in terms of 'equality' and 'justice', will reassert itself within the political imagination.

A politics that identifies justice with the form of the state is not inevitable. It is not a logical consequence of the morality of individualism. But the moral idiom of modernity, most visible in the value of legalism, lends itself to a series of subtle transformations which make this development appear both possible and desirable. At the most basic level, government consists in the deliberate variation of circumstances that affect the person. Mankind is 'rescued from the blind play of Chance'.[18] The factors which affect man are not entirely neutral phenomena. An understanding of the scope and possibilities for deliberate modification depend upon an interpretation of the character of the human person. Conceiving the person to be an 'individual', modern thinking is driven toward a specific conception of government. The methods and style of government appropriate to the individual are clearly different from those which would appear in the context of, for example, 'social man', or of the 'religious exile' whose character is completed in its journey towards heaven, and the government of which would seem to demand the creation of opportunities for grace rather than the accumulation of material wealth.[19] In these latter two cases, appropriate limitations on governance remain difficult to trace precisely, insofar as the character of 'the person' cannot be sharply delineated from the social circumstances in which it moves. The metaphysical image associated with these anti-modern characters is not that of a distinct and unified centre of motivations that is complete and intelligible on its own terms prior to its engagement with the social world. It consists in the enumeration of different personas, identified in relation to the contexts of

---

[17] William Wordsworth, 'Ode to Duty', in A Quiller-Couch (ed.), *The Oxford Book of English Verse: 1250–1900* (Oxford, Clarendon Press, 1919), no. 531. On the notions of 'duty' and 'aspiration' see L Fuller, *The Morality of Law*, 2nd edn (New Haven CT, Yale University Press, 1969), ch 1.

[18] Fuller (above n 17), 19.

[19] See e.g. Dante, *Inferno*, R Kirkpatrick (ed.) (London, Penguin Classics, 2006); Augustine, *Confessions*, H Chadwick (ed.) (Oxford University Press, 1992).

their emergence, and instantiated in a 'human person'. The unity of the person is present in its logical identity over time.[20] Completed only *in* society, and not in abstraction from it, this idea of the person is not straightforwardly compatible with a bounded conception of governance as the variation of a particular range of external conditions. Unlike the character of the 'individual', or the 'moral agent', there is not the uniformity or equality of distribution of personas (or of the capacity for their adoption) amongst 'persons' requisite to the identification of fixed limits.

Except in times of civil crisis, the metaphysical interpretation of human nature will be largely inherited, its basis and particulars buried deep and forgotten in the accumulated strata of social practice. But it is from this understanding that notions of government are formed, and from which one derives a sense of its 'inevitable' character. It should not be imagined that *fewer* limits on government exist in relation to anti-modern characters. Various personas being constituted and determined by the contexts of their emergence, it is likely that the sphere of government will be greatly diminished and that of 'natural necessity' correspondingly amplified. The question of 'limitation' is modulated into one concerning the *province* of government in relation to other elements of the social fabric (such as ecclesiastical polity as a spiritual 'estate' rather than arm of 'the state') through which the human character is nurtured and developed. In this can be observed the irony of the morality of individualism. The existence of a sharp distinction between what is internal to the individual will (as the centre of agency) and the external (social) conditions that act upon it, supplies the ideological basis for the imposition of a single condition of circumstance upon all persons. Every distinct centre of agency constituting a force 'external' to others, the identification of the limits of the range of conditions which it is proper for government to regulate, is simultaneously an assertion of a power to determine a form of life that is to be common for all individuals. This is not an incidental feature of the practice of moral individualism, for the possibility of central control can be realized only in relation to that which is fixed and uniform.

The distinction between the mode of existence experienced by 'the individual' and those of other possible characters that might be placed at the centre of politics is not a question of the *degree* to which the human

---

[20] This identity, or temporal sameness, is capable of interpretation variously as one of material substance (understood perhaps biologically), or spiritually, as in the idea of the soul, or will, psyche, ego, etc.

person is subject to or determined by external social forces. It is a question of the direction in which those forces are mustered, and the ends they might be thought to serve. Government needs to be sensitive to, and tolerant of, the directive qualities of social forces. Legalism is subject to an inevitable tendency to consolidate social conditions in a form that favours collectivism, even at the same time as it emphasizes the value of individualism. At the abstract level, the centrality and emancipatory intent of law promote the coherence of a single system of governance, and exhibit intolerance of the diversity of direction associated with the existence of relatively independent centres of power (such as churches, guilds, etc.) distributed throughout society. At the level of concrete engagement, the emergence of 'the individual' was accompanied by the recognition of a body of human rights that are appropriate to its character.[21] The delineation of these rights also involved the delineation of areas of responsibility, duty, unfreedom, etc. that correspond to the right when the external conditions of association are contemplated from the internal perspective of the will. Legalism invites a notion of the morality of social engagement as a matter for government (hence the emergence of the idea of 'political morality') rather than for individuals or for organized communities of individuals.

Ideas of 'political morality' are naturally interpreted as serving one unified vision of the material fate of mankind rather than a multiplicity of ends. By contrast, narrower communities which specify a particular mode of social engagement will not in general share the aims and ambitions for the government of the individual even if they are largely 'external' to that character. The moral contexts supplied by interpersonal communities such as congregations, professional bodies, workers' unions, etc., are generally better understood in terms of the development of the range of personas with which they are concerned, rather than the manipulation of subordinates as pawns sacrificed to some external end. Modern history (conditioned by the appearance of the individual) undoubtedly discloses the propensity of such communities to embrace movements towards tyranny, and the incipient dangers they present of

---

[21] These 'human' rights, though conceived in the character of universals, are of course a reflection of 'the human person' as presented in the moral idiom of the individual, rather than of the manifold other guises in which it appears throughout the world. See M Oakeshott, 'The Masses in Representative Democracy', in *Rationalism in Politics*, revised edn (Indianapolis IN, Liberty Fund, 1991), Essay 11; and R Geuss, *History and Illusion in Politics* (Cambridge University Press, 2001), ch 3.

sublimating and finally overwhelming individual identity. Perhaps the clearest intimation of this can be found in Marxism:

> Only when real, individual man reabsorbs into himself the abstract citizen and becomes a species-being, in his everyday life, in his individual work, and in his individual relationships; only when man recognises and organises his '*forces propres*', his own powers, as social powers, and consequently no longer separates from himself social force in the shape of political force: only then will human emancipation be accomplished.[22]

The moral idiom of 'social man', therefore, might be thought to display subjection to an internal tension of its own, readily lapsing into an antithetical state in which the character of the human person finally loses its identity except as a vehicle for the advancement of the collective existence. There may be truth in this, but if so it is a truth that requires skilful application to its historic contexts (such as that of feudalism). Yet it is in this mode of moral thinking rather than that of legalism, that the character of government is finally revealed.

Wisdom and unwisdom in politics

How should philosophers understand the character of government today? Leaving behind the ancient and medieval preoccupation with the perfection of the human character, its habits, inner attitudes and temperaments, the legalist understanding of politics concerned itself with the perfectibility of the external circumstances in which this character can pursue its own conception of human flourishing. The collective political concern with an ideal of human perfection has not disappeared, but has been mutated into the pursuit of social utopias. Those who have doubted the reality or value of utopias for the guidance of political decision have not relinquished the notion of improvement of the human lot as the overarching purpose of politics. What else but improvement can give politics its purposive, non-random character? Valuing improvement, philosophers who have avoided utopias partake of essentially the same understanding of the condition of human perfection: one that is not dependent on the cultivation of a particular persona or inward state of grace, but is both concrete and of the here-and-now. Improvement of the human situation is a worldly rather than a spiritual condition, roughly to be equated with the degree of independence of

---

[22] Marx, 'On the Jewish Question', in *Early Writings* (London, Penguin, 1992).

each individual will to pursue its own trajectory, and to achieve a level of mastery over its own situation.

Attached to this idea, jurisprudential writers have glimpsed in law a tool of government central to the creation of these external conditions. The process of creation is typically advanced through the rubric of freedom and right, but in practice it requires the bestowal of specific measures of equality where a diversity of conditions would otherwise exist. The character of this politics is a reinvention of the Pelagian heresy: an ethical vision in which human perfectibility is realizable by solely human means, and the possibility of which entails the imperative of its pursuit above all other goals. 'The fully autonomous individual' may be the final 'condition of being' associated with the state of perfection, but the pursuit of this ideal must involve the sacrifice of all particular individuals, and their divergent interests, to the final goal.[23]

Under the illusion that there are no limits to the sphere in which human powers can meet with success in identifying and attaining ends, lacking a sense of the limits of human perfectibility, philosophers have been less critical of the accumulation of limitless power at the centre as a means of organizing human effort toward the final goal. Failing to perceive its falsity, philosophers have not comprehended the unwisdom of a society conceived along these lines, forever trading current effort and hardship for an indefinitely postponed good.

The politics of modernity contain a vision of human perfection as a profane condition of things. Perfection is understood not as a preferred mode of life, but as an achievement of institutional neutrality: the equal value of all possible modes of life consonant with the character of 'the individual'. How real is this sense of neutrality? Having sanctified a certain set of worldly values, modern societies have created a specific form of life. It is a mode of life which emerges as dominant given a starting point from which all things are valued equally. By denying a spiritual dimension to the idea of perfection, no additional meaning can be found in external reality beyond the value that is placed upon it by individual predilection or desire. The spiritual significance of things

---

[23] As Kolakowski has noted, there is therefore an affinity between Pelagian thought and the Marxist ideal of the sublimation of the individual to the collective identity: see L Kolakowski, *Modernity on Endless Trial* (Chicago, University of Chicago Press, 1990), ch 7. See also Augustine, *Four Anti-Pelagian Writings* (Washington DC, Catholic University of America Press, 1992). For an alternative understanding of the consequences of Pelagian thought in modern politics see Oakeshott, *The Politics of Faith and the Politics of Scepticism* (New Haven CT, Yale University Press, 1996), ch 2.

becomes the equal significance (and thus insignificance) of all things. The goodness or otherwise of a given set of circumstances from the human point of view comes to depend upon the ascription of meaning to things, not the discovery of meaning within them. How straitening this is of the social meanings of human circumstances! There are no perfect moral democracies, just as there are no perfect social democracies; merely popular rule and common understanding. A 'market' in ideas, based as always on supply and demand. From a supposed (though never in fact real) initial position of equality, inevitably comes a narrowing of shared conceptions of the form of life that is possible and desirable.

It was above all a shared notion of the sacred that gave pre-modern society its stability and coherence, by constantly reaffirming in practice its underpinning values. Coherence was largely a cultural phenomenon, whereas the condition of modernity is one in which coherence and stability are regarded as the function of politics. Modernity brings with it the idea of the 'political culture' of a society as supplying the unity of the state, and thus it incorporates a denial of the separation of politics from culture that is essential to the recognition of the sacred in a form of life. All political ideologies are, in the end, mutable and subject to revision or abandonment. The endless pursuit of a postponed good (our conception of which is itself endlessly changing) has led to the neglect of the *logos* as the situation which ought to be contemplated, and thus central to the political system. The value of the present is subordinated to that of the future. Possibilities for exploring the manifold facets of one's present situation are reduced: for the exercise of 'choice' that is promoted by the value of legalism is related to the pursuit of opportunities which exist *within* a politically agreed mode of existence. The centralization of directive forces is likely to lead to cultural and spiritual impoverishment. For the ability to interpret one's situation as of *present* value and significance depends upon the extent to which it is not being directed towards a clear externally defined 'end', the desirability of which is in some degree independent of the means of its realization.

The tendency of modernism to denigrate the value of habit and tradition, and its promotion of the value of deliberate rule, is the result of its unwisdom. Its suspicion of conservatism stems from a hatred of hierarchy. A desire to eliminate inequality and the structures of privilege that habit and tradition serve to entrench. But a zeal to reform these structures is the misguided product of the Pelagian view of the social world. Beginning from a belief in the possibility of human redemption within history (that is, the ability of humans to bring about a state of earthly perfection through their own collective effort), Pelagianism is subject to a fatal misconception regarding the limits within which human endeavour can bring about a collective improvement of the human lot.[24]

It is the beguiling vision of a society from which all tensions and injustices have been eradicated that justifies the centralized politics of legalism: not as a finally achievable state, but as an intelligible and coherent ideal. Yet this is not the vision intimated within the view of the *logos* inherited from Christian theology. Here, original sin, or the exile from paradise, denote a form of existence defined by the constant presence of suffering and strife, from which human action cannot release us.[25] By contrast, the politics of modernity presents an alternative (but no less metaphysically derived) understanding of human existence in which the notional recovery of an ideal state is capable of directing political activity. In the grip of this ideal, we oscillate between two incorrect views of the human condition: one in which society is no more than an association between optimally free 'individuals', complete in themselves and related only through law; and the other in which each person is a subordinate part of a collective effort to bring about improvement for all.

Philosophers must learn to embrace an alternative view of the human condition. Rejecting the modernist standpoint, they must come to regard the human situation as one to which the presence of tensions, inequalities, hardships and hierarchies of privilege are enduring and permanent. It might be said that the existence of the deplorable alongside the desirable gives the human condition its very meaning. Politics faces a difficult situation. One must not sanctify privilege or inequality. It is doubtful whether any feature of society is immutable in the face of forces of deliberate revision. But politics cannot marshall its forces for the eventual dissolution of unequal structures. Can politics hope to achieve more than the management of social tensions? Dismantling established hierarchies of position or privilege, politics does not lead to the elimination of all social disparities but merely creates others. Through organized effort, it is possible to effect movement and variation in the distribution of tensions throughout society, but not their disappearance. It is necessary to a system of politics not only to recognize the forms of

---

[24] See Kolakowski, 'Can the Devil Be Saved?', in *Modernity on Endless Trial* (above n 23), 82.

[25] Aspects of this view are clearly present in Augustine's writings, but receive an unalloyed expression in Kant's late essay, 'Religion Within the Boundaries of Mere Reason' [1793]: see AW Wood (ed.), *Religion and Rational Theology: The Cambridge Edition of the Works of Immanuel Kant* (Cambridge University Press, 1996), 39.

oppression perpetuated by the conservative elements of society, but also the need constantly to reaffirm and maintain those elements. Losing sight of this, philosophers come to regard politics only in its transformative aspect. Pursuing a blueprint of 'the perfect society' or 'the just' or 'optimal' society, they do not bring about a collective improvement to the human condition, but express contempt for it.[26]

Politics in the perspective of eternity

Modern society is not a form of association from which all eschatological understandings have receded. Incorporating an interpretation of social life in terms of a vision of human perfectibility, it is a condition characterized by the reduction of all social understandings to a single eschatology: that of the 'autonomous individual'. Seeking to bring about measures of equality in social life, the purpose of much of modern politics is to effect the elimination of entrenched hierarchies. This elimination of hierarchical divisions points to a belief in a single condition of life that is appropriate for all individuals. It is unimportant that this mode of life is understood in terms of 'freedom'. It is the belief that all individuals should be presented with *the same* range of choices and opportunities which reduces all available modes of life to a single mode. The 'open society' has done nothing to alter this. One need only reflect upon the difficulty in carving out an existence that does not depend to a very great extent upon worldly measures of success. Many obstacles stand in the way of adopting 'alternative lifestyles'. Consumerism is a condition that is literally irresistible for most people.

Government should endeavour to discover means of removing obstacles to the exploration of the endless possibilities of the *logos*. Human beings standing under political order must gain an understanding of human life as one element of a wider metaphysical order, in which the ultimate significance of human actions (and of the human predicament) is apprehended through the experience of attempting to understand that

---

[26] See Chapter 9 below. Amongst jurisprudential writers it was Lon Fuller who most clearly perceived and articulated this insight, in his constant affirmation of the requirements of stability and continuity in law (see Fuller (above n 17), ch 2), and in his observation that 'the questions involved [in adjudication] are among the permanent problems of the human race' and will thus 'continue to [present men with live questions of choice] once our era has had its say about them'. See 'The Case of the Speluncean Explorers', in P Suber (ed.), *The Case of the Speluncean Explorers: Nine New Opinions* (London, Routledge, 1998), 31.

order.[27] But governments must inevitably fail to remove *all* obstacles to exploration of the *logos*. Always human beings will stand in need of common rules which modify and restrict the behaviour of all persons as a precondition of social order. The society under law will always limit the possibilities for personal development. To suppose ultimate success in achieving the ends of government is to indulge a variant of the Pelagian view of the world, upon the rejection of which wisdom in government depends.

Impeded as well as facilitated by government, the modern citizen must become something of a detached participant. Unable to avoid becoming fully immersed in society, man at the same time does not feel entirely 'at home' in the presence of every facet of social practice, custom, rule and policy. This generalized attitude has been variously described in modern philosophy. Renaissance Italian philosophy studied the character of the 'exile', of whom Socrates was the prototype and Dante, perhaps, the epitome. This was a character condemned to live apart from fellow citizens (whether literally or spiritually), cut off from what is familiar or comfortable and forced to speak and think in a different language, following foreign laws and customs. The darker tones of Germanic philosophy captured essentially the same attitude by the concept of *angst*. But it is in French existentialist philosophy that the most appropriate manifestation of this attitude is to be found: that of 'irony'. In irony we find the same essential mixture of detachment-in-immersion present in all of these understandings, but the response, or coping mechanism, is the lighter one of gentle mockery or amusement, not the defeatism and despair of *angst* and exile. Amusement, and perhaps satire, more closely approximate to the required attributes of toleration, love and mercy which constitute the objects of wise govern-ance. The disposition of the man of *angst* or exile is seldom charitable or entirely well meaning.

[27] Shortly before his confirmation as Pope Benedict XVI, Joseph, Cardinal Ratzinger said: 'Christianity must always remember that it is the religion of the "Logos". It is faith in the "Creator Spiritus", in the Creator Spirit, from which proceeds everything that exists ... Only creative reason, which in the crucified God is manifested as love, can really show us the way. In the so necessary dialogue between secularists and Catholics, we Christians must be very careful to remain faithful to this fundamental line: to live a faith that comes from the "Logos", from creative reason, and that, because of this, is also open to all that is truly rational.' Lecture to the convent of Saint Scholastica, Subiaco, Italy, 1 April 2005. Text available at: www.catholiceducation.org/articles/politics/pg0143.html.

Utopian or improving projects abound in modern politics. Present in a thousand different forms, their significance must be properly contextualized and understood. Thinking of legalism, we might ponder the words of Comenius:

> In the last place, they led me into still another very spacious lecture room where I saw a greater number of distinguished men than anywhere else. The walls around were painted with stone walls, barriers, picket-fences, plank-fences, bars, rails, and gate staves, interspersed at various intervals by gaps and holes, doors and gates, bolts and locks, and along with it larger and smaller keys and hooks. All this they pointed out to each other, measuring where and how one might or might not pass through. 'What are these people doing?' I inquired. I was told that they were searching for means how every man in the world might hold his own or might also peacefully obtain something from another's property without disturbing order and concord. 'That is a fine thing!' I remarked. But observing it a while, it grew disgusting to me ... For, in the first place, I noticed that the barriers enclosed neither the soul, the mind, nor the body of man, but solely his property, which is of incidental importance to him; and it did not seem to me worthy of the extremely difficult toil that was, as I saw, expended upon it.[28]

---

[28] JA Comenius, *The Labyrinth of the World and the Paradise of the Heart* [1631], ch 15: 'The Pilgrim Observes the Legal Profession'.

9

Political thought and the 'well-ordered society'

Let us consider in greater detail some of the ideas and implications associated with 'utopian' political thought.

Perhaps one of the most compelling themes that Rawls's *A Theory of Justice* holds for legal philosophers, is its insistence that a 'fundamental idea' of political thought is the idea of a 'well-ordered society'. It is not entirely surprising that lawyers should find the notion of order a fascinating one, particularly when placed in association with justice. When drawing out this theme of his work, Rawls has this to say: 'the fundamental idea of a well-ordered society – society effectively regulated by a public conception of justice – is a companion idea used to specify the central organizing idea of society as a fair system of cooperation'.[1] It is easy to miss the significance of the fact that Rawls is offering a *stipulative* definition here: the momentous connection of the idea of 'well-ordered society' with one 'regulated by a public conception of justice' is announced so quietly, that one might take Rawls to be rehearsing an orthodoxy. But if we contrast this statement with what Aquinas has to say on the subject, then the importance of the move begins to become apparent. Justice, in the standard Thomistic treatment of it, refers first and foremost to a special disposition of the soul, and is thus accounted as a virtue.[2] In the shift to a social perspective, justice ceases to enjoy any intrinsic connection to the soul, for it becomes concerned, not with the cultivation of virtue or moral character (Rawls has little to say on these subjects), but with the reordering of social structures according to some overarching principle or scheme: 'fairness', or something else. Its concern is with the perfection of the social order, as distinguished from that of the individual. By contrast, Aquinas says practically nothing about political regimes, and refrains from giving specific encouragement to

[1] J Rawls, *Justice as Fairness: A Restatement* (Cambridge MA, Harvard University Press, 2001), 8. See also *A Theory of Justice* (Cambridge MA, Harvard University Press, 1971), 453.
[2] Aquinas, *Summa Theologiae*, II-II, 58.8.

any particular form of society. The 'well-ordering' of society is to be understood as a product of man's sociability and his rational character, rather than explicable in terms of organizing principles.[3]

Aquinas's remarks do not altogether dissociate questions of justice from those of well-ordering. A fundamental concern for order runs throughout Aquinas: the natural law presupposes that it is a human good to live in society,[4] and all virtues are appointed by reason orientated toward the 'common good'. In this, the discussion of justice in the *Summa Theologiae* continues a tradition of reflection on society inaugurated by Aristotle's *Politics*. But the idea that one might derive, from reflection upon the virtue of justice, a general scheme for the institutional reordering of society, is an entirely different and important possibility. It is a possibility that, despite the unremarkable circumstances of its announcement, demands direct and specific consideration.

Rawls's concern with perfecting social conditions is not without antecedents. Plato's *Republic* and other texts from the classical period had exhibited a special concern with the form of the polity. Separated by an Age, a focused concern with social institutions is visible in Rousseau's compassionate investigation into the ways in which society is unintentionally responsible for the condition of its poorest or most vulnerable members. Lying in between these examples, a wealth of philosophical and literary texts purported to describe or reveal the form of the 'ideal state'. Often elaborate and intricate in their exploration of exact social conditions, these texts, which include Flavius Philostratus's *Life of Apollonius of Tyana* (c. 217 BC), and later works such as Bacon's *New Atlantis* (1627), embodied direct institutional depictions of the right or optimal way of life. Kant's *Rechtslehre* (1797) itself, perhaps the closest in method and an acknowledged source of inspiration for *A Theory of Justice*, attempts to derive the general form of society from a basis of ethical doctrine.

It is not the intellectual origins of Rawls's position which are so much in question, in drawing attention to these comparisons, but the implications Rawls's position raises for the way in which politics is understood. Much can be gained by reading Rawls in the context of some of these earlier efforts. Speaking apropos of Rousseau's remarks on social themes, Ernest Fortin suggested that:

---

[3] See Aquinas's remarks on the relationship between 'special' and 'general' justice: ibid., II-II 58.6–7. Aquinas's distinction does not precisely correspond to that of Aristotle: see *Nicomachean Ethics*, 1129b 17–31.

[4] Aquinas, *Summa Theologiae*, I-II, 94.2.

> To appreciate the overwhelming impact of Rousseau's accomplishment, one has only to observe the passionate interest evinced by later writers in such hitherto neglected classes of society as the needy, the disadvantaged, the marginalized, the criminals, and the outlaws. A classic example of this new and thoroughly Rousseauean mentality is Victor Hugo's *Les Miserables*, which places the blame for the evils that afflict human beings on society alone and whose true heros are the convicts, the fallen women, the abandoned children, and the wayward victims of poverty or oppression, for whom it expresses unbounded pity and affection. If society and its accidental structures are the primary cause of the corruption of human beings and the evils attendant upon it, they must be changed. Social reform takes precedence over personal reform; ... [b]etter institutions will give us better human beings, and not vice-versa.[5]

It is the essentially *transformative* concern that lies behind such positions, which must be considered. The desire for transformation is one that is deeply rooted in the human mind, but nowhere more evident than in visions of political 'utopias'. Thus Oscar Wilde once said, 'A map of the world that does not include Utopia is not worth even glancing at, for it leaves out the one country at which humanity is always landing.'[6]

There is, as Aurel Kolnai famously observed, a central contradiction in the thought of one whose political vision might be described as 'utopian', or transformative. Within the utopian project, man is given two contradictory roles. On the one hand, he is centrally responsible for the construction of a radically new social world. On the other, he is thought of as the passive product of the society which precedes him.[7] In Pierre Manent's words, '[Man] is thus at the same time the omnipotent master of society and its raw material or docile creation. He is both sovereign artificer and mere matter.'[8] Manent goes on to observe that one cannot avoid thinking of Thomas Hobbes in this connection, who in *Leviathan* presents man in precisely this double role. But if we wish to penetrate the underlying ideas of Rawls's position, we might gain much by returning to the first appearance of 'Utopia' in Thomas More's *Utopia*.

---

[5] E Fortin, 'Natural Law and Social Justice', reprinted in JB Benestad (ed.), *Classical Christianity and the Political Order: Collected Essays*, vol. II (Lanham MD, Rowman & Littlefield, 1996), 235.

[6] O Wilde, *The Soul of Man Under Socialism* (London, Forgotten Books, 2008), 18.

[7] See A Kolnai, *The Utopian Mind and Other Papers* (London, Athlone, 1995); also 'The Utopian Mind', reprinted in Kolnai, *Privilege and Liberty and Other Essays in Political Philosophy* (Lanham MD, Lexington Books, 1999), 121–32.

[8] P Manent, 'Introduction' to Kolnai, *The Utopian Mind* (above n 7). The essay also appears in Manent, *Modern Liberty and its Discontents* (Lanham MD, Rowman & Littlefield, 1998), 135–47.

In 1518, two years after the book's publication, More accepted a place on the privy council under Henry VIII, and began a career at court. Though having held various political positions in earlier life, More had long been deeply impressed with the idea of the monastic life, and had apparently agonized over the decision to pursue a political career.[9] At the root of More's hesitancy was a tension between two conceptions of humanism that is germane to an understanding of utopian thought. The form of political thought that was associated with Plato held to the view that a life of *otium* (literally, of peace, and therefore of freedom from involvement in public affairs) is essential for the achievement both of happiness and of our highest and proper ends. By contrast, the life of *negotium* (of business, or of strife and contestation) was to be avoided, in virtue of its inherent corruption.[10] Involvement in such a world would force the philosopher to turn away from truth, to a world of compromise, hypocrisy and worldly interest in which truth must be accommodated to the times. An alternative line of thought concluded, on the other hand, that the effort to bring about an *optimus status republicae* could hardly avoid involvement in a 'civic' scale of values; indeed, that it was the responsibility of the philosopher to labour in order to bring about the conditions for a just and well-ordered social life. This 'civic humanism' has its origins in Cicero's *De Officiis*: Cicero admits that the 'most eminent philosophers' have 'withdrawn from public affairs' in quest of serenity; but he entirely disagrees with this tendency, stating that 'duty will not suffer one to be drawn away from the active management of affairs', and that 'the reputation of virtue consists wholly in active life'.[11]

More himself offered a strong criticism of the Platonist position. The Platonic philosopher's desire to insulate himself from the world, he says, produces only a narrow scholasticism; even perhaps a failure of virtue: 'Even if you cannot pull out evil opinions by the roots, even if you cannot manage to reform well-entrenched vices according to your own beliefs,

---

[9] See Erasmus, Letter to Ulrich von Hutten (*Ep.* cccxlvii); also RW Chambers, *Thomas More* (London, Jonathan Cape, 1935), 112–17. In 1510, More had completed a translation of a biography of Giovanni Pico della Mirandola, who had definitively chosen the contemplative life.

[10] See the words of Giovanni da Ravenna, quoted by Q Skinner, 'Sir Thomas More's *Utopia*', in A Pagden (ed.), *The Languages of Political Theory in Early Modern Europe* (Cambridge University Press, 1987), 127: 'No life is more miserable, more uncertain, more self-deceiving.'

[11] Cicero, *De Officiis*, AP Peabody (trans.) (Boston MA, Little, Brown & Co, 1887), I.20 and I.6 respectively.

you must not therefore abandon the commonwealth!'[12] In many ways, Book I of *Utopia* can be interpreted as a justification of More's decision to prioritize the life of public office over that of quiet contemplation which he otherwise much admired.[13] The *optimus status republicae* that is presented in Book II is therefore not to be understood as a state for which unbounded enthusiasm should be shown, and an ultimate condition for which present forms of social life should be abandoned. *All* regimes are regarded as containing elements of negotiated order, as well as dimensions of governance in which one is obliged to entrust one's wellbeing to the hands of others. At the close of Book II, More confesses that many of the 'manners and laws' of Utopia seem to him 'very absurd'. His closing words suggest, indeed, that he wishes no radical interruption of historical traditions of governance, but that the attainment of the 'best state of a commonwealth' must come via the continual adjustment of the conditions of the present: 'I cannot perfectly agree to everything [Hythloday, the narrator] has related; however, there are many things in the Commonwealth of Utopia that I rather wish, than hope, to see followed in our governments.'[14]

The equivocation in this last sentence is characteristic of More's position in the remainder of the work. This casts a degree of doubt upon the interpretation of some scholars of the text, who regard its aim as describing the 'best' state that human reason can hope to establish in the absence of revelation: Quentin Skinner, in particular, suggests that it is More's purpose, not to lead his reader to either admiration or rejection of utopian life as a whole, but to give serious consideration to Utopia as an *optimus status*.[15] More's often ambivalent and equivocal remarks about utopian society are in stark contrast to the confidence that Rawls and other modern writers, such as Dworkin, display toward their intellectual creation. To reflect upon the utopian character of such positions, one need only consider the ease with which the political visions of *A Theory of Justice*, or *Law's Empire*, could be recast in the form of literary utopias. This tendency is perhaps especially apparent in the case of Dworkin, whose writing is of a more literary style. In a passage entitled 'Law's Dreams', he says: 'The courts are the capitals of law's empire, and judges are its princes, but not its seers and prophets. It falls to philosophers, if

---

[12] More, *Utopia* (1516), Bk I.

[13] See B Bradshaw, 'More on Utopia', XXIV *Historical Journal* (1981), 1–27; Skinner (above n 10), 134–35.

[14] More, *Utopia*, Bk II.   [15] Skinner (above n 10), 123–4.

they are willing, to work out law's ambitions for itself, the purer form of law within and beyond the law we have.'[16] But this is not simply a vision of a faraway land; it is at the same time an idealized projection of the society of the present and immediate sphere of experience (so long as it is in a 'flourishing' condition):

> [I]n a flourishing legal system, even important changes can be seen as flowing from the law in place, enriching that law, changing its base, and so provoking further change. So utopian legal politics is, in that broad way, law still. Its philosophers offer large programs that can, if they take hold in lawyers' imagination, make its progress more deliberate and reflective. They are chain novelists with epics in mind, imagining the work unfolding through volumes it may take generations to write. In that sense, each of their dreams is already latent in the present law.[17]

It is a vision that is at once present and remote: one that is the subject (unlike More's) not merely of idle wish, but of hope; hope that is directed, not only toward 'many things' in the imagined condition, but to the totality of systematic thought and circumstance that contains them. Though connected with the present through the tenuous idea of being an 'interpretation' of it, such a vision may indeed fall short of constituting a 'political philosophy' in the proper sense. A political philosophy, as Raymond Geuss observes, 'is not really an exclusively theoretical construction, but it must also be seen as an attempt to intervene in the world of politics'.[18] A similar observation can be made concerning Rawls's theory: though its conclusions and recommendations take the form of constitutional arrangements much like those of the modern United States, the argument of A Theory of Justice relates entirely to principles of institutional structure and distribution in the abstractly conceived framework of a 'well-ordered society'. Its deliberators are not citizens, but social architects working behind a 'veil of ignorance', in an 'original position' (not a socially, historically or culturally embedded one).[19] As such, the theory is not genuinely an attempt to intervene in the political realities of the present world, but a normative insistence that the totality implied by these realities be replaced by another that is both intricately elaborate and self-contained. Like Dworkin's vision, it can be accused of having confused politics with a mindless catechism.[20]

---

[16] R Dworkin, *Law's Empire* (London, Fontana, 1986), 407. [17] Ibid., 409.
[18] R Geuss, *Outside Ethics* (Princeton University Press, 2005), 35.
[19] Rawls, *A Theory of Justice* (above n 1), 137.
[20] A Badiou, *Ethics: An Essay on the Understanding of Evil* (London, Verso, 2001), liii.

What connects utopianism to politics?

However impressive the interior structures of an idealized or 'well-ordered' society, its conception is obviously intended to fulfil some practical purpose. However lacking its adherents may be in an abiding interest in the state of the world outside their universities, theories like that of Rawls purport to embody not simply a feat of intellection that is aesthetically attractive, but also a morally serious construction.[21] To say that the theory is related normatively to the reality gives little away about this ultimate purpose. Anyone who strives to establish or uncover a distinctively moral perspective on life must at some stage renounce the notion that history is normative of the content of politics. What, then, leads a writer to frame his normative considerations in terms of a structure which must be adopted *at the expense of*, and not simply by adjusting, the current form of life? Again, More's own motives offer insights into the possible rationales which lie behind the utopian project.

One possible interpretation of More's position is that he wishes to indicate the separation of properly political questions from those of the spiritual life. As Skinner observes, the main seam of humanist thought was concerned, not with the best state, but (as Erasmus put it) the proper or right way of life 'such that, if you are instructed in it, you can attain that state of mind which is worthy of a true Christian'.[22] Insofar as the 'best state' was in question in humanist thought, it tended to arise in the context of examining the relationship between the best form of the state and the attainment of that form of life 'wherein lieth the perfection of man'.[23] More separates these questions: first of all by announcing his interest as concerning only the *optimus status* in the title of the work,[24] and secondly through the attitude of the character of Hythloday. Hythloday makes clear that there are no settled religious beliefs in Utopia, indeed '[t]here are several sorts of religions, not only in different parts of the island, but even in every town'.[25] Many of these are pagan in character, sharing little but basic ideas such as the immortality of the

---

[21] For doubts about this, see Geuss (above n 18), 36–7.

[22] Skinner (above n 10), 148, quoting Erasmus, *Enchiridion Militis Christiani* [1525], 14.

[23] Ibid., quoting T Starkey, *Dialogue Between Reginald Pole & Thomas Lupset*, KM Burton (ed.) (Cambridge University Press, 1948), 26.

[24] 'De optimo republicae statu deque nova insula Utopia.'

[25] More, *Utopia*, Bk II. On the literary significance of Hythloday's name (and of More's itself), see JC Davis, 'Thomas More's *Utopia*: Sources, Legacy and Interpretation', in G Claeys (ed.), *The Cambridge Companion to Utopian Literature* (Cambridge University Press, 2010), 29–30.

soul, and the fact that the moral life is connected to religious ideas. But the Utopians also believe that 'every man might be of what religion he pleases, and though he might endeavour to draw others to it by means of argument, and by amicable and modest ways, yet it must be without bitterness against those of other opinions'.[26] Because nothing about religious creeds is certain, all must be tolerated 'with a gentle and unprejudiced mind', and none should be made the principle of the state. For Hythloday, the *optimus status* is achieved on purely rational and political grounds: the abolition of private property, and of the monetary economy. This would seem to indicate that the 'best state' is something that is achievable on the basis of rationality and human efforts alone, i.e. that it is a historical achievement potentially open to all societies, and does not depend upon any special processes of history or revelation.

But there is a deeper point lying behind More's separation of these moral/spiritual and political questions, which comes into focus when we connect its appearance to More's broader Christian humanist concerns. Hythloday is in effect advancing the Platonist argument that one's inner beliefs about the perfect life are distinct from the form taken by public affairs. Being a Christian no less than a Platonist, he even goes so far as saying that whilst the Utopians have have achieved perfection in public affairs, they have made much less progress in the optimization of individual life: lacking knowledge of the soteriological message of the Gospels, they are 'more inclinable to that opinion that places ... the chief part of a man's happiness in pleasure' rather than in virtue.[27] The figure of More in the narrative is critical of this standpoint. The *otium* required for the deepening of one's speculative thoughts upon perfection cannot be separated from the *negotiation* of order: the 'proper scene' for philosophy is the public realm itself, to the exact circumstances of which philosophy must constantly strive to 'accommodate itself'.[28] It is indeed the task of the philosopher to amend common opinions so that they 'may be as little ill as possible'; 'for except all men were good, everything cannot be right'.[29]

More argues, in effect, that there can be no appearance of the *optimus status* in the absence of the optimization of virtue in individual life: or, in other words, that the perfection of the state can be realized only when human beings have perfected their own condition. The characters of More and Hythloday in fact agree substantially upon the obstacles which

[26] Ibid. [27] Ibid. [28] Ibid., Bk I. [29] Ibid.

stand in the way of this perfectiblity: it is pride, 'that infernal serpent that creeps into the hearts of mortal men, and possesses them too easily to be drawn out'.[30] But for Hythloday, the root of this evil is *money*. Pride feeds on money: 'Pride thinks its own happiness shines the brighter by comparing it with the misfortunes of other persons; that by displaying its own wealth, they may feel their poverty more sensibly.' If monetary economy were abolished, how easily might man overcome this defect of the soul!

> Who does not see that the frauds, thefts, robberies, quarrels, tumults, contentions, seditions, murders, treacheries, and witchcrafts, . . . would all disappear, if money were no longer valued by the world?[31]

But More sweeps aside this thought with a single sentence. Of all the absurdities he identifies in Hythloday's description of Utopia, the one which 'seemed the foundation of all the rest' is precisely 'their living in common, without the use of money, by which all nobility, splendour, and majesty . . . would be quite taken away'. More implies that the corrupting factors which afflict the soul are *precisely* those which, at one and the same time, constitute the imperfection of the polity, and cannot be eradicated from the human condition. It is for this reason that he can 'wish', but fail to 'hope', that elements of Utopia can be realized in our governments.[32]

Rawls, by contrast, considers the 'well-ordered society' of his theory as being merely a 'special case' amongst 'other societies'.[33] At the same time, it is to be contrasted with 'existing societies' which 'are of course seldom well-ordered in this sense'.[34] One is powerfully reminded of Kolnai's observation that whilst 'the vision and description of an imaginary world is eminently fit to provide a framework for perfectionist speculations, yearnings and fantasies', still the 'aspiration to substitute a perfect for the imperfect human world (including man's own nature, character and morals) will quite appropriately seek a tentative expression in constructions and anticipations' providing 'a fictitious concreteness and embodied presence'.[35] The fact is that Rawls is only able to offer a vision of the well-ordered society because he removes it from the world of experience: it is 'a closed system isolated from other societies', in which '[e]veryone is

---

[30] Ibid., Bk II.   [31] Ibid.

[32] We might recall Aristotle's words in *Politics*, II.1–5, that Plato's ideal republic in instituting communism of property and of human relationships (the abolition of family), etc. is both undesirable and impossible of achievement.

[33] Rawls (above n 19), 8.   [34] Ibid., 6.

[35] Kolnai, 'The Utopian Mind' (above n 7), 121.

presumed to act justly and to do his part in upholding just institutions'.[36] The essentially insular nature of utopias is brilliantly satirized by Leszek Kolakowski's tales of the fictional Kingdom of Lailonia, which illustrate various aspects of 'human inability to come to terms with imperfection, infinitude, history and nature':

> We wasted a vast amount of time, my brother and I, on searching for the Kingdom of Lailonia. First we asked all our friends if they knew in what part of the world it lay, but no one could tell us. Then we even took to stopping strangers in the street to ask them the same question, but they all shrugged and said they didn't know. After that we started sending letters to all sorts of clever people who wrote books, so you would have thought they ought to know, and they all replied very politely and said they were very sorry they couldn't help, but really none of them had any idea where the Kingdom of Lailonia lay.[37]

If we consider what Kolnai has to say on the subject of utopias, we begin to understand that this insularity is an important dimension of utopian thinking. For him, utopian visions are 'intrinsically at war with the basic structure of reality', in being relentlessly human in their authorship and construction.[38] The principle of such societies is that they are 'determined by one unitary and sovereign human authorship: sprung from *one* human mind with its peculiar vision, scale of preferences, habits of reasoning, and imagination, although calculated to carry a more or less universal appeal'.[39] It is easy to miss the significance of the fact that, in Rawls's model, everyone can be 'presumed to act justly and to do his part in upholding just institutions': not because, in the presence of just institutions, human beings will let go of greed, envy, hate, and small-mindedness of all kinds; but because they are intrinsically creatures of the model. They move only when Rawls's mind moves them, in the ways required by the overall vision, and are not (in the way that human beings usually are) separate from the whole. No power, however concentrated, can similarly coordinate the thoughts and actions of citizens. 'Real' power inevitably 'reflects a plurality of distinct minds, attitudes, tastes, interests and wills'.[40] Like the philosophical thought of More's contemplation, thoughts of power can have no existence or reality except in continual

---

[36] Rawls (above n 19), 8.

[37] L Kolakowski, *Tales from the Kingdom of Lailonia* (University of Chicago Press, 1972), 3. One is reminded that 'Utopia' itself is a play on words: 'eutopia' (meaning the place where all things are well) and 'utopia' ('no-place').

[38] Kolnai (above n 7), 122–3.   [39] Ibid., 123.   [40] Ibid.

adjustment to the world. That is why the system of justice and the functioning of institutions in the model must be closed, and 'isolated from other societies', or centres of negotiation. Utopia can exist nowhere, or it can exist everywhere; but not merely 'somewhere'.[41]

A political vision that is utopian in its heart is therefore in the highest degree likely to exhibit intolerance toward regimes in which the ideals of the model are not central. Thus in his late work, *The Law of Peoples*, Rawls's treatment of international relations is premised upon a taxonomy of societies in which the notion of a 'liberal' state remains the 'special case' by departure from which other forms of society are measured. 'Decent' and 'benevolent' societies (those which are not liberal, but deserve to be included in a 'Society of Peoples' under a reasonable law of peoples)[42] describe the boundary of what is 'reasonable'. 'Outlaw states' are those which 'refuse to comply with' (i.e. refuse to accommodate themselves to) 'a reasonable Law of Peoples'.[43] It is 'liberal' states that possess the right to police this law, having the right to a nuclear deterrent and the right to attack outlaw states with military force if necessary to prevent breaches of human rights.[44] Underlying this intolerance is a deeper attachment to a unitary and unconditional sense of goodness or rightness, from which all values and obligations are to be derived. Hence, it is felt (because it originates in the architect's mind) that the correct understanding of this source will eliminate tension between values, for such tension is always merely apparent. Citing the example of disparities in wealth, Rawls speaks easily of 'exclud[ing] the knowledge of those contingencies which sets men at odds'.[45] How straightforwardly we could realize Utopia if men were deprived of the knowledge of such a pervasive contingency!

The 'original position' is of course merely a hypothesis; but it is not one that (as Rawls suggests) we can arrive at 'in a natural way'.[46] For a world in which motives for aggression do not arise, because their point of application has been excluded, is simply not our world: we do not experience values in the way that the hypothesis demands, and our ability to envisage them in that way will always be dependent upon the imagined

---

[41] See also Plato, *Republic*, 529a–b: the ideal city 'whose establishment we have described . . . can be found nowhere on earth, but rests only at the level of ideas'.

[42] Rawls, *The Law of Peoples* (Cambridge MA, Harvard University Press, 1999), 4.

[43] Ibid., 5.   [44] Ibid., 80–1.   [45] Rawls (above n 19), 19.

[46] Ibid. For Rawls's later discussion of the 'naturalness' of a 'sense of justice', the desire to abide by principles of justice and their institutional expression, see ibid., chs 8 and 9.

'rational agents' being no more than the projections of a single mind. For such a systematic reordering of values to gain a purchase on the 'real' world of politics, it would, as Rousseau observed, 'be essential ... that everyone should believe himself to see in the good of all, the highest good to which he can aspire for himself. But this requires a concurrence of wisdom in so many heads, a fortuitous concourse of so many interests, such as chance can hardly be expected ever to bring about'.[47] (Rousseau was later to recall that the Abbé de Saint-Pierre, upon whose scheme he was commenting, was looked upon in the French ministerial offices 'as a sort of preacher rather than as a serious politician'.[48]) Insofar as men do agree in judgments, it is not the 'pure' imperatives of reason alone that produce this concurrence, but the shared experience of living rationally: 'Only insofar as men live after the guidance of reason do they always necessarily agree in nature.'[49]

Belief in the possibility of agreement on the scale required for the utopian model is a consequence of the belief in the rightness, or more than that, the perfection, of the values upon which the utopia rests. The realization of these values amounts to no less than a vision of human perfectibility (or best form of life). But it is, as More sharply realized, the perfectionist element of utopian thought which provokes its absurdity. Its richest offerings are always seductive distortions:

> For in some senses of the word, 'perfect' things exist in the world; in some situations, 'perfect' solutions may be hit upon or elaborated; between some important values of a distinct kind, there is a natural though incomplete convergence, and happy combinations are sometimes practicable. The folly of perfectionism consists in translating this relation into the terms of automatic and ever-present necessity, and in being more interested in the convergence and the ultimate or radical identity of values than in the values themselves.[50]

This aspect of utopian thinking can be glimpsed in the case of Rawls's method of 'reflective equilibrium', a procedure for removing 'irregularities and distortions' from moral thinking.[51] In one sense, removing distortions and incoherence is unobjectionable. But how are we to understand the conflicting pulls to which we feel subject in moral

---

[47] Rousseau, 'Abstract and Judgment of Saint-Pierre's Project for Perpetual Peace', in S Hoffman and D Fidler (eds.), *Rousseau on International Relations* (Oxford, Clarendon Press, 1991), 93.

[48] Rousseau, *Confessions*, Book 9.   [49] Spinoza, *Ethica*, IV, proposition 35.

[50] Kolnai (above n 7), 128.   [51] Rawls (above n 19), 48.

experience? It is not automatically true that our sense of 'irregularities' in this experience arise because of a failure to conform our actions consistently to some specific principle. We might attribute this sense rather to our inability fully to identify the values concerned. The value of justice itself provides an example of this kind: if I seem to contradict myself, or exhibit inconsistency in my judgments concerning what is due to others, it is because I do not perfectly understand what justice is. How then can I hope to abstract from this experience, to elaborate a principle which I shall measure against those selfsame facts, and have any degree of confidence in the resultant judgments? In doing so, do I not simply allow one of these 'pulls' to assume a temporary ascendency in my thinking, and on the basis of this redistribute the burden of argument in ways I cannot immediately envisage? There is no doubt that the outcome of this procedure is to alter my perception of the relative power of the various 'pulls' (for none are without the power to influence both thought and motivation). But does this *clarify* the perception, or play havoc?

This mode of thinking receives an especially potent form in Dworkin's vision of 'the heroic judge Hercules', who thinks,

> not inside out, from more specific problems to broader and more abstract ones, as other lawyers do, but outside-in, the other way around. Before he sits on his first case, he could build a gigantic, 'over-arching' theory good for all seasons. He could decide all outstanding questions of metaphysics, epistemology and ethics, and also of morality including political morality ... He could weave all that and everything else into a marvelously architectonic system. When a new case arises, he would be very well prepared.[52]

Nothing could summarize more astutely the pathology of utopian thought. Borrowing a well-known image, Dworkin adopts the position of the hedgehog over that of the fox: 'The fox knows many little things, but the hedgehog knows one big thing.'[53] Law is to be considered as the expression of the moral ideal of 'political integrity', the 'principle that a state should try ... to govern through a coherent set of political principles whose benefit it extends to all citizens'.[54] It is coherent in that our first aim must be 'to construct conceptions or interpretations of each of

---

[52] Dworkin, *Justice in Robes* (Cambridge MA, Belknap Press, 2006), 54.
[53] Attributed to the classical poet Archilochus. See also Dworkin, *Justice for Hedgehogs* (Cambridge MA, Harvard University Press, 2011); I Berlin, *The Hedgehog and the Fox* (London, Penguin Books, 2009).
[54] Dworkin (above n 52), 13.

these values that reinforce the others', for '[u]ntil we can see how our ethical values hang together [in that mutually supportive way], we do not understand any of them'.[55]

But what is it exactly, that the Dworkinian 'hedgehog' is 'very well prepared' to do? He will be impressive, even formidable, in argument. Not only will his decisions of 'outstanding questions' equip him with ready arguments and answers for any countervailing opinions he will meet, his certainties will give him a definite advantage of confidence over all those whose sense of perplexity increases as they feel their way through the complexity and multifaceted quandaries of moral experience. Indeed, Dworkin is right in his estimation of what a mighty and difficult task the hedgehog's is: 'Nothing is easier', he remarks, 'than composing definitions of liberty, equality, democracy, community and justice that conflict with one another.'[56] But to assemble an 'architectonic system' of answers to the central questions of morality and philosophy out of all that philosophers have had to say on these subjects, is certainly a marvellous feat. Yet we might wonder whether the outcome of this mighty labour amounts to anything more than this: to have defined, and therefore rigidly fixed, a series of concepts in a way that excludes the possibility of ultimate conflicts between them. Might we not find that such rigid identities are 'invulnerable to the twists and turns [they] receive in ordinary human discourse'[57] only to the extent that our perception of moral problems has been refocused through the lens of the system that contains them? Perhaps this means only that we will have engineered in ourselves a loss of ability to recognize that 'there are various complex ways in which values can be interdependent yet nevertheless capable of conflict'.[58]

Utopian thought and the character of philosophy

It would be a mistake, in contrasting the attitude of More toward his vision of the *optimus status republicae* with the line of thinking lately described, to suggest that the message of More's *Utopia* is *anti*-perfective. For (as Dworkin's language of 'composing definitions' of values which mutually conflict implies) to define political concepts in a way that forces them to terminate in ungrounded choices between values is to supply

---

[55] Ibid., 161.   [56] Ibid., 138.
[57] NE Simmonds, *Law as a Moral Idea* (Oxford, Oxford University Press, 2007), 180.
[58] Ibid.

them with essentially the same form of rigid identities as are employed by the hedgehog. If, on the other hand, our reflective understanding is born of submissiveness toward the kaleidoscopic nature of moral experience, and thus held to be in the final analysis imperfectly realized, then who can say where such values terminate?

In fact, it is possible to interpret More's position as part of a long tradition of philosophizing which reaches back to Plato: a tradition with which, in some important ways, writers such as Rawls and Dworkin have made a decisive break. It might seem that Plato's dire warnings about the fate of the polity resonate with the way in which moral thinking is insulated from 'experience' in such theories, in order to produce perfect justice. The very possibility of knowledge is limited, in the *Republic*, to timeless and imperishable Forms inhabiting a world of intellection, in contrast to the sensible world of mutable and contingent particulars.[59] Hence the establishment of the just city depends upon the ability of the philosopher-king to rule by making particular decisions in the light of his knowledge of timeless universals; but in Book VIII, 'Socrates predicts that philosopher-rulers who possess such knowledge, and rule in virtue of possessing it, will eventually fail to master the perverse demands of the changing moment (*kairos*) and will thus initiate the downfall of their own regime.'[60] The response that Rawls and Dworkin make to this problem is to isolate diamond-hard moral demands against the complexities and dilemmas of individual things and events: by placing the decision-maker in an 'original position', or by insisting that he resolve the outstanding questions of philosophy and ethics '[b]efore he sits on his first case'. Plato's conclusion is entirely different. In the *Republic*, we are told that the ideal society which Glaucon and Socrates have been discussing and constructing 'can be found nowhere on earth, but rests only at the level of ideas'.[61] But despite its unreality, the ideal society 'is laid up as an archetype in heaven for him who wishes to contemplate it, and so beholding it, to constitute himself as its citizen'.[62] Because of this, 'it makes no difference whether it exists now or will ever come into being'.[63]

More, who had spent the year 1501 lecturing on Augustine's *City of God*, may therefore have intended his vision of the *optimus status*

---

[59] Plato, *Republic*, 476c–479e.

[60] See M Lane, 'Political Theory and Time', in P Baert (ed.), *Time in Contemporary Intellectual Thought* (Amsterdam, Elsevier, 2000), 236–7.

[61] See above n 41: *Republic* 592a–b.   [62] Ibid., 592b.   [63] Ibid.

republicae as a Platonic model to console and guide the good and wise political philosopher.[64] Augustine had adapted Plato's notion of the archetype to a specifically Christian context: the heavenly city really does exist, both as the celestial Jerusalem of the afterlife, but also 'on pilgrimage' in the temporal world, insofar as it is manifested in the good works of the faithful.[65] It is a community or people which, like Utopia, is both everywhere and nowhere. But because one can 'constitute oneself as its citizen' through acts of Christian piety, genuinely and not merely figuratively, the power of the heavenly city to console is very great.

The 'absurdities' of Utopia, if this view is correct, are not intended to moderate our admiration of the ideal state, but to suggest that its requirements can scarcely be realized within the confines of mortal life. Augustine had suggested that *all* human societies are more or less corrupted, in being built around deficient human beings who have fallen away from grace. The source of this Fall is precisely that pride (*superbia*) that More and Hythloday discuss toward the end of *Utopia*, as being the source of frauds, murders, robberies, social instability and discontent, and which takes as its central object of desire, money. So long as the human condition is characterized by pride, the various shortcomings and injustices of the polity will remain, and our attempts to reform them out of existence will not significantly transform our situation. We may 'wish' for this pre-lapsarian condition, but not 'hope' to achieve it.[66] But neither is Utopia a vision of 'perfection' in the strict sense: it is merely the *best* state of the commonwealth, an idea from a fallen perspective of a society that is un-fallen. Utopia is not heaven itself, but recalls heaven on earth: it is a vision of the form of human society that might have been achieved, if not for the Fall. The impossibility of realizing its requirements is not therefore a *sheer* impossibility, but indicates strong metaphysical grounds for believing that we shall never achieve it.

Hythloday's observation, in More's text, that the Utopians lack proper knowledge of the soteriological scheme of the New Testament, is nevertheless a reminder that the 'best state of the commonwealth' is not the

---

[64] For this suggestion see (inter alia) Davis (above n 25), 31.

[65] Augustine, *De Civitate Dei*, XIV.13.

[66] More, *Utopia*, II. Hythloday declares: 'Nor does it occur to me to doubt that a man's regard for his own interests or the authority of Christ our Saviour – who in His wisdom could not fail to know what was best and who in His goodness could not fail to counsel what He knew to be best – would long ago have brought the whole world to adopt the laws of the Utopian commonwealth, had not one single monster, the chief and progenitor of all plagues, striven against it – I mean, Pride.'

final form of the community to which pious Christians are called. The citizens of Utopia have indeed largely overcome their pride; but they are not yet 'saved'. Despite Hythloday's boundless admiration for their political achievements, he is more circumspect about the Utopians' moral progress, having confused happiness with virtue.[67] For Augustine, no human society could rightly become the object of admiration, because although a society cannot avoid making arrangements for the distribution of wealth and goods amongst its citizens, still the reasoning behind any particular distribution will be corrupted by self-interest and pride. Thus societies little differ from bands of criminals.[68] Too powerful a focus on this dimension of human experience is bound to lead to a fatalistic acceptance of the imperfect nature of present arrangements; but it was not Augustine's intention to leave his readers in darkness, bereft of hope. Hence we have the consoling vision of the City of God, which is both perfect and apart from human experience, and yet 'in some sense mixed' with the earthly city 'until they are separated at the last judgment'.[69] Significantly, however, this mixing is not of the form of existing political arrangements with another, ideal political form that is specifically revealed to the Christian. The Christian message in the New Testament contains no political teachings in this sense. It is rather a mixing of existing (more or less corrupted) arrangements, in which the Christian cannot avoid being immersed, with a way of living that is recommended for the person.[70] More's Utopia can withstand some claim to be a detailed political vision of the society implied by this way of living. Erasmus's *Adages*, which shares several important themes with More's *Utopia*, had commented in respect of Plato's proposition in the *Republic* that all things should be held in common, that 'nothing was ever said by a pagan philosopher which comes closer to the mind of Christ'.[71] Indeed, 'a community of life and resources [is] the very thing that Christ wishes all Christians to practice'.[72] In an earlier edition of the same work, Erasmus commented that:

---

[67] Ibid.   [68] Augustine, *De Civitate Dei*, IV.4.

[69] Augustine, *De Genesi ad Litteram*, XI.15.

[70] For a slightly different position, see S Bader-Saye, 'Living the Gospels: Morality and Politics', in SC Barton (ed.), *The Cambridge Companion to the Gospels* (Cambridge University Press, 2006), 264–83.

[71] Erasmus, *Adagia* [1526], proverb 1. Versions of this proverb are traceable back to the edition of 1500. For a full account of its development, see JC Olin, 'Erasmus' *Adagia* and More's *Utopia*', 100 *Moreana* (1989), 127–36.

[72] Ibid.

> If [Plato] could convince mortals of [the need for friendship based on communal property], war, envy, fraud would immediately depart from our midst; in short, a whole army of evils would march out of our lives once and for all. What other aim had Christ the prince of our religion? Truly He gave to the world only one precept, the rule of charity, and He stressed that everything in the Law and the Prophets hangs on that alone ... You see what an ocean of philosophy or rather theology has been opened up for us by so small a proverb![73]

More's *Utopia* can in part be treated as a further elaboration of this 'small proverb', giving more sustained concrete guidance on the form of life that Christians are called upon to lead whilst 'on pilgrimage' in the earthly city.

When we consider *Utopia* in this context, the role to be played by the 'best state of the commonwealth' in the thinking of the commonwealth's philosophers begins to become clear. For Erasmus, as a Christian humanist, the *communitas* of Plato (the 'well-ordered society') does not represent a free-standing possibility, neither as a dream of the intellect nor subsequently as a practical project of the will. It is instead equated with Christ's *caritas*, such that 'the peace and well-being of society is made to coincide with membership in the mystical body of Christ'[74] and expressed in the life of Christian unity and brotherhood:

> Or what else does charity urge, save that all have all things in common? Namely, it urges that joined in friendship with Christ and bound to Him by the same force that unites Him with the Father and imitating as far as we can that perfect communion by which He and the Father are one, we also become one with Him and, as Paul says, are made one spirit and one flesh in God, so that by right of friendship all that is His is shared with us and all that is ours is shared with Him.[75]

The society portrayed in *Utopia* thus represents 'an ideal that exists only in More's mind and heart, and its realization must depend on the moral rectitude of those who would create and maintain such a commonwealth'.[76] It is an ideal that 'will always remain that of a common Christian life for a whole Christian nation, but the realization of this ideal depends upon the character of its citizens, who must be as perfect in their Christianity – or as eager in their pursuit of Christian perfection – as the

---

[73] Erasmus, *Adagia* (1508 text), introduction.   [74] See Olin (above n 71), 131–2.
[75] Erasmus (above n 73), introduction.   [76] Olin (above n 71), 132.

Utopians are in their rationality'.[77] This creates a painful dilemma for the honest and wise Christian. Confronting the concrete circumstances of man's earthbound existence, and acknowledging the full extent of his greed and depravity, how should one react? By involving oneself in public life, in some measure accepting and becoming mired in its corruption? Or, by remaining detached, seeming an idealistic fool?[78] More is emphatic *both* about the necessity for involvement *and* the unavoidability of corruption: reality 'relentlessly shapes its members' expectations, aspirations and standards of behaviour'.[79] On what grounds is such involvement to be preferred? The answer is both simple and devastating: with such involvement, there is little hope of achieving the sort of social life that is proper to the Christian; but without it, there is no hope at all.

The philosophies of Rawls, Dworkin and other modern writers engaged in state-building do not squarely confront these questions. It is for this reason, particularly, that such modern utopian visions are essentially *contradictory* (in Kolnai's term). Though undoubtedly containing some elements of it, these utopias are not intended as sheer moral demands. They are taken to represent a perfection or idealized representation of dimensions of present experience that are already universally valued (at least within those communities to which the works are primarily addressed), and which therefore already reflect, in some complicated way, the values *of* the community. The present community is *both* the source of the utopian values *and* the source of those preferences and attachments which prevent its immediate realization. Consequently, the utopia is at once held to be *essentially* the free choice of rational agents (either in an 'original position' or as part of an 'interpretive community'),[80] and something that must be attained by 'the conscious and deliberate actions of an enlightened group that is in full command of the direction in which they are headed, fully aware of each stage on the way'.[81] Whenever we are made to confront such efforts, brilliant in their conception and complex in elaboration, we must constantly return to their nature as pure products of will: ultimately of a single will, which must impress itself on all the rest, or else take refuge in the insidious thought that it represents an 'interpretation' of them.

---

[77] E Surtz, *The Praise of Pleasure: Philosophy, Education and Communism in More's Utopia* (Cambridge MA, Harvard University Press, 1957), 182. (I am indebted to Olin's text for pointing out the existence of this book.)

[78] See Davis (above n 25), 38.   [79] Ibid.

[80] See Dworkin (above n 16), 179.   [81] Manent (above n 8), 138.

What is the ultimate significance of such efforts? They are reminiscent of the underlying thought of the character of the Pilgrim in what is perhaps the greatest allegory on utopian desire, Comenius's *Labyrinth of the World*, in the following passage ('The pilgrim desires to flee the world'):

> Being unable to look upon it any longer, or to bear the pain in my heart, I fled, desiring to take refuge in some desert, or rather, if it were possible, to escape from the world altogether. But my guides set out after me and catching up with me, demanded to know where I was fleeing. Wishing to repulse them by silence, I answered not a word. But when they obstinately importuned me, determined not to let me go, I exclaimed: 'I already clearly perceive that it is useless to expect better things in the world. My hope is dead. Woe is me! ... I choose rather to die a thousand times ... than to remain here where such things occur and to look upon wrong, fraud, lie, guile, cruelty. Therefore I prefer death to life.'[82]

Modern Utopians share this impatience and ultimate denial of the world. But rather than selecting exit or annihilation, they wish instead to stamp their authority and identity upon it. Only through this act does the world, and its present imperfections, become bearable to them. The spiritual significance of this cannot be underestimated, for it is an affirmation of the belief in the world as the final principle of order in the cosmos. (There is, as it were, only the world, and it must therefore be adapted.) Comenius's Pilgrim, on the other hand, finally appeals to a different source of order: 'Oh God, God, my God! If Thou exist, O God, have pity upon me, a wretched man!'[83]

The ultimate message of Comenius's work is that salvation can only be found in the soul, through the acceptance of Christ.[84] But this cannot be achieved by the individual in isolation, withdrawing from the world. Christianity is rather a fraternal religion whose watchword is *community*. Even the enmity which infects all social relationships and arises from pride, is but a distortion of the ever-present fellow-feeling that runs deeply through the human condition.[85] A similar attempt to find some

---

[82] JA Comenius, *The Labyrinth of the World and the Paradise of the Heart* [1623], ch XXXVI.

[83] Ibid.

[84] I agree substantially with N Pohl, 'Utopianism After More: The Renaissance and the Enlightenment', in G Claeys (ed.), *The Cambridge Companion to Utopian Literature* (Cambridge University Press, 2010), 51–78, though distance myself from Pohl's general view of More's text and of the concept of 'utopia'.

[85] See More, *Utopia*, I; also Erasmus, *Praise of Folly*, in AHT Levi (ed.), *Praise of Folly and Letter to Martin Dorp* (London, Penguin Books, 1971), 93–4.

measure of reconciliation between the spirit and the world of politics is what lies at the root of More's and Erasmus's earlier reflections. The task of the philosopher is to seek to amend the ills of the world, but he must do this 'in constant adjustment' to the world as it relentlessly shapes the nature of his response. This is a much more difficult and subtle task than devising an architectonic system of definitional shortcuts with which to oppose current 'values'. The nature of the philosopher's response cannot be an unyielding, impatient moral insistence. He must be the servant of the world, and not seek to be its master or saviour: above all, through such engagement, the philosopher must not lose his soul, but (as More insists) must rather find it.

10

The limits of legal ideologies

Utopian elements within modern political and legal philosophies are indeed 'the scourge of our epoch'.[1] They demand to be confronted, but their excision leaves behind a question that cannot be dismissed or avoided: the question of political forms. Politics cannot give up on its pursuit of improvements to the condition of social life, and in consequence cannot forego images of heightened political forms. The form of social organization remains important: one must not leave the fate of the poor and neglected classes entirely to the realm of private initiative. The existence of social virtue is not less important than the cultivation of private virtue. With these issues in mind, are liberals correct in assuming that liberal society represents an abundantly *rational* form of life?

Prescinding from questions concerning the 'ideal' society, one might focus attention upon the very idea of a rational form of life. The idea of the rational life has provided an object of reflection for philosophers in the Western tradition since the earliest times. In the ancient writers, law appears as an important but not pre-eminent means of securing the rationality of social life. It is above all man's sociable nature that secures rationality for the state. Law is but one facet of man's sociability. In the wake of the Reformation, law assumed a greater importance. Social instincts alone could not guarantee social peace. Order could be created by law alone. The cohesion of society depended upon the awe-inspiring structures of governance demanded by Hobbes, and others. 'Legalism' came to the fore.

In a passage from *The Morality of Law*, Lon Fuller gave concise expression to the values of legalism. As an Aristotelian who kept in mind the idea of 'good order',[2] Fuller asserted that the main purpose of law is

---

[1] See P Manent, *Modern Liberty and its Discontents* (New York, Rowman & Littlefield, 1998), 135.

[2] Fuller used the term 'eunomics' in later writings, a clear reference to Aristotle's references to *eunomia* (well-ordering) in *Politics*, IV.8. See *The Principles of Social Order: Selected Essays of Lon L Fuller*, K Winston (ed.) (Oxford, Hart Publishing, 2001), Part I.

to 'rescue man from the blind play of chance and to put him safely on the road to purposeful and creative activity', and in this way to 'create the conditions essential for a rational human existence'.[3] Fuller's assertion goes to the heart of the matter because it obliges one to ask, what exactly is meant by the idea of a 'rational human existence'? If law is itself the pre-eminent means by which rationality is to be manifested and advanced in human affairs, what assumptions does this require about the mode of life that is indicated? To what extent can it be said to complete, rather than to fight against, basic human impulses?

Certain episodes in the history of liberal thinking seem to disclose a vision of social order that must be elaborated in opposition to human impulses, except in a very 'thin' sense. Human beings aspire to the comfortable or commodious life, and require a political form to fulfil this aspiration; but their disagreement over the very circumstances in which such a life is possible (or tolerable) propels rationality out of the realm of human impulses in any deeper sense. Law and government are 'necessary evils', unfortunately required for the maintenance of social peace in a world in which conflicting ideologies must find a way to coexist. The rationality of political order does not lie in its pursuit of anterior goals that are fixed, but in elaborating a form of life that is neutral between possible goals. A hierarchy of ends in human existence is to be rejected. 'Sound' institutional arrangements are those which attempt to 'create a pattern of living that is satisfying and worthy of men's capacities'.[4] These achievements absolutely require law. They cannot be asserted in abstraction but must be worked out at a specific level, as part of the lawyer's attempt to 'impose forms of men's relations with one another'.[5]

At other times, liberals have considered the social order of the open society as intimating a political form that is itself specifically desirable. The Western conception of reason refers to that which is not merely individually preferable, but exists on a level separate from and above that of individual desires. Achieving impartiality and detachment from individual aspirations, does not the liberal legal order epitomize rational ordering, thus itself undergoing transformation into an absolute 'end' that refuses to become the mere means to anyone's relative end? Society

[3] L Fuller, *The Morality of Law* (New Haven CT, Yale University Press, 1969), 9.
[4] Fuller, 'Means and Ends', in K Winston (ed.), *The Principles of Social Order* (above n 2), 68.
[5] Fuller, 'American Legal Philosophy at Mid-Century', *Journal of Legal Education*, 6 (1954), 476.

is itself a work of man, the reflection but also the perfection of his rational nature.

It is unclear to which of these ideas Fuller refers in demanding that 'certain forms of social ordering' require to be stigmatized as 'perverted and parasitic', whilst exploring the 'conditions under which particular forms of social order may be said to approach perfection'.[6] To unravel the idea of 'rational order' one must first (or perhaps at the same time) unravel man himself.

Man's reason and social order

One vision of the reason of man that has persistently fed the Western imagination detaches this notion from any connection with the establishment of order in society. The interior order of the mind does not produce external order in the world because it must compete with countless others in order to impose its will. The works of man are naturally given to disorder: in nothing is man's design achieved fully and after his intentions, but it is subject to competition and disharmony. As a result, society requires the development of a concept of 'man' that is separate from his concrete opinions, desires and characteristics. Man as a 'citizen' is governed in abstraction from the concrete personalities that are the abstract concept's varied expressions. But what might this mean? Are there any uniting features of the human being (a kind of aggregate) that are relevant to his status as a citizen? Can we enumerate those features that in being shared, render man equal to his neighbour? Alternatively, does the existence of this impersonal aggregate declare nothing other than the independence of each citizen (as instances of it) as distinct centres of thought and impulse? In the one case, one might hope to elaborate a specific conception of society that is organized under the form of these basic equalities (much as Kant hoped to do). In the other case, even these basic equalities represent contentious opinions, man's own subjective and shifting view of himself. No single ideology is implied by the impersonal aggregate, but a chaos of conflicting ideologies that must find some way to coexist. Thus if the order of society exhibits rationality it is because it lives in fear of the organization of opinion. Ensuring that citizens are protected from having their lives shaped by the opinions of others, society works to deprive any opinion of power.

[6] Fuller (above n 2), 62.

The opposite tendency in philosophical thought has had an even greater effect upon Western societies. Reason is established in freedom from certain forms of subjective bias. Exemplified by Aquinas's idea of reason as an ability to desire universal objects, or particular objects as instances of some wider universal, or by Kant's doctrine of the Categorical Imperative, the 'objectivity' of rationality has been a constant theme of Western philosophical thought. Reason is in some sense a collective idea. Man is rational because he is not merely an individual. The category of 'the rational' must be understood to exist on a level separate from and above that of individuals, an object of the good life rather than a subject of personal preferences. In being an intrinsically social animal, the significance of man's being is not exhausted by his present situation. Linked to the realization of a social good which is larger than himself, he is an eschaton.

In the beginning of Western history's march toward rational political order, the rational and social sides of man's character were linked. Augustine, for example, gives the following definition of a 'people': 'A people ... is a gathered multitude of rational beings united in their agreement to share the things that they love.'[7] Love itself is social: it is not merely an election (or act of will), but an intellection. When Augustine speaks of 'the things that *they* love', he intends to express a collective idea, and not the 'open' choices of individuals. An act of love is an ordered cognizance of reality, through which the world is organized into those objects from which love has been withdrawn, and those toward which it is directed. Certain objects become the principle of communal organization: those which it is proper or appropriate to love, as opposed to those which must not become the ground of association. It is possible to distinguish between 'better' and 'worse' loves: 'The better the objects [of love], the better the people; the worse the objects, the worse their agreement to share them.'[8] Love is rational because it is not an arbitrary and unconditioned act of will; but it is rational also because it *includes* choice. Man's fate is not predetermined, but lies in his own hands. He is rational because he belongs to a community which appoints its objects of love (a community is a gathered multitude 'not of beasts but of rational creatures'),[9] and the rational is an object of the good life because it is at the centre of what the community loves.

---

[7] Augustine, *De Civitate Dei*, XIX.24.   [8] Ibid.   [9] Ibid.

However, a community in having adopted as its principle of association a particular constellation of goods has not 'leaped with one bound to that love which [according to I Corinthians 13:7] "bears all things, believes all things", and "never fails"'.[10] If it is only understood how high and comprehensive is the true good, 'the most that one could reasonably expect of sinful and prideful communities was some consensus on goals worth pursuing'.[11] The life of man falls short in many ways of the ideal of rationality that is appointed for him. He is not only purposeful and creative, but also lives in the presence of disorder and destruction. Politics must overcome the 'worse' loves of human beings, who too frequently rest satisfied with material goods and forget to pursue the more comprehensive good.

These two faces of man have made a lasting impression upon Western political thought. On the one hand is the image of man as a radically unstructured 'agent', an instrumental reasoner free of all fixed ends and requiring a system of laws to be erected over him in order that his exercising of free will does not lead to the annihilation of all free willing. Society is dynamic in forming an endless mass of unceasing personal activity, but it is also static in leaving man (and his reason) largely unchanged. On the other hand, man for all his personal narratives is nonetheless connected to all men and connected to history. It is through community that he can reorder his thoughts and desires, transforming himself into something greater and better than his own past. Law orders this community, and reflects this transformation.

One might have thought that the first of these images already expressed an idea sufficiently congenial to 'modernity' that it required little adaptation in order to survive into a liberal age. But the attitudes of the cynics and sceptics did in fact undergo a Protestant transformation, demanding the sanctity and priority of the individual's will as against any pre-ordering of his moral experience. The political question of what must be given to 'Caesar' must absolutely avoid determining for man the question of what is rational or spiritually significant. Order liberates. It is almost possible to say that the 'rationality' of the social realm is precisely a rationality of 'means' rather than of 'ends'.

The second image underwent a more radical transformation. Initially taking shape as an independently determined object of contemplation, the

---

[10] O O'Donovan, *Common Objects of Love: Moral Reflection and the Shaping of Community* (Grand Rapids MI, Eerdmans Publishing, 2002), 22.

[11] Ibid., 21.

idea of the 'rational' form of life came to define that area upon which human preferences converge. The existence of a rational form of life focused less upon the character of man's inner nature (his soul, and his loves), but upon the conditions of his outer relations with others. The image of humanity came once again to resemble a kind of average condition. Man is relevant to political understandings only as a unit related to other units. Understandings of the ideal form of life are refined by clarifying beliefs concerning the substance of this shared humanity. Abstracted from the totality of his impulses, 'man' needed to be reduced to finite proportions. It was necessary to comprehend man from a certain point of view. The uniting characteristics of 'the human being', considered apart from the particular lineaments of individual personality, focused attention upon a new idea: equality. Man's abstracted characteristics were understood to refer to those dimensions in which all human beings possess a basic equality. Since politics (at its most noble) concerns the advancement of the human lot through the organization and use of power, such basic equalities were naturally suggestive of an ethic in the light of which conceptions of the proper end of politics undergo their refinement. The nature of such equalities, and hence also the content of the ethic, were at the same time capable of endless interpretation. Only certain dimensions of man are relevant. Politics increasingly became concerned with the rhetorical and practical exercise of encouraging convergence upon preferred ideological principles. Nevertheless, man and politics remained objects that must be contemplated historically 'in context'. Placing the human being into a historical narrative, politics reaches beyond present realities and toward a higher state of perfection. Concerned not only with means but also with ends, politics retained a kind of transcendent dimension. It is not only of the here-and-now, but of man's future condition of life.

In whichever form it is elaborated, a vision of 'man' as the subject of law and politics cannot escape all involvement in contextual considerations. But it is necessary also to avoid reducing man entirely to these considerations. Take first the idea of man as an impersonal aggregate. What could be more context-free than this image? A 'necessary' substrate, definitive of agency, is to be contrasted with those accidental features of the concrete personality which arise adventitiously or contingently as the subjective *expressions* of this agency. Agency is the permanent truth about man, distilled from his ephemeral traits, and made the centre of political thinking. But in another way, pursuit of this image leads irrevocably back to context at every turn. Radically unstructured in his 'free' agency, *everything* about man is tied to context. None of his willing, desiring, arguing or thinking, nothing indeed except his 'capacity' for such activities, is transcendent of context. Can law and politics do anything except seek to enhance the exercise of this capacity, increasing the sphere of free willing as far as it is possible to go? By altogether ignoring context, does law chain itself entirely to context by refusing to countenance transcendent ideas?

The philosophy of equality is harder to pin down, but no less subject to these tensions. With Augustine came the thought that Adam's sin transcends history, marking us all for death. The life of man can be understood only in one way: he is 'on pilgrimage', a journey toward justification or redemption. But the realization that man is a sinner meant that sooner or later one must face up to the fact that there is nothing permanent or lasting in man upon which his communities deserve to be founded. Man's earthly communities at best provide a basis for a personal transformation, but remain as expressions of his imperfect nature. They contain no lasting monuments to the good life to which men are truly called. They provide no permanent norms. All of humanity's achievements are contextual. No political argument transcends its context.[12] Liberalism inherited this sense of division. Ideals of liberal neutrality and equality exhibit rationality in being free from dependence on specific conceptions of man and his preferred forms of life; but the weight of the democratic and social-contract traditions points in the direction of a society built entirely around men's specific visions of themselves, their preferences and the ways in which (and institutional contrivances under which) they are 'equal' to one another. There are no transcendent ideas of equality or association, merely the community's own 'best ideas' of these values.[13]

---

[12] See e.g. Quentin Skinner's remarks in P Koikkalainen and S Syrjämäki, 'Quentin Skinner on Encountering the Past', *Finnish Yearbook of Political Thought*, 6 (2002), 37, that TD Weldon, whom the young Skinner admired, had 'made it seem that our talk about "rights", and how many rights we may be said to have, is more or less meaningless, falsely assuming as it does that the notion of a right has some ontological grounding when it is merely part of a local ideological practice. I still share that view, and I suppose I have carried such scepticism even further, for it has long seemed to me that the terms in which we express such concepts as freedom, justice, equality and so forth make sense only within the cultural contexts in which they arise, so that questions of the form "but what does 'justice' or 'equality' *really mean*" seem to me virtually meaningless'. A broadly similar intellectual approach (though with some differences) is of course to be found in Hart's remarks in *The Concept of Law*, 2nd edn (Oxford, Clarendon Press, 1994), esp. ch IX.

[13] See e.g. R Dworkin, *Law's Empire* (London, Fontana, 1986), ch 6. Also *Justice in Robes* (Harvard MA, Harvard University Press, 2006), 247–8: 'judges should . . . try to identify

Less important than the question to which they are conceived as a response, Fuller's own arguments attempt to steer a course between these opposing tendencies of thought. Law itself possesses virtues, considered as a form of social ordering, that operate to 'rescue' man from irrationality even as he puts law to irrational and poor purposes. The very idea of legality is an idea of order. This order is not the simple form of 'organization', but a complex form consisting of eight dimensions, all of which are required to be present and operative to some degree: (1) avoidance of ad hoc and inconsistent regulation, the absence of rules of law, (2) non-retrospectivity in the application of laws, (3) avoidance of obscurity or unclarity in the law's elaboration of order, (4) avoidance of contradictory order, (5) abstention from the creation of demands that lie beyond the power of the ruled, (6) avoidance of instability, the result of over-frequent revision of laws, (7) proper disclosure of the law, (8) avoidance of divergence between the law's promulgation and its administration.

Human beings have it in their hands to create ruthless forms of organization through politics and legal order. When employed as an instrument for the pursuit of contentious notions of 'the good life', law can become terribly repressive. Holocausts of unimaginable scale are made possible. Hart was not wrong to draw attention to the law's unique efficiency in perpetrating harm.[14] Indeed, law cannot avoid making certain commitments to the idea of the 'good life'. Morality cannot be entirely relegated to the private realm. Law is bound to be an imperfect instrument, creating or magnifying certain injustices in its imposition of order. But however imperfect or harmful its elaboration of order may become, however 'irrational' may be its contextual ends, law in exhibiting the specific form of multi-dimensional order outlined in the eight characteristics retains a distinctness from these contextual ends with which it is associated. One might say that in characterizing and distinguishing law's 'inner' rationality, Fuller is able to explain how the image of man as

the principles of fairness or justice that best justify the law of the community as a whole and apply those principles to [each] case'; but 122: 'I would insist that citizens are not treated as equals by their political community unless that community guarantees them at least a decent minimum standard of housing, nutrition, and medical care.'

[14] See e.g. HLA Hart, *Essays in Jurisprudence and Philosophy* (Oxford, Clarendon Press, 1983), chs 3 and 9. As Nigel Simmonds has argued, however, adherence to the principles of legality reduces ruthless efficiency in the pursuit of repressive ideals in other ways: NE Simmonds, 'Freedom, Law and Naked Violence', *University of Toronto Law Journal*, 59 (2009), 381.

a social animal, author of great and humane works of reason, can be reconciled with the full extent of his depravity and inhumanity.

Reason and ideology

To what extent can this 'inner' rationality of law remain insulated against 'external' ideologies which attempt to establish for society a definite path to follow? At certain points, Fuller seems to suggest just such a division: 'In no field of human endeavour is it true that our judgments as to what is undesirable must be secretly directed by some half-perceived utopia.'[15] A 'morality of duty' only 'condemns [men] for failing to respect the basic requirements of social living'; it does not 'condemn [them] for failing to embrace opportunities for the fullest realization of their powers'.[16] In reflecting upon the demands of the conception of order articulated in the eight precepts, does one contemplate a form of rational ordering that limits attention to the perfection of man as a citizen (an individual and respecter of individuals), paying no attention to his search for directive ideals? At other points, Fuller gestures toward a perspective from which reflection upon ideas of order represents a continuous domain, in which man's efforts at aspirational order cannot be placed on a different plane to his efforts in establishing basic social order. The social bond is '[n]ever broken' in the ascent to a 'morality of aspiration'. It is obvious that '[i]f we were cut off from our social inheritance of language, thought, and art, none of us could aspire to anything much above a purely animal exist-ence. One of the highest responsibilities of the morality of aspiration is to preserve and enrich this social inheritance'.[17] It is for this reason that the classical philosophers 'took it for granted that man as a political animal had to find the good life in a life shared with others'.[18]

One might cite in this context Fuller's claim that the form of ordering instantiated by the idea of legality is not simply a 'rational' ordering but also a 'moral' ordering: an 'internal morality'.[19] Law is not equally serviceable for good ends as for bad. There is 'an intrinsic connection between law and a value that forms part of our traditional lexicon of moral or political ideas: the value of freedom, understood as independ-ence from the power of another'.[20] Law can be bent toward the service of repressive regimes, assisting their organization. But in doing so law also assists the organization of those who strive to oppose or defy repression:

---

[15] Fuller (above n 3), 11.   [16] Ibid., 6.   [17] Ibid., 13.   [18] Ibid.   [19] Ibid., 41.
[20] Simmonds, *Law as a Moral Idea* (Oxford University Press, 2007), 141.

regimes have a finite capacity for legislation, leaving open as permitted those actions that are not specified as the content of duties.[21] Certain options remain independent of the will of the state (or of others), but lie in one's own hands. Free men remain free not because of the number or even the value of the options that are open to them, but precisely in this independence of will. '[S]lavery is the very epitome of unfreedom, for however many options the slave might have available to him, those options are fully dependent upon the will of his master.'[22] Man ceases to be a political slave when his liberties depend solely upon the law.

It makes sense to say that the ideal of legality embodies a moral aspiration only if it is in some sense connected with 'good ordering' (*eunomia*) over other possible forms of ordering. Simmonds is undoubtedly right to represent Fuller's desiderata as elaborating a notion of good ordering based upon the idea of freedom. Man can only become free of the 'blind play of chance' if he is in some measure freed from the will of others. Read in one way, this might seem to suggest that the idea of 'rational ordering' can be isolated from the pursuit of particular ideologies, so that the law's 'inner' rationality does not suggest a specific form of ordering. I think this is a mistake. Freedom is a precious idea, but its very existence leads to conflicting definitions and differing institutional forms. In Raymond Geuss's opinion:

> Freedom . . . is too contested a concept to do anything foundational with it – rather than operating as a single potentially unified and unifying concept, it collapses on scrutiny into a multiplicity of highly diverse uses. The only way to deal with this is to integrate freedom into wider ethical conceptions (Luther's 'freedom of the Christian', Kant's 'autonomy', Humboldt's conception of freedom as development of the powers and capacities of the individual, Constant's 'liberty of the moderns', and so forth). But when one does that, freedom loses its apparent unity and much of its specious motivational power, and will need to be replaced by something more comprehensive and complete (Christianity, laissez-faire, existentialism, etc.) Any such more concrete replacement will of course evidently be highly controversial, replacing a mere illusion of consensus with the reality of gross disagreement.[23]

It is a supreme irony that the reality of 'freedom' in any of these contested senses would bring an end to freedom. So long as freedoms

---

[21] Simmonds (above n 14), passim.   [22] Simmonds (above n 20), 141.

[23] R Geuss, quoted in Skinner et al., 'Political Philosophy: The View from Cambridge', *Journal of Political Philosophy*, 10 (2002) 1–19, 16.

compete with one another, vying to become *the* principle of the state, the state remains free of fixed ends in the light of which it attempts to define its citizens. But the state cannot pursue a 'pure' freedom in this sense, a freedom from all fixed ideas of freedom. It is only under the rule of law that man truly experiences freedom from the will of others, but such conditions are established only under contentious notions of freedom. We cannot have a private life without the state, but whilst the law does not offer any positive resistance to Christian ideals of freedom (man's self-emancipation from worldly snares), it remains that the juridico-political order of the market society prioritizes and even treats as values instincts (acquisition, envy) that oppose such ideals.

Fuller's arguments serve as a timely reminder that there is not a 'law' that is separate from the law of a market society, or of a feudal society, or from all societies. But at the same time, law does outlast these social forms: something in the idea of ordering is preserved and continuous. Law lies at the basis of political forms, it is greater than 'mere' political ideologies, but as the above considerations demonstrate, this greatness cannot be isolated completely from its contingent ideologies. The pursuit of 'rational order' in society is irreducibly bound up with ideologies, but at the same time it is (as Fuller suggests) not therefore 'utopian'. The English common law tradition manifests an ideology of rationality in this sense. It is a form of moral thought for which the worldly arrangements of the community establish a kind of order, and a kind of love. Justice is to be understood in relation to this love and to the arrangements which secure access to its objects. They are not accidental, even if they are historical. 'Experience' is not entirely random, but shaped considerably by the appointment of collective arrangements toward what is loved and therefore representative of a society's 'common good'. The wisest societies understand that its unifying loves are not ultimate or concrete signifiers of good, but mediations of spiritual goods which are incapable of being fully revealed or manifested in social life. Glimpsed most clearly in the idea of a 'Holy Land', and the holiness of certain socio-political structures, this sense of transcendence appears everywhere in politics. The socialist dream is never completed; the capitalist's desire for stable growth is without end. But these ideal visions are not independent of historical experience. Reflection upon the historical form of one's association is not an arbitrary starting point to juridical speculations. The 'good' that is sought as an end does not require the dismantling of the entirety of a society's achievements.

A complete reordering of its priorities, except in rare instances, is not demanded. Acknowledging the imperfection of existing structures, recognizing even the imperfection of the goods around which they are ordered, a society is not compelled to reject entirely its most intimate foundational assumptions. Reflection upon justice is therefore always in part historical.

The anti-utopian direction of this juridical vision is to be contrasted with the attempt to deduce a system of general principles of morality which derive their validity in abstraction from experience. Numerous considerations conspire to suggest a divorce between experience and judgment. A society's values are not the only values. Familiar arrangements demand to be contrasted with those of other communities premised upon different principles of organization, and even with societies that can only be imagined. The hope that society can itself disclose knowledge of the good must be abandoned. Presented with these contrasts, can reason retain its connection to history? Must it not break free of all 'anthropological' associations, confronting a choice between abstracted 'systems' of value that is in essence *supra*-historical?

The ideological dimension to this distinction is clearly articulated in the first chapter of Blackstone's *Commentaries*, where he contrasts the shallow and regrettable attempts of the younger generation of MPs to legislate general solutions to social problems, with the deep, patient moral sensitivity exhibited by those who have devoted themselves to long study of common law precedents. Eager legislators with no legal knowledge are like the 'raw and inexperienced youth, in the most dangerous season of life'.[24] Citing *Nicomachean Ethics* I.5, Blackstone urges the young men keen to make a name for themselves that there are no shortcuts to wisdom, no independent and ready perspectives for the resolution of social ills: 'Jurisprudence or knowledge of [one's] laws is the principal and most perfect branch of ethics.'[25] Experience is imperfect but it remains the only possible perspective upon the good life. Writing apropos of German Nazism, Eric Voegelin drew attention to the effect of immanentist credal movements upon the fabric of national society: 'there, a science of principles will develop, and especially of

---

[24] Blackstone, *Commentaries of the Laws of England* [1765], vol. I, Introduction, s.1: 'On the Study of the Law'.
[25] Ibid.

philosophical anthropology, to the neglect of an analysis of institutions'.[26] Voegelin, like Blackstone, is optimistic about the English intellectual tradition in this sense:

> Where institutions have absorbed the political experience and wisdom of centuries; where they have proved, without a break of continuity, adaptable to the political articulation of new social groups; where immanentist creeds have not seriously disrupted the civilizational tradition, as is the case in England; there the analysis will start from the treasure of institutions, working its way cautiously toward principles in order not to lose anything of the truth that has accumulated in an organization functioning so well for so long – even at the risk of leaving principles in a penumbra where they remain indistinguishable from the state of England.[27]

It is possible to romanticize the apolitical character of common law adjudication, but there is no doubt that it represents a plane of social existence that remains distinct from the deliberate pursuit of grand political ideologies. Here, the aim of law lies not in the production of a set of ideal arrangements, nor the elucidation of a quintessential body of rules to secure their attainment, but in the creation of a means of fair and openly intelligible judgment in relation to occasions of social conflict. Law in this sense does not directly embody an ideology of the human good (of reason-in-the-world), but instead seeks to give precise expression to aspects of the background of shared understandings upon which social interaction of all kinds is based. Thus, law, more perhaps than any other social institution, articulates the meaning of historic forms of human association, and in so doing it both reflects and refines those understandings which underpin social existence.

Amongst modern philosophers, Gadamer gives clearest expression to this idea: 'Within the concrete conditions of his own historical existence – not from some position suspended above things, [the historian] sets himself the task of being fair.'[28] What is true for the historian is also true for the philosopher and, more particularly, the jurist: it is within the historic forms of language, culture and engagement that both the reality and the knowledge of our essential similarity and involvement in

---

[26] E Voegelin, 'The Oxford Political Philosophers', in *Published Essays 1953–1965: The Collected Works of Eric Voegelin*, vol. XI (Columbia, University of Missouri Press, 2000), 27.

[27] Ibid.   [28] H-G Gadamer, *Truth and Method* (London, Continuum Books, 1975), 211.

conditions of mutuality are manifested. 'Just as understanding connects the individual ego with the moral commonalities to which it belongs, so also these moral commonalities themselves – family, people, state, and religion – can be understood as expressions.'[29] Law, more than any other aspect of the institutional fabric of society, gives direct expression to the meaning of these moral commonalities.

The late-medieval and early-modern idea of common law as an 'artificial perfection of reason' gives a sense of what it means to express these meanings, which are inevitably historical meanings.[30] The human consciousness is essentially a finite source of understanding, and it embodies an intellect which is itself limited in terms of its powers of arrangement and perception. It is not something before which everything enjoys a simultaneous and equal presence. 'The earthly habitation presses down the mind as it ponders many questions.'[31] The arguments of the early natural lawyers, including Grotius, Locke and others, articulated this limitation as an inescapable frailty or imperfection of human reason, cause and consequence of the turbulent conditions of fallen man. Yet it is these same limitations which make intelligence possible: memory, perception and the submersion of the individual power of judgment within the context of historical effect are precisely functions of understanding, for they form the basis of priority and distinction. The power of distinction allows an escape from an existence of mental paralysis in which everything is equally present and co-significant. The historic consciousness is therefore inevitably a partial one. It can perceive meaning only in the part and not the whole of history; and it is this partiality that constitutes the power of judgment. Judgments made in pursuance of common law adjudication share an 'artificiality' with all judgments, but they aim nevertheless at a 'perfection' of reason that is denied to partisan interests: a measuring of all concerns without partiality.

It is not difficult to see how this understanding of common law judgment can blossom into an ideology of rationality in either of the two senses outlined above. In giving expression to the conditions of mutuality which constitute a civilized existence, we also clarify (as it would seem) a body of ideal arrangements in which the high watermark of that form of life can be identified. With what intellectual resources can these developments be resisted?

---

[29] Ibid., 213.   [30] See e.g. Coke, *Institutes* I (1628) s.128.   [31] Wisdom, 9:15.

The 'rational existence' as an object of legal thought

So how shall law advance mankind toward the rational existence? Must law escape its contextual limits, the limitations of its own time, by embracing more fully the implications of a political form? Or by asserting the contextuality of all political forms, and seeking to emancipate man by depriving all of them of final dominance? Let us examine the implications of each of these ideas.

The notion of 'good ordering', of living rightly, might seem inherent not only to the idea of organization but to any philosophy that does not result in immisericordia. The imperfections of the present demand that steps must be taken to alleviate the plight of the neglected classes. Social improvements *must* be attempted. Society must be elevated out of its present condition even if no Utopia comes clearly into mind. The very idea of order is founded upon the belief that men can be brought to 'so flourishing a state in this life that they escape being tossed around at the mercy of chance and accident'.[32] The idea that the good of man resides somehow externally to himself and not 'in himself' is familiar to Western philosophy. It predates Christianity but comes most visibly to prominence there: the supreme good of eternal life is pursued by man, but he does not possess in himself the means to it. Man's activity in this world is 'but unceasing warfare with vices, and those not external vices but internal, not other people's vices but quite clearly our own, our very own'; and to overcome these obstacles we require the help of God without which 'it is not in our power to live rightly'.[33] Meanwhile 'We are beset by evils, and we have to endure them steadfastly until we reach those goods where there will be everything to supply us with delight beyond the telling.'[34] By placing the prize in the next life, the Christian writers largely avoided diminishing the significance of man's present condition. His life holds meaning and significance aplenty, precisely because it is an ennobling struggle to live rightly for the sake of the life to come.

Where law and politics are deemed to exist so as to institute an enhanced mode of existence within this world, things stand differently. The meaning of life is placed squarely within this world rather than the next. But it is also absent or impeded, its full meaning is something postponed to a future time. It cannot completely emerge in the conditions of the present but must await a social transformation. As a

---

[32] See Augustine, *De Civitate Dei*, XIX.4.   [33] Ibid.   [34] Ibid.

result, the life of the here-and-now, of the present moment, is diminished. So long as man's perfectibility lies outside his worldly existence, the imperfection of his present situation makes total sense. Misericordia is demanded both because 'we do not enjoy a present happiness', *and* because we 'look forward to happiness' in the life to come.[35] Once man's perfectibility is located within the world, his current imperfection makes no sense. It serves no purpose, and is nothing but tragic. Hence to view present arrangements as unsatisfactory is one thing; but to view them as a mere stage of development on the road to an imagined higher earthly state is to contrast the actual imperfection of man with a vision of human perfectibility that is alien to its essential nature.

It is possible to challenge this vision of perfectibility in a number of ways, but one way of doing so rests on historical grounds. Historians have frequently pointed out the tendency, in some degree inevitable, of understanding historical events in the light of present knowledge. If this tendency is not carefully considered, one can begin to imagine history as 'something like a line of causation', the result of which 'is to impose a certain form upon the whole historical story' demonstrating 'the workings of an obvious principle of progress'.[36] Historians who wish to put ideas 'in context' are not altogether immune from this tendency. They too wish to make sense of context via a reliable historical method. As Kolakowski amusingly recounts, there are dangers inherent in all methods of historical explanation:

> My late friend Lucien Goldmann displayed admirable ingenuity in linking up the smallest details of Pascal's *Pensees* with the plight of the French *noblesse de robe* after the Fronde. One would think that he could really write the *Pensees* without reading them, solely on the basis of the historical evidence concerning the class conflicts of the time. And it is here that the crucial point lies. For if there were a reliable method for a historical explanation of culture, we would also be able to use it as a tool for prediction. To be able to explain what has happened is also to be able to predict what has not yet happened, otherwise the word *explain* would not have the meaning normally attributed to it.[37]

He concludes: 'Whoever claims to be able to explain particular phenomena in the history of music, or of the novel, can prove this claim only by

---

[35] Ibid.
[36] See e.g. H Butterfield, *The Whig Interpretation of History* (London, G Bell & Sons, 1931), ch 2.
[37] L Kolakowski, *Modernity on Endless Trial* (University of Chicago Press, 1990), 244.

writing a novel or a piece of music which does not yet exist but which will be created tomorrow by someone else.'[38]

Is the attempt to characterize an imagined state of human perfection, or of elevated human existence, any different? To claim to have discovered a general trajectory in human existence, from an initial state of barbarism to one of urban civility, and to project that into the future as a vision of a further elevated society, is to express belief in a form of historical explanation that does not exist. Shall we allow ourselves to be led astray by the thought that 'present law' contains within it 'another . . . pure law' toward which it constantly gropes?[39] The 'perfection' of common law reason cannot be generalized as the perfection of arrangements for running a society. The body of rules and decisions inherited from the past are not taken together as indicating a more perfect social arrangement; they remain a convenient set of mundane arrangements which have been tried and tested in a vast array of previous contexts, and which in virtue of this form a useful point of departure for the judgment of new contexts which lawyers decide to treat as relevantly similar to those that have gone before. The appropriate image is of a set of standards for managing the tensions endemic to a social existence, rather than a body of principles which aim, through their own gradual self-transformation, to resolve all tensions and bring about a heaven on earth.

Turning from this ideal, one might despair of the attempt to connect a 'rational form of existence' with specific political forms. History is of individuals! History is not a collection of causal processes but a living tradition, 'riddled with countless breaking-off points, and each creative act, each creative individual, is such a point'.[40] There is no single direction in which human existence moves, a collective destiny by which human existence is shaped: 'historical reality is not merely a heavy, opaque medium, mindless matter, rigid necessity against which the spirit beats in vain and in whose bonds it suffocates'.[41] It is necessary to accept

---

[38] Ibid., 245.

[39] Dworkin, *Law's Empire* (London, Fontana, 1986), 406. Dworkin asks himself whether it is optimism or pessimism in this regard which is 'wise' or 'foolish' (407).

[40] Ibid., 246.

[41] Gadamer (above n 28), 199. See also G Santayana, *The Life of Reason* (New York, Scribner, 1905), II.1: 'If man were a static or intelligible being, such as angels are thought to be, his life would have a single guiding interest, under which all other interests would be subsumed . . . In truth however, man is an animal, a portion of the natural flux, and the consequence is that his nature has a moving centre, his functions an external reference, and his ideal a true ideality.'

the idea of a form of life as reflective of the complex relationships that connect the individual to the moral commonalities to which he belongs. Law and politics cannot give a final meaning to these commonalities, instances of 'pure' values of which the world has seen no full or undistorted example. Their meaning is intensely historical, they are emergent responses to current events.[42]

If history does not exhibit rationality at the level of overarching, directive conceptions of 'progress', is the pursuit of specific political forms anything but stifling of man's capacity to invent arrangements, to explore every facet of his situation?

Inevitably, law and government consist in the production of an average condition of being. The pursuit of a particular mode of rational existence, as a single end in social life, serves to place that average condition at the heart of political and legal aspirations. Wherever organized government exists, men are governed as abstractions. As an abridgment of the complex relationships that exist between the individual and the common moral structures which that persona inhabits, government is intrinsically unsatisfying. The duties, rights and privileges that constitute the person under law will never fully or completely correspond to the actual range of interests, desires, beliefs and dispositions which belong to the concrete person. This immediately discloses an inherent tension in political and legal order. No matter how sophisticated it may be, a mere concept inevitably implies a *contrast* with real life, not its description.[43]

This tension is in a sense proper to law. Law can only secure freedom for every person by limiting the freedom of each person. Man is 'restructured' as a 'citizen' in order to avoid the nightmare of 'natural man'. Unrestrained creativity embodies anarchy: precisely the absence of regulatory boundaries to human behaviour. Society, in the proper sense of the term, demands the presence of an organized bureaucracy and the rule of law in order to contain just those forces of human creativity which mark the breaking-off points that preclude the emergence of historical

---

[42] This comes across most strongly in the context of those actions performed with a conscious regard for posterity: for the meaning of the actions of the French Revolutionaries (for example) are finally explicable only as responses to particular events which provoked them. Robespierre is as much an unrepeatable product of his time as any other historical figure.

[43] It is, as Gadamer points out, essential to an experience that it cannot be exhausted by what can be said about it or grasped as its meaning: Gadamer (above n 28), 58.

explanation.[44] One might consequently suppose that central to the notion of a 'rational' existence is the need to preserve large and concurrent areas of freedom in which to explore the self in all its particularity. Indeed, it may be thought that a rational existence involves a search for the minimal bureaucratic and legal arrangements needed to secure this personal freedom from the will of others.

Is this vision of a rational existence any less chimerical than one which seeks the implementation of a higher state of social being based on a view of human perfection? One could mention, of course, that the possibility of agreement upon such a set of minimal arrangements is on a par with that of a general consensus on 'correct' political forms. One could also say that a view of human perfection is every bit as present in this vision as in the other (how else are men to determine which forms of behaviour it is necessary to suppress within their minimal arrangements?). But I wish here to explore a different aspect of the problem. For what is common to both visions of 'rational human existence' is the assumption that the conditions required to bring that state of perfection about are external rather than internal to the self.

The elevation of social philosophies and theories of justice to the status of secular religions is to be despised precisely insofar as they present the desired form of life as a set of external conditions as opposed to an inner state of reflective awareness. It has been the hallmark of modern political thought to seek for an optimal distributive pattern of rights and liberties by reference to which all persons are treated as equals. This has led to a damaging tendency for present arrangements to harden into ideologies. But the aspect of this transformation that is most damaging is not the ongoing series of military attempts to liberate 'backward' or 'unenlightened' regimes for which such ideological developments are otherwise unattainable. It is instead the spiritual impoverishment that results from a view that a form of life is to be comprehended in terms of its outward arrangements. To have discovered the 'meaning' of life or sociality in a particular set of arrangements or mode of governance is to assume that life has less significance, less value, where such external features are absent. This is manifestly absurd: both the inner life of the spirit and the outer life of action and performance remain undiminished even in contexts wherein fundamental rights (for example) do not exist or are unimaginable, or where magic has replaced ordinary causality. Passing

---

[44] I use the word 'creativity' here to refer equally to the production of evil or destructive forces as to those of 'progress' or the good.

familiarity with Tennyson's poem 'The Lady of Shalott' or with Sieg-fried's life as presented in the *Nibelungenlied* are enough to confirm this.

If, instead, that which gives meaning to life is found not in the external conditions within which the individual moves, but in her inner spiritual life, it becomes apparent that that meaning is articulated in the endlessly variable ways in which the individual is able reflectively to transcend the present state of affairs and approach the eternal. Society is not irrelevant to the spiritual quality of life. It forms an inescapable context in which reflection is able to take place, but it is not the goal. Of course the 'individual' self only has meaning *within* society, as part of the whole world of ideas in which it is understood and given meaning. The nature of humanity as it is made transparent to us is derived from this body of ideas, and thus the ability to reflect upon the human situation is itself determined by involvement in the shared world of ideas. As Michael Oakeshott observed, a society is not finally understood as a collection of bodies in proximity, but of minds in relation.[45] It is easy to forget that, just as the production of an average condition of being falls far short of a genuine understanding of whole and part within the social world, so too does the attempt to give maximal expression to 'the individual'. An individual's experience of life is given meaning through concepts and language: phenomena that are essentially public rather than private. Such forms provide the basis for deliberation, understanding and decision. The meaning of individuality and of individual experience remain fused with the totality of social life in which they move. The meaning of an individ-ual's creative expressions, thoughts, desires and actions are constantly accompanied by the meaning of this social whole. It is necessary in consequence to think of the part neither as determined by the whole in which it operates, nor as independent of it (even relative to certain aspects or dimensions only), but of whole and part as organically connected at every point.

It is because social forms and arrangements are themselves historically undeterminable and evolving outcomes of human creativity that the shaping effect of these forces is not to be *contrasted* with the existence of personal freedom, however much they may limit immediate possibil-ities. One recognizes oneself not in contradistinction to these forces, but rather through them:

---

[45] M Oakeshott, *Religion, Politics and the Moral Life* (New Haven CT, Yale University Press, 1993), 50.

> In language, customs, and legal forms the individual has always already risen above his particularity. The great shared moral world in which he lives represents a fixed point through which he can understand himself in the face of the fluid contingency of his subjective emotions.[46]

It is this organic connectedness that undermines the two alternative ideologies of rationality. For within the creative world underpinned by common structures, there is no common object of pursuit or independence of individual direction in which to anchor the notion of a 'rational existence'. Kolakowski points to the

> simple fact that all of us, both in politics and in private life, pursue various independent objectives, irreducible to each other, inexpressible in homogeneous units, and unattainable jointly; the means we employ to achieve one objective usually limit, sometimes even destroy, the hopes of achieving another. Since we may not evaluate the objectives on a hierarchy of preferences in terms of rationality, we are often helpless in assessing the rationality of actions if they imply a choice between incompatible or mutually limiting aims.[47]

More than this, the options around which individual and collective choices and desires are structured do not come readily demarcated into discrete units; nor are such options generally functionally independent of one another. This is most clear at the political level, where party politics ensures that all but the most committed ideologues must settle for indicating support for a range of policies and objectives of which only a percentage are actually desired. The mechanics of constantly shifting majorities belie the attempt to analyze political progression in terms of the rational pursuit of consciously desired aims. At the level of individual choice and desire, each exercise of an option serves to eliminate or restrict others, or to invite unavoidable and unwanted consequences of its own. In the light of this, 'rationality' for the individual is probably limited to the deliberate avoidance, where possible, of foreseeably counterproductive actions. The complexity of all mechanisms of social choice, and the randomizing effect of interaction between millions of everyday individual decisions, means that even this restriction is insufficient for capturing a workable notion of rationality at the social level. Thus in neither sense can the purpose of law be said to consist in the pursuit of a rational human existence.

---

[46] Gadamer (above n 28), 229. (Gadamer is here commenting upon Dilthey.)
[47] Kolakowski (above n 37), 193.

Reason in society

The structure of a human society of any size or complexity is such that the connection between visible means and clearly defined ends lies beyond the scope of criteria of 'rationality' or 'irrationality'. It is perhaps a necessary feature of such societies that they seek the joint realization of objectives that are known to be mutually limiting or in conflict. The desire for minimum standards of food safety is apt to undermine the desire for low prices; the welfare state comes at the price of unwieldy bureaucracy, duplication and waste; popular elections bring about the coarsening and dilution of political debate; and all measures aimed at security (of property, of the person, of the market, etc.) are bought at the expense of freedom. That these familiar facts have not dimmed the attempt to characterize legal and political arrangements as elements in the creation of a 'rational' society is perhaps due to the enduring belief that the goal of juridical and political theory concerns the achievement of a satisfactory or correct balance between the competing aims. But the notion of 'balance' between goals which pull in mutually exclusive directions is entirely spurious. The tensions that exist between the various goals are not binary or opposite, but complex. No direct comparison of such tensions with physical forces in the context of which 'balance' has an established meaning is available. The key ingredient of a successful analogue, that the meaning of the conceptual transition is direct and clear, is missing.

If reason is manifested in society (as the great philosophers said), then it is so not at the level of policies and grand forms, but at the level of persons: not only in their 'freedom' as 'individuals' but also in their 'belonging' as 'citizens'. The person has being within a social world to some extent composed of competing causes and random effects. Being random, such forces will only ever be imperfectly and incompletely understood. External forces (fashions, manners, prices, availability, political majorities, etc.) affecting the person are not fixed or static, but constantly changing and in motion. Such forces are a permanent fact of social existence. Fuller's statement that law exists to 'rescue man from the blind play of chance and to put him safely on the road to purposeful and creative activity' might have suggested that law exists as a means of organizing the activities of persons so that they serve to converge upon specifically agreed goals, or that law operates to create domains of equal freedom from the will of others in which each person can coherently pursue medium- to long-term projects of their own. Both suggestions can indeed be useful as convenient shorthands; but they are misleading if taken for deep truths about the nature of law. When are important social goals (those significant enough to become the focus for collective pursuit) ever agreed upon, rather than converged on more or less obliquely, and with greater or lesser passion or interest, often incidentally on the road to other goals? When can the person be said to be truly free of the will of others, when we operate in a world of interpersonal cause and effect, of market interaction and multilayered influence: in short, a world of shared ideas?[48]

Law does not precisely *rescue* man from the blind play of chance, but (in forming a body of rules and decisions) offers greater stability to expectations, making the decisions of others more predictable in a world where chance cannot be eliminated. The decisions of others (deliberate or otherwise), including those of judges, may be made more transparent and predictable without ever becoming fully predictable or clear as to their total effect. We know this; but the ideologies of rationality that lie at the heart of modern jurisprudential and political thought operate as if phenomena such as 'freedom' can be given clear boundaries within which they possess an absolute, rigid existence. Moving within a world of ideas, we have lost touch with the feeling that society is not simply a collection of externally fixed rules and boundaries and interstices of freedom in which to pursue subjective desires. It is a malleable and constantly shifting product of those same ideas; our understanding of it is shaped by exactly the same linguistic and conceptual forms that give expression to our desires.

What can be concluded from this? The life of reason should not be mistaken with the life of the liberal society, or of any specific political form. Man is 'rational' when he is civilized: his reason requires a city, but it does not await the establishment of the ideal city. At the same time, the city will always offer resistance to reasonable ideals and actions. Fuller is absolutely correct to place law at the heart of a 'rational' existence. To live the life of the mind, to have room for reason, man requires order above all things. Good order and bad order alike offer occasions for the life of

---

[48] This is sadly true even of philosophy, where a market in ideas certainly exists and operates to define the orthodoxy and the accepted centre ground. It is still more true of political argument: perhaps the thought that the perceived value of ideas depends insidiously upon their popularity might do something to dent the belief that academic commentary, in virtue of being more refined, is somehow more 'rational' than lay opinion?

the mind, without thereby becoming equal or indifferent. It is well for man to ponder the problem of 'good ordering'; but it remains necessary to resist the idea that the rational life is equivalent to such ordering, as if the life of reason were the production of external conditions. General notions of human progress are to be resisted. How is such progress to be measured? Is it a matter simply of greater average standards of living? Greater material wealth and comfort might be said to lead to decadence, complacency, waste and spiritual impoverishment. Nor can progress be measured simply by technological advancement, for every such advance can be used to increase evil in the world as well as good. At every point, the general notion of 'human progress' demands the arrangement of values that are irreducible to one other into a hierarchy: values which, being mutually independent sources of good (or evil), do not admit of hierarchical arrangement on the basis of rationality.

Philosophies of politics and of law should not concern the reduction or elimination of tensions and conflicts within society according to some overarching political ideology or theory of justice. But if tensions are endemic to human society, our responses to them are not. The meaning of 'free will' is disclosed in the fact that our reaction to adversity of all kinds is open and unpredictable, which is to say that each thought and decision is a breaking-off point or creative act, not something fixed by the mechanical operation of grace or its opposite. Thus the goal of self-understanding, of the good or virtuous life, is the recognition and banishment of hatred and its replacement with the institution of the Christian ethic of neighbourly love: the avoidance of depersonalizing forces and alienating tendencies in human thought and action in favour of a compassionate understanding and fellow-sympathy. In knowing oneself, one comes to understand others. Frequently, the difficulty lies not in understanding what the good life consists in, but in actually living that life.

11

Conservatism and its dilemmas

The liberal order 'contextualizes' man, providing an ordered and stable situation in which to live. But it is also dynamic: its order is neither complete nor perfectly balanced between opposing policies, but constantly in pursuit of a thousand ideas for the improvement of man's situation. Liberal society is valued for itself, in terms of what it has provided for its citizens, but also for what it might become. Law is not poised between these alternating currents, but is deeply implicated in both. How should one read this situation?

In Part I, Chapter 5, I asked whether law is necessarily a conservative force in society, serving to entrench basic dimensions of social life and protect them from the ambitions of successive governments? Or should law be thought of as an agent of change, an instrument of governance and central means for the progress of society? We might at first be inclined to dismiss the question, by assuming both properties to coexist unproblematically in the law, and therefore conclude that no interesting issues arise from their combination. It would be a mistake to do this. The present chapter offers some further reflections upon the nature of law, drawn from the perspective of the character of conservatism. Exploration of the law's relationship with conservative thought will reveal some important associations with fundamental philosophical problems.

On the one hand, it is necessary to consider the extent to which the importation of categories and concepts of the Kantian philosophy into jurisprudence points to an indispensable condition of legal thought. On the other, one must explore the general conditions of the law's relationship to the purposes of government. The associations of conservatism, as I suggested earlier, are not *opposed* to the idea of progress, but consist in a certain attitude toward progress. Nevertheless, the conservative harbours ideas about governance which strike at the heart of modern jurisprudential understandings: often viewing government not as a means to some independently described end or ideal (such as the maintenance of peace, or the creation of liberty), but as itself describing an end. The picture of law that emerges from these reflections differs substantially from that supplied by the juridical thought of the present day. My arguments will suggest that law is neither a posited instrument, intelligible in isolation from moral ideas, nor the partial embodiment of a coherent moral ideal to which it seeks to give a deeper or fuller expression. Consequently, the central problems of jurisprudence are not with the law's disputed moral nature, but with its place and significance within the *condition humaine*.

The dilemma of conservatism

The nature of the problem I wish to consider was first pondered by Kolakowski, in a series of observations on Kant.[1] Kant has had a profound influence on the shaping of modern jurisprudence.[2] The concepts at the heart of Kant's teachings on ethics are themselves juridical: in the notion of 'the moral law', Kant articulates a form of morality that is essentially law-like. In his view, moral obligations arise not from reflection upon supposed properties of human nature, but from the capacity for objective generalization of the agent's rational determinations. 'Inexperienced in the course of the world, incapable of being prepared for whatever might come to pass in it, I ask myself only: can you also will that your maxim become a universal law?'[3] The natural form of expression for such ideas is that of a system of compossible *rights*, in the form of jointly possible domains of individual freedom structured by general rules.[4] Does such a picture represent the *necessary* form of morality? We might be tempted to suppose that it does. On the one hand, Kant's explanation gives a central place to the agent's reason, without which morality might seem to become a free-floating and essentially despotic set of impositions to which we stand as slaves. On the other hand, however, neither can morality be inferred from human characteristics or interests, at the risk of evaporating as a distinct category. '[C]an our civilization actually survive without the belief that the distinction between good and evil, between the prohibited and the

---

[1] See the essays, 'Why Do We Need Kant?' and 'The Revenge of the Sacred in Secular Culture', in L Kolakowski, *Modernity on Endless Trial* (Chicago University Press, 1990).

[2] For a valuable discussion, see NE Simmonds, 'Rights at the Cutting Edge', in MH Kramer, NE Simmonds and H Steiner, *A Debate Over Rights* (Oxford University Press, 1998), 113–232.

[3] Kant, *Groundwork of the Metaphysics of Morals* [1785], in M Gregor (trans.) and AW Wood (eds.), *Practical Philosophy: The Cambridge Edition of the Works of Immanuel Kant* (Cambridge University Press, 1996), 4:403.

[4] See Steiner, *An Essay on Rights* (Oxford, Blackwell, 1994).

mandatory, does *not* depend on our respective decisions and thus that it does not coincide with the distinction between the advantageous and the disadvantageous?'[5] Through the idea of practical reason, it is reasonable to believe Kant to have discovered the domain of the morally obligatory, without thereby relying on sources of religious certitude, or by erroneously locating that domain within the domain of the anthropological.

Spurred on by this suggestion, we might pursue the thought that juridical categories of thought are in some way intrinsic to human experience.[6] Is it not possible to regard the world as an inert realm of particulars that is given shape and intelligibility through the medium of rational *laws*? The very separation of reality into 'particulars' or 'facts' might seem to depend upon the application of rational laws, for the notion of a particular or a fact is *itself* a general intellectual category. It might seem that the essence of judgment consists in the need for general (indeed universal) rules which transcend the particular occasion. Something of this juridical spirit is reflected in patterns of thought that are noticeably anti-conservative in orientation. If the survival of civilization depends upon recognition of an absolute distinction between good and evil, then it follows that reason cannot look to past or present forms of human association as a source of moral guidance. Forms of social arrangement may be taken to embody human inclinations: they are larger than any conscious aim or design, and evolve through the realities of social interaction rather than the pursuit of a single purpose. Such 'living forms' might therefore be seen as reflecting natural inclinations, or the realities of human engagement aside from the flattering self-understandings of high-minded social idealists.[7] One cannot therefore sanctify established institutions without also suggesting that we are *justified* in following our basic inclinations.

Kant's position can be understood as reinforcing the Christian belief in the fallen condition of mankind. His moral philosophy attempts to make

---

[5] Kolakowski (above n 1), 45, emphasis added.

[6] See G Rose, *The Dialectic of Nihilism: Post-Structuralism and Law* (Oxford, Blackwell, 1984).

[7] This is one reason why a certain problematic quality may be detected in the legal philosophy of Dworkin: interpretations of social institutions which fail to portray them in their 'best light' cannot be excluded merely for that reason. See also the discussion in Simmonds, *Law as a Moral Idea* (Oxford University Press, 2007), 63n. On the dangers of 'constructivist rationalism', see FA Hayek, *Law, Legislation and Liberty* (London, Routledge, 1982), and for the idea of 'living forms' see D Hedley, *Living Forms of the Imagination* (London, T & T Clark, 2008).

sense of a situation in which evil is not ephemeral to the human condition, something to which human hands may turn amongst many options, but present (as the Crucifixion makes clear) even in the most noble actions and instincts of human beings.[8] Kant is all too aware that the search for criteria of moral obligation through reflection on concrete forms of life 'is never a means of identifying such criteria in unqualified form'.[9] Moral progress entails a process of 'letting go'; a process driven by contemplation of ethical standards that derive not from the world, not from the circumstances or characteristics of the human being, but which can arise only in abstract form through the act of judgment. Kolakowski suggests that we need Kant because renunciation of the absolute, unconditioned nature of the distinction between good and evil would bring about the loss of civilization. Without that distinction, good and evil become anthropological categories of historical success and failure, barometers of the degree of purity with which social arrangements resonate with human inclinations.

But the very forms of thought that seem to militate against a conservative standpoint *also* threaten to abolish another of the central ideas of Christianity, one that is itself intrinsic to the survival of civilization: the idea of the sacred. Every society has its sacred objects and beliefs, which continue to possess that status long after general interest in religion has declined or withered away. A society's system of divisions, its attachment to certain values (democracy, personal liberty, etc.) and particularly some of its moral attachments (its stance towards murder, incest and so on) are not amongst its negotiable objects. They form those aspects of a society's identity which, if threatened or eroded through exposure to argument, invoke in the ordinary person a sense that society itself is in danger of decline and fall. A 'feeling for the sacred' is indelibly associated with conservative attitudes of mind. It points to those matters which remain off-limits to change or revision, and may therefore claim to be the principal phenomenon through which the structure of society is stabilized and reaffirmed.

> There is no sense in asking how the sacred order imposed on secular life can be maintained without maintaining its conservative force; that force can never be detached from it. Rather, the question to ask is how human society can survive in the absence of conservative forces; in other words, without the constant tension between structure and development.

---

[8] In the context of the Crucifixion, these instincts included the punishment of blasphemy.

[9] Kolakowski (above n 1), 48.

> This tension is proper to life; its dissolution would result in death, either by stagnation (if only conservative forces remained) or by explosion (if only the forces of transformation remained, in a structural void).[10]

This is the central dilemma posed by Kant's philosophy: the absolute nature of good and evil signifies the essential mutability of social forms (which must be perpetually modified or transcended); but that same absoluteness implies the permanent importance of certain values which may be implicated within those same social forms (which must in consequence be cherished and insulated against the forces of change). Separately aware of these implications of Kant's position, Kolakowski seems to have remained less aware of the dilemma they create. Given the juridical bearing of Kant's moral philosophy, it is not difficult to comprehend the wider significance of the question with which I began; namely, the nature of law both as conservative force *and* as agent of change. The inclination to dismiss the question as unproblematic is thus revealed as premature.

Kantian vs. Aristotelian conceptions of ethics

How should one aim to respond to this dilemma? Most obviously, both sides of the problem are related to the nature of the human condition as a historical condition. Kant's position can be contrasted with an alternative standpoint on practical reason, such as that encountered in Aristotle, that might be considered as directly 'historicist'. Aristotle differs from Kant in thinking that sources of moral guidance are to be found within historical forms of human association. As Books I and II of the *Nicomachean Ethics* make clear, reflection upon these historical forms is for Aristotle a process of moral education of the agent's practical reason. Knowledge of good and evil comes not from abstract contemplation by one 'inexperienced in the course of the world', but from experience of good and evil from a position of immersion within the world of human action. Morality is only intelligible within a context of human practices; but Aristotle's point is rather that one must *learn* to be good, not through the 'interior' act of willing universally valid laws, but by educating one's capacity of judgment in concrete situations. Part of this process of moral development includes recognition of the imperfection of established practices and particular actions. Hence the form of moral knowledge

---

[10] Ibid., 70.

contemplated by Aristotle is of a kind that does not admit of neat formulation into rules and principles.[11] The notion of 'practical reason' is not that of the agent's reason being directed towards practical questions, but rather of the cultivation of a disposition or attitude. It is the exercise of judgment in practice, a form of knowledge embodied within a practical capacity, or what one might think of as an intellectual sensibility.[12]

Modern philosophers all too often associate Aristotle's moral philosophy with unacceptable ideas of 'particularism'. But in fact immersion within a form of life need not imply a focus on the unique particularity of each moral judgment. One immersed in concrete practices of judgment may develop an acute awareness of the common properties of different situations, and the necessity of continuities for the grounding of moral judgment. The historicist does not assert that there are no moral principles; he argues that all such principles are incomplete and provisional, and that a full moral understanding cannot be translated, without loss, into the form of propositional knowledge. Law might once again be taken as an especially potent source of moral understanding. For the historicist, ideas of 'the good' are reflected in the historical nexus of social institutions which nurture forms of human association. In so saying, a form of association is not *itself* the object that is prized as a manifestation of goodness. It is instead thought of as the necessary context for forms of human flourishing that can be realized only in common. Established institutions other than the law may be given a higher prominence as nourishers of human potential: the family, the market and organized religions may play significant roles. But the law, as a body of published reason, will nevertheless act as a particularly important source of reflection as the most theoretically articulate of these institutions.

Historicism has an obvious affinity to conservatism. Established forms of life are valued for their embodiment and realization of aspects of the good. Present arrangements stand as concrete moral achievements. To dismantle those arrangements (even in pursuit of a greater good) entails the dismantling of that which is good. The historicist consequently

---

[11] For discussion, see MF Burnyeat, 'Aristotle on Learning to Be Good', in AO Rorty (ed.), *Essays on Aristotle's Ethics* (Berkeley CA, University of California Press, 1980), 69–92.

[12] See, for example, Michael Oakeshott's observations on propositional knowledge vs. knowledge of a trade, in 'Rational Conduct': reprinted in Oakeshott, *Rationalism in Politics*, revised edn (Indianapolis IN, Liberty Fund, 1991), 99–131.

exhibits a greater appreciation of and sensitivity towards the value of known situations, and is less inclined to 'let go' of what is present for the promise of future gain. This, indeed, might define the essence of the conservative disposition: an attachment to the present that depends not upon its specific form so much as on its familiarity (in terms of that which makes us recognizable to ourselves). As noted earlier, for the conservative, '[w]hat is esteemed is the present: and it is esteemed not on account of its connections with a remote antiquity, nor because it is recognized to be more admirable than any possible alternative, but on account of its familiarity'.[13] The conservative is sensitive to the loss associated with every change: the equivocal character of all innovation; the uncertainty which attends the production of a total situation of which the innovation sought is but one component amongst others which can be neither predicted nor controlled.[14]

These reflections might seem to offer a simple way out of the initial dilemma. Does not the Kantian position resemble the phenomenon of legislation, whereas the historicist standpoint approximates to common law judgment? Does not this division present us with an adequate explanation of both the law's conservative nature *and* its transformative capacities? The Kantian outlook does indeed suggest clear analogies with deliberately created law. But I shall shortly argue that such analogies are more limited than they might seem. Similarly, the historicism of Aristotle's moral philosophy bears an obvious similarity to the process of common law judgment. The specific formulation of common law doctrines into fixed verbal propositions is a notoriously difficult and always controversial matter; and even 'classic' formulations (such as the neighbour principle, or the rule in *Rylands v. Fletcher*) do not represent the final word on their respective subjects, but are thought of as giving insightful or precise expression to ideas that defy a final verbal formulation.[15] Each such proposition is merely a partial expression of broader and more complex ideas. But the categories in which lawyers are accustomed to think of both of these opposing standpoints obscure the complexity of Kant's relationship to Aristotelian thought, and serve to foreclose upon the question I want to explore.

---

[13] Oakeshott, 'On Being Conservative', in *Rationalism in Politics* (above n 12), 408.

[14] See Oakeshott, ibid., 411, and also the discussion in Part I, Chapter 5 above.

[15] See e.g. AWB Simpson, 'The Common Law and Legal Theory', in *Oxford Essays in Jurisprudence, 2nd Series* (Oxford, Clarendon Press, 1973), 77–99.

Kant may be taken to address the irreducible necessity within human affairs of an absolute distinction between good and evil: one that is grounded not in understandings of human practice, nor in any scale of human values and concepts, but in the nature of good and evil as 'universals'. In Book IX of the *Metaphysics*, Aristotle also wishes to understand the nature of good and evil. Good and bad, Aristotle says, exist both as potential qualities of things, and (when their possibility is realized) as actual qualities of things. But they have this difference: whereas the actuality of 'the good' is preferable to its potentiality, it is clear that the potentiality of 'the bad' is better than its actuality. Everything that is capable of action or transformation possesses both potentialities within itself. To be potentially good is also to be potentially bad. It follows therefore that actuality, or substance, is prior to potentiality, in that potentiality can only occur if there is some actual thing that is capable of being transformed into something else. From this, Aristotle draws an important conclusion, that 'the bad does not exist apart from bad things, for the bad is in its nature posterior to the potentiality', so that 'in the things which are from the beginning, i.e. in eternal things, there is nothing bad, nothing defective, nothing perverted'.[16]

Aristotle's position allows for the absolute nature of the good whilst holding that knowledge of the good necessarily derives from the contemplation of existing things. It is therefore possible to interpret Aristotle as offering an account of ethical understanding that is related to a cosmology broadly similar to that of Christianity. The nature of the good is completely and purely represented in eternity, but human beings inhabit a fallen world in which there is but the echo of the good; and goodness is everywhere qualified, distorted, perverted or incomplete. Those who wish to become virtuous must be made aware that they may come to know the good through objects of understanding that are themselves corrupted or incomplete, and that their best efforts are never wholly free from taint. We sometimes find in Kant an idea that is similar, though opposite in its intent. For Kant, the condition of goodness is freedom of the will. Unlike Aristotle, for whom ethical understanding proceeds from an awareness of the position of human beings within a universal order of nature, Kant insists upon the need for the emancipation of the mind from all such contemplation:

---

[16] Aristotle, *Metaphysics*, in J Barnes (ed.), *The Complete Works of Aristotle* (Princeton University Press, 1984), Bk. IX.9, 1660.

[T]he practical concept of freedom has nothing to do with the speculative concept, which is abandoned entirely to metaphysicians. For I can be quite indifferent as to the origin of my state in which I am now to act; I ask only what I now have to do, and then freedom is a necessary practical presupposition and an idea under which alone I can regard commands of reason as valid ... In the same way [I] must also assume freedom of the will in acting, without which there would be no morals ...[17]

Rather than seeking to contextualize the human condition, the duty of the human being is 'to enlarge its cognitions ... and to purify them of errors, and generally to make further progress in enlightenment'. To fetter such activity 'would be a crime against human nature, whose original vocation lies precisely in such progress'.[18]

Kant's ambition is properly transcendental. He is concerned with the necessary properties, not of human nature, but of reason. It is for this reason that Kant insists repeatedly that one who is 'innocent of the ways of the world' might nevertheless discover the meaning of good and evil. His concern is ever with standards of behaviour 'of which perhaps the world has never had an example, with actions whose feasibility might be seriously doubted by those who base everything on experience, and yet with actions inexorably commanded by reason'.[19] Kant distinguishes between behaviour which, on the basis of a whole range of subjective motives (such as pity, the desire to be kind, and so on) may happen to conform to the moral law, and actions undertaken purely for the sake of that law, and it is this latter kind of which the world is said to lack an example. It is in many ways a bizarre distinction, the development of a moral persona requiring the suppression of precisely those humane virtues of benevolence, kindness and fellow-feeling which lie close to the heart of the Aristotelian *spoudaios*. But it is nevertheless an important one, for by it alone are we able to distinguish between what is good and evil (on the one hand) from what is anthropologically congenial, successful or 'natural' (on the other). Freedom, or the emancipation of the human species from its perceived historical condition, is necessary precisely because its failure effects the translation of whatever is said to represent 'natural' human inclinations into criteria of good and evil.

---

[17] Kant, 'Review of Schulz's *Attempt at Introduction to a Doctrine of Morals for All Human Beings Regardless of Different Religions, Part I*', reprinted in Kant, *Practical Philosophy* (above n 3), 10.

[18] Kant, 'What Is Enlightenment?', in *Practical Philosophy* (above n 3), 20.

[19] Kant, *Groundwork of the Metaphysics of Morals* in *Practical Philosophy* (above n 3), 4:408.

Because the identification of natural inclinations might lie in the hands of a Hitler or a Stalin, the distinction between the perceived facts of human anthropology and the criteria of good and evil must be preserved if we are not to wander (perhaps more slowly and less spectacularly) upon the same road down into the void.[20]

These reasons provide sufficient warning that easy analogies between the outlooks of Kant and Aristotle, and those of legislation and common law adjudication, are to be avoided. It is in the common law, rather than in statute, that we see a closer approximation to the effort to give shape and expression to moral ideas that lie outside the cave of conventional human understandings. We do not see, in the *ratio* of the instant case, the complete and perfect encapsulation of a moral ideal, but rather a mutable form of words, a temporary association of ideas, within which a purer form can be dimly perceived. It is through doctrinal reasoning that we 'enlarge [our] cogitations . . . to purify them of errors, and generally . . . make further progress in enlightenment'.[21] Blackstone, too, feared the consequences 'when the statute book is swelled to ten times a larger bulk'.[22] In giving a fixed and final form to common law doctrine, were not the drafters of legislation seeking to place the authority of a human parliament above that of the natural law? Blackstone's argument was fundamentally a conservative one; and the fact of this coincidence with the Kantian viewpoint, from which it is otherwise far removed, ought to serve as adequate warning not to seek for an explanation of the law's transformative and conservative characteristics in the varying forms in which legal norms are delivered.

Kantian and Platonic forms of ethicism

Plato's image of the Cave in the *Republic* is an intimation of the permanency of the idealistic mode as an aspect of human thought, which must in consequence be accommodated within ethical theory and not denied by it. It is significant that the most important source of moral instruction in Western theology, the Decalogue, does not admit of historicist forms of analysis: it is an imposition from 'outside' history. Moral ideas end up being applied to worldly situations. The philosopher must return to the

---

[20] See Kolakowski (above n 1), 47.

[21] For a famous attempt to express common law reasoning as a Kantian system of ethics, see EJ Weinrib, *The Idea of Private Law* (Cambridge MA, Harvard University Press, 1995).

[22] Blackstone, *Commentaries on the Laws of England*, I.1.

cave. But morality itself is not of the world, and the world contains only its shadow-forms. Fixating upon worldly things, who can say whether the shadows provide real information about good and evil, or distort and mislead the mind into a thousand errors? The material world imposes limits on perfection.[23] Looking for true knowledge of morality, one must turn away from the world: that is the message of the *Republic*. For all of its emphasis on the City, one must not forget that the underlying principle of the major Hellenistic kingdoms which provided the backdrop of the *Republic*'s discussion of politics, was that of empire.[24] The desire to remake the world, to universalize its culture.

Like Plato, Kant wants to emphasize how wide is the gulf between earth and heaven, experience and 'true' reality. Like the philosopher-king, he is forced to contend with shadows and images of justice, 'to dispute about notions of justice with men who have never seen justice itself'.[25] Plato speaks of the philosopher having to reacclimatize himself to the worldly situation of the cave, finding it very hard to do so amid many misconceptions. The more the gulf between truth and experience is asserted, the more difficult it becomes to see how the philosopher could become truly reacclimatized. Plato feared that the philosopher, having escaped the cave, would appear 'as a fool' in argument to those who are unenlightened.[26] Kant is more concerned that the philosopher, forced to dwell in darkness, will find his reason overtaken by foolish notions. But more than this, if the city that is demanded by the many is not truly a City, then neither is the city that excludes them, treating their demands as ill-founded and unsuitable for politics.[27]

Kant does not really resolve this tension, but his message in this context can be said to point to an indispensable condition of morality, that fundamental criteria of good and evil must be preserved, no matter how often they are violated, else all should go down in ruin. But such preservation is possible only if the traditional criteria are thought to be other than *merely* historical. For both Plato and Kant, the 'experience' of the many must somehow be overthrown; new order must be instituted. The sacred does not form part of man's world, in his extant institutions, but lies before him, or beyond the world itself.

---

[23] Cf Plato, *Republic*, 472c–473b.
[24] WL Adams, 'The Hellenistic Kingdoms', in GR Bugh (ed.), *The Cambridge Companion to the Hellenistic World* (Cambridge University Press, 2006), 35.
[25] Plato (above n 23), 517e.   [26] Ibid., 516d–e.
[27] See P Manent, *The City of Man* (Princeton University Press, 1998), 164.

Reflection upon the Decalogue's nature as moral law allows for some light to be thrown upon the nature of law in general, as a force of both conservation and innovation. Traditional legal scholarship never focused upon the law's conservative and innovative properties, but instead explored a related distinction, that of law as 'will' contrasted with law as 'reason'. The notions of will and reason are famously central to Kant's philosophy of morality. Indeed, the Kantian notion of rationality shares this with the Decalogue: that it lies outside history and experience. Moral laws are 'commanded by reason', and so 'must hold not only for human beings but for *all rational beings as such*, not merely under contingent conditions and with exceptions but with absolute necessity'; thus 'it is clear that no experience could give occasion to infer even the possibility of such apodictic laws'.[28] Being valid for all rational beings, the worth of the moral law is not to be explained in terms of human purposes. In what can the worth of actions undertaken for the sake of duty lie, if not to bring about some desired end?

> It can lie nowhere else *than in the principle of the will* without regard for the ends that can be brought about by such an action. For, the will stands between its a priori principle, which is formal, and its a posteriori incentive, which is material, as at a crossroads; and since it must be determined by something, it must be determined by the formal principle of volition as such when an action is done from duty, where every material principle has been withdrawn from it.[29]

It is this very possibility of which Kant says there has been no untainted earthly example. Despite what he shares with Plato, one might interpret (or rather re-interpret) Kant as offering a conception of morality that is reminiscent of Aristotle. Reason (on this view) is perfect and eternal, whereas the will is imperfect and finite. In consequence, the will may nowhere perceive the good in unqualified form. What then is the best that a person of good disposition can hope to do? It is '[t]o keep unspotted from the world ... not to have restricted the field of our experiences, but to have remained uninfluenced by a certain scale of values, to be free from a certain way of thinking'.[30] In contrast to this moral man, the worldly man is distinguished (in Oakeshott's words) by his belief 'in the reality and permanence of the present order of things'. He is one who:

---

[28] Kant (above n 3), 4:408 (emphasis in original).   [29] Ibid., 4:400 (emphasis in original).

[30] Oakeshott, 'Religion and the World', in *Religion, Politics and the Moral Life* (New Haven CT, Yale University Press, 1993), 30.

believes in the fundamental stability of the present order, or that it will merely evolve into another. The earth we tread, the species to which we belong, the history we make, the communities we serve, the sciences or arts to which we contribute seem to him permanent; permanent, at all events, when compared with those unstable things we call our *selves*. This belief implies what may be described as an external standard of value: things are imagined to have some worth apart from their value in the life of an individual; and consequently what is prized is success, meaning the achievement of some external result.[31]

It is scarcely possible to avoid noticing the distinctly Kantian flavour of Oakeshott's sentiments in passages such as this one. There are echoes of both Kant and Aristotle in his assertion that '[t]he other world of religion is no fantastic supernatural world, from which some activities and interests have been excluded, it is a spiritual world, in which everything is valued, not as a contribution to some development or evolution, but as it is itself'.[32] In this way, one could educate one's will, and one's judgment, not by turning from the world but by becoming more aware of the world's priorities: both what is offered, and what are its costs and limitations.

Kantian thought on morality shares this with the Decalogue. But with a difference. One must not ignore the character of the Decalogue as *revealed* moral law: one 'innocent in the course of the world' can know it precisely in virtue of its revelation, and though the will is required to *accept* it, it does not *formulate* it. For Kant, by contrast, the will must determine its categorical imperatives for itself. It is for this reason that Kant famously places reason above God: 'Even the Holy One of the Gospel must first be compared with our ideal of moral perfection before he is cognized as such ....'.[33] It is not necessary to agree with these arguments in order to perceive their importance in intimating the necessity for morality to be grounded in a metaphysical theology.[34]

The law's dualistic nature, as both a conservative force and an agent of change, can be understood against this broader background. Values that are deemed to be worth preserving transcend the particular historical and

---

[31] Ibid., 31 (emphasis in original).   [32] Ibid., 30.

[33] Kant (above n 3), 4:409. I have elsewhere criticized these arguments: see S Coyle, *From Positivism to Idealism* (Dartmouth, Ashgate, 2007), esp. ch 3.

[34] Katrin Flikschuh points out that modern liberal interpretations of Kant have sought, with only limited success, to preserve Kant's notion of freedom whilst rejecting or eliminating his metaphysical commitments. See K Flikschuh, *Kant and Modern Political Philosophy* (Cambridge University Press, 2000).

social arrangements in which they are embodied. Thus the value of sociability is not bounded by the specific social forms that have appeared in the world. What are valued are not the existing concrete arrangements, but the values for which they stand. It is this which defines the sense of the sacred. But existing arrangements will nevertheless act as a focus for conservative feelings in virtue of the values which they body forth, and their transformation or extinction will be felt as a loss. The worth of such values is determined not on the basis of will, but by reason. And yet the echo of fundamental values within present arrangements will also motivate efforts to transform society in ways that give a fuller expression to them; and such processes are effected through the will. The ideal of progress thus does not inevitably presuppose the abolishment of what is held as sacred.

Of course it would be foolish to suggest that efforts of social progress may always be reconciled with a perception of the sacred. Efforts of this kind are often directed at liberating citizens from values that are no longer judged to be sacred. Much of the rhetoric of the 'open society' proceeds on exactly this basis. But it has not been my purpose to argue that transformative activities of this kind can be ultimately reconciled with the presence of sacred ideals, nor that there is no real tension between the conservative and transformative aspects of law. It was my purpose to demonstrate that the idea of law (being informed by this dual nature) is not fundamentally incoherent, and that the opposing aspects of law can, at some level, be comprehended.

Lessons for law and government

In the political theory of the medieval period (though not always its political realities), law itself was a permanent anchor of eternal values, of which kings and rulers stood rather as trustees and interpreters than as masters. At the present day, those involved in government see themselves instead as guardians of a complex cultural inheritance that is nonetheless mutable and adaptable to the needs of the day. The label of 'conservatism' in this context stands not for a temperament or condition of being, but for a distinctive set of policies for social advancement (as conservatives see it) and renewal. One of the deepest principles of modern politics has been drawn from the interpretation of Kant's philosophy, shorn of its metaphysical commitments. It is the belief that both the authority and the stability of government are sustained by widespread allegiance to abstract principles of law and justice, and that (therefore) government, as a facilitator of individual endeavour under the law, has no immediate connection with the common cultural identity of its subjects.[35] Modern politics is thus predicated on a principle which fails to heed Michael Oakeshott's warning that a society is composed not of bodies in proximity but of minds in relation.

Modern political understandings were initially informed by anti-absolutist conceptions of governmental authority. The ideas upon which the constitutional order after 1688 was founded involved a basic acceptance of each person's possession of certain natural rights and freedoms, with which the character of government must be reconciled.[36] In one way or another, whether by contractarian analysis or some other device, the supposition was that the authority of government must be *derived* from the possession of such rights. A clear echo of this view can be seen in those political theories of the present day which, having abandoned the idea of natural rights, nonetheless offer a voluntaristic picture of politics. (Rawls's image of the 'original position' is but one heir to this tradition of thought.) Conservative ideology proceeds from an alternative thought: that no person has a natural right that is not subject to rule. Is not rule indeed the precondition of right, much as freedom (as Hobbes realized) is senseless if not defined by constraints, so that to pursue individual liberty is *at the same time* to pursue governance?

To the Kantian notion of autonomous persons willing their own laws might be opposed a different idea: that of autonomy as the development of a governed being. Governance can be thought of as relating, at the deepest level, to those aspects of the human person that are unchosen. I do not mean, those aspects of oneself which through breeding, education or example are chosen *by others*. Nor do I mean the range of possibilities that lie open to one on the basis of actions others have undertaken. I mean, specifically, what is *unchosen*. Sociability is in this sense an inescapable feature of human life. It may be conceived variously as a moral fact about human existence, or as a fact concerning reproductive necessity. But it is a myth to suggest that human beings are able to choose the manner in which this sociability is manifested or expressed: this is the error which Hayek terms 'constructivist rationalism'.[37]

---

[35] See J Gray, *Post-Liberalism: Studies in Political Thought* (London, Routledge, 1993), 44–5.

[36] For a thorough account of the differing views among the Whiggish factions during the 'English Revolution', see L Ward, *The Politics of Liberty in England and Revolutionary America* (Cambridge University Press, 2004).

[37] Hayek, *Law, Legislation and Liberty*, vol. I (London, Routledge, 1973).

It follows that the ends that the state is supposed to serve are not capable of independent description. As Roger Scruton observes apropos of the liberal end of freedom:

> Naturally, one's neighbours may interfere with one, to a greater or lesser extent, but until we are given some concrete description of the social and political arrangement, it is impossible to say whether more or less of this interference is desirable. The 'interference' proper to a rural community in Zululand is greater than anything once experienced in a Soviet city. Yet it would be sadly misguided to call it a loss of freedom, when subjection to this kind of interference is precisely what it is to *be* a Zulu.[38]

The existence of 'interference' is not (as Scruton suggests) itself a form of rule. But a structure of rule, no matter how loose, is of one piece with the limitation and ultimate organization of interference. Such a structure of rule does not require, indeed cannot conceivably be founded upon, the expression of choice. But its possibility is in the broadest terms a consequence of human nature and (were Kant's conception of rationality to be abandoned for a wider one) a manifestation of the rational nature of human beings. Explanations of government that purport to be derived from a deeper concept of personal autonomy (or natural right) fail because autonomy, properly understood, is a potential characteristic of *social* man.

How might these reflections illuminate current debates about the nature of law? I would like to suggest that they reveal the character of law as something more complex and elusive than is implied in the two most widely accepted images of the legal order at the present day: that of law as a posited instrument, capable of being understood in isolation from moral ideals, and that of law as an imperfect instantiation of a moral ideal towards which it approximates ever more nearly as it 'works itself pure'.[39] The first of these images (the positivist conception) might seem to be straightaway ruled out, if my reflections are correct, for the suggested association of law's conservative characteristics with ideas of the sacred contradicts directly the idea that law is infinitely adaptable. But the most perceptive versions of positivism (such as that of HLA Hart) have in any case maintained the necessity of a 'minimum content' of ideas and arrangements which, no matter how they are endowed with specific form and substance, must be present within the fabric of a

---

[38] R Scruton, *The Meaning of Conservatism*, 3rd edn (London, Palgrave, 2001), 40.
[39] See L Fuller, *The Law in Quest of Itself* (Chicago, Foundation Press, 1940), 140.

society's governance.[40] It is therefore not with the suppression of the sacred that the difficulty lies, but with an image of the ethical life that, in centring upon our subscription to abstract moral principles, divests experience of any intrinsically ethical dimension.

Law belongs to society, and because this mode of belonging is necessary and not adventitious, it can be said that the notion of 'law' is capable of being understood in isolation from whatever purposes or moral projects a particular society might happen to be in pursuit. One might think, in consequence, that law can be understood under two different modes of perception: the first in its relation to society regarded as no more than a form of human association; and the second in its relation to society as the organized pursuit of numerous projects and ideals. But if we *also* think (however tacitly) that in contemplating the first of these modes, we perceive the contribution of law to society in complete abstraction from its ethics, then insight has given way to illusion. There is not a division between 'moral man' and 'natural man' (who has no morality), but an idea of *social* man considered at different levels of development and sophistication. The existence of social man is one, even considered in abstraction from its purposive qualities, the meaning of which is revealed only through the lens of a metaphysical theology. Neither does one penetrate the depth of law's mysteries if one considers it only in relation to the organized, collective pursuit of certain goals and moral ideals. For this is to consider government in relation only to its purposes and not its existence. But it is not in its chosen goals, or its self-image, that a society is most fully and clearly perceived as a moral entity, but in its total and unchosen mode of existence.

I began with some of the philosophical dilemmas posed by conservatism, and their manifestation in the dualistic nature of law as both a conservative and a progressive force. The burden of the chapter was to suggest how these dilemmas can be faced, and consequently how a deeper appreciation of the conservative nature of law affects an understanding of the relationship between law and government. Law can be considered under various aspects. The modern period in jurisprudence has dwelt particularly upon law as contemplated in its relationship to moral ideals and purposes, and in its separability from those ideals and

---

[40] HLA Hart, *The Concept of Law*, 2nd edn (Oxford, Clarendon Press, 1994). The question, often raised, whether the admission of such an inner core effectively undermines the theory's claim to be offering a *positivist* account of law, is to a large extent a definitional one which is of no concern to the theme I am exploring.

purposes. My suggestion has been that neither of these images of law fully discloses its essential nature as a phenomenon of governance. Seeking to comprehend this nature, one must look rather at the broader ethical significance of the *condition humaine.* Insofar as the purposes of government are grounded in this condition, law and government require contemplation not in their contribution to or production of it, but in the way the human condition is manifested, and sometimes transformed, within them.

In the final chapter of this section of the book, I would like to attempt to bring some of these themes together. What is one finally to make of the 'open' nature of liberal society versus the perception of liberal government as a political 'form'? The very presence of 'form' confirms the existence of unchosen phenomena, grounded in man's 'sociable' rather than his 'autonomous' nature. As much as any political form, liberal politics demands the presence of order. Without this order, man's freedom would cause the unravelling of society. At the other extreme, the 'chosen' aspects of social order, its progressive and transformative ideals, cannot exhaust the meaning of 'order' without bringing about the closure of the 'open' society. I have spoken previously of the connection between the notions of order and justice, and have set out to challenge some extant conceptions of their significance for modern liberal order. The following chapter offers some further thoughts on order in the light of the foregoing discussion.

12

Liberal jurisprudence and its order

In the eleventh chapter of *Leviathan*, Hobbes strikes upon the central chord of 'modern' man's experience: that he has no longer any end fixed in his nature, but he still has a future.[1] Devoid of 'nature' as such, man possesses no form in terms of which he can supposedly see not only what is, but also what is naturally good and desirable. Indeed one might say that it becomes impossible for man to be moved by the good, for he has no essence of which this good is the fulfilment, in reference to which the good has the power of attraction over man. Man has not one future but many possible futures. In the absence of anything else, man's possible futures are determined by the 'last appetite' of his will.[2]

These ideas entail the destruction of the scholastic and the classical images of politics, but it is not clear what should be put in their place. No longer shall man know tranquillity or contentment (the fulfilment of his essential needs), but desires without end. Moved constantly by dissatis-factions and hungers more than by noble ends, each person is out to improve their situation in the world, placing them on the path to a conflict that is without limit. Political power can no longer be wielded for the sake of a common good, but extends to all things, knowing no boundaries. On the basis of these considerations, Hobbes conceives a politics of authority terrible in its implications, but constructed out of an image that is thoroughly recognizable to liberals and democrats: that of a 'people' incorporated only by the fact of their subjection to common government, and otherwise unravelling into a chaos of individuals. More tolerant of freedom, liberals have constructed a politics premised upon the reconciliation of individualism with the realities of a society's demand for incorporation. It is the individual's freedom to search for truth that is paramount, and not Truth itself. Faced with the contradictions of a 'free

---

[1] Hobbes, *Leviathan* [1651], ch 11; see P Manent, *The City of Man*, M LePain (trans.) (Princeton University Press, 1998), 130.

[2] Hobbes (above n 1), ch 6.

people', liberal politics proclaims its openness when in reality it is threatened with a kind of paralysis. Liberal society 'in putting everyone on the same level . . . undermines the sense of individuality. The citizen is absorbed by the people, the people by humanity, and humanity itself by an undifferentiated Nature'.[3] Like its people, liberal politics is unable to give a clear answer to the most basic question: do we desire to become more of what we already are, or something other than we are?

In pondering this situation, it is necessary to understand the bearing that the liberal attachments to individualism and freedom have upon a central idea of Western political society: *order*. Commenting on this very notion, Aquinas says that the 'unity' of a society is precisely a 'unity of order', as distinguished from a substantial unity or 'absolute oneness'.[4] Individuals belong to society and indeed compose it, but are not annihilated by it as if understandable as mere parts of a single whole. The 'good' of society is not something that is outside of a person, but remains a perfection intrinsic to them (*bonum suum*) even if realizable only through the composition of social order.[5] Being both genuinely common *and* genuinely personal (i.e. promotive of one's nature and development), the life of society is truly appointed to a kind of order. On the contrary, when all traces of the intellection of ordered ends have been removed from the idea of society, what remains is less than an 'order', but can be described only in terms of 'regulation' or 'regimentation'. Everything that might have been an end is reduced to the status of personal preferences which, lacking further significance, cannot be structured into an order, but only regulated or regimented according to specific intellectual schemes. Do liberals truly understand what has been left behind with the notion of order?

For modern thinkers willing to grasp head-on the new ideas of freedom and individual self-determination, the absence of order appeared to offer exciting opportunities for analysis or, even more ambitiously, the creation of a new type of social bond. In the ninth chapter of *The Concept of Law*, Hart had gone so far as to declare that human survival itself is but a contingent desire, and not an end that is antecedently fixed.[6] Laws which regulate social life in ways that promote that end (placing

---

[3] E Perreau-Saussine, *Catholicism and Democracy: An Essay in the History of Political Thought* (Princeton University Press, 2012), 1.

[4] Aquinas, *Commentary on the Nicomachean Ethics*, I.1.5.

[5] Aquinas, *Summa contra Gentiles*, III.24.2 and 6–7.

[6] HLA Hart, *The Concept of Law*, 2nd edn (Oxford, Clarendon Press, 1994), 192.

restrictions on violence, regulating harm, distributing necessary resources, and so on) are not to be considered as an immutable order, but as one possible way of regimenting human affairs which shall remain only as long as such desires continue to hold widely amongst men. The seeming permanence of certain desires is to be understood not as a response to the power of attraction of the 'good' of the objects that fulfil them, but by reference to the structure of thought and language. It is a fact about our *thinking*, and not about our *being*. Indeed, what is reflected is nothing other than the profundity of linguistic structures 'in terms of which we describe the world and each other'.[7] Such ways of thinking may be very deeply imbedded: '[i]t is latent in our identification of certain things as human *needs* which it is *good* to satisfy and of certain things done to or suffered *by* human beings as *harm* and *injury*'.[8] This way of thinking is so ingrained that:

> We could not subtract the general wish to live and leave intact concepts like danger and safety, harm and benefit, need and function, disease and cure; for these are ways of simultaneously describing and appraising things by reference to the contribution they make to survival which is accepted as an aim.[9]

Heady in its rejection of deeper ideas of order, Hart's position begs certain questions. What processes (ratiocinations, even) explain the presence, and seeming inarguability of such linguistic structures? Is the wish to survive intelligible on its own terms, or does it become so only in conjunction with further assumptions such as the assumption that one will continue to undergo bearable experiences, or the belief that only certain kinds of life are worth living? May not other ends than survival occupy a similarly fundamental place in human thinking, and therefore in law and politics? What shall explain their presence?

Similarly keen on tearing down mythologies, the political historian Quentin Skinner's insistence upon a mode of history in which grand narratives are echewed resembles Hart's position in a number of ways.[10] But Skinner, perhaps more aware that the elimination of 'order' requires something to be put in its place, compromises his contextualism by

---

[7] Ibid., 192.   [8] Ibid., 190.   [9] Ibid., 192.

[10] For a classic statement of Skinner's historical methodology see Q Skinner, 'History and Ideology in the English Revolution', reprinted in Skinner, *Visions of Politics*, vol. III (Cambridge University Press, 2002), 238.

asserting a kind of narrative of his own, fashioned around a standpoint of republicanism.[11] It is not history which leads us to republicanism (except perhaps our recent social history) but reflection upon our own situation. As the old hierarchies of British society collapsed, unable to endure long without their religious underpinnings, what was to take the place of the old moral certainties? A civic virtue, grounded in ideas of equality, citizenship and responsibility to one's homeland, would henceforth inform the bonds of socio-political belonging that integrate the British 'people', replacing heavenly virtue.[12] Despite being unable to turn to history (tradition) as a source of duties, 'public obligations' of citizens should be fashioned out of more than 'the minimum demands of social life'.[13] Why? Skinner, ever drawn toward what can be extracted from Machiavelli, thinks that the answer lies in a republican theory of liberty. He could with equal justification have pointed to Hobbes, who writes in Part II of *Leviathan* that there is 'no obligation on any man which ariseth not from some act of his own'.[14] But he thinks that Hobbes's political priorities point in the wrong direction. Founded on nothing except what is necessary for social cohesion (agreement to give up one's rights, to accept the rule of a sovereign), Hobbes grants too little to liberty, a thin and mutable condition. People must be more involved in the creation of their socio-political circumstances. Their liberty will be the product of their own labours, not of the single act of recognizing the will of a sovereign.

But republicanism was not the only option for those searching out a new basis for law and order. An incipient Kantianism, dormant for a while in the face of utilitarian and intuitionistic political philosophies, burst forth afresh at the end of the 1960s. At the hands of writers such as Rawls, the guiding force behind people's political labours would come to be understood in relation to an idea of autonomous reason. Skinner's contextualism wants to deny both 'reason' understood as ordered by a tradition and 'reason' ordered by the intellect's own internal order. The only 'order' that one can point to is the ordering achieved in the

---

[11] See Skinner and M van Gelderen, *Republicanism: A Shared European Heritage* (Cambridge University Press, 2002). See generally E Perreau-Saussine, 'Quentin Skinner in Context', *Review of Politics*, 69 (2007), 106–22.

[12] Skinner, 'The Republican Ideal of Political Liberty', in G Bock (ed.), *Machiavelli and Republicanism* (Cambridge University Press, 1990), 293–309.

[13] Ibid., 308.   [14] Hobbes (above n 1), ch 21.

construction of civic life: a kind of regulation, one that is rational but based on the equation of moral with civic virtue.

In light of the deficiency of these explanations, is there some strand of modern political thinking to which the classical notion of order stands as a central idea, distinct from prospective visions of regimentation?

Order and its absence

Republicans emphasize civic freedom because they understand that the character of liberal society demands to be validated according to broader criteria than the satisfaction of middle-class desires or 'interests'. They resist the idea of freedom as a choice between a thousand 'false' needs, the mere absence of constraints. But what lies at the basis of the more demanding political order that republicans wish to construct, founded upon more than a minimal agreement, more than the autonomy of practical reason?

Liberty is so pervasive and of such paramount importance to all that can be achieved in modern societies that it can easily be mistaken for an end, but it is in fact unintelligible as a value unless it is directed toward a more substantial idea: the pursuit of happiness.[15] There is no value in choice as such: the 'free' conditions of the state of nature are 'nasty, brutish and short' precisely because there is no real possibility to pursue happiness.[16] Men in modern societies desire greater choice because they are surrounded by things that are in some sense *worth* having. They would not desire freedom with the same urgency if there were not opportunities to engage with or experience these things. Hobbes was not wrong to think that conditions of 'mere' nature are an insufficient basis for liberty to establish itself as a value. In the absence of all those things listed in the thirteenth chapter of *Leviathan* as demanding the presence of a 'common power' (industry, arts, letters, machines, society), liberty is experienced as a source only of anxieties, bringing forth nastiness and brutality. In order for liberty to be a means to something substantial, it requires a context not simply of 'nature' but of works of men that enrich the natural order, as it were, sub-creatively. It is therefore not contradictory to say that liberty must be maintained

---

[15] See Manent, *Modern Liberty and its Discontents* (Lanham MD, Rowman & Littlefield, 1998), 220.
[16] Hobbes, *Leviathan*, ch 13.

within the scope of a superior order, and that the exercise of this freedom must sooner or later redound to this order, and in some sense confirm it.[17]

For modern liberty to become explicable, it is essential not to lose sight of either side of man's character, neither his innate freedom nor his intrinsically social nature:

> The community requires liberty as much as does the individual; and the individual requires community ... Man requires freedom in his social organization because he is 'essentially' free, which is to say, that he has the capacity for indeterminate transcendence over the processes and limitations of nature. This freedom enables him to make history and to elaborate communal organizations in boundless variety and in endless breadth and extent. But he also requires community because he is by nature social. He cannot fulfill his life within himself but only in responsible and mutual relations with his fellows.[18]

If most liberals are happy to concede the appropriateness of Hobbes's characterization of social organization as a kind of artefact, they tend to be more demanding about the kind of organization they are willing to tolerate. Hobbes wanted known and settled laws; we 'want laws that are not merely known, but democratically enacted; that are not merely democratically enacted, but just'.[19] This raises an acute question. Can a Skinner be sure that people will give any priority to equality, citizenship or responsibility to one's homeland (that is, exhibit civic *virtue*)? Can a Rawls safely assume that 'all reasonable people' would 'affirm' a commitment to liberalism?[20]

Readers of Aquinas – the philosopher of order *par excellence* – not unnaturally look to new natural lawyers for guidance on these issues. And indeed John Finnis has this to say to advocates of political liberalism:

---

[17] See Hegel, *Elements of the Philosophy of Right* [1821], s.260: 'The principle of modern states has prodigious strength and depth, because it allows the principle of subjectivity to progress to its culmination in the extreme of self-subsistent personal particularity, and yet at the same time brings it back to the substantive unity, and so maintains this unity in the principle of subjectivity itself.'

[18] R Neibuhr, *The Essential Reinhold Neibuhr: Selected Essays and Addresses*, McAfee Brown (ed.) (New Haven CT, Yale University Press, 1986), 162.

[19] O O'Neill, 'Would Making Laws Better Make Better Laws?', *Jurisprudence*, 3 (2012), 1–13, 3. (O'Neill makes these remarks apropos of Locke rather than Hobbes, but the point remains valid.)

[20] See J Rawls, *Political Liberalism* (New York, Columbia University Press, 1996), 39.

Rawls fails to take seriously the fact that 'political liberalism' of his or any other kind may need to demonstrate its positions in the face of an existing or emerging anti-liberal 'consensus' or would-be consensus, not to mention the curious and the uncommitted. We may not be able to ignore this indefinitely, if large Muslim minorities or even, a bit later, majorities emerge in, say, European countries, and if these adhere, for whatever reason, to that important variety of Islam – probably the religion's authentic central form – which teaches the legitimacy of compellingly induced conversion, expulsion of anti-Islamic views and practices from the public domain, and the capital guilt of apostasy from Islam. Where is the defence of freedom or religious (including irreligious) expression and practice to come from? Even setting aside the unreasonable self-denying ordinances proposed in Rawls's theory of liberalism, where are we to find the bases for a defence of that freedom, or for a defence of the radical equality of men and women?[21]

In his most famous book, Finnis selected Aquinas's remarks as his starting point for a consideration of order: 'Order stands to reason in four ways.'[22] Human beings are capable of having intellections of a natural order that they do not themselves bring about ('natural order'); but there is also the order or coherence of thought itself. By exercising their powers, human beings can bring into existence further order, reducing aspects of nature to their control ('sub-creative order'), and can introduce a domain of order to their practices through intelligent choice and action.[23] In each case, 'order' is to be understood as 'a set of unifying relationships'.[24] The order of communities is in part a physical and biological unity, but also in part the coherence of its established fields of knowledge, a unity of thought and (to some extent) of judgment. Part of the community's order is its cultural and linguistic artefacts (cultural unity), but also its unity of action in directing and shaping a common life. Requiring unity in all four orders, human community is concerned

---

[21] J Finnis, 'Religion and Public Life in Pluralist Society', reprinted in Finnis, *Religion and Public Reasons: Collected Essays*, vol. V (Oxford, Clarendon Press, 2011), 42–55, 53. On Rawls's 'self-denying ordinances' (his call for an overlapping consensus devoid of appeal to one's 'comprehensive worldview'), see Rawls (above n 20), 151–3.

[22] Aquinas (above n 4), I.1.1. See Finnis, *Natural Law and Natural Rights*, 2nd edn (Oxford, Clarendon Press, 2011), 157n. Finnis also notes Germain Grisez's references to Aquinas on order. Previously Aquinas had said (in the same paragraph) that 'wisdom is the most powerful perfection of reason whose characteristic is to know order'.

[23] Finnis (above n 22), 136–8. (The designations in quotation marks are mine.)

[24] Ibid., 136. See also Finnis, *Aquinas: Moral, Political and Legal Theory* (Oxford University Press, 1998), ch 2.

above all with order in the fourth sense (the order that is brought to actions and dispositions through intelligent deliberation).[25]

When giving an account of social order, Finnis (consistent with his Thomism) looks to Aristotle who, in the *Ethics*, considers social relationships in relation to three sorts of *philia*.[26] Community consists in part of 'relationships of utility' in which the collective pursuit of a common interest demands coordination and cooperation ('the maintenance of [an] ensemble of conditions'[27]) even though each person may remain indifferent to others' success in pursuing the objective. Such relationships are distinguishable from those Aristotle terms 'relationships of pleasure' in which 'the activity or performance is valued by the participants for its own sake, and is itself the source of their pleasure or satisfaction', such that the coordination of action is itself the objective of the various parties.[28] But Aristotle thinks of full friendship as the central case of *philia*, in which there is 'unity' not only in the conditions and the commonality of means toward what is desired, but also in the mutual enjoyment of the object. In some cases the wellbeing of one person is so bound up with that of another that acting for that person's interest is also to enhance one's own wellbeing, whilst one's own wellbeing must be valued because it is a constitutive element in the wellbeing of the other:

> The reciprocity of love does not come to rest at either pole. Thus self-love (the desire to participate fully, oneself, in the basic aspects of human flourishing) requires that one go beyond self-love (self-interest, self-preference, the imperfect rationality of egoism . . .). This requirement is not only in its content a component of the requirement of practical reasonableness; in its form, too, it is a parallel or analogue, for the requirement in both cases is that one's inclinations to self-preference be subject to a critique in thought and a subordination in deed. The demands of friendship can thus powerfully reinforce the other demands of practical reasonableness, not least the demands of impartiality as between persons (though it is obvious that friendship complicates those demands and can, if unmeasured, compete with and distort them).[29]

As Aristotle was aware, the boundaries between the three sorts of *philia* are not always clear and precise. Finnis nevertheless thinks that there is no possibility of understanding the classical tradition of natural law teachings on order, nor his own, if the strongest associations of true

---

[25] Ibid., 138. [26] Aristotle, *Nicomachean Ethics* VIII.2–4.
[27] Finnis (above n 22), 139. [28] Ibid., 140.
[29] Ibid., 143. On the differences between Finnis's account and Aristotle's, see 159n.

friendship are left out of consideration. In particular, it is this paradig-
matic form of 'unity in association' that explains the necessity of individual freedom and of a 'private domain', and the compatibility of these
realities with order. Political philosophy has long entertained ideas for
the development of communist utopias in which all things (land, goods,
even persons) are held in common: friendship amongst citizens in its
widest and most enthusiastic form. Plato's vision of the ideal society in
the *Republic* therefore demanded the ordering of the community toward
the most extensive sharing of its 'assets', such that even children and
sexual partners are banished from the realm of what is by nature private.
It was accordingly necessary for Aristotle to begin the *Politics* by elaborating its order through a proper understanding of *philia*.[30]

It is impossible to will the good of one's friend without committing
oneself to assisting in the other's participation in basic aspects of human
flourishing (or self-constitution). But there can be no 'commitment' in
this sense if one cannot turn aside from the endless number of alternative
commitments that one might have made, just as one can give nothing to
a friend unless one has something of 'one's own' to give. Much that one
has to give, can only be given to a few; and much can only be fully given
to a few with whom one has a permanent relationship. Only families (or
permanent close friendships) can build up reserves of affection, knowledge, memories, 'rapport': the enrichment and consolidation of unity in
the four orders. From this point of view, Plato's suggestions for the
reconstitution of the *polis* constitute a radical watering-down of friendship even as the new society is built in its name.

But the first book of the *Politics* also reminds us that the family
(though 'natural' in this sense) is insufficient in its own terms to ensure
the good of its members, unless it is first liberated from the need for all
hands to work relentlessly to ensure basic material necessities. The family
will accordingly flourish more fully if without dissolving itself, its
members 'enter into a whole network of associations with their neighbours'.[31] One might say that Plato's proposal in the *Republic* envisages
the complete absorption of the family into the community, so that (to use
Aquinas's term) the order that is produced is one of substantial unity, in
which the parts do not retain distinctness from their involvement in the
whole. Though Aristotle does not want to dissolve the family, he insisted
from the outset of the *Politics* that the form of association that is 'natural'

[30] I summarize here and in the next two paragraphs Finnis's line of argument.
[31] Ibid., 145.

in being truly self-sufficient and promotive of the good of its members, is the *polis* itself. All of this leads Finnis to say that 'The point of this all-round association would be to secure the whole ensemble of material and other conditions, including forms of collaboration, that tend to favour, facilitate, and foster the realization by each individual of his or her personal development.'[32] This ensemble of conditions is equivalent with 'the common good',[33] so that one can say that the community exists for the sake of the common good.

Finnis's concern with order has attracted much less attention than it deserves amongst theorists of liberal democracy, who remain focused on the idea of individual freedom but who have much less to say about the liberal state that such freedom requires. Where Skinner and Rawls pass over in silence the question of what ultimately guarantees an attachment to civic virtue or the convergent agreement in judgments, Finnis can call upon the whole edifice of practical reasonableness, itself a dimension of the common good, in explaining how human deliberation is already a kind of order: an order-producing order, one might say. But on the all-important question of what guarantees this order, Finnis's explanation is decidedly unsatisfactory in several respects.

Ordo virtutum

Toward the end of his discussion of community and order, Finnis offers a reminder to the reader that the 'common good' understood as a kind of order (or 'ensemble of conditions') is possible only because the fundamental goods of life, friendship, freedom in practical reasonableness and so forth are 'good for any and every person', and because 'each of these human values is itself a "common good" inasmuch as it can be participated in by an inexhaustible number of persons in an inexhaustible variety of ways or on an inexhaustible variety of occasions'.[34] Pursuit of such values, in any of the numerous forms and variations open to each person, equates to human fulfilment or 'flourishing', and Finnis had devoted the preceding chapter of his book to a demonstration of how

---

[32] Ibid., 147.

[33] Ibid., 155: the common good is 'a set of conditions which enables the members of a community to attain for themselves reasonable objectives, or to realize reasonably for themselves the value(s), for the sake of which they have reason to collaborate with each other (positively and/or negatively) in a community'.

[34] Ibid.

the analysis of those values results in the elaboration of various dimensions of practical reasonableness. Many of the dimensions of practical reasonableness are either directly or indirectly order-giving: to avoid actions which threaten or oppose the basic values, refrain from arbitrary preferences amongst persons, or indeed amongst the values themselves, and not least to foster the common good. It is because of this infusion of the basic values with 'freedom in practical reasonableness' (again, itself a dimension of the good) that Finnis is able to speak of the common good as above all 'a set of conditions which enables the members of a community to attain for themselves reasonable objectives, or to realize reasonably for themselves the value(s), for the sake of which they have reason to collaborate with each other (positively and/or negatively) in a community'.[35]

Finnis's language and the substance of his position reflect closely the Catholic Church's position on liberal society as set out in numerous encyclicals, including *Dignitatis Humanae* (1965), *Rerum novarum* (1891) and *Centesimus annus* (1991):[36] a position itself informed by consistent adherence to Thomism as the *philosophia perennis*.[37] Finnis wishes to present the structure of practical reasonableness as a precise working-out of Thomist *prudentia* for one demanding 'more determinate' guidance.[38] But one cannot draw an immediate equivalence between these ideas. Aquinas's remarks in the *Summa Theologiae* make it clear that *prudentia* is at once right reason in matters of action (*recta ratio agibilium*) but also 'rightly ordered affection', the application of which to concrete situations requires not only knowledge of the good but also correctness of desire.[39] On the other hand, practical reasonableness 'functions exclusively as an intellectual capacity whose role ... is to deduce from the postulated basic values the best, and possibly the only decent, set of rules governing human conduct. The soul, its passions, and

---

[35] Ibid.

[36] The Church was not always so supportive of liberal order or 'freedom of conscience': see the encyclical *Mirari Vos* (1832), Pope Gregory XVI's insistent call for the restoration of Catholic truth in the face of 'evil and dangerous times' in which 'sound doctrine is perverted and errors of all kinds spread boldly' (5–6).

[37] See the encyclical *Aeterni Patris* (1879) of Pope Leo XIII.

[38] Finnis (above n 22), 102: 'Someone who lives up to these requirements is thus Aristotle's *phronimos* and has Aquinas's *prudentia*.'

[39] Aquinas, *Summa Theologiae*, II–II.47.2, 47.4, 47.13. He thus refers to *prudentia* as an intellectual virtue (as distinct from moral virtues, such as temperance or moderation). See also T Hoffman, 'The Intellectual Virtues', in B Davies and E Stump (eds.), *The Oxford Handbook of Aquinas* (Oxford University Press, 2012), 327–36.

the reordering of those passions do not enter into account'.[40] The common good remains an 'ensemble of conditions' that certainly depends upon cooperation for its continued existence, but which requires no fundamental conversion from a self-centred concern with the pursuit of private projects to a genuine stirring in the soul for the plight of one's neighbours.

In speaking of friendship as the central case of *philia*, Finnis does indeed give nascent expression to an ideal of civic virtue, and of society as a covenant of love. But it remains that he says far too little about the virtues. 'Countless' aspects of 'human self-determination and self-realization' (such as courage, generosity, moderation, gentleness, etc.) are excluded early on from the status of 'basic values', regarded instead to be 'modes of pursuing the basic values, and fit (or are deemed by some individual, or group, or culture, to fit) a person for their pursuit'.[41] The power of love and of desire to 'compete with and distort' the pursuit of basic values is mentioned by Finnis in his discussion of friendship,[42] but he says very little concerning the mediating agency of virtue in moderating the desire that the basic goods hold for us, which can easily become 'unmeasured'. Indeed, the fundamentality and equal priority of the basic goods entirely excludes any deeper sense of order that mirrors an order in the soul. One can shift one's focus and one's priorities at will, dependent upon one's present 'horizon of opportunities'.[43] Thus 'if one focuses on the value of speculative truth, it can reasonably be regarded as more important than anything; knowledge can be regarded as the most important thing to acquire; life can be regarded as merely a precondition, of lesser or no intrinsic value'.[44] Should one say that the great philosopher or mathematician, upon seeing a neighbour drowning, is justified in refusing to risk himself to go to the rescue? In such circumstances, is one merely 'inclined to shift one's focus to the value of life simply as such'?[45] And what would be the basis of this inclination?

---

[40] E Fortin, 'The New Rights Theory and the Natural Law', reprinted in JB Benestad (ed.), *Classical Christianity and the Political Order: Collected Essays*, vol. II (Lanham MD, Rowman & Littlefield, 1996), 271. My argument roughly agrees with Fortin, though I think he exaggerates the 'Rawlsian' character of Finnis's position vis-à-vis its roots in Aquinas.

[41] Finnis (above n 22), 90–1.   [42] Ibid., 143 (and see above).   [43] Ibid., 92–3.

[44] Ibid., 92.

[45] Ibid. I adapt Finnis's example: he has in mind the situation in which it is oneself who is drowning.

In the absence of the virtues, it seems impossible to say why one should put faith in the strength and surety of people's practical reasonableness in sustaining a mutually advantageous 'ensemble of conditions'. What holds people to the 'determination not to be a free-rider',[46] if not the all too far-off possibility of bringing about the eventual dissolution of society? Indeed from the point of view of the natural law tradition, happiness alone (or 'flourishing' in Finnis's terminology) is not a sufficient explanatory basis for adherence to order. The natural law is not 'merely' a law of human flourishing, but also a law that is 'proper' or commanded, ultimately coercive in its nature. By insisting upon the equivalence of natural law and natural 'rights', Finnis comes close to the reasoning of the early- and proto-utilitarian thinkers who, perceiving that the full force of the substantive doctrines of jurists such as Grotius (who famously declared that such doctrines would hold in the absence of God's existence) was borne by considerations of felicity, declared that no further motivating force was necessary, and so dismissed the deontic force of natural 'law' in favour of utility itself.[47] For Finnis, the natural law is indeed 'only analogically law'.[48]

'Order' in its classical sense demands more than the application of reason to practice. If the virtues are merely 'modes' of engaging with the good which may or may not fit (or be deemed to fit) the actual circumstances in which the good is being pursued,[49] then what shall prevent repeated depredations of order, or even of one's loves? The virtues are nothing if not practical, but their meaning is not entirely exhausted by the phenomenon of participation. A certain correspondence with 'the good' certainly exists (if I lack moderation, my health is likely to suffer; if I lack generosity, I am not likely to be loved, and so forth); but virtue does not simply redound to, or reduce to, prudence. What the virtues in fact redound to is a morality: a body of commandments which (at the

---

[46] Ibid., 149.

[47] For an account see NE Simmonds, *The Decline of Juridical Reason* (Manchester University Press, 1982), 60–6. See Grotius, *De Iure Belli ac Pacis*, Prolegomena, 11.

[48] Finnis (above n 22), 280.

[49] Ibid., 90–1: they represent 'modes' rather than 'means'. This perhaps carries the suggestion that 'virtues' relate to the question of how basic goods are pursued in the circumstances at hand, and neglects their importance in developing lasting dispositions and good character. A brief passage in the postscript (421–2) suggests that Finnis regards the language of 'practical reasonableness' as a more satisfactory and precise way of making claims than the language actually used by Aquinas, who 'arranges' his largest discussion of morality 'under the various cardinal virtues'. My arguments above suggest that this purported equivalence is at best problematic.

uttermost limit) 'do not merge or blend into the operation of life concerns but only circumscribe it; ... they do not partially constitute or
embody but only *punctuate* practice'.[50] Howsoever strong is the desire to
connect attainment of the good with morally good action (bliss or
contentment as the reward of virtue), stronger is the distinction between
the cunning man, the prudential man protective of his deepest interests,
and the 'good' man. Indeed Aristotle insists that for some it is only
through being commanded to good habits that they will eventually take
virtue into their heart, learning to love goodness for its own sake.[51] It was
never in Aristotle's thought that one participates in the virtues in order to
become happy. Habituation to the virtues leads to the agent's flourishing,
as it were, in the distance; but the process is that of learning to find
fulfilment and enjoyment in being good. The 'cardinal' virtues concern
above all control: wisdom (*prudentia*) pertains to the ability to discern
the correct position between different extremes; temperance being
reason's restraint of one's inclinations to self-preference; justice one's
listening to reason's governance and moderation of selfish impulses in
the face of one's relations with others; courage (*fortitudo*) the control of
fear, which might otherwise prevent one's exercise of the virtues in
difficult situations.[52]

What Finnis says concerning friendship might seem to imply an
engagement with virtue, for in treating the other's wellbeing as an aspect
of one's own, and one's own wellbeing as worthy of advancement because
it is likewise an aspect of the other's, a person moves beyond self-love and
self-interest. 'The reciprocity of love does not come to rest' with one's
own concerns having the final word or upper hand.[53] One's practical
deliberations take place within a context of loves that are not utterly
absorbed by selfish concerns. It is indeed true that, through familial or
filial ties, one may bind one's good so firmly and inexorably to that of
another (or several others) that consideration only of 'one's own' interests becomes all but impossible. As Augustine makes clear in chapter
XIX of *City of God*, however, there are 'better' and 'worse' loves.[54] But at
this crucial point, Finnis has only this to say:

---

[50] A Kolnai, *Ethics, Value and Reality* (New Brunswick NJ, Transaction Publishers,
2008), 116. See also J Annas, *The Morality of Happiness* (Oxford University Press,
1993), 108–09.

[51] Aristotle, *Nicomachean Ethics* I.3 and X.9.

[52] Indeed the early Church added to this list (inter alia) humility (*humilitas*), submission to
the will of God.

[53] Finnis (above n 22), 143; and see n 29 above.   [54] Augustine, *De Civitate Dei*, XIX.24.

> In friendship one is not thinking and choosing 'from one's own point of view', nor from one's friend's point of view. Rather, one is acting from a third point of view, the unique perspective from which one's own good and one's friend's good are equally 'in view' and 'in play'. Thus the heuristic postulate of the impartial benevolent 'ideal observer', as a device for ensuring impartiality or fairness in practical reasoning, is simply an extension of what comes naturally to friends.[55]

This perspective is quite inadequate to determine the propriety or impropriety, the wisdom or unwisdom, of one's loves. Finnis rightly observes the need for one's inclinations to self-preference to be 'subject to a critique in thought and a subordination in deed'.[56] But such a critique demands a wider horizon than the 'impartiality or fairness' of the situation in which one's interests are pursued to their fulfilment. Even the internal organization of the criminal gang is a kind of justice, but it is a distortion or perversion of justice.[57] Without an 'order of the virtues' in the soul, order becomes a kind of relative organization, 'a gathered multitude of rational beings united by an agreement to share the things they love'.[58] This is a possibility that, as Augustine makes clear, is compatible with the very worst sort of order.

Of course, Finnis is aware of the possibility that familial and friendship ties can distort the demands of practical reasonableness, and are themselves vastly diluted across society. Human beings give their love unevenly, and only fully to a few: this is intrinsic to the possibility of order. He therefore devotes a chapter to a value that has, throughout the history of political philosophy, been considered as essential to the very possibility of order: *justice*.

The problem of justice

Finnis's grounding of order in the common good puts political and legal thought on a path that is definitely worth following, but it is interesting to contrast his treatment of human flourishing with what Augustine has to say on the subject. In an early treatise on the 'happy life' (*De Beata Vita*), Augustine contended that happiness arises from attaining the good, and the good is attained through virtue: specifically moderation (*modestia*), that comes from 'just measure', which is itself an order in the soul (*modus animi*), through which a person at once avoids excess, but does

---

[55] Finnis (above n 22), 143.   [56] Ibid.   [57] Augustine (above n 54), IV.4.
[58] Id. XIX.24.

not fail to achieve that of which it is capable.[59] Citing Book IV of the *Republic*, Finnis is convinced that one must avoid the image of 'justice as an order in the soul [which] then becomes the model for and cause of justice as right order in society', considering it an analogical 'extension' of the idea of justice based on 'word-play'.[60] This expulsion of justice from the soul goes far beyond any 'discreet stewardship of the truth'[61] in the face of an academic culture focused on practical reason in ethics.

Certainly, justice as elaborated by Finnis establishes a kind of order. The 'ensemble of conditions' is appointed to enhance the wellbeing of each person only as an aid to their self-fulfilment, and not as a kind of 'common stock' or 'common enterprise'. Whatever else justice demands, it remains that 'where individuals, or families, or other relatively small groups, can help themselves by their own private efforts and initiatives without thereby injuring ... the common good, they are entitled in justice to be allowed to do so'.[62] In order to do this, they require private property, and a certain freedom to deal with and dispose of property after their own pursuits.[63] Thus a community stands in need of principles by which its store of accumulated resources, and the burden of shared responsibilities, are to be meted out. Justice is above all an exploration of the concrete implications of practical reasonableness, an assessment of 'what practical reasonableness requires of particular people in their dealings with other people'.[64] Its emphasis therefore lies not on equality (except in a residual sense) but the common good: the flourishing of all members of the community.

With this in mind, a basic concern of justice is always going to consist in the fulfilment of people's basic needs. Beyond the threshold where such needs are met, other considerations may become more important. Functional possibilities and capacities also take a certain priority (higher education to those who are capable of benefiting from it), as do

---

[59] Augustine, *De Beata Vita*, 4.33. See also Carol Harrison, who does not fail to note the Stoic influence on this passage: C Harrison, *Augustine: Christian Truth and Fractured Humanity* (Oxford University Press, 2000), 81.

[60] Finnis (above n 22), 162, citing Plato, *Republic*, IV 441c–444a.

[61] Finnis (above n 21), 43: defined as 'presenting always what is true, withholding no more of the relevant truth than the ignorance or prejudices of one's hearers would prevent them from properly understanding and assessing'.

[62] Ibid., 169.

[63] Finnis regards this as a matter of both distributive and commutative justice: ibid., 169. But it is not an absolute requirement of justice but relative to times and circumstances: 170.

[64] Ibid., 175 (parentheses and emphasis suppressed).

considerations of desert, and rewards for risk-takers in business.[65] Since these demands involve a commitment of wealth and energy, it is not reasonable (at least as between persons) to give equal weight or concern to the interests of every person whose interests it is possible to ascertain or affect. Not least, there will be duties of commutative justice: the keeping of contracts and promises, and the correction of wrongs and injuries. There is (says Finnis) no absolute distinction between these concerns. Common endeavours produce gains for the parties but economic activity also generates wealth for society generally. Where such endeavours break down, causing loss for one or more parties, should this situation be considered commutatively (as demanding the redress of wrongs perpetrated, such as breaches of contract), or distributively (a question of how risks and burdens of wealth-creating activities should be spread)?

Finnis is right to observe that his theory of justice 'is not restricted (like Rawls's) to the "basic institutions" of society',[66] and that it does not require (as does Rawls) ideal conditions of compliance to principles and institutions of justice.[67] One can know a measure of justice in an unjust world. Much can be said in favour of the view that the concern of the state is to get its members to act as good *citizens*, without also enquiring into their goodness as *persons*. Only deeds matter: one discharges one's responsibilities in justice by paying one's taxes, performing one's contracts, meeting one's obligations, howsoever resentfully or prudentially motivated. The state cannot demand virtue from its members, nor discover the secret policies of people's hearts. But from the proposition that the state does not demand virtue from its citizens, it does not follow that society can know law and order in the absence of virtue; still less that justice is related to virtue only 'analogically' and 'by extension'. Not by accident was justice (*iustitia*) numbered amongst the cardinal virtues, the virtues that are *cardo* (hinges) in the sense that the moral life hinges upon their presence in the heart and soul.[68] Can one be truly confident that order could be created or maintained without a sufficient tendency amongst persons to spontaneous virtue? Would prudential motives genuinely carry sufficient strength (and indeed

---

[65] Ibid., 174–5.

[66] Finnis (above n 22), 163, citing Rawls, *A Theory of Justice* (Cambridge MA, Belknap Press, 1971), 4, 7, 84 and 109.

[67] Ibid., 164 and 170.

[68] See Saint Ambrose, *Expositio Evangelii Secundum Lucam*, V.62.

precision) to ensure 'right judgment' in the heat and causal complexity of specific situations?

The virtue of *iustitia* was centred explicitly, not upon self-interest or what would ultimately redound to self-interest, but the proper moderation between self-interest and the rights or needs of others. Accordingly the traditional definition of justice always spoke of the constant will to give to others what is properly due to them.[69] A person may of course perform the actions that are required in justice (paying debts, etc.) without exhibiting this will. But what shall guide the reason to the right decision in each case if a concern with the interests of others, or a concern with doing the right thing, is absent? Absorbed entirely in self-interest, the unrighteous person will hardly in all cases deem the outward form of just action to conform to the eventual satisfaction of his desires. Finnis is entirely correct to say that man therefore stands in need of law, which 'has to determine the requirements of justice in a society where persons are only partially compliant and imperfectly just'.[70] But he mentions only *en passant* a fundamental and very revealing proposition: 'No system of law can secure justice if its subjects, let alone its officials, are themselves careless of justice.'[71] Finnis clearly means by this, 'careless of the demands of practical reasonableness', and not 'careless of one's own self-interest'. But nevertheless, one is brought back to the point that the immoderate and selfishly focused person, careless of the needs and claims of others, is not likely to regard such demands as all that reasonable if (as they must) they place restrictions upon the fulfilment of one's desires, and deny altogether the satisfaction of certain (entirely legitimate) preferences one might have. Indeed, this sense of dissatisfaction is likely to be compounded in the light of the law's own intrinsic limitations: '*General* and clear rules about procedure, proof, notification, time, appeals, etc, must be adopted, notwithstanding that their very generality and clarity – the source of their value in the effort to do justice – will sometimes occasion the failure of particular parties to secure the satisfaction of their just claims.'[72]

The association of law with questions of order inevitably invites consideration of the bearing of 'rights' upon the issues under consideration. Finnis claims that 'almost everything' in his book is about rights, and that the 'extensive and subtle' grammar of rights expresses 'virtually

---

[69] Cicero, *De Legibus*, I.15.   [70] Finnis (above n 22), 191.   [71] Ibid.

[72] Ibid. Particularly so since '[t]he basic human goods are not abstract forms, such as "life" or "conscious life": they are good as aspects of the flourishing of a person' (ibid., 195).

all of the requirements of practical reasonableness'.[73] Since we encounter justice in Finnis's argument as a working-out of the concrete implications of practical reasonableness, it is not surprising to find that ideas of justice in chapter VII are articulated in terms of this splendidly pliable and incisive mode of discourse. Reflecting on the purposes underlying the law on bankruptcy, one may consider the desirability of provisions designed to prevent attempts by debtors to evade their debts, to enter into new debts without means of repayment, to live beyond their means at others' expense, or to give preference to one creditor over others without lawful reason. Such laws, as Finnis notes, exist to serve at once the needs of distributive justice and commutative justice. The law recognizes the commutatively just claims of each of the creditors (each person's just claim to satisfaction of the debt out of the debtor's property regardless of the claims of others), but it also takes into account that the enforcement of the full extent of one or more of these claims might exhaust the debtor's assets before other equally just claims can be satisfied. The law in treating the bankrupt's assets as the common property of the creditors thus recognizes the commutatively just claims of each creditor; but in dividing it amongst them it performs an act of distributive justice (recognizing also the claim of the debtor to that which he needs to avoid slavery and indigence, and to retain such earnings as are necessary for the maintenance of dependants, including employees).[74]

Without the idea of a person's claim lying in a *right*, claims of justice on the part of parties affected by the debtor's behaviour would indeed lose determinacy and precision. Limiting the possibility of recovery to those situations in which another has infringed an 'entitlement', the law ensures that not all damage or loss caused to another will result in the award of a remedy. Recognition of 'pervasive and infinitely variable' forms of *damnum absque iniuria*[75] is essential to the maintenance of that freedom from the will of others that is central to liberal (and indeed tolerable) societies. Part of that freedom consists in the freedom from constant or frequent interference by others who find one's daily activities objectionable even if they do not cause injury: the loss of customers to one's business caused by my opening of a rival store next door being a

---

[73] Ibid., 198.

[74] *Re Wilson Ex p. Vine* (1878) 8 Ch D (CA) 364 at 366. Considered by Finnis (above n 22), 189n.

[75] See Simmonds, 'Straightforwardly False: The Collapse of Kramer's Positivism', *Cambridge LJ*, 63 (2004), 98–131, 128.

clear example, but equally including my practising of a religion that my neighbour deems to be against truth and objectionable on that ground. The extent of one's rights against others (such as one's proprietary right to light through a window for example)[76] may indeed be subject to dispute and contestation; but there is no doubt that the language of rights, informed inter alia by Hohfeld's analysis of 'jural relations',[77] provides a specificity that is unavailable to more generalized moral concerns.

At the same time, if the language of rights is allowed to stand for the whole of what may be claimed morally, the consequence is an impoverishment of the law's moral horizons. There is little doubt that the language of rights (whatever its correlativity with notions of duty) encourages a concern with what is due to one, to the exclusion of the other's interests. In the mouths of many people, justice concerns more than anything the ability to secure 'what is due to them, what they are entitled to, what is rightfully theirs'.[78] Limiting the analysis of bankruptcy law to these considerations, one may regard with dissatisfaction the abatement of justified claims *pari passu*, wondering why the unfulfilled part of the claim is not in all circumstances merely suspended, and why there should be any situations in which it is cancelled. But the traditional concern of the natural law was not limited to such concerns. The question was indeed 'not about rights and their vindication, but about what is right'.[79] Judgment concerning 'what is right' in such situations may involve other virtues than those of commutative and distributive justice. The moderating demands of *caritas* (generosity, sacrifice) and of *humanitas* (compassion) lie at the basis of the law's provisions on such matters as the ranking of preferred creditors.

Considering justice only in the light of practical reasonableness, Finnis is left with fewer resources with which to explain the law's moral complexity. He is able to explain adeptly how the law establishes minimal (and imperfect) thresholds of justice as a precondition of order in an imperfectly just world, but he gives little if any recognition to the fact that order also depends upon the law's embodiment of standards of

---

[76] *Aldred's Case* [1610], 77 All ER 816.

[77] WN Hohfeld, *Fundamental Legal Conceptions as Applied in Juridical Reasoning, and Other Essays* (New Haven CT, Yale University Press, 1919): for Finnis's reliance on Hohfeld see Finnis (above n 22), 199ff.

[78] Finnis (above n 24), 133.

[79] Mario Conti, Bishop of Glasgow, quoted in T Rowland, *Culture and the Thomist Tradition After Vatican II* (London, Routledge, 2003), 152.

compassion, mercy, moderation and other virtues. These too must be minimally present in society, but must also be present widely and spontaneously, for the possibility of order. The question of 'what is right' is undoubtedly clarified by the language of 'rights': it helps us to understand, for example, that the exercise of other virtues (such as compassion) comes at a price (the debtor does not recover what is owed to him).[80] But if the language of rights, and of practical reasonableness, is allowed to eclipse altogether other bases of moral understanding, then this will overthrow and distort the explanation of social 'order':

> Whereas in the older patristic and medieval traditions God's right established a matrix of divine, natural and human laws or objective obligations that constituted the ordering justice of political community, in the newer traditions, God's right established discrete rights possessed by individuals originally and by communities derivatively that determined civil order and justice.[81]

As might be expected of a writer in the Thomist tradition, Finnis gives a much more satisfactory account of order than any of the modern republicans, Kantians and positivists reflecting on the basis of liberal society today. In the end, it is sad that his attachment to the idea of 'practical reasonableness' prevents systematic reflection upon the problem of justice in an imperfect world. Ultimately he has very little to say about the engagement of justice with important virtues that are also all too imperfectly practised in this life. Given the importance of justice to a consideration of order, I propose to devote the final chapters of this book to an exploration of justice, investigating some of its many dimensions.

---

[80] I am grateful to Tobias Schaffner for this example, and for his thoughts on the relationship of natural rights and the virtues.

[81] JL O'Donovan, 'Historical Prolegomena to a Theological View of Human Rights', *Studies in Christian Ethics*, 9 (1996), 54, also quoted in Rowland (above n 79) 153.

PART III

Justice

13

Justice without mercy

The jurisprudential thought of the modern era has maintained a steady focus on the idea of justice, but it has paid much less attention to an important concept, that of *mercy*. The neglect of mercy is not altogether inexplicable, for it is famously associated with a number of paradoxes. For example, the idea of mercy depends upon its being conceived as a virtue that is in some way distinct from, and irreducible to, justice. Mercy is said to moderate the operation of justice because it lies apart from the realm of law and justice, belonging instead to the domain of love, or compassion. Mercy *transcends* justice; but this transcendence seems to involve a departure from justice (and therefore bring about injustice). Were mercy always coeval with the requirements of justice, it would lose its identity as a separate virtue. Thus, mercy is either reducible to justice or, in undermining justice, ceases to be comprehensible as a virtue.[1]

Given its apparently paradoxical character, it is not surprising that the major theories of justice largely ignore the idea of mercy. It has been fashionable since the publication of Rawls's book *A Theory of Justice*, to place questions about justice at the heart of jurisprudential debates about the character of law and politics.[2] Justice representing the *highest* ideal at which the enlightened polity should aim, the perfection of society would appear to demand the constant refinement and realization of that ideal rather than its abandonment in specific situations. Any imperfections arising from the operation of justice are interpreted as shortcomings in

---

[1] I summarize here Jeffrie Murphy's argument in 'Mercy and Legal Justice', in J Murphy and J Hampton, *Forgiveness and Mercy* (Cambridge University Press, 1988). Other recent discussions of mercy include R Harrison, 'The Equality of Mercy', in H Gross and Harrison (eds.), *Jurisprudence: Cambridge Essays* (Oxford University Press, 1992) 107; NE Simmonds, 'Judgment and Mercy', *OJLS*, 13 (1993), 52; J Tasioulas, 'Mercy', *Proceedings of the Aristotelian Society*, 103 (2003), 101.

[2] Raymond Geuss has remarked upon the inherent strangeness of placing a theory of justice at the centre of a 'liberal' theory of politics: see R Geuss, *Outside Ethics* (Princeton University Press, 2005), ch 1. See also above, Part II, Chapter 9.

our perception of the ideal, and not indications of the limits of any such ideal. This attitude, which might be called 'the idealization of politics', is unfortunate. It is no accident that its most corrosive effects have received deepest exploration not in philosophy, but in literature. The tendency towards idealization and abstraction impedes exactly that humane understanding of which it is the function of literature to give expression. Morality is encountered, in literature as in life, as an active sensibility rather than a framework of general propositions. It is only through a heightened awareness of this sensibility that one may come to appreciate (as Trollope did) the dangers inherent in the ambition: 'Let justice be done though the heavens may fall.'[3]

My aim in this chapter is to offer an alternative understanding of the relationship between justice and mercy. My argument will attempt to demonstrate the centrality of mercy to an understanding of political society, and of the place of the juridical realm within it.

One might first consider what a 'paradox' of mercy implies. No tension could be felt between the ideas of justice and mercy if those ideas, 'justice' and 'mercy', did not possess an internal coherence and superficial plausibility. At the same time, there is a certain asymmetry about the relationship of those ideas. Mercy does not deny the operation of justice nor the validity of its ambitions, but justice leaves no room for mercy. More comfortable with the idea of justice, Western thought thus attributes a paradoxical character to its less practised virtue. The paradox is 'generated' by the application of a set of premises to an established body of ideas about reality. Because, generally speaking, the premises are not alighted upon wholly independently of the existing ideas but are in some way suggested by them, the correct response to a paradox is not to attempt to overcome the contradiction implied by those ideas whilst retaining as much of their integrity as possible, but rather to challenge the entire picture suggested by them, and find another way of looking at the world.

Mindful of this, my initial discussion will focus not upon the character of mercy, but on the nature of human understanding of society. I shall argue that our understanding of the social world crucially depends upon the articulation of mercy as a value, and that unconsciousness of this dimension of value is one of the most damaging effects of the idealistic

---

[3] This phrase appears a number of times in Anthony Trollope's works, but can be seen for instance in chs 61 and 62 of *The Last Chronicle of Barset*, new edn (Harmondsworth, Penguin Classics, 2002).

view of politics. Mercy, I shall argue, must be understood by reference to its roots as a religious concept, and I shall suggest that any political analogue of mercy must retain certain features of that intellectual inheritance if it is to make a genuine contribution to understanding.

Law, justice and society

There are good reasons to expect that political thought could be resistant to the religious associations of mercy. In contradistinction to Plato, Aristotle's vision of politics was focused very much on *this* world, and does not need to call upon any supernatural ideas in order to explain its forms and ambitions. Politics, like man himself, is of nature. The influence of Aristotle's preference over Western political thought was profound, influencing even Aquinas. Upon its disintegration in the early-modern period, the political vision that replaced it did not do so by invoking the supernatural, but by asserting the ultimately conventional basis of social arrangements. Human beings confront the world as a set of conditions which, despite being sufficient in all essential ways of supporting and sustaining life, are nevertheless imperfect when contemplated from the perspective of the ideal or preferred mode of life. Some of these conditions may be interpreted as 'natural' or 'given' states whereas others are brought about through human efforts. Human agency can therefore reasonably seek to alter existing worldly conditions in various ways. In undertaking such efforts, the overriding goal must be the production of *improved* conditions rather than impoverished ones, and this requires some set of standards to guide the understanding of what represents improvement to the human lot. Human beings stand in need of some practical notion of what the 'good' or preferred mode of existence consists in.

All such systems of understanding (whatever their vision of 'the good' or the means of reaching it) deserve to be called 'moralities'. Since it is the function of morality to seek to *change* the world, philosophers are driven to the distinctly un-Aristotelian thought that moral insight (or whatever passes for it) cannot derive from an understanding of worldly conditions, but must come from elsewhere. Hence it is often supposed that morality consists of general principles or ideals which together form an independent outlook upon the world of mundane and variable fact.

In virtue of the fact that the institution of the ideal form of association requires contemplation of the world, and of human action, from the perspective of general rules, a close and permanent relationship exists between justice (as a component of the ideal life) and law, as the form in which justice is both articulated and realized. The idea of justice is therefore simultaneously abstract and autonomous vis-à-vis the worldly conditions upon which it sits in judgment, and yet intelligible only within the context of collective social conditions. Accordingly, the attempt to implement justice in the world is always and everywhere the attempt to bring about the just *society*. This creates an interesting problem. Justice, being a creature of law and of society, must always be associated with the suppression of human freedom. The meaning of 'society' and of a 'form of association' involve precisely the avoidance of a state of total freedom, or anarchy. It is therefore inevitable to the character of justice that the effort to realize within the dynamic forces of human society a tolerable justice, must end with the continual alternation between intolerable anarchy and intolerable tyranny.[4] (I refer here to the coexistence of anarchic and tyrannical elements *within* a form of association, rather than as names of specific kinds of association.)

Liberals employ a thousand means and definitions to escape the need to dwell on this problem. Natural lawyers, who often upheld and affirmed the rational explicability of politics, a sense of the orderliness of this world on its own terms, nevertheless took the underlying problem far more seriously.[5] The natural and conventional order of this world was to be contrasted with the perfect order of the next. If human existence belongs to a rationally ordered cosmos in which it has an ultimate purpose and direction, nevertheless the full and final expression of that purpose lies outside the circles of the world. Divine law is the law that is natural and proper to the human condition; but it is always human effort and human interpretations which form the actual rules by which societies are governed.[6] So long as the *lex divina* was present within the world only in a reduced and attenuated form, human beings must confront a world that is chaotic and random as well as

---

[4] I borrow this image (though not the sentiment expressed) from Reinhold Niebuhr. See R Niebuhr, 'The Christian Witness in the Social and National Order', in R McAfee Brown (ed.), *The Essential Reinhold Niebuhr: Selected Essays and Addresses* (New Haven CT, Yale University Press, 1986), 99.

[5] See e.g. Grotius, *De Iure Belli ac Pacis*, Prologomena, 11: remarks on natural order would retain 'a degree of validity even if we should concede that which cannot be conceded without the utmost wickedness, that there is no God, or that the affairs of Men are of no concern to Him'.

[6] See for example Grotius (above n 5), II.2.vi.91.

cosmically meaningful.[7] The secular moralities of the present day present a different and more ambiguous role for transcendent morality. In forming an autonomous standpoint for reflection, morality is presented not only as the source of meaning of the human world but also its judge. This is an interesting intellectual position, depicting in an especially direct way the failure of modern philosophy to resolve the tension of historical immanence and transcendence. Morality embodies the absolute meaning of associative human relationships and not simply their present meaning, and in this it is transcendent. But it is also the *goal* of human society, and thus considered to be capable of historical implementation. It is the crucial failure of the jurisprudential and political thought of the present that it employs the idea of transcendence so as to absolutize rather than to criticize these partial achievements of history.[8]

This absolutizing tendency is premised upon certain assumptions concerning the historical significance of human efforts and the operative range wherein they can meet with success. 'Law' and 'Justice' represent accomplishments that, in being rational, express the highest potentialities of the human spirit, bringing order where before was chaos, and meaning to life where there had been mere existence.[9] In this there is an important bridge between the tradition of natural law thinking and the secular political theories that came after. Even if such efforts are interpreted as having their source in the divine will, it became increasingly clear to the ancestors of liberals that such divinity is imaginable only in virtue of its rationality. This eventually paved the way for the removal of theological presuppositions from political thought: Kant observing that, 'Even the Holy One of the Gospel must first be compared with our ideal of moral perfection before he is cognized as such'; and this ideal is one 'that reason frames a priori and connects inseparably with the concept of a free will'.[10]

---

[7] The theme of 'the frailty of human reason' in interpreting the divine law was present in various forms throughout the canon of natural law writing in the seventeenth and early eighteenth centuries, and perhaps especially acute in Locke: see Locke, *Essays on the Laws of Nature*, W von Leyden (ed.) (Oxford, Clarendon Press, 1954).

[8] See further Niebuhr, 'Optimism, Pessimism and Religious Faith', in McAfee Brown (above n 4), 6.

[9] Perhaps the clearest expression of this view is to be found in Hobbes's characterization of the transition from the state of nature to that of civil society: see *Leviathan*, ch 13.

[10] Kant, *Groundwork of the Metaphysics of Morals*, M Gregor and AW Woods (eds.) (Cambridge University Press, 1997), 4:409.

The detachment of theology from politics encouraged a focus on rationality as the ultimate instrument of order and significance in the world. Law and justice, the supreme incarnation of rational principles, gave impetus to a view of human societies as the ultimate centres of order in the world. As a result, it became possible to view the value systems of these societies as the final arbiters of human good and evil. The upward potentialities of these efforts seemed limitless. Such sentiments, as Matthew Kramer has observed, lie at the heart of a liberal vision of politics:

> [T]he liberal philosophers had to introduce a new tone of public discourse to match their substantive outlook. Just as liberalism had overall been a salutary response to what had preceded it, so its characteristic tone would improve upon the tenor of discourse that had prevailed under the *ancien regime*. Christianity had been pessimistic, murderously intolerant, fanatical, and dogmatic; liberalism would hence be optimistic, generously open-minded, cool-headed, and responsive to rational persuasion. Truth would be tied no longer to sacred writings and divine revelations, but would be seen henceforward as the product of close analysis and wide-ranging debate.[11]

Arguably the most direct expression of this optimism is that encountered in Rawls's mighty book, *A Theory of Justice*.[12] It will be recalled that Rawls sought to demonstrate, by this work, that the idea of justice could be elucidated on the basis of uncontentious propositions that are accepted as a rational starting point for further reasoning. The book (and the method) were to have a profound re-orientating effect upon political philosophy that is partly explained by its advance over the intellectual environment into which it emerged. That environment was dominated by a utilitarianism that depicted the modern society as a realm of conflicting preferences, the goal of politics being to maximize overall satisfaction of those preferences. The notion of justice was marginal to such concerns, the focus of politics lying not upon the value or soundness of the preferences but rather upon their strength. Where justice was discussed, it tended to be viewed as an issue of the practical and provisional balance to be achieved between randomly colliding syndicates advancing interests that must find some way to coexist. By grounding his argument in an 'original position' wherein rational

---

[11] MH Kramer, 'The Rule of (Mis)recognition in the Hart of Jurisprudence', *OJLS*, 8 (1988), 401.

[12] J Rawls, *A Theory of Justice*, revised edn (Cambridge MA, Belknap Press, 1999).

individuals seek to articulate, from behind a 'veil of ignorance', a set of principles for the structuring and administration of society, Rawls produced a powerful vision of justice that was appropriate to conditions of pluralism in that an understanding of it *precedes* contentious understandings of 'the good'.

It is (as Raymond Geuss observed) remarkable that such a complex theory, consisting of more than five hundred pages of dense and sustained argument, should culminate in a vision of the just and well-ordered society that is so striking in its resemblance to present constitutional arrangements of the United States. Moreover, '[i]t strains credulity to the breaking point to believe that "free and rational agents" (with no further qualifications), even if they were conducting a discussion from behind an artificial veil of ignorance ... would light on precisely *these* arrangements'.[13] Despite the serious redistributive aims of *A Theory of Justice*, the points of convergence between the theoretical model and actual features of the liberal democratic society are sufficiently profound as to encourage belief in the notion that such enlightened polities embody Rawlsian moral concerns. The 'meaning' of this form of human association (and by extension, all human association) is thus believed to be supplied by the precepts that belong to the theory.

An obvious antidote to the belief that meaning is given to human affairs via the autonomous standpoint of theory has received little emphasis in modern jurisprudential argument: that the present condition of the liberal society owes much more to the social movements and culture of 'permissiveness' which arose in the 1960s than to developments within the rarified world of academic philosophy.[14] Had more attention been paid to this aspect of social progress, the efforts of philosophy might have reflected to a greater extent the realization that important dimensions of social meaning arise out of historical actions that are independent of philosophical concerns.[15] The present point I wish to explore, however, concerns the consequences that result from

---

[13] Geuss (above n 2), 22.

[14] *A Theory of Justice* was first published in 1971 (though early versions of some of the book's arguments had appeared in article form in academic journals from the 1950s). It is perhaps worth emphasizing that I focus on Rawls here as the most *direct* embodiment of the trends I wish to examine. The philosophical methodologies (reflective equilibrium, etc.) integral to those trends have seen widespread use throughout political philosophy since the publication of Rawls's book.

[15] See also above, Part I, Chapter 3.

those tendencies within modern philosophy that operate to deify certain features of the present social order.

I have suggested that the attitude implicit in the Rawlsian theory of justice (and similarly conceived theories) could be described as 'the ideal-ization of politics'. Social arrangements and institutions are taken as implying certain ideals. The imperfection of present arrangements is treated as an indication that some refinement (and perhaps in some cases abandonment) of the established ideals is required, the better to reflect our most sophisticated and appealing conceptions of justice. Having con-ceived the goal of politics to be the identification and realization of an ideal of justice, secular liberal philosophies take for granted that the social grouping (or form of association) is the ultimate source of meaning in human affairs. Rawls (for example) considers that rational agents in the 'original position' will agree that issues of justice arise only in a context of scarce resources and conflicting preferences. If the allocation of resources to each individual carried no implications for the others, no one would care who received what, and no question of justice would arise. Thus, the idea of justice makes sense only within the context of a shared form of association where men live in permanent proximity to one another. All values make sense in terms of a mode of association, making the social grouping the ultimate source of meaning in human affairs, and the final centres of order in an otherwise random and chaotic world.

Where a general theory of justice is the ultimate source of value and meaning in this way, there is indeed no room for mercy in the adminis-tration of human affairs. The history of human effort can be regarded as the progressive attempt to replace conditions of chaos with conditions of order and stability. The moralities which guide such efforts, inevitably, are moralities of *rules*, for which law supplies the archetype. Since mercy seeks specific *departures* from the rules, it will seem that mercy is on the side of the chaotic elements of human history against which the general part of human effort is set. Standing in opposition to justice, the value of mercy remains unintelligible within the structures of meaning that ground the understanding of the human condition.[16] It is not difficult

---

[16] Nietzsche's view of the character of mercy is further demonstration of this: mercy, for Nietzsche, was the prerogative of the powerful sovereign to be employed as an emblem of power. Forbearance toward challenges to the sovereign authority demonstrated the security of that power, and its lack of diminishment in the face of challenges that lack the significance of a *necessary* response. See Nietzsche, 'The Wanderer and his Shadow', in *Human, All Too Human*, RJ Hollingdale (trans.) (Cambridge University Press, 1996), s.33. This line of thought is inherited from Seneca: see JM Cooper and

to trace the logic of this outlook. The meaning of history as a realm of human choice and action, is progress: the gradual removal of ignorance and immaturity, and the realization of ultimate meaning. Insofar as this ultimate meaning, and its attendant possibilities of order, are embodied in a *particular* form of association (the desired, or just society), the first moral duty of humanity is to seek the universal implementation of this social form: the elimination of 'outlaw states' and the conversion of all regimes to that of the ideal.[17]

These dangerous and corrosive effects of the idealization of politics are all too familiar in the international politics of the day. Rather than explore their implications further, I would like to propose an alternative.

Mercy and society

All human efforts can be understood as the attempt to find meaning in the world, perhaps nowhere more widely or deeply than in philosophy. Amongst the wisest thinkers, one glimpses the realization that this meaning is not to be discovered only through the analysis of social forces, but it requires a metaphysical perspective that relates the significance of those forces to an ultimate source of meaning which lies beyond them. In spite of the general hostility felt towards metaphysics within modern analytic philosophy, the mainstays of that tradition – the distinction of fact and value, the depiction of morality as an abstract and autonomous perspective on the world, emphasis on voluntarism, etc. – enshrine a metaphysical position whereby ultimate meaning within human affairs (that which ought to be) is held to transcend the meaning of present conditions (that which is). One might profitably reflect upon the history of attempts to locate this ultimate source of meaning.

It might be supposed that if there is meaning in the world, it can derive only from one (or perhaps both) of two sources. Either it must come from human history (as a realm of freedom and action), or else it must derive from nature (as a domain of forces that are in play independently of human action). The ultimate meaning of the human condition might then be thought to lie within the relationship between the two. A tradition of thought has existed from the earliest times that attributed

---

JF Procope (eds.), *Seneca: Moral and Political Essays* (Cambridge University Press, 1995), Essay 2: 'On Mercy', 134.

[17] For the notion of 'outlaw states' see Rawls, *The Law of Peoples* (Cambridge MA, Harvard University Press, 1999).

to nature a moral significance. Natural events (the rich harvest, the poor harvest, the storm at sea) came to be interpreted as judgments upon the sinful condition of mankind, which could be influenced by prayer. This twofold attitude toward the external world (of fearful obedience and thankful piety) generated two distinct but related interpretations of the relationship between humanity and the world. Both interpretations are present in the biblical account of Genesis: on the one hand was the assumption that God had created the earth as a home for mankind, rich in resources and appropriate to the purposes of human flourishing; on the other, the earth was viewed as a hostile environment with no particular sympathy to human aims, to be conquered and tamed by human agency.

The history of legal thought offers many examples of both interpretative tendencies, but they are perhaps most clearly to be observed in the diverse canon of natural law philosophy in the seventeenth and eighteenth centuries. The seventeenth century proved to be an especially rich period for the development of juristic thought. The disintegration of religious unity in Europe, coupled with a gradual shift from old jurisdictional notions of 'kingdoms' to something more closely resembling the modern 'state', combined to produce a new understanding of human society, and thus of the place of the human being within the world. These new jurisdictional orders were no longer to be thought of as projections of the divine will, manifested in the claims of the ruling dynasties, but rather as independent zones of power and interest.[18] No grand plan could be discovered in the relations between states whereby a final peace would emerge according to God's law. Nor did continual warfare signal the painful birth-pangs of the new order of peace and harmony amongst nations, but simply betokened the inevitable posture to be assumed between such independent sources of absolute power. Perpetually in competition with each other, these independent jurisdictions could no longer be thought to exist in order to realize or secure a common good, but had to be conceived simply as alternative domains of power operating to preserve their independence vis-à-vis one another. As jurists strove to understand the moral relations between these independent entities, it came to seem inevitably that relations between individuals within states must be treated in the same way. Lacking an idea of the common good,

---

[18] Such developments in thought did not, of course, occur overnight. Their discovery rather had the character of a gradual and deepening awareness of the implications of these new theoretical assumptions.

the moral basis of the state could not concern the promotion of conditions conducive to the realization of this preferred existence, but must instead consist in the protection and preservation of spheres of personal autonomy wherein the individual remains free of the will of others.[19]

These currents of thought served to place individuality at the heart of political understandings, but they were capable of development in various ways. Two understandings in particular were of special importance for the future direction of juridical thought concerning the relationship between law and society. The first was that of Grotius. Under his particular variation on the Aristotelian philosophy, the purpose of law was the systematic protection of entitlements governing the moral relations between individuals who pursue independent and potentially conflicting goals. Such entitlements were thought to derive from a basic right of self-preservation inherent in the notion of a 'human being', and expressed in the idea of the *suum* (or that which properly belongs to a person).[20] This was essentially an eschatological notion, in that the existence of the *suum* was inferred on the basis of a theological view of the world as created by God so that man may survive and flourish. (Only in such terms could there be a *right* to the means of survival, *suum ius*). Here was an image of the world as a domain of order and purpose in which the existence of man is subsumed within a wider cosmos that is ultimately related to and expressive of God's intentions. Viewed in such terms, the world is a domain of non-overlapping entitlements for which positive law is required simply for the purposes of their clarification and enforcement. On the other hand was the view of Hobbes, for whom the basic premise of self-preservation implied indeed not a harmonious realm of compossible entitlements, but a lawless world in which human interaction naturally takes the form of a war of each against all. In such a world, none but the most primitive set of assumptions could exist to guide human endeavour toward the attainment of peace. Law could only emerge as fabricated response to these basic conditions of the human predicament. In this way, Hobbes rejected the idea of a rationally ordered cosmos (such as that of Aristotle) structured by compossible domains of

---

[19] For a deeper account of this connection, see R Tuck, *The Rights of War and Peace: Political Thought and the International Order from Grotius to Kant* (Oxford University Press, 2001). See also Part II above.

[20] See Grotius (above n 5), I.1.iii.18. For an argument that Grotius 'deserts' Aristotelianism, see Tuck, *Natural Rights Theories: Their Origin and Development* (Cambridge University Press, 1979), ch 3.

ius, and instead represented the world beyond the boundaries of human society as a hostile environment from which escape, at almost any price, is necessary.[21]

Present within these variant pictures of the world were two distinct views of the character not only of law, but of all human value systems. The tension between them has in large measure shaped all subsequent thought about the nature of morality and law. We are accustomed to addressing this tension from a number of related standpoints: from the perspective of pluralism vs. absolutism; moral objectivity vs. moral subjectivity; ethical relativism vs. ethical realism; and so forth. But there is also a neglected, eschatological dimension to the tension which is of central importance for jurisprudential thinking on the relationship between justice and mercy. For it forces us to confront two distinct understandings of historical reality: one for which the world of human experience is interpreted pantheistically as domain in which all things that come to pass do so for a reason and have significance relative to an ultimate purpose; the other for which concrete reality is a corrupted realm of crude matter from which the spirit must detach itself. This latter perspective is informed by a kind of dualism which has itself taken numerous forms in the history of religious thought. It is present in the Hebrew division between the imperfection of the existing age and that of the perfect age to come; and it featured too, as a dualism of material and spiritual interests, in early Christian notions of the religious person's renunciation of material and earthly connections.[22]

Are either of these perspectives satisfactory? In supposing the ultimate meaning of existence to fall within the present world, neither has any difficulty in asserting that historical reality admits of a purely rationalist explanation. A pantheistic interpretation effectively sanctifies history, for every event and process is a contribution to the ultimate meaning of things. What view could be more congenial? But its comfort is deceit. We do not know the meaning of the Holocaust, but we rob it of its tragedy if we believe its presence in history to be ultimately redeeming. Yet dualism represents no advance over this view, for a world in which events are

---

[21] See Hobbes, *Leviathan*, chs 13–22. For detailed discussion see Harrison, *Hobbes, Locke and Confusion's Masterpiece* (Cambridge University Press, 2002). Specific dimensions of Hobbes's treatment of *ius* and *lex* are analysed in my article: S Coyle, 'Thomas Hobbes and the Intellectual Origins of Legal Positivism', *Canadian J of Law and Jurisprudence*, 16 (2002), 243–70.

[22] For an insightful discussion, see M Oakeshott, 'Religion and the World', in T Fuller (ed.), *Religion, Politics and the Moral Life* (New Haven CT, Yale University Press, 1993), 28.

wholly unrelated to transcendent values that make sense of them, is intolerable. To assume that the Holocaust has no meaning beyond the brute facts of its occurrence, to accept that all human laws and endeavours are reflective of nothing but temporary meanings and base desires, is to condemn the world completely as a home for the spirit and to render all motivation finally otiose.[23]

These points reveal a good deal about the assumptions that structure modern thinking on justice. Sharing with these perspectives the belief that rational historical explanations are possible, modern juridical thinking is able to locate all structures of meaning within the realm of possible experience. The 'transcendent' context in which the present meaning of human affairs is related to its absolute meaning turns out to be human history itself. Hence the final balance of judgment in all things falls within the scope of what is historically intelligible. We are left with the possibilities that the ideal form of the just society is (in principle) a realizable goal, or (alternatively) that there is nothing more to the idea of justice than can be discovered within the actual structures of meaning by which human thought proceeds. I am not concerned with the differences between these positions, but with their essential commonalities. The crucial presupposition that unites both cases is that human communities represent the ultimate centres of order in the world. Accordingly, such structures represent the only means by which evil can be redressed. In constituting the ultimate possibilities of order, human societies erect the final limits within which the forces of evil and disorder are contained. Historical progress is equated with the eventual suppression of the randomizing effects of human effort (and of nature), and the abolishment of unchecked evil. History itself is taken to represent the transition from barbarism and ignorance toward the highest forms of civility.[24]

The implications of this thinking are profound. The only possible response to evil and disorder is the imposition of justice. Disorder is suppressed because a scheme of justice includes certain distributive goals in terms of which material goods, powers and liberties are apportioned so as to produce a rationally defensible outcome.[25] The response to evil is achieved by way of judgment, and a fair and organized system

---

[23] I owe the basis of this argument to Neibuhr (above n 4), 15.

[24] See e.g. F Fukuyama, *The End of History and the Last Man* (London, Penguin, 1993), and my extended discussion in Part I, Chapter 1, above.

[25] See e.g. R Dworkin, *Law's Empire* (London, Fontana, 1986), 165.

of punishment. As a *social* virtue, justice leaves no room for mercy in either context. For mercy in its purest sense represents the remittance of the consequences of evil by modification of the response to it. Evil *demands* a response (if it is to he held in check); but the exercise of mercy is the decision not to exact the whole of what is due from the wrongdoer as the one responsible, but to reserve some of the suffering to oneself. Mercy is therefore always and exclusively the prerogative of the victim of evil. It is not a virtue that can be exercised (except by dubious extension) on behalf of another. As a result, mercy is incapable of being exercised by the organs of the state, or by any collective institution. The intelligibility of justice, as a social virtue, rests upon the demand 'that the state act on a single, coherent set of principles even when its citizens are divided about what the right principles of justice and fairness really are'.[26] Any attempt by organs of the state to exercise mercy *on the part of* the victim would therefore involve a readjustment of this single set of principles, not the simultaneous application of two distinct systems of value.[27]

This aspect of mercy and its relationship to society, has been explored by Ross Harrison.[28] Harrison's discussion is informed by a slightly different perspective, in that it concerns the close relationship that exists, in his eyes, between mercy and autonomy (the source of the merciful impulse being vital in falling within the choice of the person who bears the risks of his leniency). In being responsible for its citizens, the state must rather make its decisions on the basis of their content, for which the appropriate criteria must be rationality and justice. Mercy is not open to the state precisely because it embodies the denial of that keystone of formal justice, that like cases must be treated alike.[29] The details of this position are not of direct concern to the present argument, but attention needs to focus on one of the assumptions upon which it rests. This assumption is manifested most clearly in the responses to Harrison's claims. One such response appears in an important essay by John

---

[26] Ibid., 166.

[27] Finnis, who does not have much to say about mercy in his most famous work, might possibly argue that the state can exercise mercy insofar as acts of injustice harm the common good. This is by no means a straightforward possibility, giving rise to a thousand questions as to who 'owns' the act of mercy. At the same time, Finnis's conception of justice in being substantially different to that put forward by Rawls and others, certainly leaves the door more open for mercy.

[28] Harrison (above n 1), 117.

[29] Ibid., 108–9. I have necessarily compressed Harrison's argument here.

Tasioulas, upon which I shall very briefly focus.[30] According to Tasioulas, Harrison's understanding of the character of mercy belongs to a long-established sceptical tradition which challenges the rationality of mercy: 'The obvious problem with this contrast between individuals and organs of the state ... is that mercy is inherently other-regarding, impinging heavily on the interests of those liable to punishment.'[31] In belonging to this matrix of interests, mercy seems to belong to the same area of ethical thought as justice. Thus, 'Harrison's understanding of mercy as rationally ungoverned leniency leaves it mysterious what value it realizes, unless capricious deviations from justice are implausibly accorded value.' Hence also, 'he dresses mercy in the irrationalist garb favoured by its detractors, not its supporters'.[32]

The assumption that I wish to tease out is that if mercy is understood as a facet of practical reason, then it must be understood (as is justice) by reference to its ability to transform the structure of relationships that hold *within* a system of interests. If the role of mercy is to be explained in this context, then (by the usual meaning of 'explanation') there must be a certain consistency in its treatment of specific cases, and therefore a degree of abstraction in the criteria which govern its exercise. The intention of my remaining argument will not be to question this inference, but to undermine it at the root. I shall call into question the very idea that mercy belongs to this system of interests at all, and hence I aim to show that the comprehensibility of mercy transcends the narrow idea of 'rationality' associated with this view.

The character of mercy

I have suggested that a modern outlook on politics can be loosely identified with a belief that human societies represent the possibility of meaning in a world that is otherwise chaotic and random. At the same time, modern thought inherits from natural law the awareness of a possible (and indeed actual) gap between the present meaning of collective arrangements, and their absolute meaning. One cannot look to the world for a sense of this absolute meaning, because it is yet to be fully realized by any worldly conditions. It must instead belong to a

---

[30] Tasioulas (above n 1). Again, it is not my intention to explore this argument in detail, but simply to highlight an assumption. I hope therefore that the reader can excuse the very short treatment of a rich and complex argument.

[31] Ibid., 104.   [32] Ibid., 104 and 106.

transcendent horizon of morality by reference to which existing conditions (or that which is) can be compared to a set of ideal conditions (or that which ought to be). But since this transcendent horizon is itself thought to be the product of human reflection (the original position, the act of interpretation, the 'reasoned conviction', etc.), the absolute meaning of the human condition is thought nevertheless to be represented by a form of collective social organization. Morality is assumed to concern, not the situation of human existence within a wider cosmos, but the much narrower realm in which human effort can manipulate and vary aspects of the social situation. It is, as I have tried to argue, difficult to see how mercy can inform this process.

Fixing human social order as the ultimate source of meaning in the world, modern political thought can be said to have adopted a perspective in which 'law' has replaced 'God' as the supreme mover against evil and disorder. In this sense one may say that modern liberalism, especially in its utopian and idealistic versions, gives expression to a kind of secular religion. Life, in the modern polity as much as in the primitive 'state of nature', is subject to various confusions and frustrations, but unless there is some sense of an ultimate order by which evil is punished and good rewarded, there is nothing beyond the chaos of circumstances to lend it coherence. Hence, in *Leviathan*, Hobbes is moved to observe that the recognition of certain structural possibilities even within the 'state of nature' can be exploited in order to effect escape to a better condition of life in which evil is checked and order imposed.[33] By giving these transitional postulates the character of 'theorems' (that is, ratiocinations rather than externally imposed norms), Hobbes regards the worldly instantiation of peace and harmonious order as emphatically human achievements. Modern political thought has followed Hobbes in this, both secular philosophies *and* exponents of religiously inspired politics sharing the basic belief that justice in the world is realized through human action. Either there is no God, and we stand alone as bringers of order to a chaotic world, or God exists and we are His instruments, effecting the suppression of evil in His name. In both cases, justice (and by implication mercy) must be understood as *legal* virtues, for they seemingly represent a scale of values that cannot be understood apart from law.[34]

---

[33] See Hobbes (above n 21), ch 14.

[34] See e.g. Simmonds (above n 1), 52: '... mercy is not, as might first appear, a recognition of the extent to which non-juridical values such as that of love transcend the abstract and

The position of 'the moderns' in relation to justice gives tacit recognition to the connection between justice and an inescapable political phenomenon: *power*. If justice is to exist as more than merely an abstract idea, if it is actually to be done in the world, it must be exercised through law. Howsoever law might be said to place restraints and limitations upon power, its existence also depends upon and presupposes power. Justice in the world is thus not independent of power. Power in this sense is political power (the power to vary or regulate relationships in a *polis*), and insofar as it requires enforcement it involves also military or executive power. Though not an intrinsically evil idea, power cannot thereby be entirely divorced from evil ambitions and effects: for it is always and everywhere the projection of human ideals and interests which hold themselves out as sufficient or final centres of order in the world. Consequently, the imposition of justice by human agency does nothing to suppress or eliminate evil in the world. Though it may effect the suppression of particular instances of evil, the administration of justice actively perpetuates the struggle between opposing ideologies. This fact has received greater acknowledgement in the sphere of international politics than elsewhere (illustrated by contemporary concern over the Treaty of Versailles, for example), but its obvious implication has never successfully penetrated political consciousness: that the domain in which human agency can achieve its goals is much more limited than has been supposed.

Historically, political thought was able to avoid dwelling upon this implication due to the impact of the Judeo-Christian religion upon the juridical categories of the West. The religious man lived his life under the guidance of moral laws, finding an ultimate source in the divine will. Human evil is an affront to such laws, and thus also to the authority of God. As such, all evil ultimately demands to be contained within a greater power which limits and judges it. That power, historically and theologically, was manifested not through the Almighty's direct intervention in the world, but was assumed to be effected by earthly princes who serve as God's instruments. In this way, the foundation of political or prerogative power was presented as an extension of the divine authority. Such assumptions have not disappeared from the modern polity: the oath of allegiance and loyalty, at all levels of the political system, terminates in

formal claims of law. Rather, mercy is itself inseparable from the framework of juridical thinking, exhibiting its distinctive and autonomous character only in the specific context of judgment.'

an act of recognition of monarchical authority deriving from the coronation. Even today, these ideas have not entirely receded to the status of ceremonial relics. The Coronation of Queen Elizabeth II in 1953 was marked not by a political proclamation but by a religious rite that continues to be central to its constitutional meaning. It is nevertheless true to say that, today, the detailed business of the day-to-day administration of the law pays little attention to these ideas. But insofar as government and officers of the law continue to believe their exercise of power to be other than groundless and arbitrary, so long as the organization of their efforts is informed by considered values rather than random impulses, the underpinning assumptions have not receded utterly into the background but have undergone a transition. The demands of religion and Church have been supplanted by the demands of 'one's country'. Even democracy and liberalism themselves have taken on the status of ultimate values, proclaimed from the mouths of politicians and presidents on the world stage as the ground of righteousness. Religious impulse has not disappeared; it has merely elevated the 'secular state' to the level of an object of faith and worship.

Yet the same religious ideas that gave form and direction to Western political thinking also pointed consistently to a more humbling conclusion, one that has tended to receive less political expression. Resistant of too close an association between the will of God and the works of Man, Christians ever dwelt upon how limited were the things that human beings achieve. Realms and societies were not the final, but only premature and inadequate centres of order in the world. The ideas of justice, and of mercy, could extend far beyond what human beings could accomplish historically. The order of nature and of the *polis* were of course rationally interpretable, but demanded to be contemplated from a perspective outside history in order for their final significance to become known. Situated firmly within history, human beings are in the position of knowing that the world has meaning, but not being able to comprehend fully what that meaning is.[35] Believing in the reality of a moral order in nature (i.e. the moral significance of natural and historical processes), rejecting the nihilistic possibility that life has no meaning at all beyond the fact of its subsistence, man must nonetheless abandon belief in any straightforward, intelligible correlation of morality with natural and historical processes. He must see in the world evidence of

---

[35] See e.g. Neibuhr (above n 4), 14.

the essential impartiality of divine justice. God's Creation of the world as something apart from Himself involves the realization of freedom within it. But the creation of such freedom necessitates also the creation of ultimate limits in relation to the defiance that this freedom implies. These limits must operate within the world (if the world is not to be dismissed as utterly spoilt and irredeemable), and not simply become present as judgment in the afterlife. However, in the absence of direct intervention, the justice by which evil is checked must fall impartially as a judgment upon all: upon the good as much as upon the sinners. If any natural process is to be interpreted as belonging to this moral order (the death of an enemy from disease; the poor harvest; the shipwreck of a missionary voyage, etc.) then it must be regarded as possessing no immediate or discoverable meaning, but an ultimate and incomprehensible meaning.

The full meaning of the moral order is not at the same time exhausted by these ideas, for the very impersonality of justice (the wrath of God) seems incompatible with the idea of God as present within the Judeo-Christian tradition. The full meaning of the moral order is thus completed by God's *mercy*, manifested in the image of the crucified Christ. Mercy can therefore be explained in the following terms. Divine justice (the manifestation of God's power in the world) is an inescapable consequence of human freedom. But the nature of such justice is to be impersonal, so that the sun shines on both good and evil, and the rain falls on the good man and the bad alike. The justification for God's judgment is characterized by the fallen state of man. 'The good man' is never absolutely good, the worst of men not irredeemably bad, and therefore (as with all justice) its imposition is deserved. As beings (according to the Christian story) men are imperfect, forever giving in to sin. Thus, if men are to be saved it cannot be justice which achieves this salvation, but rather mercy. It is mercy that is manifested in the Crucifixion of Christ: God the Father judges the world, but gives the world His only Son, and in submitting to rather than refusing agony, it is God the Son who 'takes away the sins of the world'.[36] The Crucifixion represents God's mercy (specifically that of Christ) in remitting the full consequences of justice by taking the final such consequences to Himself. Where otherwise there would be inescapable damnation, there is the possibility of redemption.

---

[36] The words of the *Agnus Dei*, taken from John 1:29: 'Agnus Dei, qui tollis peccata mundi, miserere nobis.'

I have set out these views about the nature of mercy because they seem to me to represent the only finally satisfactory understanding of the meaning of mercy. The paradoxes concerning the character of mercy are dissolved, because the framework in which mercy is finally comprehensible is not that of the attempted balancing of competing interests in society. Within that narrower framework, mercy seemed to be paradoxical for it did not make sense in terms of the conceptions of rationality that structure the framework.[37] Rather than accepting that framework as the ground for dismissing mercy as a coherent idea, I suggest that we instead retain mercy and dismiss the framework. Within the broader framework I have outlined, the tension between justice and mercy becomes finally explicable. Mercy tempers justice, in mitigating its punitive consequences, but it does so by simultaneously standing as the culmination and fulfilment of justice.[38] I do not claim that in order to comprehend the value of mercy one must *accept* the Christian story (for of course many do not). I simply claim that an *understanding* of the story is a prerequisite for grasping the true meaning of mercy. In the following section I shall attempt to indicate some of the implications of this view of mercy for a jurisprudential understanding of law and society.

The role of mercy in the world

I began this chapter by mentioning the absence of serious discussions of mercy in the arguments of modern jurisprudence. The reason for such lack of discussion can be put down to the general acceptance amongst jurisprudential scholars of a conceptual framework in which mercy has no obvious place. Modern jurisprudential arguments contain many fiercely competing understandings of the implications of this framework, but they do not often exhibit a willingness to make the framework itself an object of criticism. I have attempted in the foregoing discussion to bring into focus some of the main features of this framework: the focus on personal interests, the mechanism of justice, belief in rational solutions, the perfectibility of society, and so on. These ideas I have brought loosely together under the term 'the idealization of

---

[37] Thus Murphy (above n 1) dismisses mercy as a juridical virtue in categorical terms, stating that there 'is simply no room for mercy as an autonomous virtue with which [a judge's] justice should be tempered. Let them keep their sentimentality to themselves, for use in their private lives with their family and pets' (at 174).

[38] I borrow the expression from Neibuhr (above n 4), 30.

politics'. Because the idealization of politics involves the belief that the meaning of society itself is ultimately comprehended by a theory of justice, modern jurisprudential scholarship can be described without too much exaggeration as recommending the pursuit of justice 'without mercy'. I believe this to be an unfortunate and damaging direction of thought, and that its central claims, as well as its questions and focal concerns, ought to be given up.

The operations of mercy, I have suggested, are not historical (though they are manifest in history), but belong to a supra-historical moral order. The appearance of paradox within the character of mercy is the result of a failure to grasp this fact. Mercy seems to be paradoxical because it is thought to concern the rational adjustment of relationships amongst interests that have already been determined by the value of justice (and thus to be in conflict with justice). Properly understood, mercy does not concern the further refinement of the balance between personal interests, but in fact transcends the rational computation of interests in terms of which its relationship to justice remains incomprehensible. Mercy (in the broader terms I am suggesting) does not *annul* justice, for justice remains historically present as a necessary absolute limit to evil in the world. Yet it completes the eschatological meaning of that justice in its recognition of the limits of the justice of social arrangements.

An example will suffice. A owes certain goods or services to B under contract which has been performed on B's side, but falls into bankruptcy. On the one hand, we could say that B has a right in justice to the delivery of the goods. Justice itself might demand that B refrain from pressing this claim until such time as A is solvent again (basic necessities for life being always 'due' to A in justice), but B's claim would revive (in justice) upon A's solvency.[39] But once A is declared solvent, B may exercise mercy by waiving his right. He may do this with an eye to many things: a concern that A's financial position is still somewhat precarious; or ultimate doubts as to whether fulfilment of the claim is really necessary to B's future financial security, whereas non-delivery would have a greater positive impact on A and A's dependants. The exercise of mercy comes at a cost: by forgiving the debt, B does not recover what is due to him. Justice (the computation of what is due to a person) shows that B is entitled to the performance he has waived. Thus mercy does not involve a

[39] I ignore for the moment the English law on bankruptcy which demands the abatement of creditors' claims *pari passu*. I owe this example to Tobias Schaffner.

re-calculation of 'what is due' to A and B, but a virtuous decision by B to ignore or moderate these calculations. It does not 'depart' from justice, because the sense of what is due in justice remains intact. The same would be true if B were one of A's ordinary creditors, and decided to waive his claim, being (as he judges) in a better position to absorb the loss than others, so that their claims can take a larger slice of the common pool of assets, *pari passu*.[40] Above all, B might cultivate a merciful and compassionate temperament out of a sense that what is due to him under the *ius positivum* may not correspond to objective justice, and that he lacks a sure sense of how extensive his entitlements under those objective standards truly are.

Grounded in virtue, exercises of mercy are not instances of 'rationally ungoverned leniency', nor do they represent 'capricious deviations from justice'.[41] They will appear so only to those for whom justice itself is treated as a dimension of practical reason with no connection to the idea of virtue. Rawls's treatment of justice as a property of the 'basic structure' of society is the epitome of this approach. It fixes the mind upon an idea of justice as the creation of a set of social conditions.[42] Where this idea takes hold, political philosophy will have little time for mercy, for mercy does not suggest any particular set of social arrangements as necessary or desirable. Indeed this captures the importance of mercy for modern thinking. Mercy promotes a greater sensitivity to the mutable and imperfect nature of all 'progress', whether theoretical or practical. It avoids 'the illusion that pursuit of the common good is pursuit of a once-for-all attainable objective'[43] terminating in 'ideal conditions'.

Moral deliberation is best understood as an active sensibility which addresses a continually disordered array of values and circumstances that are permanently in motion. The processes of detachment and abstraction that inevitably inform moral decision are naturally inclined to suggest a picture of morality as a juridical structure of rules, rights and principles. A representation of morality along these lines vastly impoverishes ethical

---

[40] Having exercised a legal power to waive his rights, B creates a new situation for justice: because new expectations arise from B's act upon which A may rely, it would then be unjust to seek to reassert the original claim.

[41] See Tasioulas (above n 1), 104.   [42] See Rawls (above n 12), 454.

[43] See J Finnis, *Natural Law and Natural Rights*, 2nd edn (Oxford, Clarendon Press, 2011), 193. See my discussion in Part II, Chapter 12, for the complaint that Finnis pays insufficient account of the virtues (including mercy).

understanding,[44] but its most corrosive effects lie in the elimination of mercy from the evaluative judgments concerning human relationships. Locating justice in social institutions, isolating individual rights from the moral demands of the other virtues, we may come to find that a certain destructive mercilessness also characterizes social institutions through which such values are projected, defying all attempts to perceive within them a full and satisfactory expression of even the most basic moral concerns.

[44] See my discussion in Coyle, *From Positivism to Idealism* (Dartmouth, Ashgate, 2007), ch 2.

14

Justice and moral judgment

Having said something about the relationship of justice to the idea of mercy, I would now like to turn to a different dimension of moral experience which, despite belonging to the rational part of man's character (like the virtues), is altogether ignored by present-day reflections upon political morality. I am referring to the idea of conscience.

It might be thought that conscience, so important an idea in the realm of personal morality, has little to do with 'political morality'. But if this is true it can only be because the morality of the political realm is utterly discontinuous in meaning with that of ordinary persons. One might of course try to distinguish two disjointed senses of 'morality', but such a suggestion is largely irrelevant to the understandings I intend to explore in this chapter, for these are held to proceed directly from the moral judgments of individuals, thinking *as* individuals in their mode of belonging to a collectivity.

In the 'original position' of Rawls, for example, the personal characteristics of the deliberators are 'veiled' from sight, but they are not absent. Each participant approaches the major questions of society from the perspective of how beings such as themselves are to relate to one another. They do not deliberate from some drastically novel vantage point! Appropriately, the notion of justice that emerges from the original position is based upon an idea that is immediately intelligible to those who reflect on questions of personal morality: that of fairness. The absence of ideas of conscience from discussions of 'political morality' is perhaps in part a legacy of attempts, particularly since the great works of Sidgwick, to discover a 'method' of moral reflection in politics.[1] For clearly the processes of conscience are not amenable to methodological analysis. In order to illustrate the bearing of conscience upon methods of political reflection (such as that of 'reflective equilibrium') I shall

---

[1] See H Sidgwick, *Methods of Ethics* (Indianapolis IN, Hackett Publishing, 1981).

concentrate upon a widely influential example of such a method: that owing to Dworkin. Dworkin does not of course have anything to say about conscience. But such is the extent of the incompatibility of methodical reflection with the processes of conscience that one cannot treat this omission as a simple oversight, capable of being remedied by their later inclusion. Recognition of the importance of conscience entails the rejection of the modern political understandings.

I will focus initially upon Dworkin's notion of 'integrity', suggesting that it conflicts with important elements of ordinary moral experience. Then, I propose to say a little more about the connection between moral philosophy and the contemplation of 'ultimate questions' (of religion, metaphysics and theology). These aspects of the discussion are not strictly separable, because the nature of one's ordinary moral intuitions might be said to depend upon their relationship to ultimate questions. Nevertheless I will endeavour to separate the two stages of the discussion as much as possible: relying in the first stage only upon a description of ordinary moral experience, as this has developed in the West, without exploring the connection of such intuitions to fundamental metaphysical ideas (or to their denial). The second stage of the argument will then deepen the approach by exploring the connection of morality to ultimate questions.

Integrity and conscience

In his recently published work, Dworkin announces an intention to interpret legal practices 'in a general way', in terms of 'the mix of values that best justifies the practice and that therefore should guide us in continuing the practice'.[2] Within this 'mix', a central place must be given to the 'ideal of political integrity, that is, to the principle that a state should try so far as possible to govern through a coherent set of political principles whose benefit it extends to all citizens'. Integrity, in this sense, is a 'dimension of equality'.[3] These claims necessitate some prior clarifications.

It is not unreasonable to suggest that, because integrity is a 'political' value, the argument must be taken to refer specifically to the domain of 'political morality'.[4] Can one therefore say that the argument pertains to intuitions that may differ from those of morality in the ordinary,

---

[2] R Dworkin, *Justice in Robes* (Cambridge MA, Harvard University Press, 2006), 12–13.
[3] Ibid., 13.   [4] Ibid., 15.

unadorned sense? The idea of 'political morality' is not as transparent as it might first appear. Implying mobilization of the state's resources, it may be thought to coincide with the idea of 'public morality' as opposed to 'private morality'. But as judgments of political morality might in some cases concern the location of the boundary between 'public' and 'private' morality, this explanation is not very helpful. Similarly, the notion of 'positive morality' might be thought to capture some of the sense that political morality differs from one's 'pure' moral judgments, but this fails adequately to reveal the reflective character of political morality. Perhaps one should simply say that 'political morality' brings together the domains of politics and 'ordinary' morality into a continuum. The idea of integrity therefore 'infuses political and private occasions each with the spirit of the other to the benefit of both'[5] and thereby 'fuses citizens' moral and political lives'. In doing so, integrity 'expands and deepens the role individual citizens can play in developing the public standards of their community'.[6]

Understood in this way, integrity (and by extension, political morality) defines a scale of values that exhibit commonality in a domain of disagreement. Taken as a whole, such values will therefore stand in various degrees of distinctness from the personal moralities of individual citizens, without being utterly discontinuous with personal moral values. Perhaps this is what prompts Dworkin to say that the most important aspect of 'integrity' is its representation of political morality as an essentially 'Protestant idea': 'fidelity to a scheme of principle each citizen has a responsibility to identify, ultimately for himself, as his community's scheme'.[7]

The Protestant character of political morality is intrinsic to its structure and language. Moral reflection upon 'public standards' is said to consist in the exploration and deepening of one's moral convictions. Such reflection is prompted, Dworkin says, by a worry about whether one's moral convictions are sound. Moral reasoning is 'taken up' as a response 'to felt uncertainty or vulnerability in [one's] moral convictions' or because people want 'to satisfy themselves that these convictions are

---

[5] Dworkin, *Law's Empire* (London, Fontana, 1986), 190. See also Dworkin (above n 2), 34–5: law and political theory are described as 'departments of morality' distinguished only on the basis of their embodiment of distinct institutional structures.

[6] Ibid., 189.

[7] Ibid., 190. Dworkin refers to 'protestantism' without capitalization, presumably in order to avoid raising suggestions of an implicit spirituality in his moral outlook. In the second part of this chapter I discuss my reasons for thinking that this evasion is unsuccessful.

not inconsistent with the more general principles or ideals that they endorse on other occasions'.[8] On the face of it, this is an odd way of speaking. For to possess a 'conviction' is to be convinced of something. How can one doubt one's own convictions! At first, we might be tempted to conclude that no great matter turns upon what is perhaps a fairly common way of speaking. It may be that to speak of 'doubting one's convictions' or worrying about their soundness, is just a short and convenient way of implying that one is no longer convinced of certain beliefs. That one's certainties have been, or are in the process of becoming, eroded. But after further reflection, we might come to believe that a deeper and more serious problem affects this way of speaking. Is the suggestion that we 'take up' moral reasoning only in situations where we have *lost* our convictions? That moral reasoning seeks to direct action precisely in those situations where we *no longer* possess a 'sound' understanding of right and wrong?

Could the introduction of further distinctions sufficiently dispel the sense of oddness that attaches to these suggestions? Can one for example distinguish between earlier and later convictions, or between 'provisionally held' convictions and the 'deeper' convictions that arise out of the process of reflecting upon the provisional beliefs? Or could one speak of the refinement of one's convictions (and so on)? But on reflection the effect of such distinctions is simply to devalue the notion of 'conviction'. Provisional beliefs are working hypotheses, not convictions. The refinement of one's convictions is an evasive way of referring to their alteration, or replacement. Still missing is an explanation of why (prior to 'taking up' moral reflection) a person should come to doubt their earlier convictions, or feel dissatisfaction with old certainties.

In one sense the notion of a moral 'conviction' may be viewed as implying the modest belief that one may, for all one's certainty and diligence, be wrong. The psychology of such an implication is in practice difficult to entertain consistently. One feels a most unsatisfactory tension between the propositions, 'I am sure I am right about this', and 'I may be wrong'. Acceptance of both propositions will usually result in a process of abstraction: an acceptance 'in principle' of the possibility of error, but in a way that effectively shields the particular belief in question from the broader implications of scepticism. Entertaining the potential for error as an abstract possibility, we leave our sense of the truth of our particular

---

[8] Dworkin (above n 2), 79.

beliefs undisturbed. One's modesty is therefore accommodated without any diminishment of one's sense of being sure. The seeming disparity between the possession of moral convictions and the reasons for 'taking up' moral reasoning is thus not dissolved by the introduction of distinctions between different kinds of convictions.

I raise these questions about the nature of conviction in order to highlight some latent ambiguities, or problems, in what might otherwise seem to be a transparent and unproblematic concept. Such doubts about 'convictions' may invite the suggestion that reference to conviction is but one idiom in which the central ideas of Dworkin's moral philosophy may be set out, and that the objections I have so far raised require no more than a rephrasing of those central ideas. I do not think that would be a useful manoeuvre. References to 'convictions' pervade Dworkin's published writings to such a degree that it would prove highly difficult to eradicate them without disturbing the substance of his theses. Even were this possible, any alternative terminology must preserve the distinction between truth and belief implied in the idea of a 'conviction', as well as providing sufficient certainty required of grounds for action. Let the unconvinced reader therefore attempt to eliminate the idea of conviction without thereby precipitating a general revision of major doctrines, or otherwise simply reproducing the substance of 'convictions' by the use of equivalent terms.[9]

Thus far I have only pointed to the presence, within the idea of 'convictions', of troubling ambiguities and difficult implications. This by itself would not establish disparities between Dworkin's view of moral reasoning and that of 'ordinary morality', but only (perhaps) the need for further explanation concerning the nature of moral convictions. But I shall now suggest that Dworkin's position is alien to the traditional forms of ordinary moral experience.

The traditional form to which Dworkin's position is most congenial is that of Lutheran Protestantism. Like the early Luther, Dworkin insists that all forms of communal reasoning and tradition can be trusted only if they find a source in the interpretations of 'free minds' that are informed by their own, independent reflections upon the appropriate texts and standards. Moral reasoning, on Dworkin's account, is not consonant with an agent's thinking and acting from a position of immersion within a

---

[9] I shall not for the present press my point beyond this invitation; but in the second part of this chapter I offer an explanation of the centrality of convictions to a Protestant account of morality such as Dworkin's.

communal tradition, but begins at the point at which the agent adopts a
critical posture towards that tradition and its values.[10] It is in this sense
that moral reasoning is said to depend upon the conscious adoption of a
moral perspective. Central motifs of the Lutheran position – the equal
potential for all to engage in moral reasoning, and the necessity of a
personal relationship with God – are translated in Dworkin's moral
philosophy as the rejection of unthinking reliance on inherited standards
and the personal responsibility of each agent to 'identify . . . his community's scheme'.

At the same time, Dworkin makes important departures from Lutheranism. Whether or not Lutheranism is accepted as embodying a correct
understanding of morality, it can certainly be understood as an intelligible form of moral experience. Dworkin's departures, I shall now suggest, give his position only a dubious connection to moral experience.

One question that can be asked of Lutherans is what constitutes a 'free
mind', and to what extent a free mind can or should detach itself from
established values. In the case of Dworkin, the answer is to be found in
his earlier discussion of practices of courtesy.[11] He imagines a society
given to following certain rules or practices in an 'unstudied', 'mechanical' or 'runic' way. Gradually, people develop an 'interpretive attitude'
towards the practices. They begin to understand that the practices do not
simply exist, but have some point or purpose. Eventually, in the light of
this purpose the particular requirements of the practice might come to be
modified or re-described. One could say that the mind becomes free in
achieving a certain distance from the practices in which it is immersed: it
ceases to be 'mechanistically' attached to them. Such minds 'impose
meaning on the institution' and then 'restructure it in the light of that
meaning'.[12] Freedom of the mind is not the complete abandonment of
established practices, but (as it were) intellectual mastery of them. Such
mastery 'is a matter of *imposing* purpose on an object' so that there is
'interaction between purpose and object'.[13]

Dworkin recognizes what might be called the 'contextualism' of moral
reasoning. Morality presupposes a context of shared practices and social
interaction. The freedom or intellectual mastery required is above all
mastery *of a practice*. Dworkin therefore shares with Lutheranism the
sense that the dimension of values forms a separate domain to that of 'the

---

[10] Cf. Dworkin's remarks on the adoption of an 'interpretive' attitude (in contrast with 'runic
traditionalism'), and the status of integrity as an interpretive concept: above n 5, ch 2.
[11] Ibid., 46ff.   [12] Ibid., 47.   [13] Ibid., 52 (my emphasis).

facts' upon which they are called to judge. Indeed, it may seem to be
intrinsic to the idea of moral judgment that its standards and assumptions derive from something other than the facts which must be adjudicated. But Dworkin makes some crucial movements away from
Lutheranism in his account of how this voluntarism structures moral
experience.[14] The mind's need for detachment from customs and traditions (if it is to become 'free') comes, in Luther's view, from the essential
corruption of mankind after the Fall. In light of man's fallen state, mired
in sin and wickedness, established contexts of practice and tradition
cannot act as a source of moral guidance for one who seeks to be good.
The good man must rely not upon the customs in which he is immersed,
but solely upon the guidance of sacred scripture. But how is one to
interpret scripture? How, from amongst possible understandings, must
its lessons be understood? The answer cannot lie in intuitions, for these
are the very intuitions which must be educated through contemplation of
the scriptures. It lies rather, according to Luther, in the *character*: that of
an individual who (as Aquinas wrote), 'realize[s] his weakness, and
acknowledge[s] his need of grace',[15] in whom God has instilled an inward
sense of charity, love and readiness to obey. Only through possession of
the appropriate character can the individual hope to approach moral
truth.

Such an attitude is the opposite of one driven by 'convictions'. As
Luther observes, 'For so long as the opinion of righteousness abideth in
man, so long there abideth also in him incomprehensible pride, pre-
sumption, security, hatred of God, contempt of His grace and mercy.'[16]
Dworkin, by contrast, makes it clear that he regards moral reasoning as a
matter of 'creative' or 'constructive' interpretation, through which values
are then *imposed* upon reality as standards of judgment. The locus of
such values can be nothing other than the 'will' of the reasoning agent.[17]

---

[14] My arguments here do not address the general sustainability of moral voluntarism, but
are confined to the issue of whether Dworkin's voluntarism is compatible with ordinary
moral intuitions.

[15] Aquinas, *Summa Theologiae*, I–II 106.3.

[16] Luther, 'A Commentary on St. Paul's Epistle to the Galatians', in J Dillenberger (ed.),
Martin Luther: Selections from his Writings (New York, Doubleday, 1961), 141.

[17] The classic attempt to reconcile the notions of reason and will is that of Kant's
Rechtslehre. I discuss the problematic character of that purported reconciliation in
S Coyle, *From Positivism to Idealism* (Dartmouth, Ashgate, 2007), ch 2. For the purposes
of the present argument, however, it makes little difference whether one focuses upon the
idea of a free-floating will, or upon the idea of a free-floating rationality. See also Part II,
Chapter 6 above.

What we are left with is, in the memorable words of FH Jacobi, 'Lutheranism without the Bible': a position in which the agent 'finds the only source of value within himself' and who therefore threatens to become 'such an egomaniac that he is convinced that he is God'.[18]

Having rejected religion, modern man may indeed see himself as the God of Morality. But he will nevertheless not, in ordinary contexts of moral judgment, think of his values as matters of ungrounded *choice*. This is nonetheless the logic of a voluntarism along the lines espoused by Dworkin. The nature of such a choice serves to create values that are autonomous and oppositional. Ethics (on this representation) is a complex structure of values, so that it becomes the task of moral reasoning 'to construct conceptions or interpretations of each of these values that reinforce the others'.[19] Dworkin argues extensively against moral pluralism: 'Nothing is easier [he writes] than composing definitions of liberty, equality, democracy, community, and justice that conflict with one another. But not much, in philosophy, is harder than showing why these are the definitions that we should accept.'[20] Yet moral values remain oppositional within Dworkin's account. In direct consequence of his rejection of pluralism, Dworkin argues that we are not, morally speaking, 'beholden to two independent sovereign powers' because 'we are drawn to each of the rival positions through arguments which, if we were finally to accept them as authoritative, would release us from the appeal of the other one'.[21] In other words, convictions are reached by a process of argument in which rival positions are opposed to one another, until one has arrived at the 'right' or 'best' answer, in the form of the best argument or set of definitions, whose power and appeal release us from the appeal of imaginable alternatives.[22]

---

[18] FC Beiser, *The Fate of Reason* (Cambridge MA, Harvard University Press, 1987), 83. See also FH Jacobi, *Werke*, III (Leipzig, Gerhard Fleischer, 1825), 49. One is also reminded of Lessing: 'If God were holding all truth in His right hand and the erring search for it in His left, and then said, "Choose!" I would humbly fall upon His left hand and say, "Father give! Pure truth is for Thee alone".' (Quoted in Beiser, *The Fate of Reason*, 98.) See also the discussion in Part II, Chapter 6, above.

[19] Dworkin (above n 2), 161.   [20] Ibid., 116.

[21] Ibid., 111. The 'two sovereign powers' refer here to freedom of speech and the punishment of racist speech. Clearly however the argument must extend to other values if similar conflicts are to be resolved.

[22] See Dworkin's remarks on the truth of legal and moral propositions in the introductory chapter to *Justice in Robes*. The 'right answer thesis' is sufficiently familiar to legal theorists to avoid the need for extensive rehearsal; but the notion of 'right answers'

Is this a plausible depiction of moral reasoning? Faced with situations of moral perplexity, do we feel that some clear thinking, and enough time and effort, would be enough to resolve feelings of moral unease or conflicting intuitions? Dworkin's understanding of moral reasoning seems to neglect a dimension of central importance to ordinary moral experience: conscience.

One could say that the notion of 'integrity' implies conscientious judgment, in that one who acts with conscientious consistency invites a certain kind of moral approval, even though the values he conscientiously serves are (in others' view) wrong. Conscience itself may seem able to fall into moral error, and in that sense resemble the idea of 'conviction'. Equally, conscientious consistency possesses moral value, for a person in whom all sense of conscience is absent, but who *happens* to act (as we think) rightly, is ordinarily worthy only of a heavily qualified form of moral praise. Conscience is thus an intrinsic dimension of moral experience. But it has this difference from the idea of a 'conviction': it serves, ordinarily, not as the voice of certainty, but as a questioner and a voice of doubt. If we truly believe in the existence of right and wrong, as standards distinct from what is conscientiously believed (i.e. believe 'morality' to be something more than 'conscience'), integrity must be taken to be, not the goal of moral reasoning, but merely its precondition.

Conscience is manifest within moral experience in a range of variant guises, of which the presence of 'conviction' is but one possible expression. It therefore represents 'a catholic receptivity of mind' to dimensions of moral experience which are incapable of expression in the form of convictions.[23] The conception of moral reasoning implied by 'integrity' carries the danger of reducing the notion of conscience to that of 'reason' (in making judgments and selecting ends), or else of will (in making conscious demands). Yet conscience is more elusive and more complex than either of these ideas. For it seems to embody *both* a faculty of judgment, which stands in a critical relationship to one's 'reasons', *and* a form of immanent moral sensibility that transcends wilful intentions.

---

stands in obvious contrast to the Lutheran postulate that all human traditions and institutions are tainted with the sinful characteristics of fallen man.

[23] See AK Rogers, 'Conscience', *International Journal of Ethics*, 41 (1931), 161. The notion of conscience may seem to have a particular resonance within Protestantism, since it is a distinctively *interior* source of judgment. But any conscience must be educated; and the education of conscience through personal scriptural study is no *more* valid a form of education than that based in communal efforts of reasoning and teaching. The idea of 'Catholic conscience' is therefore by no means deficient or retarded.

As such, the voice of conscience makes room for facets of moral experi-ence (that is, complex moral attitudes) that are either problematic for or otherwise wholly excluded by, the notion of moral integrity.

By way of example, the experience of 'remorse' is difficult to accom-modate within the picture of moral reasoning offered by integrity. Con-sider the case in which a person's own earlier states of conscience are reflected upon at a distance: where a person acts fully in accordance with their conscience, but later comes to believe his conscience to have fallen into moral error. Such a person might be said to have acted with 'integrity' (for one cannot know one's present conscience to be errone-ous); but we would nevertheless tend to identify in that person a moral defect implying some level of guilt. The man of 'integrity' is likely to respond to this kind of situation by seeking to identify and correct mistakes in his earlier 'convictions'. Such errors, one may suppose, result from some deficiency in the agent's attempt to achieve 'reflective equilib-rium' amongst his existing convictions. These errors could lie either in his general moral intuitions, or in his more specific convictions about the way in which the general moral principles 'fit' the context of particular facts.[24] But here, there is a danger of translating moral deficiencies (which involve the character) into purely intellectual errors: the moral 'blame' involved being relative to a sense of what the agent 'ought to have known' or understood.

Implicit in Dworkin's conception of practical reason is its intrinsic propensity to bring about moral progress. Each occasion on which the agent 'takes up' moral reasoning is one on which he refines his convic-tions as to how his actions, decisions or practices can be further perfected (made 'the best example of their kind that they can be'). The agent's 'established convictions' may thus be represented as a particular body of arguments and counter-arguments, to which each successive thought adds a further argument. It is tempting to suppose that each additional argument extends, or further completes, moral knowledge: one has, as it were, the existing level of excellence *plus* the new insight. Yet the voice of conscience is not an opposing Socratic presence in an internal, dialectical argument, but the lodestone of one's moral experience. It is this which shapes the character of remorse. Remorse is not to be trivialized as the shame of having fallen into a moral error from which intellect or

---

[24] See Dworkin's remarks on his attachment to the method of reflective equilibrium; above n 2, 161. Dworkin, unlike Rawls, extends the method to the area of 'personal morality and ethics'.

conscience has now rescued one. Remorse may indeed be felt on such occasions; but it will also be felt in situations in which the action towards which one feels remorse still appears to be the best, or only, thing that one could have done thus placed. It is only in regard to our grossest moral mistakes that we will find ourselves 'release[d] . . . from the appeal' of the opposing view.[25] On many occasions, we may instead be struck by the awareness that *every* possible avenue of action or inaction that is open to us has foreseeably evil consequences as well as ones that are foreseeably good. This admixture of good and evil is disguised even by the terminology of 'best' decisions or 'imperfect' decisions, for such terms lead us to ignore the fact that it is an *additional* evil that is done, alongside the good, in performing the action, and not simply an incomplete reduction of evil within a situation.[26]

To take but one example: the 'best' or 'morally correct' course of action may require a degree of dishonesty on the part of the actor. One instance of this is famously supplied by Dworkin himself: that it may be better for a judge in a Nazi regime to lie about the law (but there are many more trivial examples of the sort, which the reader will find little trouble in imagining). But any sense one may have that deception may occasionally be required by 'the right thing' in no way disrupts the categorical connection with 'the cruder and more blatant forms of dishonesty with which it is frequently and significantly, though not necessarily, associated'.[27] The additional evil that is done is easily demonstrated by considering the result of such deception coming to light. There may be no further consequence other than the essentially negative experience of realizing that one has been deceived.

It may be objected that these thoughts presuppose a philosophical doctrine that Dworkin explicitly denies: that of moral pluralism. But this is not the case. Dworkin urges that the apparent impasse between seemingly conflicting values cannot be a *conclusion* of practical reason. If argued into an impasse, 'we cannot then think that our reflection has been a success, that we have earned the right to stop. We are only stuck,

---

[25] Ibid., 111.

[26] For a theological defence of this possibility, see R Niebuhr, *The Essential Reinhold Niebuhr: Selected Essays and Addresses*, R McAfee Brown (ed.) (New Haven CT, Yale University Press, 1986).

[27] A Kolnai, 'Erroneous Conscience', in Z Balazs and F Dunlop (eds.), *Exploring the World of Human Practice: Readings In and About the Philosophy of Aurel Kolnai* (Budapest, CEU Press, 2004), 66.

which is different'.[28] But such an impasse need not be a consequence of values that are independent of one another and standing in mutual opposition. Values may also be mutually limiting whilst at the same time dependent on one another both for their intelligibility and their realization. (Liberty, for example, may be said to limit equality, but at the same time presupposes some degree of equality in its very idea.) The fact, as Aurel Kolnai has observed,

> is that we constantly choose on some grounds what we would reject on some other grounds, or conversely. This is precisely what choice means: our numerous, and in part changing, concerns clash mutually in various ways, and we cannot pursue them except by restricting and postponing them, by choosing to favour one and renounce another temporarily or perhaps definitively. The mutual attunement, scaling and ordering of our concerns, with 'ends and means' as one of its aspects, is called Practice.[29]

Dworkin's remarks on 'pluralism' emphasize his notion of practical reason as concerning the formation of 'convictions'. In Dworkin's eyes, the situation of doubt and mutual accommodation described by Kolnai must fail to represent a coherent moral situation or genuine *moral* experience. He encourages us to view it rather as, at most, an intermediate stage on the way to the formulation of a conviction. But the notion of practical reason as the successive adjustment and endorsement of convictions is not likely to foster the development of self-awareness and sensitivity in one's moral understandings. Those dimensions of moral experience (remorse, doubt, reluctance, nagging conscience, moral discomfort, the heavy heart, etc.) that signal the troubled conscience are not problems to be *overcome* by a more enlightened morality, but are part of the very presence of the moral attitude, as factors which educate the conscience even where one's substantive decisions remain unchanged. Thus understood, the central problem with Dworkin's view of morality is that it treats judgment as effectively equivalent to decision. He consequently feels puzzlement as to how we might (for example) *both* have a right that racial insults be punished *and* an unrestricted right of free speech.[30] But the conflict at the heart of this puzzlement is generated only if moral sensibilities can be translated, without loss, into juridical ideas (such as that of right), which have the effect of bringing judgment within the realm of decision.

---

[28] Dworkin (above n 2), 162.   [29] Kolnai (above n 27), 67.
[30] Dworkin (above n 2), 111.

In practice, moral error is not typically occasioned by intellectual delusion. The education of one's conscience is often as much a matter of educating the emotions (learning moderation and other virtues, bringing about a rational order of the passions) as educating the mind. Therefore, morality resembles not so much the attempt to articulate and 'fit' general moral principles to imperfect worldly conditions, as learning to love in a context of persons and actions that are in turn defined by imperfection.[31] The Dworkinian man of practical reason, the (perhaps) generous and high-principled, but rather self-willed servant of good causes,[32] is neither, I therefore conclude, the ideal nor even the typical moral persona.

Morality and metaphysics

There is a curious, but easy and seductive state of mind known as the 'alienated conscience'. It occurs when the agent's conscience ceases to take as its central principle and authority the contemplation of moral absolutes and allows instead some non-moral authority to usurp that place.[33] Kant, of all philosophers, was most aware of the tendency and fought most insistently against it, opposing the idea of freedom (of the 'will') against the immature propensity to cling to familiar authority; to allow others, or the past, or the Church, to 'think for us' and thereby impede the contemplation of 'pure reason'.[34]

Much of philosophy might be said to consist in such a state of mind, for it comes upon us whenever we, glimpsing some aspect of the truth in the writings of a Hobbes, a Locke, a Kant or a Rawls, become fixated upon the doctrine in which it is bodied forth and forsake the pursuit of that which we originally sought. It is present in the philosopher's self-description as a 'Kantian' or a 'Rawlsian', as a 'liberal' or as a 'communitarian'. The feeling that the true way is to be found more readily or more completely in a particular doctrinal position, and is to be studied in relation to that doctrine to the exclusion of others, confers upon the

---

[31] See Augustine, *De Civitate Dei*, XIX. Compare also the contrast in the New Testament between the morality of the Scribes with that of the law of love. In both cases, this is not of course to deny that love and virtue are rational, intellectual experiences.

[32] I adapt the type described by Kolnai (above n 27), 65.   [33] Ibid., 71.

[34] See Kant's essay, 'What Is Enlightenment?', in MJ Gregor and AW Woods (eds.), *Practical Philosophy: The Cambridge Edition of the Works of Immanuel Kant* (Cambridge University Press, 1996), 17–22. Kant speaks repeatedly of the human being's 'self-incurred minority'. See also the discussion in Part II, Chapter 6 above.

thinker a powerful and easily assimilated identity. But it bestows also forgetfulness that the great philosophers of the past, be they ever so wise, 'can appear in the capacity of witnesses, pleaders and experts only'.[35] Absorbing such an identity,

> the thinker is no longer a pupil whom his master has taught how to see the Object but a moon-struck sectarian whose gaze remains fixed upon the master, with the Object yielding its place, in his vision, to its mere reflection in the master's mind.[36]

So determined was Kant's revolt against this possibility, that he created a space for genuine contemplation of the truth, separated from all experience, all authority, and all presupposition, that is void and hopeless. One is left with the necessity of educating one's conscience in its pursuit of moral truth by reference to the existing stock of human thought, whilst at the same time preserving its autonomy and finality in judgment. This is not an easy task. For just as the mind cannot be expected to receive an uninterrupted image of the truth by casting away the particulars of human experience behind a 'veil of ignorance', neither may it move towards that image by way of convictions born of present experience, even in 'reflective equilibrium'.[37]

How is the task to be accomplished? By reference to which authorities should we be guided? In the course of this book, I have suggested that the spirituality of modern jurisprudence has been shaped in part by Lutheran ideas, especially as they have been re-imagined (and perhaps distorted) by Kant. This inheritance must be rejected. In its place we must pursue a moral vision infused with a Catholic temperament.[38] Kant must be rejected because of the falsity of his central moral idea. One could say that morality, in the widest sense, concerns 'the good'. (We might avoid making any presuppositions as to the nature or characteristics of 'the good', so that it may be agreeable, thus far, to utilitarians as much as to virtue ethicists, eudaimonists or sceptical subjectivists.) The idea of 'the

---

[35] See Kolnai, *Ethics, Value and Reality* (New Brunswick NJ, Transaction Publishers, 2008), 35.

[36] Ibid.

[37] The notion of the 'original position' – like that of Cartesian doubt – is especially troubling; for what picture of the human being can sustain the thought that identities, or even preferences, can be discarded as one might remove one's outer garb?

[38] I leave aside here the ritualistic dimensions of Catholicism versus those of the Protestant confessions, being concerned only with the authorities of moral guidance. For I wish to leave open the question as to what extent the specific ritual observances prescribed by the Church are an indispensable constituent of the moral life: though see below. For Augustine, the *philosophia perennis* was that of Plato: see *De Civitate Dei*, VIII.

good' is inconceivable without some reference to its power of attraction in respect of those who pursue it.[39] But precisely such an idea, shorn of its attractive properties, is the principle upon which the Kantian philosophy is founded. Thus, the true image of the thing being pursued is not to be found in Kant.

If 'the good' requires some connection with the good of the agent who pursues it, nevertheless the good cannot be judged equivalent to what is 'good for the agent', even if this is taken in its most objective sense. Something that is 'good of' or 'for the agent' may be so in two separate senses. In the first place, one could make a straightforward equation with the notion of 'pleasure'. A subjective vision of this kind is of course contrary to the category of conscience; but it is also contrary to experience. Advocating a kind of subjective vision of the good, Hobbes observes that each person's 'good' is particular to them, and to advance one's own interests is to curb that of others. Why then, if pleasure is the ultimate ground of action, is not all humanity unremittingly evil, when judged according to the lights of (the mistaken category of) conscience? But ultimate satisfaction, perhaps, is not a matter of sensation only, yet also concerns man's rational qualities. Thus Hobbes asserts that escape from the darkness of the 'condition which man by nature is placed in' is effected only partly by the desire for commodious living, but partly also by man's rationality.[40] Though Hobbes suggests that reason is but a *means* to escape (supplying 'convenient articles of peace') and defines not the goal, yet his subsequent discussion does not bear out this distinction. Nor can it: for whether the 'laws of nature' suggested by reason are genuine norms of behaviour, imperative in character, or mere 'theorems of prudence',[41] it is they which determine the shape of the commodious life and consequently cannot be understood apart from it. Implementing the 'laws of nature' we have, not preconditions for the good life which are yet not of that life, but rather the essentials of its reality and substance. (We have, as it were, not 'the form of peace' but its actuality, of which the form is part.)

Recognizing this, we are obliged to regard the human being as more than an animal of sensuous urges, but also a creature of reason. Whether or not reason is ultimately the slave of the passions (as Hume averred), nevertheless it plays some part in their modification, and restraint. This suggests a second sense of what is good of, or for, the agent: that which,

---

[39] See Kolnai (above n 35), 74.   [40] Hobbes, *Leviathan*, ch 13.   [41] Ibid., ch 14.

deriving from Aristotle, we view as *perfective* of the agent's nature. Pleasure is not the stuff of goodness, but accompanies in some measure its pursuit. But the matter cannot rest with Aristotle. For as Augustine pointed out, whilst the good man finds pleasure in virtue, pleasure is by no means confined to the doing of good. If there is to be a distinction between good and evil (so that 'the good' of the agent refers not to one determined to become perfectly *bad*), one must find a wider significance in the distinction between what is sensual or 'brutish' in human nature, and what is spiritual or rational. The significance of morality therefore does not end with human nature: a significance to be found in the following, most Augustinian, pattern of thought:

> [M]an's mind enables him to turn to all kinds of things and by judgment and intelligent choice reach for the good that suits him best. However, if man is an image of God he is also an embodied animal and his soul partly a machinery of sensuous urges; his reason both controls and ennobles his sensuality but at the same time is vulnerable to its warping influences. For the somehow god-like height and wealth of his mode of life ... he pays with the possibility of erroneous judgment and vicious choice, nay, an innate inclination to misuse his powers, allow his unbridled desires to stray into ways of degradation, and fall short of his essential stature. While always of *a priori* necessity pursuing a conceptual semblance (*species*) of good, he may pursue a merely *apparent* and disregard the *true* good. To avoid this and ascend to his 'natural' perfection, he needs education ...[42]

Absent from this sentiment, but to be found (for example) in much of Philip Allott's writing, is the specific need for a collective effort to renew the social forms which perpetuate misuse of powers on an international scale. Morality is in this sense '[a] revolution, not in the streets, but in the mind'.[43]

The ability ultimately to distinguish between right and wrong demands a frame of reference that is wider than that of human interests. Neither is the intelligibility of goodness *exclusive* of such interests. Moral thought therefore demands a mode of belief that is informed by a

---

[42] Kolnai (above n 35), 74–5. A similar sentiment can be found in *De Civitate Dei* VIII: 'For if man has been so created as to attain, through the special excellence in man's being, to that excellence which is superior to all other things, that is, to the one true God of supreme goodness, without whom no being exists, no teaching instructs, no experience profits, then we should seek him in whom for us all things are held together, we should find him in whom for us all things are certain, we should love him, in whom is found all goodness.'

[43] PJ Allott, *Eunomia: A New Order for a New World*, 2nd edn (Oxford University Press, 2001), 257.

sense of the place of human beings within a broader cosmological order. It is for this reason that morality cannot be finally separated from 'ultimate questions' concerning the nature of that cosmological order. Despite the focus in Protestant belief, the significance of such an order is not exhausted by the character of one's personal relationship to God, but requires a sense of the collective achievement (and failure) of a community of believers. In the language of Idealism, we confront an Absolute: and in so confronting it we become aware of our relationship to it, and involvement in it. But such a relationship, though it may be personal, is neither perfectly private nor particular, for others too have the same manner of involvement in it, and form part of what it must mean for us.

Clearly the 'absoluteness' of morality demands a certain alienation of self and interest to something acknowledged to be greater than oneself. One's own 'good' must be acknowledged as something distinct from and lesser in degree than the good absolutely. But if this act of subjugation is to make any sense, neither can the absolute good involve a wholehearted *denial* of what is good for one. Above all, this manner of involvement with an absolute morality is not particular, but is common to all beings capable of comprehending its character. Thus, if in acting compassionately toward another I may be said to have sacrificed something of my own interests, the meaning of this sacrifice is grounded not in the interests of the other alone, but in the absolute good also of which the other's interests are but an imperfect reflection, and of lesser degree. For the act of compassion is itself meaningless, unless done for the sake of a greater notion of good.[44] (Why not otherwise act for the earthly interests of moral monsters as much as for those in whom one has recognized some good after which one strives oneself?) It is this which Augustine intends in the tenth book of *City of God*:

> Thus the true sacrifice is offered in every act which is designed to unite us to God in a holy fellowship, every act, that is, which is directed to that final Good which makes possible our true felicity. For that reason even an act of compassion itself is not a sacrifice, if it is not done for the sake of God ... Hence a man ... is in himself a sacrifice inasmuch as he 'dies to the world' so that he may 'live for God'. For this also is related to compassion, the compassion that a man shows towards himself.[45]

---

[44] Recall the discussion of Finnis's treatment of self-sacrifice in Part I, Chapter 1 above.
[45] Augustine, *De Civitate Dei*, X.

The ethic of neighbourly love itself becomes intelligible when understood as the expression of the involvement of others in a single absolute (no matter how variously described or understood). For the sacrifice of one's interests is not done merely for the furtherance of others (or else morality would be a matter of the character of one's actions towards those whom one was, as it were, romantically or emotionally attached only), but for the approximation of things to the way they should be. In bringing about such an end one is oneself moved into closer approximation to the absolute that is in view, though one's interests had to be denied in order to achieve it. But at the same time, one can perceive the character of the absolute good only in the reduced sense in which it appears in what is immediate and close at hand, being 'dazzled by the clearest objects of nature, as the owl is dazzled by the light of the sun'.[46]

At all events, the law of neighbourly love (which is to be exercised towards friends, strangers and enemies alike) is indistinguishable from a love of goodness in its absolute sense, from the realization that one's own involvement in it is not splendidly independent of that of others, and from the desire that all should be moved closer towards it. And to know it more completely, to know what it *must be*, is therefore to know it in the context of a community. Identifying the absolute, in this sense, with God, Augustine writes: 'For we are His temple, collectively, and as individuals. For He condescends to dwell in the union of all and in each person. He is as great in the individual as He is in the whole body of His worshippers.'[47]

In this way one can comprehend more clearly the complexity of the relationship between the individual's own 'good' and that of morality. For beyond the self-love of interests, upon which it is all too easy to fix one's eye, there is the self-love of what Augustine calls 'felicity', meaning one's proximity to God which, referring not to one's interests but to one's humanity, is the gateway to neighbourly love:

> For in order that a man may know how to love himself an end has been established for him to which he is to refer all his action, so that he may attain to bliss. For if a man loves himself, his one wish is to achieve blessedness. Now this end is 'to cling to God'. Thus, if a man knows how

---

[46] Aristotle, *Metaphysics*, II.i.

[47] Augustine, *De Civitate Dei*, X. Thus also, Augustine observes that 'it immediately follows that the whole redeemed community, that is to say, the congregation and fellowship of the saints, is offered to God as a universal sacrifice'.

to love himself, the commandment to love his neighbour bids him do all
he can to bring his neighbour to love God.[48]

It is this dimension of experience that the cold rationality of Kant is
unable to fathom. So too is it missed by the modern Protestant thinker
(in this chapter exemplified by Dworkin) who, armed with his convictions, views the world rather as an arena of action in which one must
strive to remain true to one's inner standards. It has always been the
weakness of such approaches that the domain of 'political morality' (by
which is meant the morality of, or applicable to, the collectivity) is seen to
arise through a process of agreement in judgments; an effort to arrive at
coherent definitions or understandings of moral concepts that is a joint
effort only because it arises in a joint domain, in which each actor must
adapt his patterns of thought and action for the sake of a mutual
accommodation. But the supposed condition of autonomy which generates this opposition in turn undermines any reason to believe that each
person's 'convictions' should converge in practice to such an extent that
mutual accommodation between them is possible. The idea that this
process of adaptation is achieved through 'reflective equilibrium' is a
poor substitute for the required explanation. For those commonalities
upon which one is supposed to reflect in attuning one's abstract beliefs (a
shared language, culture, structure of concepts, etc.) are precisely those
things the existence of which must *be* explained as products of common
patterns of thought and action.[49]

The aim of this chapter has been to offer a direct challenge to the
dominant understanding of 'political morality'. I have tried to show that
it is both necessary and possible to comprehend morality in terms which
perceive no distinction between the morality of the common domain and
that of the individual person. The result is a picture of morality far
removed from the notion of 'integrity' that is said to inform the morality
of law. Whilst being a morality of absolutes, it is not a morality of ideals
in the usual sense. It represents a form of morality that is largely absent
from jurisprudential discussions of the nature of law even amongst those
identified as 'natural lawyers' (except perhaps Finnis).[50] I shall therefore
endeavour to indicate briefly its meaning for law, and for politics and
society in general.

---

[48] Ibid.   [49] See my discussion in Coyle (above n 17).
[50] See J Finnis, *Natural Law and Natural Rights*, 2nd edn (Oxford, Clarendon Press, 2011),
chs 5 and 13.

The morality of the law

Few perhaps have pondered the full significance of the title of Lon Fuller's most famous book.[51] In it he considers not the connection between two independent objects of contemplation, law and morality, nor the extent to which one is included in or by the other. It is accordingly not the morality *in* law that interests him, but the morality of the law itself. This, it seems to me, is the correct starting point, but one from which it is possible to strike out in various directions.

Building on the general direction of argument pursued in the second part of this book, one could say that law deserves to be understood as a process for creating conditions in which the mode of sacrificial love explored in the foregoing section can flourish and grow within social conditions in which it is presently absent. Present society does not endure a complete absence of that love, but carves out an existence always in its less-than-full presence. To speak in such terms is itself an averaging of social conditions which are by nature highly various, in which the presence of love in human relations is here greater and there less, but never everywhere the same. Law must therefore address the whole spectrum of such conditions, the greater and the less, and its character is shaped by this need. 'Modern' jurisprudence (by which is meant theories of law that developed after the Protestant Reformation) is in large part premised upon a contrast between law and love.[52] The meaning of this contrast might be taken to reflect the fact

> that law is abstract, impersonal, objective, deliberate, whereas love is concrete, personal, subjective, spontaneous. But such a notion is a caricature both of love and of law. It makes love sentimental and romantic, and law wooden and sterile. Law, by which I mean society's effort to establish just relations among people, to resolve conflicting interests, to regulate social life, and love, by which I mean the sacrificial sharing of one's life with God and with one's fellow men, stand in a complementary relationship to each other. Love needs law to give it structure; law needs love to give it direction and motivation.[53]

Love, no less than law, requires rules and procedures when it extends beyond the relationships of more than only a few people. Berman's

---

[51] L Fuller, *The Morality of Law*, revised edn (New Haven CT, Yale University Press, 1964).

[52] See e.g. NE Simmonds, 'Protestant Jurisprudence and Modern Doctrinal Scholarship', *Cambridge LJ*, 60 (2001), 271–300.

[53] HJ Berman, *Faith and Order: The Reconciliation of Law and Religion* (Grand Rapids MI, Eerdmans, 1993), 314.

remark touches a deep truth about law. Both law and love concern human relations: relations in which love is present in varying degrees. It would of course be facile to suggest that the adjudicative context is one in which love is always entirely or mostly absent, for lawsuits are begun and pursued for a host of reasons, not all of which presuppose the hatred of the defendant by the claimant. Law itself, beyond its existence as a set of rules and procedures, is a mode of relationship between people. And '[l]ove in the Christian sense is not more excluded from legal relationships than from any other type of human relationships'.[54] In one obvious sense, adjudication represents the desire to deal fairly with the person who has harmed one, and not to pursue one's claim against the person through violence, deceit, fraud, or other means.

Application of the law's rules to the specific situation is said to demand 'interpretation'. This notion has perhaps been partially responsible for the controversies that have dogged the jurisprudential debates of the modern age. For one must ask whether the standards or procedures by which one 'interprets' the rules of authority are to be viewed as wholly internal to the law as an institution, or whether at least some of these lie outside law as such. Are such controversies relevant to a deep understanding of law? Their character is altered as soon as one recognizes that for 'interpretation' in this context must be read 'judgment'. The judge in the instant case is obliged to decide upon the legal position as it affects the parties. In this he might be said to be guided by a number of factors. One factor inevitably concerns the guidance offered by reflection upon previous cases through the doctrine of *stare decisis*. Another concerns the facts of the instant case, including the behaviour of (and thus the particular relationship between) the parties. It is often said in this context that law excludes certain aspects of the 'total situation' as between the parties, and concentrates upon their character as right- and duty-bearers only. But this statement must not be allowed simply to repeat the facile distinction between 'law' and 'love'. For we have not as yet established any reason why the notions of right- and duty-holder should be deemed to be intelligible only in isolation from ideas of love, or from other human values that inform relationships between persons.

How shall one account for the law's abstraction from 'the total situation'? Unless it is completely dehumanized and divorced from justice, the judicial application of law must exhibit sensitivity to the particular

---

[54] Ibid., 315.

features of the case. To accept this is to admit that nothing less than the 'total situation' is relevant to the deliberation of the judge, though ultimately her judgment is grounded on certain aspects of the situation only. Such a process of narrowing is one of appreciating which aspects of the total situation assume particular significance in the light of doctrine, policy, and so on. No aspect of the 'total situation' that is presented before the court is *ab initio* excluded. But neither can the judgment be based *exclusively* upon the relationship between particular individuals. The character of law, and of love and justice also, are such that they must apply to situations that are unlike the present situation in numerous respects. Because there is no 'average condition' in society concerning the extent to which love, or justice, or true morality is present in human relationships, the law must supply it. The judge must therefore be sensitive to this need for generality, as well as for specific attention to the features of the instant case.

The resulting body of standards, doctrines and judgments (which are nowhere the product of one mind, nor of a single point of view) might be collectively referred to as a 'secular morality'. They are secular in being specific products of human thought and action that are addressed, not to the law of Christian love directly, but to a situation in which the law of love is only imperfectly realized and heavily qualified. For this reason, law can be said to embody, in Fuller's words, a morality of minimum duty.[55] But precisely in that it does *not* embody a fully realized law of love, precisely insofar as it addresses an imperfect reality, the law can also be said to instantiate a 'morality of aspiration': one which makes possible, in laying down minimal conditions for civilized behaviour, the contemplation of, and striving for, a 'higher morality'. This, it seems to me, is what is essential to the character of law as a moral, political and social institution. And the fact that law can also exhibit immorality, can close off avenues for the further realization of Christian love, is immaterial to the question I have been contemplating: the question of what morality and goodness *must mean*, and how law may be said to be related to it.

In the light of these suggestions, I propose to devote the final two chapters to a consideration of the meaning of law, and of justice in particular, in the context of a chronically imperfect world.

---

[55] Fuller (above n 51), ch 1.

15

Fallen justice

In a letter to Nectarius, Augustine takes to task the political philosophers of the Roman polity for their failure to secure justice for the earthly realm. Though philosophy correctly identifies justice as a central concern of politics, learned men are powerless to realize the just society except in thought and speech.[1] At times, Augustine seems to argue that 'real' cities (not those which exist only in speculative thought) do not, and perhaps cannot, contain true justice. The basis of peace in the earthly city is 'an ordered agreement of mind with mind'[2] that is limited to 'the establishment of a kind of compromise between human wills about the things relevant to mortal life'.[3] Such societies are founded not upon 'common acknowledgement of right' but on 'common agreement as to the objects of their love'.[4] In the absence of truly cordial and just relations with one's neighbours, politics becomes a matter of instituting a kind of average condition of being, but one that is deficient in many respects. Perhaps, in such conditions, justice is a virtue that can be satisfactorily explored only in private life: 'what consolation have we in this human society,' Augustine asks, 'so replete with mistaken notions and distressing anxieties, except the unfeigned faith and mutual affections of genuine, loyal friends'.[5]

Passages such as these find Augustine expressing ideas that are not widely adrift of those of Hobbes. The law of the earthly city has as its primary purpose the maintenance of peace and good order; yet in a world in which there are no agreed conceptions of justice, this is not the bliss which comes when each person is accorded what is rightly due to them, but the fragile armistice between competing interests which correctly perceive that without law, things would go worse. Because the human condition is a fallen one, the sum of human efforts to realize true justice in the world will meet with little success.[6] Law has no intrinsic

---

[1] Augustine, Epistle 91, 4.   [2] Augustine, *De Civitate Dei*, XIX, 13.   [3] Ibid., XIX, 17.
[4] Ibid., XIX, 24.   [5] Ibid., XIX, 8.   [6] Augustine, *De Libero Arbitrio*, I.

connection to justice, but provides the common body of rules and standards required by a community in the absence of justice.

At other times, however, Augustine pursues a quite different understanding of the importance of justice. Whilst still accepting that some injustice is inevitable in the government of any society, he declares that a Roman commonwealth 'never existed, because there never was real justice in the community'.[7] Rome 'was a commonwealth to some degree', but 'true justice is found only in that commonwealth whose founder and ruler is Christ'.[8] Here, Augustine adopts 'the more plausible definition' of a society, as something that exists by degrees according to the extent to which justice is present within it. Unlike his first definition of society (as an association from which justice may be, and largely is, absent), the second treats society as intrinsically related to ideal justice. An association is to be recognized as a society only insofar as it approximates to, and realizes, that ideal. Furthermore, an association is only fully a society if it enjoys a *Christian* government. This second definition allows Augustine to recognize that pagan societies (such as those of Athens and Sparta) are 'commonwealths' insofar as they contain elements of justice and of right, but that they instantiate the ideal society only partially and imperfectly. States cannot be entirely without justice, or there would be no society at all; but this is, at the same time, but a relative and internal justice.[9]

Augustine was nevertheless pessimistic about the prospects for human justice even within Christian societies. Though he seldom articulates his views in terms of 'natural law' (except in the *De Libero Arbitrio*), Augustine's standpoint is clearly that human justice cannot give even so much as a partial or conditional expression to the justice embodied in the eternal law; it offers at most a suggestion, or pale echo of that justice. Consequently, it is not possible to speak of human law as *embodying* the demands of true justice or of the natural law. The role of politics is not to cultivate virtue, it is a remedial institution arising due to sin. It can create nothing that is morally good, but merely maintain peace.[10] To find a less darkened view of politics, we must turn to the other great figure of the classical natural law tradition, Thomas Aquinas.

---

[7] Augustine (above n 2), II, 22. See also XIX, 21 and 24.   [8] Ibid., II, 22.

[9] See E Perreau-Saussine, 'Paradise as a Political Theme in Augustine's *City of God*', in M Bockmuehl and G Stroumsa (eds.), *Paradise in Antiquity: Jewish and Christian Views* (Cambridge University Press, 2010).

[10] See H Deane, *The Political and Social Ideas of St Augustine* (New York, Columbia University Press, 1963), 78; also PJ Burnell, 'The Status of Politics in Augustine's *City of God*', *History of Political Thought*, 13 (1992), 13–29.

Famously, Aquinas distinguishes the notion of 'eternal law' from that of 'natural law', and in so doing he creates room for optimism concerning the capacity of human actions to implement justice. He does not reject Augustine's view that the fall of man corrupts and obscures understanding of the *lex aeterna*, but resists the conclusion that human institutions are utterly sinful and removed from that law, doing little good but serving to restrain evil. Eternal law (God's divine wisdom) remains unknowable to human beings, but the natural law is that part of the eternal law that is accessible to human understanding in respect of humans' rational nature.[11] Thus 'human law' is yet 'derived from the eternal law, but ... is not on a perfect equality with it'.[12] For 'every human law has just so much of the nature of a law, as it is derived from the law of nature': 'wherefore the force of a law depends upon the extent of its justice'.[13] Human law is 'given for the correction of the natural law, either because it supplies what was wanting to the natural law; or because the natural law was perverted in the hearts of some men'.[14] Here, Aquinas points in the direction of Augustine's second definition of society (as an approximation to justice), but his distinction between *lex naturalis* and *lex aeterna* allows him to conclude that earthly social arrangements can after all hope to implement true justice. One can therefore extract from Aquinas's premises the view that 'the demands of the natural law can somehow be met on the level of civil society and hence do not have to be diluted in order to become applicable'.[15]

Though they point in different directions, the ruminations on justice found in Augustine and Aquinas present an unfamiliar standpoint from which to contemplate a central jurisprudential problem, that of the relationship between law and justice. To political writers of the modern day, justice is visible as a political ideal concerned specifically with the reordering of socio-political arrangements, and hence this visibility is a question of the extent to which 'principles' of justice are embodied in the standards of that most articulate and order-producing of social institutions, law. In the works of modern political philosophers, amongst them Rawls, Dworkin and Korsgaard, are to be found conceptions of justice, equality and right that, in belonging specifically

---

[11] Aquinas, *Summa Theologiae*, I–II 94.2.
[12] Ibid., I–II 93.3.   [13] Ibid., I–II 95.2.   [14] Ibid., I–II 94.5.
[15] See E Fortin, *Classical Christianity and the Political Order: The Collected Works of Ernest Fortin*, vol. II, JB Benestad (ed.) (Lanham MD, Rowman & Littlefield, 1996), 211.

to liberal democratic social structures, are judged already to have been partially realized in the political societies of the present. By contrast, neither Augustine nor Aquinas is straightforwardly a *political* thinker. The true justice that is to be discovered in the *lex naturalis* is not of a kind that establishes or recommends particular forms of social arrangement. Christianity, being a universalist religion, is not dependent upon specific political forms, but lays down commandments and intimations of the good life (characterized by a loving disposition, forgiveness, the exercise of mercy, and so forth) that offer little if any guidance on concrete political problems of distribution, civic obligation, questions of 'corrective justice' or punishment. In this, the Christian notion of a 'natural law' as it appears in Augustine and Aquinas differs markedly from the Law that features centrally in the dominant religions of the East: the Judaistic Talmud, Islamic Sharia, and so on.

Despite their qualified enthusiasm for Cicero's *De Republica*, neither writer strictly belongs to the Ciceronian tradition of reflection upon justice and the question of how it is to be implemented politically.[16] Justice is a property of the natural law, and only in a qualified sense to be woven into the concrete political structures of human societies. The question that is squarely faced by the classical natural law writers is therefore of a fundamentally different nature to that of modern politics. At its heart is not the production of perfected or transformed social institutions (though the question of how institutions are to be transformed cannot be eliminated from it). Human societies are fallen, but the imperfection of social institutions is not the cause of human imperfection; it is because human nature is sinful and corrupted that social arrangements, which are an expression of that nature, are incapable of perfection. Consequently we must ask: to what extent can human beings hope to realize justice in their relations, and under what conditions will it appear?

I shall attempt to get to the heart of the visions of justice that are found in Augustine and Aquinas. I will then offer suggestions as to how the relationship between law and justice should be properly conceived. Above all, I hope to pose questions about justice that have been suppressed by the dominant approaches to justice in the political and jurisprudential writings of the present day.

---

[16] See e.g. Augustine, *De Civitate Dei*, II, 21.

Augustine: justice without the law

Augustine's separation of the two 'cities' in the *City of God* supplies the context in which he thinks about questions of justice. It is also a significant factor in the intellectual backdrop which informs Thomas's writings on the subject. Augustine distinguishes between the earthly and heavenly cities according to their objects of love: 'In one city, love of God has been given first place, in the other, love of self.'[17] The city of God is at once the eternal heavenly community *and* a dimension of present life, where it exists 'on pilgrimage' in the acts of love and charity demonstrated in the earthly city. In consequence, 'those two cities are interwoven and inter-mixed in this era, and await separation at the last judgment'.[18] True justice, associated with the heavenly city, has its source in love: both the love of God and, derivatively, love of one's neighbours.[19] Such love is said to be a matter of being rightly ordered in one's own mind. Being rightly related to God, a person is properly related within himself and to those around him.[20]

If the circumstances of real politics do not prevent the exercise of Christian virtue, they nevertheless offer resistance to all attempts to deal with others in the way that justice suggests. Quoting Terence, Augustine says:

> Wrongs and suspicions, enmities and war – Then, peace again! Have they not everywhere filled up the story of human experience? Are they not of frequent occurrence ... [a]nd even peace is a doubtful good, since we do not know the hearts of those with whom we wish to maintain peace, and even if we could know them today, we should not know what they might be like tomorrow.[21]

Thus, '[t]he larger the city, the more is its forum filled with civil lawsuits and criminal trials' and it is never free from 'the alarms or – what is more frequent – the bloodshed, of sedition and civil war'. Yet a society cannot be wholly without common bonds of affection amongst its members, nor wholly without attempted acts of justice, unless it ceases to resemble a society at all: 'Remove justice, and what are kingdoms but gangs of criminals on a large scale?'[22] The mutual relations of men in most

---

[17] Ibid., XIV, 13.   [18] Ibid., I, 35. See also XVIII, 34.

[19] Augustine, *On the Morals of the Catholic Church*, I.15: 'justice is love serving God only, and therefore ruling well all else, as subject to man'; I.26: 'we can think of no surer step towards the love of God than the love of man to man'.

[20] Ibid., I.25. See also Plato, *Republic* IV.   [21] *De Civitate Dei*, XIX, 5.

[22] Ibid., IV, 4.

situations may resemble more closely those of the 'mob' than of a 'people', but nevertheless the presence of justice within the internal ordering of the polity raises it higher than a mere mob. Actual societies will manifest neither 'city' in unqualified form,[23] being divided in the nature of their love.

The image of societies as a 'fallen' context in which justice will struggle to break out is one that lies somewhere between Hobbesian and Averroist ideas. In his Commentary on Aristotle's *De Anima*, Averroes wrote that Man cannot wholly dedicate himself to the pursuit of his intellectual perfection so long as he lacks peaceful relations with his fellow men.[24] Similarly, in *Leviathan*, Hobbes famously suggests that justice and injustice are values that relate only to men 'in society', and that outside such a context, such ideas have 'no place'.[25] The 'natural condition of man' is placed by Hobbes somewhat beneath that of the robber band, for the latter (on Augustine's definition) is yet characterized by internal organization and concord. But in the state of nature, men are doomed to 'become enemies; and in the way to their end ... endeavour to destroy or subdue one another'.[26] Lying between Averroist perfection and Hobbesian warfare, civil relations in actual societies are not of a kind that encourage, even when they allow for, the expression of the agapic love that is the source of true justice.

Augustine raises here what is perhaps the central problem of Western politics and jurisprudence. Perfected individuals require perfected institutions. Does this mean that by perfecting and improving social institutions, one *thereby* hopes to perfect individuals?[27] Augustine's reply is negative: governments cannot hope (any more than individuals) to avoid becoming polluted by the very vices they exist to control. True goodness is to be found neither in actually existing arrangements nor in any plan for what should be.[28] Like Machiavelli, Augustine wishes us 'to follow the truth of the matter rather than the imagination of it'.[29] Justice

---

[23] Ibid., XV, 1 (Augustine states that he is speaking of the two cities 'allegorically').

[24] See AL Ivry, 'Averroes's Middle and Long Commentaries on the *De Anima*', *Arabic Sciences and Philosophy*, 5 (1995), 75–92.

[25] Hobbes, *Leviathan*, ch 13.   [26] Ibid.

[27] See, for example, Rawls's discussion of the 'original position': J Rawls, *A Theory of Justice* (Cambridge MA, Belknap Press, 1971), ch 1.

[28] Augustine does not respond directly to this question, but his reply can be distilled from *De Civitate Dei*, XIX, 17–22. See also RA Markus, *Saeculum: History and Society in the Theology of St Augustine* (Cambridge University Press, 1970), xix–xx.

[29] Machiavelli, *The Prince*, ch XV.

is not an abstract idea, but a concrete set of dispositions and practices. The *form* of justice is that proposed by Aristotle: it is 'that virtue which assigns to everyone his due'.[30] But its impulse is not a political principle of fairness, or equality. It is a habit of virtue cultivated by one whose love for God, and thence for his neighbours, carries over from his intellectual life into the world of practical dealings.

Justice nevertheless cannot avoid receiving expression in the form of a tracery of *civic* relationships: the city of God is itself a *city*. The *amor dei* is not mystical, but social. It manifests itself as a concern for the 'weal of the people'. The love that informs justice is not sacrificial, but limited and incapable of detachment from self-interest. It contains an element of calculation, of what is *due* to a person, rather than of what *may* be given to them. Such 'impurity' of love of neighbour is present even within the most intimate of human relationships: marriage is itself based upon a considerate calculation of what is due to the other, without which its harmony breaks down, just as absolute self-abasement is not a sound basis for family life. But if such calculations are not themselves infused with love, married life becomes a parody of itself, rooted in cynicism and personal transactions of a prudential nature.[31] Similarly in social relationships, one cannot go about as a sheep amongst lions if one is to maintain one's responsibilities towards others. In speaking of earthly justice as a concern for the 'weal of the people',[32] Augustine does not divide the life of self and that of society into opposing camps of 'interests', but regards society as a context of competing claims made upon the self by numerous considerations of general welfare. One's responsibilities may require one to give precedence to the interests of one's family over those of the stranger; or to what is owed to a political ally as opposed to the claims of a favoured interest group; to consider what is due to some subsection of one's community over another, and so on. One cannot do this if inspired by a selfless agape, even if such a state were possible. But uninformed by love, these calculations become in turn calculations merely of collective self-interest, not of genuine concern for the 'weal' of one's neighbours.

Yet there is no reason to think that the nature of these conflicts is static, or amenable to fixed formulas: we do not know the hearts of those

---

[30] *De Civitate Dei*, XIX, 21; citing Aristotle, *Nicomachean Ethics*, 5.5.2.
[31] Augustine, *De Civitate Dei*, XIX, 14–15. See also P Reynolds, *To Have and to Hold: Marriage and its Documentation in Western Christendom 400–1600* (Cambridge University Press, 2007).
[32] *De Civitate Dei*, XIX, 21.

with whom we would be at peace, 'and even if we could know them today, we should not know what they might be like tomorrow'.[33] As a political principle, justice does not suggest any specific or permanent form of social ordering. Earthly justice cannot take a fixed form because that which is owed to others is owed as much to what they can or will become, as to what they are. The justice that Augustine regards as possible within the earthly city is not directed towards 'ultimate' conditions or solutions, but to the establishment of relative and sufficient harmonies.

At times, Augustine seems to think that all manifestations of human association embody corruption and injustice. In XIX, 16, we find him declaring that God 'did not wish the rational being, made in His own image, to have dominion over any but irrational creatures, not man over man but man over beasts'. There is in nature no room for kings of men; these arise as a result and reward of a fallen nature in which sin must be restrained. Societies do not conform to some norm or historical pattern of natural law: endless in their variety, they subject men to a governance without which the institutions of civilization could not exist; but the subordination to the rule of men is itself unjust, so that all societies have injustice permanently woven into their fabric.[34] The source of this injustice is pride (*superbia*) or self-love. Through self-love, a man turns from what is due to God and neighbour, and seeks to make of himself an end, and a focus of interests around which the community is to be structured.[35] This is not a mere weakness of the flesh or will, which may be overcome by devotion to a law of 'pure reason', but a problem of the fallen soul itself, 'making a bad use of the body to wander from the law of God'.[36] Because it is not a defect of reason which causes and strengthens the impulse to self-love, neither can law nor reason reveal anything about the means by which justice may be implemented, and self-interest qualified or overcome.

Much of book XIX of *City of God* is concerned with the contrast between ultimate order (God's final judgment upon good and evil) and the endless and temporary forms of social order. Augustine's ruminations upon justice stand out because he is acutely aware of how easily the concern for the weal of a people turns into a corrupted form of

---

[33] Ibid., XIX, 5.

[34] Ibid.: 'Without injustice, the republic would neither increase nor subsist. The imperial city ... could not rule without recourse to injustice. For it is unjust for some men to rule over others.'

[35] Ibid., XIX, 4–5 and XV, 6.   [36] Augustine, *De Sermone Domini in Monte,* 1.16.46.

collective self-interest. The original sin (pride) characterizes the fallen state, for it encourages such transformations. Always we are apt to perceive in our political visions not an endless sequence of temporary accommodations, but a final centre of order in the earthly realm as the goal to be obtained. But these political goals are to be obtained only *as against* other possible forms of ordering: socialism as against free-market capitalism; liberalism as against aristocratic governance, and so forth. None of these forms of political ordering are themselves free of imperfection. We escape the evil of 'unfeeling' capitalism only to run into the arms of 'repressive' socialism (and vice versa). All of them operate in a way which violates the basis of social order ('do no harm to anyone' and 'help everyone wherever possible').[37] Of all judgments passed by men upon their fellow men, Augustine says: 'How pitiable, how lamentable do we find them!'[38] The political ambitions even of the most committed lover of justice involve the tyrannous advancement and imposition of collective self-interests.

It is of the first significance that Augustine avoids any real reference in his thinking on politics and justice to ideas of natural law. Both the classical tradition of thought which existed before him, in Aristotle and Cicero, and the medieval and modern thought which came after him, perceived an eternal order in history after which human societies are normatively patterned. In Book V, chapter 7 of the *Nicomachean Ethics*, Aristotle argues that despite the historical variety of forms of government, 'only one is naturally the best', for each 'stands as a universal in relation to particulars'. For Aquinas, similarly, 'human law has just so much of the nature of law, as it is derived from the law of nature'.[39] The same basic orientation is evident in modern philosophy, insofar as it is informed by Kantian ideas of universal laws of reason that are applicable to the concrete institutional realities of human society: those in the 'original position' transcend the imaginative limitations imposed by historical context in order to engineer society according to only very general and permanent considerations (the 'circumstances of justice', basic economic laws, and so forth).[40] In departing from this tradition, Augustine places speculation about law and justice onto an entirely

---

[37] *De Civitate Dei*, XIX, 14.   [38] Ibid., XIX, 6.

[39] Aquinas, *Summa Theologiae*, I–II 95.2.

[40] See Rawls (above n 27), 441. We might also see a similar pattern in the method of 'reflective equilibrium': the oscillation between general norms and scattered particulars (or eternity and temporality).

different path. Augustine does not think of human societies as being guided by an ideal that is 'external' to them, but by a dynamic that is internal. All forms of human association are doomed to give first place to order amongst their priorities (for without order, 'society' does not exist); but justice must enter somewhere into this order, for 'unsatisfied desires are bound to challenge every order'.[41] Human beings are enjoined to an eternal law that, in belonging to God's will, is mysterious and unknown to them. Consequently, they are not called upon to implement a law of perfect justice in the earthly realm, but to draw upon the resources of a love that is present within that realm in order to modify the endlessly variable patterns of human behaviour in which they are enmeshed.

By grounding justice in love rather than law, Augustine is not being an idealist, but perhaps the most uncompromising political realist. Where the spontaneous, agapic love of neighbour is absent, the production of a top-down order of governance is necessary so as to maintain the peace and order that are essential to society. Such descending order is always tyrannous, assuming power over human beings but being wielded by human beings who are no closer to the truth, or to virtue, than anyone. The vices which frustrate peace are not conquered but merely forced to submit, 'repressed under a rule still troubled by anxieties'.[42] But where such love is present, it may be reflected in the legal order so that executive power does not produce it, but lends precision and structure to harmonies that already exist.[43] The justice that is found in a context of social practices will therefore not be free of the 'taint' of power, but is more valuable in being free in its origin.

Augustine provides for justice in the earthly realm by acknowledging its fundamentally fallen character. Justice is not altogether absent from the world, for the very idea of injustice requires the partial presence of its opposing force. But its presence in human relationships depends upon a form of agapic love that cannot fully manifest itself in worldly political conditions, and is moreover corrupted insofar as it is manifested. Law is related to justice because love alone is an insufficient basis of order and peace in the earthly city. Law gives structure and specificity to human

---

[41] See R Niebuhr, *Love and Justice: Selections from the Shorter Writings* (Philadelphia, Westminster Press, 1957), 14.

[42] *De Civitate Dei*, XIX, 27.

[43] For the argument that law is necessarily *both* reflective *and* constitutive of social order, see my article: S Coyle, 'Positivism, Idealism and the Rule of Law', *Oxford Journal of Legal Studies*, 26 (2006), 257–88.

relationships which are relevant to justice (or which, as Rawls says, provide the 'circumstances of justice'), and is perhaps unimaginable unless it offers some reflection of social harmonies which precede it. Nevertheless, law *corrupts* justice because it forms part of a context of power which, although necessary, possesses no inherent justification. The challenging nature of Augustine's vision of human justice lies in his refusal to countenance a 'middle order' of law or principle, elevated above the black-letter of positive legal arrangements and standing towards it as a form of 'higher' law: the 'law beyond law' or the ideal body of principles according to which the law 'works itself pure'.[44]

Aquinas: The justice of the law

Despite the darkness of his political vision, Augustine's conclusions about the context of justice allow him to escape certain problems that are faced by Aquinas. In Aquinas, we see something approaching more nearly our own understandings of justice, for his position blends Augustinian concerns regarding the eternal law with the main Ciceronian tradition of reflection upon justice. His starting point is that of Aristotle: human beings are fundamentally social creatures, and cannot be understood apart from the society they inhabit. The man who discovers the completion of his nature in separation from society is thus either less than fully human, or else God-like and above humanity.[45] Society implies some ordering of relations between men. The primordial context of justice (that is, of right relations) is therefore the political *regime*. Justice for Aquinas represents a political ideal essentially, and not derivatively. The regime is prior to love as a basis for an understanding of justice, because it is society that constitutes man as a linguistic and a thinking being, and therefore a being fitted for love. This places the Thomist philosophy much closer to the Averroist understanding. The society which constitutes man as an intellectual being (capable of loving and reflecting upon justice) is not the Hobbesian 'natural condition', but an ordered existence in which justice is in some measure already present. Cordial social relations do not represent an *achievement* of 'rational man', but something that is natural to him, and the condition of his rationality. Justice is then a feature of social relationships *before* it is an

---

[44] See R Dworkin, *Law's Empire* (London, Fontana, 1986) ch 10; L Fuller, *The Law in Quest of Itself* (Chicago, Foundation Press, 1940), 140.
[45] Aquinas, *Commentary on Aristotle's Politics*, I.1.22.

expression of love, or an object of knowledge. In this way, Aquinas is able to account for the fact that infidel rulers can nevertheless preside over regimes that are in some way just.[46]

For Aquinas, the provisional intimations of justice that are present in civic relations are not merely natural, but reflect natural *law*. The legal character of justice is not metaphorical: 'right' (*ius*) is the object of justice (the just thing itself), and law (though not identical with right) is the expression of right.[47] Famously, Aquinas defines genuine law as a written decree, and therefore he says that natural law is 'written on the hearts' of men.[48] Through this 'middle order' of law, 'all things participate in some way in the eternal law, insofar as they receive from it inclinations towards their own acts and ends'.[49] Human societies are therefore amongst the things that participate in the eternal law: the natural law (the expression of right) is present not only in reason, but in action also. Human societies do not fail utterly to implement justice, except in thought and speech. Though their implications may become obscured by sin, the principles of the natural law cannot be abolished from the human heart.[50] Real justice remains present, though in qualified (but not corrupted) form.

As a consequence of this less darkened vision, Aquinas is immediately embroiled in several difficult problems. How is the presence of an ineradicable natural law reconcilable with the full measure of human depravity? If all human societies contain within them a strain of the eternal and universal good, then how can we avoid canonizing even the vilest regimes yet dreamt by human beings? If it is present to some degree in all societies, how is the natural law to take account of the distinctively scriptural character of Christian ethics?[51] Does not the wide variety of forms of human association and the supposed 'freedom' of man not render impossible the task of defining schemes of justice in terms of 'necessary' standards? Is one not doomed simply to infect the definition of justice with specific details drawn from the given realities of one's own social order?[52] In seeking to implement such a justice, do we not establish rather an egotistical corruption of justice?

---

[46] Aquinas, *Summa Theologiae*, I–II 90.3, glossing 2 Romans:14–15: 'When the Gentiles, who have not the law, do by nature the things contained in the law, these, having not the law, are a law unto themselves: Which shew the work of the law written in their hearts'. See also I–II 63.2 and 65.2.

[47] Ibid., II 57.1.   [48] Ibid., I–II 94.6.   [49] Ibid., I–II 91.2.   [50] Ibid., I–II 94.6.

[51] See J Porter, *Natural and Divine Law* (Ontario, Novalis, 1999), 165.

[52] See Niebuhr (above n 41), 48, and A MacIntyre, *Whose Justice? Which Rationality?* (London, Duckworth, 1988), ch 1.

None in the Ciceronian tradition of thinking on the subject of justice, perhaps, can escape such questions, either with or without the Christo-logical dimension. Thomas's writings on justice display in an especially potent form the apparently irresistible tendency of politico-legal concep-tions of justice to invite a unitary and convergent socio-historicism: all societies, in all times and places, insofar as they are 'good' must approxi-mate to the final form in which true justice is revealed.[53] Such concep-tions of justice do not moderate, but rather give encouragement to the tendency inherent in political regimes to conceive of themselves as the sole basis for progress and human wellbeing. Isaiah Berlin is the principal figure in modern times to have resisted such temptations; it is therefore instructive that it is in a book that is highly critical of Berlin that one recent writer, in discussing America's 'most fundamental contribution to political morality' urges: 'We have been envied for our adventure and we are now increasingly copied all over the world . . . Let's not lose our nerve when all over the world other people, following our example, are gaining theirs.'[54] Liberalism itself, if raised to the level of a spiritual good, paradoxically becomes the basis for a vision of the universal civilization that is to come.[55]

The scale of Thomas's problem becomes evident if we consider that one central feature of Christianity as a social religion, is its lack of direct interest in political questions. Both the Hebrew Scriptures and the Qur'an set forth a law by which the faithful community is to be governed. But to the extent that Aquinas grounds the natural law in revealed texts, he does so only in relation to the moral legislation of the Old Law (the Deca-logue) as *distinguished* from its judicial legislation.[56] The Hebrew and Islamic religions needed no natural law precisely because they directly embodied a legal tradition, spelling out the form of life that the faithful must live. The natural law, by contrast, offers little or no concrete guidance on the form of social relations one must participate in if one is to remain true both to real justice and to the laws and customs of one's

[53] See e.g. F Fukuyama, *The End of History and the Last Man* (London, Penguin, 1993).

[54] Dworkin, *Justice in Robes* (Cambridge MA, Belknap Press, 2006), 138–9.

[55] See J Gray, *Enlightenment's Wake* (London, Routledge, 1995). Perhaps the most perni-cious feature of the images of 'personal freedom' (autonomy) imparted by the liberal tradition is its tendency to require that such freedom be *imposed* upon societies and cultures which lack it. Such freedoms, in being implacably hostile to the forms of tradition (especially foreign tradition), become blind to the extent to which they are themselves embedded in traditional forms to which they give expression.

[56] See Aquinas, *Summa Theologiae*, I–II 100–4, and Fortin (above n 15), 210–15.

country. It is through natural law that human beings participate in God's eternal law (true justice), but 'human reason cannot have a full participation ... but according to its own mode, and imperfectly'.[57] The natural law is not, therefore, a law of a *fallen* nature, but frail human reason knows only its general principles, 'but not proper knowledge of each single truth'.[58] To a great extent, 'man was left to the direction of his reason'.[59] He must construct his own laws, which are 'given for the correction of the natural law, either because it supplies what was wanting to the natural law, or because the natural law was perverted in the hearts of some men',[60] and because 'practical rectitude is not the same for all, as to matters of detail, but only as to the general principles'.[61] Our comprehension of justice is abstract and imperfect, and it is therefore not our part to implement it, but rather to achieve it.

One must therefore treat with caution the arguments of modern-day 'Thomist' writers who attempt to derive from Aquinas's writings a set of concrete propositions about justice. To a considerable extent, it is possible to think of the natural law as giving concrete advice on the structure of social relationships only if one can derive from Thomas's remarks on 'objective right' (*ius*) a series of propositions concerning 'subjective rights' (*iura*). One significant such attempt is that of John Finnis: in *Natural Law and Natural Rights*, Finnis indicates (in chapter VIII, and elsewhere) that the titular concepts are not to be regarded as finally distinct, but that '[a]lmost everything in this book is about human rights ("human rights" being a contemporary idiom for "natural rights" ...)' and that '[t]he reader ... will readily be able to translate most of the previous discussions of community and justice, and the subsequent discussions of authority, law, and obligation, into the vocabulary and grammar of rights'.[62] Aquinas adopts the Ciceronian definition of justice as a willingness to accord another his own right (*ius suum*).[63] This right is objective (the objective state of affairs that justice seeks to realize), but Finnis claims that all the elements necessary for a recognition of subjective *iura* are already present in Thomas's definitions. In his discussion of justice, Aquinas lists injuries (being killed or harmed, subjected to loss of

---

[57] Ibid., I–II 91.3.   [58] Ibid.

[59] Ibid., I–II 91.4, glossing Ecclesiasticus 15:14: 'God left man in the hand of his own counsel.'

[60] Ibid., I–II 94.5.   [61] Ibid., I–II 94.4.

[62] J Finnis, *Natural Law and Natural Rights* (Oxford, Clarendon Press, 1980), 198.

[63] Aquinas, *Summa Theologiae*, II 58.1.

property or damage) which amount to injustices. 'Such a list of *iniuriae* – violation of right(s)', Finnis says, 'is implicitly a list precisely of rights to which one is entitled simply by virtue of one's being a person.'[64] Thus, although Aquinas speaks always of 'the right thing', his treatment of the natural law as it relates to what is due to a person implies (as in Roman law) the presence of a series of discrete 'rights' as instruments of disputation.[65]

Though he was influenced by the Roman law, Aquinas does not express himself in these terms. Nevertheless, it might seem that the ease with which later Spanish Thomists adopted the language of 'natural rights' lends credence to Finnis's point.[66] Finnis posits a clear connection between natural law and the system of natural rights, for law is the basis of right (*ratio iuris*).[67] But Aquinas is careful to avoid the suggestion that there is a pattern of deductive reasoning from the natural law to concrete systems of right: our knowledge of the natural law extends only to its first principles; 'the more we descend to matters of detail', the less do we find that 'truth or rectitude is the same for all'.[68] Though Aquinas speaks of deduction, his examples suggest that only very general conclusions may be derived from the first principles: from the principle that 'one should do no harm' comes only the conclusion 'one must not kill'.[69] But '[t]he general principles of the natural law cannot be applied to all men in the same way, on account of the great variety of human affairs'. Human laws and customs are required because of the lack of concrete guidance given by the natural law to specific contexts of civic life.[70] The absoluteness of 'that which is truly right' ensures that *ius* exists as a purely spiritual idea, in which the concrete distributions of *iura* in the civic polity may participate only by degrees: 'every human law has just so much of the nature of law, as it is derived from the law of nature', 'wherefore the force of a law depends upon the extent of its justice'.[71]

---

[64] Finnis, *Aquinas: Moral, Political and Legal Theory* (Oxford University Press, 1988), 136. See Aquinas, *Summa Theologiae*, II 122.6.

[65] See A Brett, *Liberty, Right and Nature: Individual Rights in Later Scholastic Thought* (Cambridge University Press, 1997), 92.

[66] Finnis's arguments form part of a long-standing controversy over the presence of natural rights in Thomistic thought. One exchange on the subject can be found in a Symposium in *Harvard Journal of Law and Public Policy*, 20 (1997), 627–731 and another in *Review of Politics*, 64 (2002), 389–420. I do not intend to digress too deeply into this debate in the present context.

[67] Finnis (above n 64), 135.   [68] Aquinas, *Summa Theologiae*, I–II 94.4.

[69] Ibid., I–II 95.2.   [70] Ibid., I–II 94.5.   [71] Ibid., I–II 95.2.

It has been said that Finnis's attempt to derive from 'natural law' a concrete set of personal rights ultimately owes less to Thomistic conceptions than to Kantian ones: it consists in deriving, by way of practical reason, conclusions of right from universal moral laws. In doing so, Finnis has been accused of giving encouragement to a specific conception of social relations, redolent of the cultural milieu in which it is written. Finnis:

> sees the common good as constituted by an ensemble of 'conditions' that makes it possible for the members of a community to collaborate with one another 'positively and/or negatively' in the pursuit of the basic values in terms of which human flourishing has been described. Human beings are not united in a common dedication to a common goal. They are not 'parts', as Thomas Aquinas still taught, but atomic wholes, open to others and often in need of them, but nonetheless free to organize their lives or devise their 'life-plans' as they see fit, provided they do not interfere with the freedom of others.[72]

This is perhaps a little uncharitable to Finnis. But as I have argued in Part II, Chapter 12 above, Finnis's isolation of natural rights from the moral demands made by the virtues allow those rights to operate outwith the scope of a natural moral order that (as Aquinas suggests) can make incredibly complex demands in particular cases. By treating justice as a dimension of practical reasonableness, ignoring the language of virtue in favour of that of rights, Finnis pulls the Thomist philosophy toward a much more specific idea of justice (terminating in the assessment of people's rights) than the account in the *Prima Secundae* suggests is possible.

The lesson from Aquinas is that justice is not entirely absent from the world, though it contains a wide variety of regimes, based on many different principles of social ordering. The world is not saturated in the blood of a universal Hobbesian 'natural condition' though its many laws may be 'a perversion of law'.[73] Aquinas is ready to concede that the second table of the Decalogue is present in the form of natural law, independent of its promulgation to Moses, because he wishes to account for the presence of virtue and justice in pagan societies: 'Christian theology stands in need of a category of natural goodness apart from Christian Revelation or grace. Without some such category, it is impossible to preserve the doctrine of the Creation, except as a bare abstraction.'[74] Justice in general implies 'complete rightness of order',[75] but the world does not contain complete order. Justice requires that act wherein to each is rendered his due, but the

---

[72] Fortin (above n 15), 271–2.   [73] Aquinas, *Summa Theologiae*, I–II 95.2.
[74] Porter (above n 51), 177.   [75] Aquinas, *Summa Theologiae*, I–II 113.1.

absolute equality demanded by the full act of justice gives way, in the circumstances of the world, to 'a certain proportional equality'.[76] General justice aims at the common good, which surpasses the private good of the individual. The individual's private good cannot be wholly opposed to the common good (if it genuinely is a *common* good), but 'wherefore nature inflicts a loss on the part, in order to save the whole', so the justice of earthly laws must 'impose proportionate burdens'.[77] Justice in the world does not produce stable and final order, nor does it imply harmony.

It is our doom, thinks Aquinas, to know something of true justice, even, perhaps, to participate in it, but never to realize it fully in this world. Consequently, the world cannot experience that 'complete rightness of order' that is the culmination of justice. Yet the vision of Aquinas remains less dark than that of Augustine, despite its recognition of the presence of elements of disorder. For Augustine, war is merely the limiting case of social disorder:

> in it, we come face to face in their extreme form with the tensions endemic in all forms of social living, and in circumstances where the normal agencies of law enforcement are inoperative. War is the coercive power inseparable from the social existence of fallen human beings, exercised in this extremity. It is no more – and no less – objectionable than any other use of coercive power to enforce what is right, and always subject to the same moral imperatives that stand above all human action, if they are to be thinkable as human.[78]

But for Aquinas, political regimes contain traces both of sin *and* ratio dei. Human powers to implement justice always amount to much less than is given to us in conceptions of just relations, but politics and society are never utterly remote from justice in this sense: it is present in more than mere 'thought and speech'.

Justice and its implications

We are accustomed to think of justice as being one of the great human achievements, however weak and small-minded human beings might otherwise become in their attachment to self-interest. But the lesson that is repeatedly handed down by the natural law writers of the Western tradition is that it is man's very greatness which betrays him, through the instrument of a pride which seeks to conceal his weakness. The sense that

[76] Ibid., I–II 96.4.   [77] Ibid.   [78] Markus (above n 28), xiii.

the dominant political theories of the age sometimes function as 'compensatory fantasies', diminishing our perception of the depravities of society through the distorting lens of rational reconstruction, occasionally shines through.[79]

How is justice to achieve some presence within the structures of civil society? Central to all questions of justice is its relationship to the political regime. The early writers understood that justice must have some presence in the regime if it is to be visible, to have a reality beyond that of hopes and thought and speech. But they were less willing to give to this the name of true justice, justice in its fullest sense. If we want to understand how Thomas allows more room for a genuine (if attenuated) justice in society, and why modern writers on justice still feel able to draw upon his writings, we must come to realize that the *social* dimension of justice relies upon a fundamental shift from an agapic to a eudaimonistic point of view. Aquinas thinks of laws as being appointed for the common good.[80] Though he is very aware that law is often used for the advancement of personal or sectional interests,[81] it is necessary to understand that the proper function of law is directed toward the creation of a benevolent regime. If human beings are social animals, requiring the society of others for their completion or perfection, then law (as the final instrument of order and transformation in society) has as its proper function the creation of a benevolent regime in which human flourishing can take place. Aquinas conceives of this common good as demanding the harmonious functioning or peace between the distinct parts which combine to form the whole society.[82] The final unity of a society requires some measure of mutual accommodation as between the competing claims of the sectional interests within it: not so that they are reconciled into one single interest, but taking each into due consideration as they are adjusted to the whole.[83] The common good is therefore not the same as the private good of the individual, but (in being prior to it, as a condition for its pursuit and realization) the common good is obviously not unconnected with the good of the individual.[84]

Within the structures of a large society, the lover of justice will direct his attention not towards the immediate circumstances of his fellow

---

[79] See R Geuss, *Outside Ethics* (Princeton University Press, 2005), 34–5.

[80] Aquinas, *Summa Theologiae*, I–II 96.1 and 95.4.

[81] Ibid., I–II 96.4.   [82] Ibid., I 103.3.   [83] Ibid., I–II 105.1.

[84] Ibid., II–II 47.10. It is, as it were, the *proper* good of an individual (if he is indeed a social animal), as distinct from his private good.

citizens, but towards the body of rules which govern the interests of all citizens. The impulse to justice is not *primarily* the love that seeks to ensure the wellbeing of particular individuals (neighbours or strangers), but that which is concerned with the morality and fairness of social arrangements generally. The good citizen may fend for others in part by expending time and other resources upon the effort to alleviate their situation directly, by manipulating or adjusting it. But he best defends their *interests* by seeking to bring into service the mighty machinery of the state for their aid. Agapic expressions of justice tend to require adjustments or redistributions that are particular and immediate. But it is a well-understood feature of law that it operates to remove elements of particularity and immediacy from the treatment of lawsuits. Such disputes are not responsive to the full range of emotions and commitments of the parties, but adjudicated by reference to stable rules and concepts. They are not immediate, but subjected to protracted and organized procedures; not spontaneous, but dispassionate. The point is not that one cannot love an abstraction (for the commandment of neighbourly love is precisely that one should love the other irrespective of his particular virtues or vices), but that settled procedures of adjudication have as their central concern, not the peculiar interests of certain individuals, but arrangements for the wellbeing and smooth functioning of society as a whole. It therefore became common for later writers in the Western tradition to distinguish the realm of law and justice from that of the 'law of love': the former pertaining to correct distributions of 'perfect' (i.e. enforceable) rights, and the latter relating to 'imperfect rights' the realization of which depends upon perception of worthiness or esteem.[85]

But if we establish a context for social justice in this way, what can be said about its content? Can indeed *anything* be said about its content that is not completely dependent upon considerations of a contextual and historical nature? We must take care to separate two distinct dimensions of this question: (1) does justice point to a permanent idea, as distinguished from the great variety of its concrete realizations? (2) Does justice represent a final centre of ordering in human affairs, or merely an endless sequence of temporary accommodations?

The justice of property rights provides a useful example in which to explore this distinction. Suppose one were to contrast English property rights of, say, the eighteenth century with those of the current century.

---

[85] See e.g. Grotius, *De Iure Belli ac Pacis*, I.4.7.

We might note that property in an aristocratic regime is subject to a great many constraints that are not present today: the system of entails, fees, rules of primogeniture, sosage, and so forth, operate to define and preserve a 'landed class', and to keep land out of the hands of the majority of citizens. The extension of the capital, land and labour markets created conditions in which such rules would gradually become qualified or disappear. The commodification of land contributes to its liberalization: land becomes a commercial object that may be freely traded, and (through the system of mortgages) a resource in which virtually all can share. But a shallow comparison which might suggest that modern liberalized arrangements are more just, is impeded by the thought that this liberalization of property rights cannot be finally separated from the capitalism that gives rise to it; a capitalism which brings with it the sense of dislocation within communities, division into 'haves' and 'have-nots', wage- and mortgage slavery, the erosion of communal ties, and so on. Arguably, the implications of this destruction are only now beginning to become clear.[86] But the difficulties of comparison lend weight to the suggestion that no content can be given to the idea of 'justice' that is not at the same time irrevocably tradition-bound and contestable. How is freedom to be compared to poverty? Wage-slavery and inequality of bargaining power to the plight of labourers in Blake's 'dark satanic mills'? Stifling social hierarchies to the aspirations and failures of the welfare state?

Alasdair MacIntyre famously suggests that in relation to such questions, there is 'no neutral set of criteria by means of which the claims of rival and contending traditions could be adjudicated'.[87] Philosophical reflection is a means of 'clarifying issues and alternatives but not of providing grounds for conviction on matters of any substance': consequently, the abstraction from concrete traditional contexts that would be required for drawing such comparisons will produce ideas of justice that are 'far too thin and meagre to supply what is needed'.[88] Similarly, Stuart Hampshire argues that '[t]here is no way in which entirely abstract arguments from the bare concept of justice can by themselves produce a determinate conclusion about the justice of a particular social

---

[86] For an extremely informative discussion of some of these themes, see E Perreau-Saussine, 'What Remains of Socialism', in P Riordan (ed.), *Values in Public Life: Aspects of Common Goods* (Berlin, LIT Verlag, 2007), 11–34.
[87] MacIntyre (above n 52), 334.   [88] Ibid., 334–5.

practice'.[89] Unlike contexts of theoretical reasoning (such as mathematics) in which the conclusion is unaltered by the number of steps different people take to reach it, '[t]he practical conclusion of a debate on policy ... is not similarly independent of the particular arguments which have led to the conclusion. The arguments that have led to the conclusion may be entered into the full characterization of the conclusion itself.'[90] Accordingly, Hampshire suggests that the 'basic concept of justice, taken by itself, is primarily procedural' in referring to 'a regular and reasonable procedure of weighing claims and counter-claims, as in an arbitration or court of law'.[91] But if Hampshire thinks that justice and fairness, at the most abstract level, are 'specifications of the notion of practical rationality',[92] MacIntyre's thesis is principally famous for regarding notions of practical rationality themselves as interior products of intellectual traditions. One does not increase one's understanding of justice by standing outside tradition, but by refining one's traditional ideas as the 'tradition shows itself in successive encounters [with rival traditions] able to furnish the necessary resources and achieve the necessary transformations [of its concepts]':[93] to survive, in other words, as a vibrant and viable outlook on the world.

Both Hampshire and MacIntyre may appear here to come to certain conclusions about question (1), when in fact their conclusions relate to question (2). Their arguments put into question whether there is some final ordering of social arrangements that is the objective form upon which all just societies converge. (There is not.) They do not concern the question of whether the endless variety of efforts to implement justice within concrete civic arrangements concern, not one idea ('justice'), but an infinite variety of homophonic but ultimately distinct concepts. (For how else would they be intelligible as arguments *about justice*?)

How then is justice to be understood in civic contexts? We seem to confront a social situation that is not wholly devoid of any justice, but which fails to exhibit justice in its fullest or undistorted form. It has long seemed to writers in the Western intellectual tradition that our understanding of justice is guided by reference to an ideal (or theoretical model) of justice: one which is only partially fulfilled by the practices and arrangements of the moment. The identity of this ideal is taken to be one of the most important and pressing questions of modern political

---

[89] S Hampshire, *Innocence and Experience* (Cambridge MA, Harvard University Press, 1989), 61.
[90] Ibid., 52.   [91] Ibid., 61 and 63.   [92] Ibid., 53.   [93] MacIntyre (above n 52), 327.

thought. If justice is related to the common good, for example, then what is the content of the latter concept? Is it the harmony and unity required for mutual survival?[94] Or does it involve the effort to foster other forms of 'human flourishing', such as knowledge, friendship, practical reasonableness and so forth?[95] What of the inclusion of other 'goods', such as freedom, or meaningful labour? Indeed, is the notion of common good capable of finite description? Or, given the proliferation of different 'forms of the good' which to some extent vie and compete, should the guiding ideal of justice be identified, not by reference to the good, but rather with the rule of law itself?[96]

These are important questions. The tendency to pursue versions of the latest of these theses (the prioritization of the right over the good) is perhaps responsible for converting the art of politics, as Aristotle, Aquinas, and even Hobbes knew it, into a 'science' of social and economic administration. Such reductive conversions promote, not the good of individuals via the privatization of the means of its pursuit, but a mere flattening or averaging of social existence and its attendant moral and spiritual horizons. But it would be a mistake to think that some alternative ideal, or idealized understanding of the common good, offers assistance to a concrete understanding of justice. To suggest this is to posit some particular form of political regime (at whatever level of abstraction) as a final centre of order in human affairs: the abolition of contrary forms of order where they appear in society appearing to be the abolition of evil itself. If, on the other hand, we answer question (2) above in the negative, then we understand with Augustine that the idea of justice gives encouragement to *no* particular political form: 'A view of politics as a choice between economic systems for distributing material goods would strike Augustine as a choice between two roads to Hell.'[97]

The political philosophies which dominate the thinking of the present day (those of Rawls and his interlocutors) offer little systematic reflection

---

[94] See e.g. HLA Hart, *The Concept of Law*, 2nd edn (Oxford, Clarendon Press, 1994), ch IX; Hobbes, *Leviathan* (various edns), ch 13.

[95] See Finnis (above n 62), ch 4.

[96] This corresponds roughly to Rawls's position: see *Justice as Fairness: A Re-statement* (Cambridge MA, Harvard University Press, 2001), 8–24. See also N Sagovsky, *Christian Tradition and the Practice of Justice* (London, SPCK, 2008), ch 8, and R Plant, *Modern Political Thought* (Oxford, Blackwell, 1991), 86.

[97] O O'Donovan, *Common Objects of Love: Moral Reflection and the Shaping of Community* (Grand Rapids MI, Eerdmans, 2002), 23. For an exploration of the liberal bases of Finnis's argument, see Fortin (above n 15), 271–6.

upon these themes. Nor is the mood of modern philosophy very receptive to the questions which drive them. But the result of their abandonment is a debate about justice which, on all sides, vastly inflates the
perception of the area wherein human effort can meet with success. It is
such a misperception which sustains Rawls's optimism that 'political
injustice' may be 'eliminated by following just (or at least decent) social
policies and establishing just (or at least decent) basic institutions'; and
that by following this method, 'great evils will eventually disappear'.[98]

Augustine is right that the tendency to make social structures of order
the ultimate scales of value in human affairs is to be resisted. But a society
cannot avoid making arrangements for the distribution of material goods,
nor refrain from implementing rules governing matters of transfer and
restitution. In thinking of such matters, it is impossible to exclude questions of justice. But deliberation in these contexts should not be conceived
as receiving guidance from an ideal of justice (as it were, from 'above'). It
is to be explored by reference to our ability to understand when justice is
absent. Familiarity with instances of injustice (being present) is more
articulate, more poignant, and more immediate than comprehension of
an absent ideal. For human beings see more clearly what is missing, than
what is absent: we can articulate what is wrong in an imperfect game of
chess with more success than we can imagine a perfect game; the artist
refines his work by reference to what is imperfect in its expression, not by
some perfect image he is trying to capture. As Amartya Sen writes, 'What
moves us ... is not the realization that the world falls short of being
completely just – which few of us expect – but that there are clearly
remediable injustices around us which we want to eliminate.'[99] The ability
to give expression to the wrongness of immoral situations precedes an
understanding of what is ideally right. Aristotle's doctrine of the mean
assists understanding in these contexts. Our understanding of courage
(for example) is shaped not by knowledge of that virtue, but by contemplation of its absence or distortion: foolhardiness, on the one hand, and
timidity, on the other, define opposing points on a continuum of possibilities where true courage is absent. The wise person understands that
courage lies somewhere toward the centre of this spectrum, but perception of the true virtue comes into focus not by searching for its positive
expression, but increasing one's knowledge of the forms in which it is
corrupted or absent in various degrees or dimensions.

[98] Rawls, *The Law of Peoples* (Cambridge MA, Harvard University Press, 1999), 126.
[99] A Sen, *The Idea of Justice* (London, Penguin Books, 2010), vii.

I would like to conclude with the thought that our understanding of justice is formed in a similar way. We refine that understanding not by focusing contemplation upon an ideal that we know to be absent from concrete situations, but by giving careful examination to the actual situations of injustice that we meet constantly in actions, in rules and arrangements. In all such situations, justice is absent in some degree.[100] But our deliberations are clarified if, instead of comparing actual injustices to some imagined ideal that we take to be a positive expression of justice, we take thought concerning the incompleteness, or corruption, of the arrangements of the present. Common lawyers especially understand this. Criminal lawyers, tort lawyers, contract lawyers: all have their definitions and working understandings of justice. Yet despite the tendency of jurisprudential writers to represent the common law as the embodiment of a 'system of justice', common lawyers understand that these working definitions are but fragmentary and imperfect attempts to achieve justice. Judicial decisions do not state 'principles of justice', but articulate justifications addressed to the litigants in light of the concrete circumstances of the case.[101] The application of these justifications outside these concrete circumstances is acknowledged to be problematic, and to require a constant process of adaptation, modification, rethinking and distinction: justice is not achieved according to a fixed understanding, but through the guidance of precedents which we acknowledge to be imperfect and incomplete. The adjustments which suggest themselves on this basis will also, inevitably, reveal themselves as in turn corrupted and unjust in some measure. But we are better able to articulate the imperfection of social arrangements, and to avoid sanctifying political principles, if we accept that our understandings are guided 'from below' in this way. Above all, we grow in awareness if we adopt as our intellectual guides not Kant, or Rousseau, or Rawls, but rather Augustine and Aquinas.

---

[100] We might of course take comfort from the realization that neither are our practices perfect expressions of *injustice*.

[101] I have in mind particularly Dworkin, Rawls and others who, in representing the common law as a body of abstract principles, seem to me to misunderstand fundamentally the nature of common law adjudication.

16

Freedom and justice in a democratic age

Writing in 1991, after the spectacular collapse of communism in the former Soviet republics, Pope John Paul II asked whether capitalism is the victorious social system, the path to true economic and civil progress. His answer is cautious, and complex. Freedom and promotion of human creativity in the economic sector is to be welcomed and affirmed, but that same economic freedom will come to be despised if it is not 'circumscribed within a strong juridical framework which places it at the service of human freedom in its totality, and which sees it as a particular aspect of that freedom, the core of which is ethical and religious'.[1] A similar note of caution about the ultimate direction of capitalism is sounded by the English political philosopher John Gray. The market society has incalculable advantages over earlier, feudal and socialistic forms of social ordering, but subverts these advantages at the moment that its central institutions become free-floating and autonomous (as perhaps logically they must), detached from the fabric of the communities which they originally served.[2] How is one to respond to this tendency in capitalism? By deepening one's commitment to its noble aspects, or by distancing oneself from too enthusiastic an embrace of capitalist ambitions? *Centesimus annus* shies away from offering a general theory of society: 'The Church has no models to present; models that are real and truly effective can only arise within the framework of different historical situations, through the efforts of all those who responsibly confront concrete problems in all their social, economic, political and cultural aspects, as these interact with one another.'[3]

The Church's hesitancy over capitalism provides a useful context in which to examine the significance of the two great political 'models' of

---

[1] See the encyclical *Centesimus annus* of 5 January, 1991, 42.
[2] See e.g. J Gray, *Enlightenment's Wake* (London, Routledge, 1995), 89–121; also Gray, *Beyond the New Right* (London, Routledge, 1993), chs 2 and 3.
[3] *Centesimus annus* (above n 1), 43.

modern times, capitalism and socialism. The life of modern man may be said to be governed by two great ideas which produce in him a tension. In the domain of action, it is governed by the idea of freedom.[4] In the domain of the intellect, it is governed by the idea of justice. First in Europe and then elsewhere, the synthesis of these ideas (initially as phenomena and then as 'values') became a central focus of the political imagination.

The historical forces which made such a synthesis necessary are extremely complex. One might say that the problem of modernity stems precisely from a sense of this complexity: the non-lineal nature of its most cherished ideas. Freedom is an agreed language for moderns, but they disagree about its meaning and form. In one sense, freedom resembles the escape from convention, a life lived outside the scope of conventional forms and manners. In Book 4 of the *Politics*, Aristotle reacts against this 'cynical' definition of freedom, opposing one of his own: living for the moment means being dominated by the moment, and by one's transitory appetites. True freedom lies in self-mastery, a posture of responsibility toward others. The problem of modernity addresses an altogether more profound difficulty than is raised by these classical disagreements: the presence of multiple definitions and conceptions of freedom, and the question of how they are to be harmonized. The life of the *phronimos* has a different shape to that of the cynic.[5] How shall they live in common?

In what was to be one of the *ancien régime*'s last great political works, Hobbes offered one answer to this question. The divergent conceptions are to be coerced into a unity, brought under the jurisdiction of the state. There are still measures of freedom possible under the iron rule of the 'mortal god', but in a profound way the basic political freedoms cherished by the classical philosophers are all but extinguished. The classical idea of autonomy, brought to life in Rousseau's image of man as a 'perfect and solitary whole',[6] is not permitted to exist. Man cannot be his own master. More than his freedom, man must learn to love that necessity of the commodious life that only the state can provide: *security*.[7] Hobbes is perhaps the first philosopher to grapple systematically with the question of modernity, but his solutions are anti-modern. Hobbes shared

---

[4] P Manent, *Modern Liberty and its Discontents* (Latham MA, Rowman & Littlefield, 1998), 170.

[5] See R Guess, *Outside Ethics* (Princeton University Press, 2005), 30.

[6] Rousseau, *Social Contract*, II.7.   [7] See generally Hobbes, *Leviathan*, ch XIII.

with the classical philosophers the idea that good government represents harmony, so that the excellent society is a harmonious one. In the course of the following century, a new framework of thought appeared. Adam Smith's work points the way to this new understanding: that good government recognizes the permanency of conflict and competition, and seeks to harness its forces for the purposes of creativity. The worst instincts of man cannot be excluded by the 'correct' form of government, but must be put to work for the good of all society. Left to themselves, man's needs to accumulate and acquire wealth lead only to destruction. Resources and labour are stripped from the hands of the less skilful and placed in those of the most productive. Efficiency is indeed ruthless in what it destroys. Capitalists and proto-capitalists wish instead to place human greed within a creative framework: the open market. This 'invisible hand' will succeed in redistributing wealth to areas of need in a way that has little to do with what each person actually intends.[8]

Except in those few instances where communist ideas successfully established themselves, arguments between capitalists and socialists have taken the liberal political order as their battleground. This did not happen by accident. Capitalism is properly defined not against socialism but against traditional societies in which production and consumption, in being governed by tradition, religion, ritual and custom, are essentially unchanging. The notion of 'class' served to justify and reinforce stark divisions of wealth and privilege. Capitalism might increasingly tear down and challenge such structures, increasing social mobility, but its liberalization of society would not bring an end to exploitation. The problem with freedom is that it cares too little about justice. The wealthy will continue to dominate and exploit the poor. Socialists insisted upon a class struggle that would bring an end to this injustice. Inequalities must be vanquished.[9] If freedom cannot bring about the desired condition, then society needs to be convulsively reordered in a revolution that will place land, labour and the means of production in the hands of an all-powerful state apparatus.

Smith's own works illustrate the tendency of capitalist ideas to instigate a broader social transformation. In his earlier text of 1759, *The*

---

[8] Adam Smith, *An Inquiry into the Nature and Causes of the Wealth of Nations*, IV.2: 'he intends only his own gain, and he is in this, as in many other cases, led by an invisible hand to promote an end which was no part of his intention'.

[9] See e.g. Marx, *Critique of the Gotha Programme* [1875], s.II; H Saint-Simon, *Letters from an Inhabitant of Geneva to his Contemporaries* [1803].

Theory of Moral Sentiments, the invisible hand is first presented as a functional working of the structures and political assumptions of the class system. Vanity, which sets in motion the imagination of the wealthy classes, both animates and feeds the economic system: in 'expand[ing] itself to everything around', the imagination of the rich shall prompt them 'to cultivate the ground, to build houses, to found cities and commonwealths, and to invent and improve all the sciences and arts, which ennoble and embellish human life'.[10] By 1776, the fingers of the invisible hand have grown longer: tied no longer to the actions only of the rich, the invisible hand is the product of the behaviour of 'every individual', whose pursuit of gain causes them 'necessarily' to labour in a way that redounds to the benefit of society.[11] Modes of exchange that were traditionally embedded within social structures from which they derived their meaning (such as the feudal exchange of land for service) are now 'open'. The removal of barriers to trade (economic liberalization) brings with it social liberalization.

Proponents of the free market like to point to these processes as examples of capitalism as a creative force, but in fact they function equally as representations of the market's tendency to produce social *destruction*: the collapse of social organization and the system of meanings that the 'market' was originally meant to serve. Once the process of economic liberalization has begun, it is very difficult to prevent its spread to all areas of life. Kinds of human behaviour that are not intended to be profit-maximizing become engulfed by the market. The activities of universities provide one example of this. Above all, capitalism depoliticized society. The aristocracy and the lower classes no longer had distinct political functions, but a monistic economic function that left them undifferentiated. Henceforth, wealth would determine one's 'standing'. The notion of 'function' could not easily survive this movement, the market steadily transforming politics into a domain of 'interests'. What the state could no longer 'direct' it could now only 'represent'. Thus powerful impetus was given to democracy as the preferred, and perhaps the only legitimate form of politics.

In the face of these new freedoms, capitalists and socialists laboured to show how a society unfolding in the presence of the market could yet find room for the expression of man's other great idea: justice. According to its defenders, the capitalist economy and a liberal social order are

---

[10] Smith, *The Theory of Moral Sentiments*, IV.1.   [11] See *Wealth of Nations*, IV.2.

necessary given the basic orientation of the human condition. Socialists try to deny the necessity of greed as a basic instinct, but their constructions, which are intended to eliminate its operation, produced misery and poverty on a scale far greater than anything the free market has delivered. Capitalists are quick to seize upon these facts in order to justify their vision of a liberal society orientated toward free enterprise. But their own position is not less open to problems. Capitalism does not eliminate poverty, but tries to argue that the deepening division between rich and poor, haves and have-nots, is nevertheless accompanied by a steady enrichment of the vast majority of society, including the predicament of its poorest sectors. Inequalities between rich and poor are not justified, but they are inevitable consequences of a necessary system. In the light of this, socialists have modified their claims. No longer seeking revolution, an end to the open market and to democratic politics, they insist instead upon injecting more order into an otherwise too-free system.

Let us not neglect to consider the significance of this remarkable situation. Does the eventual defeat of communist regimes around the world (which seems assured) suggest that there are no alternatives to the form of life indicated by the path of Western societies? By limiting their calls for equality and fraternal political community to moral critiques of the market they once opposed, have socialists confirmed what capitalists all along suspected, that justice presupposes a specific political structure akin to that of the market societies of the West? Prominent works of modern political theory seem to confirm this view. In the opening pages of Rawls's *A Theory of Justice*, the idea of justice appears as a property of the 'basic structure' of society.[12] Justice is to be associated not only with the form of the polity (its institutional arrangements), but with a specifically liberal institutional form. The idealized and abstracted considerations that inform the basis of argument for this conclusion (the 'veil of ignorance' and 'original position') suggest strongly that liberalized economic and social order are somehow inevitably definitive of justice. The liberal arrangements that took shape at the hands of capitalism are especially elevated to the status of permanent contributions to man's sociability, the solution to a problem of which the ancients were scarcely even aware.

Does either capitalism or socialism provide the means to resolve the tensions between freedom and justice, man's two great ideas? One

---

[12] J Rawls, *A Theory of Justice*, revised edn (Cambridge MA, Harvard University Press, 1999), 6.

century before the appearance of *Centesimus annus*, the Church confidently proclaimed solutions to the predicament of the neglected classes. The encyclical *Rerum novarum* called for a fundamental Christian critique of the market.[13] Socialism is to be resisted. The market and private property can be harnessed for the common good. Capitalist institutions can be made just, built upon a foundation of Christian justice. Solutions must come from the Church and from Christians specifically.[14] By 1991, the Church sounds more cautious. With the collapse of communism in the East, the predicament of the poor across the world has deepened. Evils have proliferated, creating new struggles for justice. Each age of the world will bring 'new things' that must be confronted.[15] Poverty threatens to assume massive proportions, whilst 'tragic crises loom on the horizon'.[16] Christians and non-Christians alike must bear responsibility for creating just arrangements.[17] There are no theories, but only actions; no answers, only deeds.

In the light of the failure of conservative and socialist perspectives on the market to address the plight of the vulnerable classes, what if anything can be learned from their philosophies? The proliferation of centrist positions on both the left and the right testifies to the inadequacy of both positions to confront the realities of vulnerability in the liberal order. I intend to ignore this central ground, home to 'capitalists with a conscience' and free-market socialism, except insofar as demanded by the context of liberal political order. I will consider what might be taken from these rival positions, and in the light of this I will offer some thoughts on the difficult relationship between justice and freedom in a democratic age. Above all, I would like to impart some sense of the Church's insight that doctrinal possibilities can confer a fatally misleading sense of what is achievable in practice, and consider where this leaves us.

Freedom

Defenders of the capitalist economy like to proclaim the overriding significance of freedom. Full of ideas of personal liberty, they insist that as the state increases its organization of the welfare of the private sphere, people will become less resilient. Individuals must learn to stand on their own two feet if society is not to produce a class of dependent people. They have a point. Individuals will only become masters of their situation

---

[13] See the encyclical *Rerum novarum* of 15 May 1891, 16.   [14] Ibid., 16, 27 and 55.
[15] *Centesimus annus*, 61.   [16] Ibid., 57.   [17] Ibid., 60.

if they are allowed to create their own arrangements. Human freedom is a more effective solver of problems than the government's legislative schemes. Classics of liberalism and capitalism indeed lauded the new strengths supposedly created by the market. The absence of economic barriers leaves man free to trade and to accumulate, but it also opens the door to exciting social freedoms: the ability to choose one's own profession, and to determine one's own priorities. Individuals, but also land and labour, are liberated from the social structures in which they were previously embedded, free to find new meanings. No longer in the hands of an oligarchy, man's destiny lies increasingly in his own hands.

But the same processes of liberalization also invoke feelings of vulnerability and dispossession. The individual in becoming free of social structures also becomes a commodity. Those who are less skilful, who have less to offer, face the prospect of unemployment. The same market forces that distribute resources and labour to the most productive are also responsible for creating high rents and mortgages, wage-slavery and joblessness. Markets create not only wealth but also poverty: new obstacles to social mobility. Those who suffer most from the ruthless operation of market forces feel that their fate is governed by unseen forces. Their destiny lies not in their own hands but truly in 'invisible hands' that remain staunchly indifferent to their needs.

Socialists rightly criticize supporters of the market for their failure to understand the things that cause people to stand in need of justice, and to desire limitations to the market's operations. Many of the things that make people vulnerable (economic poverty, health, treatment of minority groups) do not abate in the face of increased opportunity. A social philosophy which leaves people to sink or swim will not render individuals more resilient in the face of their vulnerabilities, nor force them to become resilient enough to overcome them. Advocates of capitalist society will always fail to take questions of justice seriously because the premise of their position is founded upon an appeal to the prosperity that market institutions deliver.[18] Considerations of justice can only intrude to modify free-market forces that are already in operation: trespassing upon the freedom of the market by imposing order upon it. A certain reluctance (if not hostility) toward attempts to *structure* resilience, redressing the balance between haves and have-nots, remains a deep-seated feature of capitalist thinking.

[18] See Gray, *Beyond the New Right* (above n 2), 67.

Pointing to the ruin created by socialist central planning in communist regimes, toward the waste and crushing poverty associated with such systems, the market's supporters attempt to occupy the high ground. They argue that it is an illusion to think that there are real alternatives to the capitalist system. There are no superior social systems. The proper context in which considerations of justice operate is the free-market society. The collapse of many communist systems in the East reveals the inevitability of failure in attempting to pull out the market at the roots, by replacing it with systematic organizational ideas. Justice cannot *precede* the market!

Convinced of the necessity of the market, governments in developed countries shall always favour growth over equality. They rightly accuse socialist regimes of achieving (measures of) social and economic equality only at the most appalling levels of poverty and unfreedom. At the same time, capitalists are wrong to equate prosperity with moral progress. They argue that societies make moral progress only when they can afford to do so: the abolition of slavery in the West depended on the affluence of the classes who could afford to dispense with them. Material security is necessary in allowing human beings the luxury to think and have ideas about their situation. Their predicament is not necessary (all that they can afford), but amenable to change. But in another sense, markets have been accused of bringing about moral degradation. Market societies respond only to those needs that are 'solvent'.[19] Where even basic needs are divested of purchasing power, they are condemned to remain unfulfilled. Free economies respond only to 'marketable' needs: pornographic and many other forms of exploitation are permitted to flourish in response to monied demands, whereas deeper needs (such as dignity and resilience) find it difficult to be recognized. There is no doubt that markets, in promoting consumption, generate 'false' needs at the expense of 'real' needs. Are socialists right to argue that Western governments fail to take issues of justice seriously?

Justice is inseparably bound to questions of order or structure. It is in this sense systematic. In one sense, defenders of the capitalist economy do not make any systematic attempts to alleviate inequalities or ensure any 'common' good. Allowing market forces to take their course, vulnerabilities and advantages are left to lie where they fall. The majority of vulnerabilities (those created or exacerbated by poverty) are not

---

[19] *Centesimus annus*, 34.

distributed according to specific plans, but by the operation of the 'invisible hand' that in distributing the benefits of the market also distributes harm: low wages, job insecurity, unemployment, high rents and unaffordable commodities, and thus also health- and welfare-related problems. For a whole range of reasons (amongst them the perceived inability of the state to be responsive in the face of an ever-changing situation), the first and most prolific line of defence against such problems is the transactional behaviour of those most deeply affected, who shall contract and bargain their way to a better situation.

In another sense, capitalists cannot avoid systematic distributive implications. The market itself is a mechanism for distribution, and in this sense 'orders' society. The very freedom of the market is the removal of restrictions on trade stemming from social structures within which exchanges of products previously operated. The decision about what is to be left to market forces and what is to remain or be placed within the determination of social considerations, is nothing other than a question of 'structuring'. A free market is not that which remains once all regulation and control have been withdrawn. Markets are not fully spontaneous but require constant direction. Without this direction the market would extinguish itself either through dissolution or by pursuing its other tendency into monopoly. Modern markets constantly threaten to unravel as the result of a thousand complications that are internal to their own operation. In the absence of all intervention, the market would be indistinguishable from chaos. Markets cannot function without a stable system of contract law for the enforcement of bargains, and a system of property law for the recognition of claims. The image of the market as having gained 'independence' from the social structures in which it was embedded is an illusion. Markets always presuppose a larger social context into which they fit. The question is to what extent the social structures have ceased to be serviced by the market, but exist largely or solely in order to sustain the market's operations. (One sees this for example in arguments about the classification of the law of contracts as a branch of commercial law vs. its traditional association with a law of obligations.)

Overwhelmingly dominated by economic considerations, capitalists frequently conceive of justice in the only terms the market understands: basic needs. Aware of poverty, they argue that the economy needs a safety net. Schemes and programmes for the least well-off. Two assumptions underpin this understanding. The first is that the state's obligations to justice are met insofar as basic needs are addressed through its resources. The second is that justice has been done if individuals can be placed in a position in which they are capable of meeting their own needs. Taken together, these ideas might seem to imply a principle of justice that is widely regarded as sound in Catholic social teaching: subsidiarity.

As Pope Pius XI wrote in the encyclical *Quadragesimo anno*, 'It is a fundamental principle of social philosophy, fixed and unchangeable, that one should not withdraw from individuals and commit to the community what they can accomplish by their own enterprise and industry.'[20] Capitalists can easily speak in this language, but in fact their ambitions point in the opposite direction. The Church's position states that the proper function of the polity is to assist its members to help themselves 'or, more precisely, to constitute themselves through the individual initiatives of choosing commitments ... and of realizing these commitments through personal inventiveness and effort'.[21] It holds that all forms of society (from the family to the state itself) should be in the service of the individual, and that the purpose of government is to create the conditions required for the development of the individual as a human and social being. The individual should not be absorbed by 'the common good', so that individuals, families and other mediating institutions must be allowed to pursue their own independent initiatives if they do not thereby injure the common good.[22] What capitalists propose is not really a form of *subsidium* (assistance). They wish above all to make individuals responsible for their own problems. The context of their assertion is not the fostering of a common good, but the imperatives and ideals of open market competition. Their real question is how far the state can go in withdrawing its assistance. Reliance on state benefits is therefore stigmatized as a failure, or in many cases a refusal, to exercise one's talents in a reasonable way.

The ideals of subsidiarity demand a vision of the common good: respect and assistance for man as a social being. As much as their vision is limited by the horizons of the market, the market's supporters fail to appreciate that justice is a question not simply of need but also of an individual's total situation. People need society as well as economy if they are to achieve their aims. People are not in the main (or without great loss) 'self-sufficient' but require the society of others for their completion.

---

[20] See the encyclical *Quadragesimo anno* of 15 May 1931, 79.

[21] J Finnis, *Natural Law and Natural Rights*, 2nd edn (Oxford, Clarendon Press, 2011), 146.

[22] Ibid., 169, and see Part II, Chapter 12 above.

The human being is not an *ens completum*. When in the presence of strong family, friendly and neighbourly ties, the individual is less vulnerable, more supported. It is well known that market forces erode these ties. As market imperatives come to dominate political policy, the wellbeing of the community is progressively divorced from measures of its structural strength and integrity, the wisdom and fittingness of its customs, and comes to be associated with a different measure: economic growth. The privatization of wealth brings with it the privatization of family life, the huge expansion of the 'private realm'. Individuals are more private, but their vulnerabilities and insecurities also become largely private matters, 'public' only to the extent that state-organized welfare mechanisms provide relief from them.

Under sustained capitalist conditions, 'communities' are no longer sufficiently organized to respond to the issues that affect them. Crime is more shocking not because it is more widespread but because it is individuals who must deal with its effects. Inequalities of wealth are less pronounced but more difficult to bear for those who depend upon the state for their income. The community is no longer concerned with the plight of the poor, but has replaced this feeling with another one: fear. Suspicion of an underclass that might reasonably be supposed to covet or resent the blessings of the middle classes. Driven by the market, aware of the prosperity it has brought, communities eventually absorb capitalist assumptions into their modes of thinking, and voting. They end up asking why those on benefits, or those who turn to crime, cannot simply use the market and their own initiative to better their situation, gathering wealth for themselves? The underclass is largely responsible for its own vulnerabilities!

Critics of neo-conservative capitalism appeal to such considerations in an effort to demonstrate that the advance of the market does not ensure moral progress, but brings about moral and social disintegration. Markets privatize vulnerability and injustice just as effectively as they privatize wealth. The loosening of neighbourly bonds frees the individual, but also robs him of the very thing that makes him resilient in the face of his vulnerabilities.

Justice

Aware that freedom alone is not sufficient to enable people to lead a decent life, socialists prefer to emphasize modern man's other great idea: *justice*. Following their instinct for greater organization, they demand that help must be available to those who are powerless to take charge of their situation. Difficult to argue with, there is however no doubt that this creates new focuses for dependence. Capitalists are right to be suspicious of systems that produce complacency or dependence upon state benefits. Alleviating the effects of certain forms of vulnerability, socialists have encouraged people to become vulnerable in other ways, reliant on systems of support over which they have no meaningful control.

One dynamic of the socialist understanding of justice is often overlooked. In giving priority to welfare need, socialists have in effect sided with capitalists in arguing that the market shall finally provide the required solutions. The market is not to be abolished, but reordered. Its existence is not to be called into question, but it requires more structure, more direction. Their concern is not to question the market's priorities, but to ensure their wider distribution. Free-market capitalism is to be replaced by state capitalism. Those in poverty do not want a different way of life from that of the middle classes, but wish to emulate them, accessing and enjoying the same goods. They no longer wish to annihilate the middle classes but aspire to join their ranks. The underlying values of society and of the market itself are not denied but reinforced: society is not appointed to a public, collective good, but to the protection of private lives and private property.[23] Socialism will always play second-fiddle to neo-conservatism in liberal societies for the reason that it will always be predominantly the ideology of an underclass which does not want to challenge the priorities of the middle classes, but wishes instead to share in their wealth.

The instinct of socialists that the most acute injustices stem from, or are exacerbated by, poverty is essentially correct. However, they are wrong to regard poverty as largely a monetary phenomenon. The unsatisfactory situation of the less well-off cannot be cured through redistribution alone. Understood less in monetary terms but 'situational' ones, the predicament of the poor is a product of phenomena such as the breakdown of families and of good relations amongst neighbours. As social traditions are eroded by the market, more is lost than merely an instinct of responsibility and fellow-feeling. Skills and trades cease to be practised or communicated, leading to lack of mobility and increased dependence. The idea of 'social needs' becomes lost or subsumed under the idea of 'wealth'. Whereas advocates of private enterprise place

---

[23] See E Perreau-Saussine, 'What Remains of Socialism', in P Riordan (ed.), *Values in Public Life: Aspects of Common Goods* (Berlin, LIT Verlag, 2007), 11.

responsibility upon the poor themselves for their situation, socialists invest responsibility in an altogether abstract and faceless entity: the community 'as a whole'. Voting replaces action. Taxation and welfare schemes become a surrogate form of social responsibility in a system in which no one bears responsibility.

Socialist-minded liberals also resemble capitalists in associating the individual's predicament with a key liberal phenomenon: mobility. Socialists and free-market capitalists approach this idea from different ends, but their assumptions are otherwise remarkably similar. Where individuals are vulnerable or dispossessed it is because they lack the power to alter their situation, to change things for the better. They must be moved out of the path of the considerations which make them vulnerable. Where supporters of free enterprise seek to increase social mobility through the very absence of organization, socialists understand that unstructuredness can itself result in lack of mobility. The achievement of large-scale social mobility requires organization. For the market's supporters, nothing matters more than the elimination of structures that inhibit freedom. The defeat of this last enemy will allow men to escape all others: surely no one who is the author of his own situation can claim to be beset by injustices? More aware of the enormous range of potential inequalities, socialists prefer to put the power of the state behind the effort to mitigate them. It is not individual freedom but distribution that shall triumph. The poor are to be lifted out of desperation through the wealth of the rich.

Socialists (like advocates of the free market) blind themselves unnecessarily to aspects of human vulnerability that are situational rather than need-based. It is not only lack of money that causes people to become stuck in disadvantageous situations or downward spirals. As the market redefines the needs of the more affluent classes, the demand for certain skills drops, causing problems for those who lack skill-mobility. Family breakdown and instability cause people to become more reliant on their own meagre resources, resulting in lack of opportunity. The ubiquity of the middle-class lifestyle, the inescapable power of advertising, reduce the ability of society to distinguish between 'real' and 'imagined' needs. The result is a market in debt, with the burden falling heaviest upon the least well-off, further reducing their room for manoeuvre.

Socialists (at least liberal socialists) do nothing to address these factors, being essentially uninterested in challenging the picture of man as a creature in pursuit of the fulfilment of his desires. What they wish to do is combine this image with a mode of organization that will limit each person's pursuit of his private goals in the name of equality for all. They no longer investigate the causes of social breakdown because they regard it as synonymous with the 'liberal freedom' that they wish to secure for all. They wish only to place man's acquisitive instincts, and his private enterprise, within the scope of a superior organization. The original socialist dream has propagated beyond the confines of 'true' socialism to become the desire of many liberals: the just society, based not upon the just instincts of its citizens (who may pay taxes very reluctantly) but upon the very foundations of the liberal order, the 'basic structure of society' in Rawls's terminology.[24]

It could be said that Rawls's theory itself resembles a socialism that has given up the class struggle. Informed by powerful instincts of equality, concerned to provide for the least well-off in society, its primary aim is to argue for a fair distribution of 'primary social goods', amongst which feature prominently: liberty, opportunity, income and wealth. Intended to be unbiased between possible conceptions of the good life, it has nevertheless been suggested that Rawls's theory inherently gives preference to acquisitive or individualistic lifestyles: each of the 'primary' goods is a central constituent of a lifestyle founded upon the accumulation of 'goods' and profit, even if they do not erect barriers to other priorities. Shall one say that money and liberty also offer assistance to other forms of life (such as the founding of a spiritual community), even if they are not central to them, and are in this sense 'neutral'?[25] That is perhaps the case, but the centrality of liberty, opportunity and ideals of wealth accumulation actively oppose the rebuilding of a more integrated, close-knit society. The just society shall not fetter a man with too many responsibilities: only taxation. The individual shall not 'know his place', but create his own. The liberality of Rawls's theory equates to a more honest socialism for socialists who have limited their critiques of capitalism to calls for a wider distribution of the benefits of growth. They fail to address, and even compound, the defining characteristic of the modern citizen: alienation.

It is by being alienated from his fellow men, more than by being poor, that the individual's predicament becomes most precarious. Valuable, indeed essential, in so many other ways, it is the market itself that is responsible for this dislocation. This situation will continue so long as

---

[24] See Rawls, *A Theory of Justice*, revised edn (Cambridge MA, Belknap Press, 1991), ch 1.
[25] See e.g. NE Simmonds, *Central Issues in Jurisprudence*, 3rd edn (London, Sweet & Maxwell, 2008), 67–8.

market priorities are allowed to become independent of and unfettered by the communities they previously served. Socialists wish to contain the market's freedom within a broader justice, but they ignore the social dimension of justice ('the common good'). The market must be put back into the service of the community to a much greater extent, and society must be more cohesive, if people are to become truly capable of facing their vulnerabilities.

The state

Neither the Left nor the Right holds out much hope for a resolution of the central problems of man's existence. Recipes for the transformation of society into a just political order have not fulfilled their promise. The image offered of the liberal polity by Rawls, and others, is but an idealized distortion of actual conditions, masking the fact that divisions between rich and poor have become more entrenched.[26] The dream of socialism itself terminates in the nightmare realities of communism. In democratic societies, socialist parties will never fulfil their promises because they rely upon middle classes that will never vote taxation upon themselves in the levels required for the realization of the socialist's dreams. At the same time, the dreams of the market's loudest enthusiasts have been no less unsatisfying. Freed from traditional social customs, individuals did not rise up and claim for themselves the prizes offered by the market. The worst-off did not escape their poverty. The market's invisible hands turned out to be far more powerful and far more capricious in their effect than the hands of either individuals or the government.

Resisting the capitalist's tendency to demand the withdrawal of the state from the 'private' and 'economic' spheres, should one insist upon a larger role for the state? But despondent about the limitations of socialist government, its tendency to authoritarianism and stifling bureaucracy, how shall one avoid its most oppressive implications? Indeed one could ask, what *is* the state for these purposes?[27] The ideologies of the market encourage one to think of institutions such as the family and the corporation, as private entities, handled through private ordering. But one must not forget that such institutions are 'constructed and evolving' and that

[26] See R Geuss, *Outside Ethics* (Princeton University Press, 2005), ch 2.
[27] A question asked by Martha A Fineman, 'The Vulnerable Subject: Anchoring Equality in the Human Condition', *Yale Journal of Law and Feminism*, 20 (2008), 5–6. I am grateful to Fineman's analysis which has influenced my thoughts in the analysis that follows.

'[b]oth intimate and economic entities are creatures of the state, in the sense that they are brought into legal existence by the mechanisms of the state'.[28] Law determines the boundaries within which such entities are both recognized and entitled to act in society. Forms of private ordering are themselves dependent upon contracts that are constituted and controlled by the laws of the state.[29] As such, one must recognize that the state is manifested not only in the classical organs of government, but 'through complex institutional arrangements'[30] that are not altogether outside the scope of public authority. In themselves potentially unstable, susceptible to corruption and market fluctuations, and prey to a thousand affecting forces, such institutions can also exhibit injustice, making reliance upon them particularly frightening.[31]

In the light of these concerns, and concerns over costs, Western societies have witnessed the progressive withdrawal of the state's responsibility for the functioning of public institutions. Increasingly, the management of public provision in the fields of education, healthcare, energy and other sectors, and essential aspects of social services (such as refuse collection) are carried out by private corporations. Competitive tenders reduce costs for the state which can no longer afford to supply essential goods and services. The worry is that corporate concerns will be less willing to pay attention to the concerns of the vulnerable, be less concerned with acting justly, responsive first and foremost to the expectations of their own shareholders. Regimes created and administered by private concerns are not of a kind to maximize opportunities for individuals to develop the range of assets and skills they require to become resilient in the face of their vulnerabilities.[32] Corporate interests shall dominate over the needs of the individual. As private enterprises swallow up the roles traditionally performed by the state, the fate of the individual indeed lies increasingly in 'invisible hands' that he is fundamentally unable to identify, and against which he has no real recourse.

How should one respond to this situation? The state's control and its structuring of corporate interests need to become more visible. The fingers of the state have not truly withdrawn, but have become inactive. Echoing the sentiments of *Rerum novarum* and *Centesimus annus*, one could demand that the state become more active in its pursuit of justice, ensuring to the extent possible that public goods are distributed according to values that are truly social rather than merely

---

[28] Ibid., 6.   [29] Ibid., 7.   [30] Ibid., 6.   [31] Ibid., 13.   [32] Ibid., 20.

corporate.[33] One could insist 'that the laws and institutions, the general character and administration of the commonwealth, shall be such as ... to realize public well-being and private prosperity'.[34] Both *Rerum novarum* and *Centesimus annus* envisage a far more responsive role for the state in ensuring the distribution of the market's benefits to all in society.[35] The state cannot be excluded from the domain of private contract: under no circumstances must it permit 'unbridled capitalism' to press forward unhindered.[36] The state 'has the duty of watching over the common good and of ensuring that every sector of social life, not excluding the economic one, contributes to achieving that good'.[37]

Can one share in this hope, the hope that the state may find ways to escape the boundaries of the market and establish a more thorough and sensitive regime of equality?[38] Market mechanisms alone cannot establish a just regime, cannot safeguard the common good. Surely it is the state's role to implement public values! But it is unclear whether one can any longer rely on this independence even at the theoretical level. Privatization is one option open to governments that can no longer realistically afford to supply public goods and services on the traditional model. It is axiomatic that private providers in areas such as transport, the criminal justice system and infrastructure industries will only enter such markets if they remain free to turn significant profits. Reliant upon the cooperation of large corporations in complex ways, the boundaries within which governments can regulate such industries are not as wide as might be desired. Modern governments more than ever find themselves tied to the success of the economy, including its largest corporations. Arguably, given the constraints within which governments operate, significant restrictions upon competition must come primarily from the international rather than the domestic level if the nation is not to lose business, become less competitive, more reliant upon imports and foreign investment, and generally less affluent. Operating ever more in a globalized context, the assumptions of turbo-capitalism are increasingly incapable of being reversed 'unilaterally'.[39]

---

[33] Ibid., 8.   [34] *Rerum novarum*, 32.
[35] See e.g. *Rerum novarum*, 47–8; *Centesimus annus*, 33–42.
[36] *Centesimus annus*, 7–8.   [37] Ibid., 11.   [38] See Fineman (above n 27), 20, 23.
[39] See Finnis (above n 21), 149–50, who casts doubt on the Aristotelian self-sufficiency of the *polis*.

The importance of civil society

Both Left and Right versions of liberal politics in neglecting the idea of 'the common good', fail to accord sufficient priority to something that remains an important dimension of modern man's experience: civil society. Partha Dasgupta recalled the tendency of Marxism to operate as as elite theory, predominantly employed by intellectuals whose promises turn out to be 'words, words and words, and got lost along the way'.[40] The impact of Marxism upon the value systems of the poor in Asia and elsewhere has been very limited; there is 'little evidence that the poor householders in rural Asia or Africa are interested in much more than tilling the soil, raising a family and relating to neighbours. These are the central concerns of anyone wishing to live, not merely that [sic] of the peasant'.[41] But elsewhere, in societies where communist totalitarianism took hold, civil society was ruthlessly dismantled: the only organization compatible with the 'national security' state is the organization of the state itself. All institutions, from the family to the corporation, must be placed under state control, becoming instruments of 'policy'.[42] But the conditions of market capitalism have not been kinder to communities, diminishing their cohesiveness. Successive governments in the West have progressively eliminated those intermediate institutions, especially trades unions, which in modifying or limiting the 'free' operation of market priorities are guilty of 'restrictive practices'.[43] Today, the individual 'is often suffocated between two poles represented by the State and the marketplace'.[44]

The predicament of the modern man needs to be understood above all by reference to the progressive erosion of civil society. It is not as individuals that the most vulnerable in society become resilient. Typically, vulnerable persons do not have the internal resources necessary to face or overcome their vulnerabilities. Liberals need to learn to accept that persons are completed by society. Human beings are indeed social animals. Their resources for dealing with problems of living are not

---

[40] P Dasgupta, quoted in Q Skinner et al., 'Political Philosophy: The View from Cambridge', *Journal of Political Philosophy*, 10 (2002), 5.

[41] Ibid.

[42] For observations on the absence of civil life under the Soviet regime, see Gray, *Post-Liberalism: Studies in Political Thought* (London, Routledge, 1993), ch 14.

[43] See e.g. N Boyle, *Who Are We Now? Christian Humanism and the Global Market from Hegel to Heaney* (University of Notre Dame Press, 1998), 19.

[44] *Centesimus annus*, 49.

exhausted by their own strength, but possess a social dimension. Liberal politics in a democratic age operates to suppress this dimension: a society of atomic individuals increasingly only constituting themselves as 'a community' when exercising their democratic right at the ballot box, then immediately dissolving again. But wiser minds (Aristotle and Augustine, for example) perceived that it is the proper role of politics to foster and exalt civil society. The power of vulnerabilities over the vulnerable is finally diminished not by right order alone, but where men learn to be good neighbours.

The encyclical *Rerum novarum* leaves no doubt as to the essential characteristic that is required: *justice*. Economic and civil freedom must be allowed to exist, but under unbridled market prerogatives the essence of this freedom can become 'self-love carried to the point of contempt for God and neighbour'.[45] Individuals must absolutely learn to accept that their self-interests are limited by demands of justice. Where there is no faith in the inclination of individuals to grant justice, an enlargement of the state's interventionist policies is likely to operate to the detriment of both civil and economic freedom. Men will only grant what they are obliged by law to grant. Socialist societies are in this sense just as unfeeling as those driven by private enterprise. Civil society manifests justice at the level of deeds which are conditioned not by principles but by the love of neighbour, a respect for the dignity of other persons. Self-love must itself be conditioned by love of others. Such love is not of course ecstatic and spontaneous, but requires order: 'recourse ... to societies or boards'[46] such as trades unions and workers' guilds, mutual associations and fraternal societies, and various institutions for welfare and charity.

At the close of the nineteenth century, Pope Leo XIII called for such institutions to be run by and according to the principles of men of Christian piety.[47] As the twenty-first century came into view, his successor widened this call: 'intermediate communities' which 'give life to specific networks of solidarity' constitute 'real communities of persons and strengthen the social fabric, preventing society from becoming an anonymous and impersonal mass'.[48] The strengthening of civil society is the work not only of Catholics but of all men, as a shared responsibility.[49] In 1991, there was 'a reasonable hope that the many people who profess no religion will also contribute to providing the social question with the necessary ethical foundation'.[50]

---

[45] Ibid., 17.   [46] *Rerum novarum*, 45.   [47] Ibid., 53.   [48] *Centesimus annus*, 49.
[49] Ibid., 51.   [50] Ibid., 60.

Popes Leo XIII and John Paul II called for a kind of 'guild capitalism' to replace the turbo-capitalism of modern times, and to dismiss the spectre of Marxist promises to transform society, which 'create utter confusion in the community'.[51] They demand a moderate social and economic freedom, accompanied by moderate levels of state intervention. The state should use its powers only to support the institutions of civil society, to provide them with adequate resources and to ensure their fair operation, sometimes protecting them from the market. But governments should never lose sight of the fact that 'needs are best understood and satisfied by people who are closest to them and who act as neighbours to those in need'.[52] They must not surround protective institutions in red tape and bureaucracy. Above all else, it is the responsibility of civil society to extend its benefits to all men, not simply to a specific class: 'We are not dealing here with man in the "abstract", but with real, "concrete", "historical" man. We are dealing with each individual.'[53]

The Church calls for a 'responsive' state in conjunction with civil freedom, but the state must respond in the right way. Too excessive a mode of political interference will erode civil society, which requires the freedom to organize itself toward the common good. But neither must the state withdraw too much, leaving fundamental issues of the common good to the realm of private initiative or at the mercy of corporate interests. The needs of justice cannot be met without the state's involvement, but are not capable of systematic integration into society unless the community itself becomes more integrated, more responsive to the needs of others.[54]

What can be drawn from this? The market-driven society famously leads to social fragmentation and disintegration. As jobs and even families become less secure, less permanent, individuals increasingly face their problems alone. The rejuvenation of civil society is absolutely necessary. The idea of civil society is the community's own organic structures of responsibility and mutual assistance ('fellow-feeling'). Men must rebuild social ties, a sense of civic responsibility or pride in one's community. Above all, justice must come before excessive self-interest. Unfortunately, the free market works against such instincts. Men are fundamentally placed in competition with one another. Declining advantages that are illegitimate or exploitative will not prevent others from

---

[51] *Rerum novarum*, 4.   [52] *Centesimus annus*, 48.   [53] Ibid., 53.

[54] Cf. the Church's recognition that genuine relief for the poor and the vulnerable 'may mean making important changes in established lifestyles': *Centesimus annus*, 52.

pursuing them instead. Insofar as people's livelihoods depend on the market, many are literally powerless to avoid such options.[55] In a world in which the market has significantly diminished organic notions of civic responsibility, it falls to the state to regulate interpersonal relationships in a more formal way.

I have suggested that the power of the state to mitigate the effects of the market is much more limited than we would like to admit. Increasingly, it is the demands of the economy that control government rather than vice versa. To some extent trapped by the realities of a globalized economy and the limitations of the ballot box, it lies outside the power of state and citizens to instigate social change on a large scale. One is thrown back on the informal resources of civil society, asking what it is possible to achieve. The Church is correct when it places its faith in 'all people of good will' to do what they can to change things.

But there will always be a considerable disparity between the possibilities that are open to the civil order, and what it actually achieves. It is unrealistic to think that citizens of the liberal order would be willing to give up their privacy and independence in order to feel less vulnerable. Attempts to foster resilience within communities will therefore always be severely limited. But liberals on the left and the right have compounded this problem through their disinterest in a civil order that they have given up trying to direct, devoting their energies instead entirely to the structure of the political order of society. Socialists and free-market advocates must refocus their attention. They must cease to fight vulnerability through the class struggle or the market. A politics that aims to establish a genuine resilience in its citizens must turn its gaze toward civil society. Its watchword should be neither regulation (as with socialism) nor freedom (as with capitalists and neo-conservatives), but enablement. Resilience is created and fostered at the level of communities that have taken justice into their hearts.

---

[55] It is necessary to reflect on the fact that those whose livelihoods are most vulnerable are least able to adopt an 'ethical' approach to advantages.

BIBLIOGRAPHY OF WORKS CITED

Primary sources

Althusius, J, *Politica*, S Carney (ed.) (Indianapolis IN, Liberty Fund, 1995).

Ambrose of Milan, *Expositio Evangelii Secundum Lucam*, M Adriaen (trans.) (Turnhout, Brepols, 1957).

Anselm of Canterbury, *Opera Omnia* (Edinburgh, Thomas Nelson & Sons, 1940–61).

Aquinas, T, *Commentary on Aristotle's Politics*, RJ Regan (ed.) (Indianapolis, Hackett Publishing, 2007).

    Summa Theologiae (Cambridge University Press, 2006).

    Summa Contra Gentiles, CJ O'Neil et al. (eds.) (South Bend IN, University of Notre Dame Press, 1997).

    Commentary on Aristotle's Nicomachean Ethics, CI Litzinger (ed.) (Chicago, Dumb Ox Books, 1993).

Aristotle, *Nicomachean Ethics*, R Crisp (trans.) (Cambridge University Press, 2000).

    The Politics and the Constitution of Athens, S Everson (trans.) (Cambridge University Press, 1996).

    De Anima, DW Hamlyn (ed.) (Oxford, Clarendon Press, 1993).

    Metaphysics, in J Barnes (ed.), *The Complete Works of Aristotle* (Princeton University Press, 1984).

Augustine of Hippo, *De Libero Arbitrio*, P King (trans.) (Cambridge University Press, 2010).

    On the Morals of the Catholic Church (Whitefish MT, Kessinger Publishing, 2010).

    Letters 1–99, Part 2, vol. I, JE Rotelle (ed.) (New York, New City Press, 2001).

    Political Writings, M Atkins and R Dodaro (eds.) (Cambridge University Press, 2001).

    Confessions, H Chadwick (ed.) (Oxford University Press, 1992).

    Four Anti-Pelagian Writings (Washington DC, Catholic University of America Press, 1992).

    De Genesi ad Litteram, J Quasten et al. (eds.) (Mahwah NJ, Paulist Press, 1982).

    De Civitate Dei, H Bettenson (trans.) (London, Penguin, 1972).

    The Enchiridion on Faith, Hope and Love (Washington DC, Regnery Publishing, 1961).

De Sermone Domini in Monte, in P Schaff (ed.), *Select Library of Nicene and Post-Nicene Fathers of the Christian Church* (Grand Rapids MI, Eerdmans, 1956).

Contra Academicos, JJ O'Meara (ed.) (Westminster MD, Newman Press, 1951).

De Beata Vita (Washington DC, Catholic University of America Press, 1944).

Bacon, F, *The New Organon* [1620] L Jardine and M Silverthorne (eds.) (Cambridge University Press, 2000).

Bayle, P, *Dictionnaire Philosophque et Critique* [1697]. Selections in Bayle, *Political Writings*, SL Jenkinson (ed.) (Cambridge University Press, 2008).

Bentham, J, 'Nonsense Upon Stilts', in P Schofield et al. (eds.), *Rights, Representation and Reform: Nonsense Upon Stilts and Other Writings on the French Revolution* (Oxford University Press, 2002).

Bernard of Clairvaux, *On Loving God* [c.1121] (Nepi, Cassia Press, 1999).

Blackstone, W, *Commentaries on the Laws of England* [1765], W Morrison (ed.) (London, Routledge, 2001).

Cicero, *On the Commonwealth and on the Laws*, JEG Zetel (ed.) (Cambridge University Press, 1999).

De Officiis, AP Peabody (trans.) (Boston MA, Little, Brown & Co, 1887).

Coke, E, *The First Part of the Institutes of the Laws of England (Coke upon Littleton)* (New York, Legal Classics Library, 1823).

The Second Part of the Institutes of the Laws of England [1671] (London, E & R Brooke, 1797).

Coleridge, ST, *The Friend: A Series of Essays to Aid in the Formation of Fixed Principles in Politics, Morals and Religion*, vol. I, B Rooke (ed.) (Princeton University Press, 1969).

Comenius, JA, *The Labyrinth of the World and the Paradise of the Heart*, [1631] (Whitefish MT, Kessinger Press, 1992).

Dante, *Inferno*, R Kirkpatrick (ed.) (London, Penguin Classics, 2006).

Donne, J, *Sermons on the Psalms and Gospels*, EM Simpson (ed.) (Berkeley CA, University of California Press, 1963).

Erasmus, *Adages* [1526], W Baker (trans.) (University of Toronto Press, 2001).

Praise of Folly and Letter to Martin Dorp, AHT Levi (ed.) (London, Penguin Books, 1971).

Enchiridion Militis Christiani [1525], R Himelick (trans.) (Bloomington IN, Indiana University Press, 1963).

Fortescue, J, *De Laudibus Legum Angliae* [c.1470] (London, T Evans, 1776).

Grotius, H, *De Iure Belli ac Pacis* [1625], R Tuck (ed.) (Indianapolis IN, Liberty Fund, 2005).

Hegel, GWF, *Elements of the Philosophy of Right*, [1821], HB Nisbet (trans.) (Cambridge University Press, 1991).

Hesiod, *Theogony and Works and Days* (Oxford University Press, 1999).

Hobbes, T, 'A Dialogue Between a Philosopher and a Student, of the Common Laws of England', in A Cromartie and Q Skinner (eds.), *Thomas Hobbes: Writings on Common Law and Hereditary Right* (Oxford, Clarendon Press, 2005).

Writings on Common Law and Hereditary Right, A Cromartie and Q Skinner (eds.) (Oxford, Clarendon Press, 2005).

De Cive [1649], R Tuck and M Silverthorne (ed.) (Cambridge University Press, 1998).

Leviathan [1651], R Tuck (ed.) (Cambridge University Press, 1996).

Humboldt, W von, *The Limits of State Action*, JW Burrow (ed.) (Cambridge University Press, 1969).

Hume, D, *An Enquiry Concerning the Principles of Morals* [1777], TL Beauchamp (ed.) (Oxford, Clarendon Press, 2006).

Dialogues Concerning Natural Religion (Oxford University Press, 1993).

Enquiry Concerning Human Understanding, LA Selby-Bigge (ed.) (Oxford, Clarendon Press, 1975).

Jackson, T, *Treatise of the Divine Essence and Attributes* [1628], in *The Collected Works of Thomas Jackson*, vol. V (Oxford University Press, 1844).

Jacobi, FH, *Werke* (Leipzig, Gerhard Fleischer, 1825).

Kant, I, *Anthropology from a Pragmatic Point of View*, R Louden (trans.) (Cambridge University Press, 2006).

Critique of the Power of Judgment: The Cambridge Edition of the Works of Immanuel Kant, P Guyer (ed.) (Cambridge University Press, 2001).

'Religion Within the Boundaries of Mere Reason', in AW Wood (ed.), *Religion and Rational Theology: The Cambridge Edition of the Works of Immanuel Kant* (Cambridge University Press, 1996).

Groundwork of the Metaphysics of Morals [1785], in M Gregor and A Wood (eds.), *Practical Philosophy: The Cambridge Edition of the Works of Immanuel Kant* (Cambridge University Press, 1996).

'An Answer to the Question: What Is Enlightenment?', in M Gregor and A Wood (eds.) *Practical Philosophy*.

'Idea for a Universal History with a Cosmopolitan Purpose', HB Nisbet (trans.) in H Reiss (ed.), *Kant's Political Writings* (Cambridge University Press, 1970).

Laertius, D, *Lives of Eminent Philosophers* (Cambridge MA, Loeb Classical Library, 1925).

Leibniz, GW, *Theodicy* (New York, Open Court, 1988).

Locke, J, *Two Treatises of Government* [1689], P Laslett (ed.) (Cambridge University Press, 1988).

An Essay Concerning Human Understanding [1690], P Nidditch (ed.) (Oxford, Clarendon Press, 1979).

Essays on the Laws of Nature, W von Leyden (ed.) (Oxford, Clarendon Press, 1954).

Luther, M, *Martin Luther: Selections from his Writings*, J Dillenberger (ed.) (New York, Doubleday, 1961).

    Werke (Weimar, Hermann Bohlaus & Co, 1883).

Machiavelli, N, *The Prince* [1532], Q Skinner and R Price (eds.) (Cambridge University Press, 1989).

Marx, K, *Critique of the Gotha Programme*, in *Essential Writings* (Detroit MI, Red & Black Press, 2010).

    'On the Jewish Question', in *Early Writings* (London, Penguin, 1992).

    The Grundrisse: Foundations of the Critique of Political Economy, new edn, M Nicolaus (trans.) (London, Penguin Classics, 1973).

    Early Texts, D McLellan (ed.) (Oxford University Press, 1971).

Mill, JS, *An Examination of William Hamilton's Philosophy* [1865], in J Robson (ed.), *The Collected Works of John Stuart Mill*, vol. IX. (London, R&K Paul, 1963–91).

Montesquieu, C de, *L'Espirit des Lois* [1748], AM Cohler et al. (eds.) (Cambridge University Press, 1989).

More, T, *Utopia*, G Logan and R Adams (eds.) (Cambridge University Press, 2002).

Nietzsche, F, *Human, All Too Human*, RJ Hollingdale (trans.) (Cambridge University Press, 1996).

Plato, *Republic*, D Lee (trans.) (London, Penguin, 2007).

    Cratylus, B Jowett (trans.) (Middlesex, The Echo Library, 2006).

    Theaetetus, R Waterfield (trans.) (London, Penguin, 1987).

    Politicus, in L Campbell (trans.), *The Sophistes and Politicus of Plato* (Oxford, Clarendon Press, 1867).

Pufendorf, S, *De Iure Naturae et Gentium* [1672] (Buffalo NY, WS Hein, 1995).

Rousseau, J-J, *The Social Contract, and Other Later Political Writings*, V Gourevich (ed.) (Cambridge University Press, 1997).

    'Abstract and Judgment of Saint-Pierre's Project for Perpetual Peace', in S Hoffman and D Fidler (eds.), *Rousseau on International Relations* (Oxford, Clarendon Press, 1991).

    Confessions, J Cohen (trans.) (Penguin, 1973).

Saint-Simon, H, *Letters from an Inhabitant of Geneva to his Contemporaries* [1803], in *Selected Writings* (London, Croom Helm, 1975).

Seneca, *Moral and Political Essays*, JM Cooper and JF Procope (eds.) (Cambridge University Press, 1995).

Smith, A, *The Theory of Moral Sentiments* (London, Penguin, 2010).

    An Inquiry into the Nature and Causes of the Wealth of Nations, A Skinner (ed.) (London, Penguin, 1982).

    Lectures on Jurisprudence, R Meek, D Raphael and P Stein (eds.) (Oxford, Clarendon Press, 1978).

Spinoza, B, *Ethics* (Middlesex, The Echo Library, 2006).

Starkey, T, *Dialogue Between Reginald Pole & Thomas Lupset*, KM Burton (ed.) (Cambridge University Press, 1948).

Secondary sources

Adams, WL, 'The Hellenistic Kindgoms', in GR Bugh (ed.), *The Cambridge Companion to the Hellenistic World* (Cambridge University Press, 2006), 35.

Allott, PJ, *Eunomia: A New Order for a New World*, 2nd edn (Oxford University Press, 2001).

Annas, J, *The Morality of Happiness* (Oxford University Press, 1993).

Armitage, D, *The Declaration of Independence: A Global History* (Cambridge MA, Harvard University Press, 2007).

Austin, J, *The Province of Jurisprudence Determined* (London, John Murray, 1832).

Bader-Saye, S, 'Living the Gospels: Morality and Politics', in SC Barton (ed.), *The Cambridge Companion to the Gospels* (Cambridge University Press, 2006).

Badiou, A, *Ethics: An Essay on the Understanding of Evil* (London, Verso, 2001).

Balazs, Z and Dunlop, F (eds.), *Exploring the World of Human Practice: Readings In and About the Writings of Aurel Kolnai* (Budapest, CEU Press, 2004).

Balfour, AJ, *Essays and Addresses*, TG Appleton (ed.) (Ann Arbor MI, University of Michigan Library, 2009).

Beiser, FC, *The Fate of Reason: German Philosophy from Kant to Fichte* (Cambridge MA, Harvard University Press, 1987).

Berlin, I, *The Hedgehog and the Fox* (London, Penguin Books, 2009).

Berman, HJ, *Faith and Order: The Reconciliation of Law and Religion* (Grand Rapids MI, Eerdmans, 1993).

Berman, HJ, *Law and Revolution, Volume I: The Formation of the Western Legal Tradition* (Cambridge MA, Harvard University Press, 1983).

Black, A, 'The Individual and Society', in JH Burns (ed.), *The Cambridge History of Medieval Political Thought c.350–c.1450* (Cambridge University Press, 1988).

Boyle, N, *Who Are We Now? Christian Humanism and the Global Market from Hegel to Heaney* (University of Notre Dame Press, 1998).

Bradshaw, B, 'More on Utopia', *Historical Journal*, 24 (1981).

Brett, A, *Changes of State: The Nature and Limits of the City in Early Modern Natural Law* (Princeton University Press, 2011).

    Liberty, Right and Nature: Individual Rights in Later Scholastic Thought (Cambridge University Press, 1997).

Burnell, PJ, 'The Status of Politics in Augustine's *City of God*', *History of Political Thought*, 13 (1992), 13.

Burnyeat, MF, 'Aristotle on Learning to be Good', in AO Rorty (ed.), *Essays on Aristotle's Ethics* (Berkeley CA, University of California Press, 1980), 69.

Butterfield, H, *The Whig Interpretation of History* (London, G Bell & Sons, 1931).

Callus, DA, 'The Date of Grosseteste's Translations and Commentaries on Pseudo-Dionysius and the Nicomachean Ethics', *Recherches de Théologie Ancienne et Médiévale*, 14 (1947), 101.

Canning, JP, 'Ideas of the State in Thirteenth and Fourteenth-Century Commentators on the Roman Law', *Transactions of the Royal Historical Society*, 33 (1983), 1–27.

Chadwick, O, *The Secularization of the European Mind in the 19th Century* (Cambridge University Press, 1975).

Chambers, RW, *Thomas More* (London, Jonathan Cape, 1935).

Coffa, JA, *The Semantic Tradition from Kant to Carnap: To the Vienna Station* (Cambridge University Press, 1993).

Collingwood, RG, *Essays in Political Philosophy*, D Boucher (ed.) (Oxford, Clarendon Press, 1989).

Coyle, S, 'The Reality of the Enlightenment', *British Journal for the History of Philosophy*, 17 (2009), 849.

    From Positivism to Idealism (Dartmouth, Ashgate, 2007).

    'Positivism, Idealism and the Rule of Law', *OJLS*, 26 (2006), 257–88.

    'Thomas Hobbes and the Intellectual Origins of Legal Positivism', *Canadian J of Law and Jurisprudence*, 16 (2002), 243.

    and K Morrow, *The Philosophical Foundations of Environmental Law* (Oxford, Hart, 2004).

Davis, JC, 'Thomas More's *Utopia*: Sources, Legacy and Interpretation', in G Claeys (ed.), *The Cambridge Companion to Utopian Literature* (Cambridge University Press, 2010).

Deane, H, *The Political and Social Ideas of St Augustine* (New York, Columbia University Press, 1963).

Devigne, R, *Recasting Conservatism: Oakeshott, Strauss and the Response to Postmodernism* (New Haven CT, Yale University Press, 1994).

Doe, N, *Fundamental Authority in Late Medieval English Law* (Cambridge University Press, 1990).

Duxbury, N, *Patterns of American Jurisprudence* (Oxford University Press, 1995).

Dworkin, R, *Justice for Hedgehogs* (Cambridge MA, Harvard University Press, 2011).

    Justice in Robes (Cambridge MA, Belknap Press, 2007).

    Law's Empire (London, Fontana, 1986).

    Taking Rights Seriously (London, Duckworth, 1978).

    'Lord Devlin and the Enforcement of Morals', *Yale LJ*, 75 (1966), 986.

Ewin, RE, *Virtues and Rights: The Moral Philosophy of Thomas Hobbes* (Boulder CO, Westview Press, 1991).

Farr, A, *Sartre's Radicalism and Oakeshott's Conservatism: The Duplicity of Freedom* (London, Palgrave, 1998).

Fineman, MA, 'The Vulnerable Subject: Anchoring Equality in the Human Condition', *Yale Journal of Law and Feminism*, 20 (2008), 1.

Finnis, J, *Natural Law and Natural Rights*, 2nd edn (Oxford, Clarendon Press, 2011).

'Religion and Public Life in Pluralist Society', reprinted in Finnis, *Religion and Public Reasons: Collected Essays*, vol. V (Oxford, Clarendon Press, 2011), 42.

'Aquinas on *Ius* and Hart on Rights: A Response to Tierney', *Review of Politics*, 64 (2002), 407.

Aquinas: Moral, Political and Legal Theory (Oxford University Press, 1998).

Flikschuh, K, *Kant and Modern Political Philosophy* (Cambridge University Press, 2000).

Fortin, E, *Classical Christianity and the Political Order: Collected Essays*, vol. II, JB Benestad (ed.) (Lanham MD, Rowman & Littlefield, 1996).

Human Rights, Virtue and the Common Good: Collected Essays, vol. III (Lanham MD, Rowman & Littlefield, 1996).

Frost, S, *Lessons from a Materialist Thinker: Hobbesian Reflections on Ethics and Politics* (Stanford University Press, 2008).

Fukuyama, F, *The End of History and the Last Man* (London, Penguin, 1993).

Fuller, L, *The Principles of Social Order: Selected Essays of Lon L Fuller*, K Winston (ed.) (Oxford, Hart Publishing, 2001).

The Morality of Law, revised edn (New Haven CT, Yale University Press, 1964).

'American Legal Philosophy at Mid-Century', *Journal of Legal Education*, 6 (1954), 476.

The Law in Quest of Itself (Chicago, Foundation Press, 1940).

Gadamer, H-G, *The Idea of the Good in Platonic–Aristotelian Philosophy* (New Haven CT, Yale University Press, 1986).

Truth and Method, new edn (London, Continuum Books, 2004).

Gerencser, SA, *The Skeptic's Oakeshott* (New York, St Martin's Press, 1990).

Geuss, R, *Politics and the Imagination* (Princeton University Press, 2010).

Philosophy and Real Politics (Princeton University Press, 2008).

Outside Ethics (Princeton University Press, 2005).

History and Illusion in Politics (Cambridge University Press, 2001).

Girardet, R, *Nationalismes et Nation: Questions au XXes* (Brussels, Editions Complexe, 1996).

Goldsmith, M, 'Hobbes on Liberty', *Hobbes Studies*, 2 (1989), 23.

Gray, J, *Enlightenment's Wake* (London, Routledge, 1995).

Beyond the New Right (London, Routledge, 1993).

Post-Liberalism: Studies in Political Thought (London, Routledge, 1993).

Green, EHH, *Ideologies of Conservatism* (Oxford University Press, 2002).

Hampshire, S, *Innocence and Experience* (Cambridge MA, Harvard University Press, 1989).

Harrison, C, *Augustine: Christian Truth and Fractured Humanity* (Oxford University Press, 2000).

Harrison, R, *Hobbes, Locke and Confusion's Masterpiece* (Cambridge University Press, 2002).

'The Equality of Mercy', in H Gross and R Harrison (eds.), *Jurisprudence: Cambridge Essays* (Oxford University Press, 1992) 107.

Hart, HLA, *The Concept of Law*, 2nd edn (Oxford, Clarendon Press, 1994).

'Definition and Theory in Jurisprudence', in *Essays in Jurisprudence and Philosophy* (Oxford University Press, 1983), Essay 1.

'Problems of the Philosophy of Law', in *Essays in Jurisprudence and Philosophy*, Essay 3.

'American Jurisprudence Through English Eyes: The Nightmare and the Noble Dream', in *Essays in Jurisprudence and Philosophy*, Essay 4.

'1776–1976: Law in the Perspective of Philosophy', in *Essays in Jurisprudence and Philosophy*, Essay 5.

'Rawls on Liberty and its Priority', in *Essays in Jurisprudence and Philosophy*, Essay 10.

'Social Solidarity and the Enforcement of Morality', in *Essays in Jurisprudence and Philosophy*, Essay 11.

Law, Liberty and Morality (Stanford University Press, 1963).

Hayek, FA, *Law, Legislation and Liberty* (London, Routledge, 1982).

Hedley, D, *Living Forms of the Imagination* (London, T & T Clark, 2008).

Hochstrasser, TJ, *Natural Law Theories in the Early Enlightenment* (Cambridge University Press, 2000).

Hoffman, T, 'The Intellectual Virtues', in B Davies and E Stump (eds.), *The Oxford Handbook of Aquinas* (Oxford University Press, 2012), 327.

Hohfeld, WN, *Fundamental Legal Conceptions as Applied in Juridical Reasoning, and Other Essays* (New Haven CT, Yale University Press, 1919).

Horwitz, MJ, *The Transformation of American Law 1780–1860* (Cambridge MA, Harvard University Press, 1977).

Hunter, I, *Rival Enlightenments* (Cambridge University Press, 2001).

Hylton, P, *Russell, Idealism and the Emergence of Analytic Philosophy* (Oxford, Clarendon Press, 1990).

Inge, WR, 'Theism', *Philosophy*, 23 (1948), 38.

Ivry, AL, 'Averroes's Middle and Long Commentaries on the *De Anima*', *Arabic Sciences and Philosophy*, 5 (1995) 75.

Jacobson AJ and B Schlink (eds.) *Weimar: A Jurisprudence of Crisis* (Berkeley CA, University of California Press, 2000).

Koenigsberger, HG, 'Monarchies and Parliaments in Early Modern Europe', *Theory and Society*, 5 (1978), 191.

Koikkalainen, P and S Syrjämäki, 'Quentin Skinner on Encountering the Past', *Finnish Yearbook of Political Thought*, 6 (2002), 37.

Kolakowski, L, *The Two Eyes of Spinoza* (South Bend, IN, St Augustine's Press, 2004).

Modernity on Endless Trial (Chicago IL, University of Chicago Press, 1990).

The Presence of Myth (University of Chicago Press, 1989).

Tales from the Kingdom of Lailonia (University of Chicago Press, 1972).

Kolnai, A, *Ethics, Value and Reality* (New Brunswick NJ, Transaction Publishers, 2008).

'Erroneous Conscience', in Z Balazs and F Dunlop (eds.), *Exploring the World of Human Practice: Readings In and About the Philosophy of Aurel Kolnai* (Budapest, CEU Press, 2004).

Political Memoirs, F Murphy (ed.) (Lanham MD, Lexington Books, 1999).

Privilege and Liberty and Other Essays in Political Philosophy (Lanham MD, Lexington Books, 1999).

The Utopian Mind and Other Papers (London, Athlone, 1995).

Korsgaard, C, *Creating the Kingdom of Ends* (Cambridge University Press, 1996).

Kramer, MH, *Where Law and Morality Meet* (Oxford University Press, 2004).

In Defence of Legal Positivism: Law Without Trimmings (Oxford University Press, 2003).

'The Rule of (Mis)recognition in the Hart of Jurisprudence', *OJLS*, 8 (1988), 401.

Kries, D, 'In Defense of Fortin', *Review of Politics*, 64 (2002), 411.

Lacey, N, *A Life of HLA Hart: The Nightmare and the Noble Dream* (Oxford University Press, 2004).

Lane, M, 'Political Theory and Time', in P Baert (ed.), *Time in Contemporary Intellectual Thought* (Amsterdam, Elsevier, 2000).

Laslett P (ed.), *Philosophy, Politics and Society* (Oxford University Press, 1956).

Laursen, JC, 'Oakeshott's Skepticism and the Skeptical Traditions', *European J of Political Theory*, 4 (2005), 37–55.

The Politics of Skepticism in the Ancients, Montaigne, Hume and Kant (New York, Brill, 1992).

MacIntyre, A, *Whose Justice? Which Rationality?* (London, Duckworth, 1988).

Secularization and Moral Change (Oxford University Press, 1967).

Manent, P, *Modern Liberty and its Discontents* (Lanham MD, Rowman & Littlefield, 1998).

The City of Man, M LePain (trans.) (Princeton University Press, 1998).

Marcuse, H, *One-Dimensional Man: Studies in the Ideology of Advanced Societies* (London, Routledge, 1964).

Markus, RA, *Saeculum: History and Society in the Theology of St Augustine* (Cambridge University Press, 1970).

Mason, H, 'Optimism, Progress and Philosophical History', in M Goldie and R Wokler (eds.), *The Cambridge History of Eighteenth Century Political Thought* (Cambridge University Press, 2006), 195.

McCarthy, VA, *Quest for a Philosophical Jesus: Christianity and Philosophy in Rousseau, Kant, Hegel and Schelling* (Macon GA, Mercer University Press, 1986).

Meynell, H, 'In Defence of the Humanities', *New Blackfriars*, 81 (2007), 327.

Midgley, M, *The Myths We Live By* (London, Routledge, 2004).

　Heart and Mind (London, Routledge, 1981).

Murdoch, I, *Metaphysics as a Guide to Morals* (London, Chatto & Windus, 1992).

Murphy, J, 'Mercy and Legal Justice', in J Murphy and J Hampton, *Forgiveness and Mercy* (Cambridge University Press, 1988).

Niebuhr, R, *The Essential Reinhold Niebuhr: Selected Essays and Addresses*, R McAfee Brown (ed.) (New Haven CT, Yale University Press, 1986).

　Love and Justice, DB Robertson (ed.) (Louisville KY, John Knox Press, 1957).

Oakeshott, M, *The Politics of Faith and the Politics of Scepticism* (New Haven CT, Yale University Press, 1996).

　Religion, Politics and the Moral Life, T Fuller (ed.) (New Haven CT, Yale University Press, 1993).

　Rationalism in Politics, revised edn (Indianapolis IN, Liberty Fund, 1991).

　Hobbes on Civil Association (Indianapolis IN, Liberty Fund, 1975).

　Experience and its Modes (Cambridge University Press, 1933).

O'Donovan, JL, 'Historical Prolegomena to a Theological View of Human Rights', *Studies in Christian Ethics*, 9 (1996) 54.

O'Donovan, O, *Common Objects of Love: Moral Reflection and the Shaping of Community* (Grand Rapids MI, Eerdmans Publishing Co, 2002).

Olin, JC, 'Erasmus' *Adagia* and More's *Utopia*', *Moreana*, 100 (1989), 127.

O'Neill, O, 'Would Making Laws Better Make Better Laws?', *Jurisprudence*, 3 (2012), 1.

Pennington, K, *The Prince and the Law 1200–1600* (Berkeley CA, University of California Press, 1993).

Perreau-Saussine, A, 'Immanuel Kant on International Law', in J Tasioulas and S Besson (eds.), *The Philosophy of International Law* (Oxford University Press, 2008).

　'An Outsider on the Inside: Hart's Limits on Jurisprudence', *University of Toronto LJ*, 56 (2006), 371.

Perreau-Saussine, E, *Catholicism and Democracy: An Essay in the History of Political Thought* (Princeton University Press, 2012).

　'Paradise as a Political Theme in Augustine's *City of God*', in M Bockmuehl and G Stroumsa (eds.) *Paradise in Antiquity: Jewish and Christian Views* (Cambridge University Press, 2010).

　'Quentin Skinner in Context', *Review of Politics*, 69 (2007), 106.

　'What Remains of Socialism', in P Riordan (ed.), *Values in Public Life: Aspects of Common Goods* (Berlin, LIT Verlag, 2007), 11.

Plant, R, *Modern Political Thought* (Oxford, Blackwell, 1991).

Pohl, N, 'Utopianism After More: The Renaissance and the Enlightenment', in G Claeys (ed.), *The Cambridge Companion to Utopian Literature* (Cambridge University Press, 2010), 51–78.

Porter, J, *Natural and Divine Law* (Ontario, Novalis, 1999).

Quine, WVO, 'Two Dogmas of Empiricism', in *From a Logical Point of View*, new edn (Cambridge MA, Harvard University Press, 1980).

Quinn, PL, 'Original Sin, Radical Evil and Moral Identity', *Faith and Philosophy*, 1 (1984), 188–202.

Rawls, J, *Political Liberalism*, 2nd edn (New York, Columbia University Press, 2005).

Justice as Fairness: A Restatement (Cambridge MA, Harvard University Press, 2001).

The Law of Peoples (Cambridge MA, Harvard University Press, 2001).

Lectures on the History of Moral Philosophy, B Herman (ed.) (Cambridge MA, Harvard University Press, 2000).

A Theory of Justice, new edn (Cambridge MA, Harvard University Press, 1999).

Raz, J, *Between Authority and Interpretation* (Oxford University Press, 2009).

'On the Nature of Law', *Archiv fur Rechts und Sozialphilosophie* (1996), 1.

Reynolds, P, *To Have and to Hold: Marriage and its Documentation in Western Christendom 400–1600* (Cambridge University Press, 2007).

Rogers, AK, 'Conscience', *International Journal of Ethics*, 41 (1931), 161.

Rommen, HA, *The Natural Law* (Indianapolis IN, Liberty Fund, 1998).

Rose, G, *The Dialectic of Nihilism: Post-Structuralism and Law* (Oxford, Blackwell, 1984).

Rowland, T, *Culture and the Thomist Tradition After Vatican II* (London, Routledge, 2003).

Rubenstein, N, 'The History of the Word *Politicus*', in A Pagden (ed.), *The Languages of Political Theory in Early-Modern Europe* (Cambridge University Press, 1997), 41.

Sagovsky, N, *Christian Tradition and the Practice of Justice* (London, SPCK, 2008).

Santayana, G, *The Life of Reason* (New York, Scribner, 1905).

Schneewind, JB, *Essays on the History of Moral Philosophy* (Cambridge University Press, 2010).

Schofield, P, *Utility and Democracy: The Political Thought of Jeremy Bentham* (Oxford University Press, 2007).

Scruton, R, *The Meaning of Conservatism*, 3rd edn (London, Palgrave, 2001).

Sen, A, *The Idea of Justice* (London, Penguin Books, 2010).

Sidgwick, H, *Methods of Ethics* (Indianapolis IN, Hackett Publishing, 1981).

Simmonds, NE, 'Freedom, Law and Naked Violence', *University of Toronto Law Journal*, 59 (2009), 381.

Central Issues in Jurisprudence, 3rd edn (London, Sweet & Maxwell, 2008).

Law as a Moral Idea (Oxford University Press, 2007).

'Law as a Moral Idea', *University of Toronto LJ*, 55 (2005), 61.

'Straightforwardly False: The Collapse of Kramer's Positivism', *Cambridge LJ*, 63 (2004), 98.

'Protestant Jurisprudence and Modern Doctrinal Scholarship', *Cambridge LJ*, 60 (2001), 271.

'Rights at the Cutting Edge', in MH Kramer, NE Simmonds and H Steiner, *A Debate Over Rights* (Oxford University Press, 1998).

'Judgment and Mercy', *OJLS*, 13 (1993), 52.

'Between Positivism and Idealism', *Cambridge LJ*, 50 (1991), 308.

The Decline of Juridical Reason (Manchester University Press, 1982).

Simpson, AWB, 'The Common Law and Legal Theory', in *Oxford Essays in Jurisprudence, 2nd Series* (Oxford, Clarendon Press, 1973), 77.

Skidelski, E, 'The Strange Death of British Idealism', *Philosophy & Literature*, 31 (2007) 41.

Skinner, Q, 'History and Ideology in the English Revolution', reprinted in Skinner, *Visions of Politics*, vol. III (Cambridge University Press, 2002).

'The Republican Ideal of Political Liberty', in G Bock (ed.), *Machiavelli and Republicanism* (Cambridge University Press, 1990), 293.

'The State', in T Ball, J Farr and RL Hanson (eds.) *Political Innovation and Conceptual Change* (Cambridge University Press, 1989), 112.

'Sir Thomas More's *Utopia*', in A Pagden (ed.), *The Languages of Political Theory in Early Modern Europe* (Cambridge University Press, 1987).

and M van Gelderen, *Republicanism: A Shared European Heritage* (Cambridge University Press, 2002).

and P Dasgupta, R Geuss et al., 'Political Philosophy: The View from Cambridge', *Journal of Political Philosophy*, 10 (2002) 1.

Smith, TW, 'The Glory and Tragedy of Politics', in J Doody, KL Hughes and K Paffenroth (eds.), *Augustine and Politics* (Lanham MD, Lexington Books, 2005).

Soames, S, *Philosophical Analysis in the Twentieth Century*, vol. I (Princeton University Press, 2003).

Steiner, H, 'Working Rights', in MH Kramer, NE Simmonds and H Steiner, *A Debate Over Rights: Philosophical Inquiries* (Oxford University Press, 1998).

An Essay on Rights (Oxford, Blackwell, 1994).

Suber, P (ed.), *The Case of the Speluncean Explorers: Nine New Opinions* (London, Routledge, 1998).

Surtz, E, *The Praise of Pleasure: Philosophy, Education and Communism in More's Utopia* (Cambridge MA, Harvard University Press, 1957).

Tasioulas, J, 'Mercy', *Proceedings of the Aristotelian Society*, 103 (2003), 101.

Tierney, B, 'Natural Law, Laws of Nature and Natural Rights. Continuity and Discontinuity in the History of Ideas', *Catholic Historical Rev*, 93 (2007), 111.

'Natural Law and Natural Rights: Old Problems and Recent Approaches', *Review of Politics*, 64 (2002), 389.

Tolstoy, L, 'The Three Questions', in *Walk in the Light and Twenty-Three Tales* (Maryknoll NY, Orbis Books, 2003).

Tseng, R, *The Sceptical Idealist: Michael Oakeshott as a Critic of the Enlightenment* (London, Imprint Academic, 2003).

Tuck, R, *The Rights of War and Peace: Political Thought and the International Order from Grotius to Kant* (Cambridge University Press, 2001).

'The Dangers of Natural Rights', *Harvard J of Public Policy*, 20 (1997), 683.

Natural Rights Theories: Their Origin and Development (Cambridge University Press, 1979).

Tur, R, 'The Notion of a Legal Right: A Test-Case for Legal Science', *Juridical Review*, 21 (1976), 177.

Twining, W, *Karl Llewellyn and the Realist Movement* (London, Weidenfeld & Nicholson, 1973).

Voegelin, E, 'Necessary Moral Bases for Communication in a Democracy', in E Sandoz (ed.), *Published Essays 1953–65: The Collected Works of Eric Voegelin*, vol. XI (Columbia, University of Missouri Press, 2000).

'Science, Politics and Gnosticism: Two Essays', in *Modernity Without Restraint: The Collected Works of Eric Voegelin*, vol. V (Columbia, University of Missouri Press, 2000).

'The Oxford Political Philosophers', in *Published Essays 1953–1965: The Collected Works*, vol. XI (University of Missouri Press, 2000).

Ward, L, *The Politics of Liberty in England and Revolutionary America* (Cambridge University Press, 2004).

Warnock, GJ, *English Philosophy Since 1900* (London, Oxford University Press, 1958).

Watson A (ed.), *The Digest of Justinian* (University of Pennsylvania Press, 1997).

Weinrib, EJ, *The Idea of Private Law* (Cambridge MA, Harvard University Press, 1995).

Wendell Holmes, O, Jr, *The Common Law* (Cambridge MA, Harvard University Press, 2009).

Wilde, O, *The Soul of Man Under Socialism* (London, Forgotten Books, 2008).

Zucker, MP, 'Do Natural Rights Derive from Natural Law?', *Harvard J Public Policy*, 20 (1997), 695.